T0318891

WORKING WITH TEXT

Tools, Techniques and Approaches for Text Mining

CHANDOS
INFORMATION PROFESSIONAL SERIES
Series Editor: Ruth Rikowski
(email: Rikowskigr@aol.com)

Chandos' new series of books is aimed at the busy information professional. They have been specially commissioned to provide the reader with an authoritative view of current thinking. They are designed to provide easy-to-read and (most importantly) practical coverage of topics that are of interest to librarians and other information professionals. If you would like a full listing of current and forthcoming titles, please visit www.chandospublishing.com.

New authors: we are always pleased to receive ideas for new titles; if you would like to write a book for Chandos, please contact Dr Glyn Jones on g.jones.2@elsevier.com or telephone +44 (0) 1865 843000.

WORKING WITH TEXT

Tools, Techniques and Approaches for Text Mining

Edited by

EMMA L. TONKIN

GREGORY J.L. TOURTE

AMSTERDAM • BOSTON • CAMBRIDGE • HEIDELBERG
LONDON • NEW YORK • OXFORD • PARIS • SAN DIEGO
SAN FRANCISCO • SINGAPORE • SYDNEY • TOKYO
Chandos Publishing is an imprint of Elsevier

CHANDOS
PUBLISHING

Chandos Publishing is an imprint of Elsevier
50 Hampshire Street, 5th Floor, Cambridge, MA 02139, USA
The Boulevard, Langford Lane, Kidlington, OX5 1GB, UK

Notices

Knowledge and best practice in this field are constantly changing. As new research and experience broaden our understanding, changes in research methods, professional practices, or medical treatment may become necessary.

Practitioners and researchers must always rely on their own experience and knowledge in evaluating and using any information, methods, compounds, or experiments described herein. In using such information or methods they should be mindful of their own safety and the safety of others, including parties for whom they have a professional responsibility.

To the fullest extent of the law, neither the Publisher nor the authors, contributors, or editors, assume any liability for any injury and/or damage to persons or property as a matter of products liability, negligence or otherwise, or from any use or operation of any methods, products, instructions, or ideas contained in the material herein.

British Library Cataloguing-in-Publication Data
A catalogue record for this book is available from the British Library

Library of Congress Cataloging-in-Publication Data
A catalog record for this book is available from the Library of Congress

ISBN 978-1-84334-749-1

For information on all Chandos Publishing
visit our website at https://www.elsevier.com/

Working together
to grow libraries in
developing countries

www.elsevier.com • www.bookaid.org

Publisher: Glyn Jones
Acquisition Editor: Glyn Jones
Editorial Project Manager: Jennifer Pierce
Production Project Manager: Omer Mukthar
Designer: Greg Harris

Typeset by SPi Global, India

CONTENTS

CONTRIBUTORS

B. Alex
School of Informatics, University of Edinburgh, Edinburgh, UK

S. Ananiadou
University of Manchester, Manchester, UK

H. Barjat
Barjat Consulting, Langley, Macclesfield, UK

W.J. Black
University of Manchester, Manchester, UK

K. Bontcheva
University of Sheffield, Sheffield, UK

H. Bretz
Thomson Reuters, NYC, NY, USA

A. Charlesworth
University of Bristol Law School, Bristol, UK

G. Bueno-de-la-Fuente
University Carlos III of Madrid, Madrid, Spain

L. Derczynski
University of Sheffield, Sheffield, UK

J. Greenberg
Drexel University, Philadelphia, PA, USA

C. Grover
School of Informatics, University of Edinburgh, Edinburgh, UK

B. Hachey
University of Sydney, Sydney, Australia

M. Haeussler
University of California, Santa Cruz, CA, USA

L. Hawizy
Department of Chemistry, University of Cambridge, UK

E. Klein
School of Informatics, University of Edinburgh, Edinburgh, UK

B.N. Lawrence
National Centre for Atmospheric Science, Natural Environment Research Council; Centre for Environmental Data Archival, STFC Rutherford Appleton Laboratory; Department of Meteorology, University of Reading, UK

C. Llewellyn
School of Informatics, University of Edinburgh, Edinburgh, UK

J. McNaught
University of Manchester, Manchester, UK

M. Miwa
University of Manchester and Toyota Technological Institute

J. Molloy
University of Cambridge, Cambridge, UK

P. Murray-Rust
University of Cambridge, Cambridge, UK

C. Oppenheim
Queensland University, Brisbane, Australia

C.L. Pascoe
National Centre for Atmospheric Science, Natural Environment Research Council;
Centre for Environmental Data Archival, STFC Rutherford Appleton Laboratory, UK

D. Rodríguez Mateos
University Carlos III of Madrid, Madrid, Spain

A. Rowley
University of Manchester, Manchester, UK

F. Schilder
Thomson Reuters, NYC, NY, USA

S. Singh
Thomson Reuters, NYC, NY, USA

M. Thomas
Thomson Reuters, NYC, NY, USA

R. Tobin
School of Informatics, University of Edinburgh, Edinburgh, UK

E.L. Tonkin
Department of Digital Humanities, King's College London, London, UK; Department of
Electrical & Electronic Engineering, University of Bristol, Bristol, UK

G. J.L. Tourte
School of Geographical Sciences, University of Bristol, UK

T. Vacek
Thomson Reuters, NYC, NY, USA

M. Zampieri
Saarland University, Saarbrücken; German Research Center for Artificial Intelligence
(DFKI), Saarbrücken, Germany

PREFACE

In collaboration with UKOLN, University of Bath, Elsevier is very pleased to publish this book. Complimentary access to the e-book is available, as open access, on ScienceDirect (http://www.sciencedirect.com/). On behalf of UKOLN, University of Bath, and Elsevier, we hope that you enjoy the contents of this work.

ACKNOWLEDGEMENTS

As with any lengthy endeavour, there are many people to acknowledge.

I would first like to thank Stephanie Taylor for her invaluable support in the development of this book. Although Steph agreed to co-edit this volume, to my lasting regret, the cessation of funding to UKOLN meant that intensive collaboration became impossible. I would also like to congratulate Steph on her role as a Senior Consultant in Academic Research Technologies at the University of London Computer Centre.

Juggling jobs and projects is never easy and has been rendered harder still by disruptive change. As such, this book owes much to the support of the wonderful people who generously helped to make it happen. I would like to thank Larissa Tonkin for applying her organisational brilliance to the coordination of this book and Greg Tourte for his support, advice and forbearance throughout the process.

Special thanks also go to Paul Walk, now of EDINA, without whom this would not have happened at all, and to Henk Muller, who introduced me to Professor Markov and the Reverend Bayes.

I am also grateful to the presenters and attendees at the Open Repositories 2012 Working with Text workshop and the LOV-HIVE workshop in Spain organised by Jane Greenberg and Eva Mendez.

Finally, I would like to thank all the people who have shared their knowledge and views with me during the development of this book, particularly those who agreed to interviews.

CHAPTER 1

Working with Text

E.L. Tonkin[*,†]
[*]Department of Digital Humanities, King's College London, London, UK
[†]Department of Electrical & Electronic Engineering, The University of Bristol, Bristol, UK

1.1 INTRODUCTION: PORTRAITS OF THE PAST

The year is 1439, and a curly-haired, hawk-nosed young man in his early thirties is about to indulge his argumentative streak by starting an argument with the Catholic church. The man's name is Lorenzo Valla, and it has fallen to him to share his contentious findings with the public. Like many others, he has come to the conclusion that the *Donation of Constantine*, the *Constitutum Constantini*, is a fake. It is a matter of more than academic importance. Purportedly, this document grants broad powers to the pope, including rank, political powers and most significantly control over Italy and the Western provinces. The document is used by the Church to justify dominance over Italy. Emperor Constantine the Great is reported to have written the document upon the occasion of his baptism and cure from leprosy. It is said to date from the earlier years of the third century AD, more than 1000 years ago, so any eyewitnesses to the process of the document's creation have been dead for well over 900 years. How can the young man prove his case?

In the event, Valla found the solution in his remarkable knowledge of Latin style, grammar and rhetoric. He had authored a previous work, the *Elegantiae latinae linguae*, which he himself described with characteristic modesty as of greater practical use than "anything written for the past six centuries in the fields of grammar, rhetoric, dialectic, civil law, canon law or semantics" (Cronin, 2011). In this work, Valla dealt almost exclusively with the details, *res minusculae* – the little things, from the choice of pronoun (*illi* or *sibi*?) to the turns and flourishes of the writer's rhetorical style. Using this approach, he saw, would provide him with plenty of supporting evidence upon which to base his argument (Coleman, 1922). From the *Donation of Constantine*, Valla picked out anachronistic terms and usages, such as the word "satraps", which came into current usage only in the eighth century. He noted that the document drew on knowledge that the supposed author could not have had. Using his knowledge of Latin, he demonstrated to the eventual satisfaction of his audience that the style of the text was more consistent with medieval Latin than with the document's supposed origin. Valla won his case, at least in part – society would take some time to come round to his views – and moved on to apply his method to other documents. But his habit of questioning the orthodox did not gain him the gratitude of the pope. Not until the present pope died would he be rewarded for his work.

Although he did not know it, Valla was in the vanguard of a very modern tradition: the comparative analysis of texts, intended to answer questions about the text in question. Certain methods that Valla uses, such as analysis of relative word frequencies, place him not far from the field of text mining, the use of computational methods to extract knowledge from a text. Today, similar methods are likely to be used for different purposes, such as search and retrieval, analysis of word frequencies and patterns, and identifying the topics covered within a group of texts. Valla's interest in the attribution of authorship places him firmly at the head of the lengthy family tree of stylometry, the study of structure and writing style for purposes such as author attribution, categorisation of genres and styles, and study of macro patterns in groups of authors.

Valla's text-first approach to the analysis of authorship makes him the earliest regularly cited example of stylometric analysis, but he is far from alone in seeking information about authorship from the *res minisculae* contained within a text. Consider Delia Bacon (1811–1859), a New England girl and daughter of a Calvinist minister whose death during her early childhood flung the family into relative poverty. She had just one year of secondary schooling and began to teach at the age of 15 (Baym, 1996). Bacon's attention was caught by Shakespeare's plays, then by Shakespeare the man, who she came to view as an imposter. In a transformative reimagining, Bacon characterised the plays as "republican polemics" (ibid.), authored primarily by Francis Bacon (to whom she was unrelated, despite the coincidence of their names). To this, one may identify a political dimension, an appropriation of the quintessentially English playwright to support another nation's narrative. Bacon's arguments leant heavily on textual interpretation of the plays. She wrote, and theorised, extensively. In support of her arguments she travelled to England to pursue her research, declaring eventually that the proof that would vindicate her views could be found in Shakespeare's grave. Soon thereafter, she would suffer a breakdown from which she was never to recover, escorted back to the United States to spend her last months in an asylum.

The story of Bacon is essentially one of human interest, incidental to the mathematics, science or practicalities of text analysis, yet it casts light on the complex and intensely felt relations between text, authorship and society. Whatever may be said of Bacon's scholarship and motives – and much has been said and written on both subjects – she lived her life according to the philosophy that an afternoon spent exploring Shakespeare's texts is an afternoon spent in the proximity of the author itself. To spend time in the company of a text is to learn something about the author: through the playwright's texts shall ye know him. What we know of an author may inform us about the text: what we know of a text may inform us about the author – and if both are well-understood, our knowledge of text and author may lead us to conclusions about the reader, the third member of the triad, who is drawn to the text and perhaps to the personality that created it.

Rockwell (2003) tells the story of Father Roberto Busa, an Italian Jesuit priest. Following the completion of a thesis at the Papal Gregorian University of Rome, which explored the work of Saint Thomas Aquinas, Busa decided on his next challenge: the creation of what is known as a concordance – an index of Aquinas's work – which Busa began in 1946. The task in hand was huge; it would, to say the least, be the work of a lifetime. In 1949, he travelled to the United States looking for an automated alternative to replace the 10,000 hand-written index cards that his work had already generated. After visiting about 25 American universities, his search led him to IBM, where he met the company's founder, Thomas J. Watson Sr. (Winter, 1999). It seemed unlikely that IBM could help; their technology couldn't achieve what was required. But Busa would not concede defeat so easily. He took an IBM poster with him into the meeting and showed it to Watson: it was printed with the now-familiar slogan "The difficult we do right away; the impossible takes a little longer". Watson agreed to support Busa's work.

Busa's undertaking evolved with the available technology, from paper index cards to punch cards to eventual publication on compact disc. Text analysis, unlike data mining, was not "born digital". Rather, it is an area that originally relied upon manual input, painstaking review of ancient manuscripts, collation and statistics gathering. Nonetheless, it is a subject that has benefited a great deal from the increasing availability and variety of text analysis tools and automation, and should perhaps be seen as both an inspiration and an ancestor for, as well as a modern-day user of, the suite of tools and techniques currently collectively referred to as text mining. Busa is sometimes now described as the founding father of humanities computing (Jockers, 2013; Gouglas et al., 2013).

A few years later, the Founding Fathers of the United States would become the subject of computational text analysis. The Federalist Papers, published by the three authors Alexander Hamilton, James Madison and John Jay under the shared nom de plume "Publius", include several articles for which no authorship information had been made available. Anonymous speech was not only a wise precaution but also a colonial-era tradition (Boudin, 2011). The Founding Fathers' predilection for anonymity would provide an irresistible opportunity for textual analysis. For many years the Federalist Papers had attracted labourious manual analysis. When such methods became possible, it was inevitable that computational stylistic analysis would be applied to determine the true (or at any rate most probable) authorship of disputed papers.

The analysis of these papers was taken up by Frederick Mosteller, founding chair of Harvard University's statistics department, alongside collaborators Frederick Williams and, later, David Wallace. Their authorship attribution study, *Inference and Disputed Authorship: The Federalist*, represented an early application of Bayesian inference; it evaluated the probability of various hypotheses according to a known basis of evidence. Mosteller and Wallace created a knowledge base of information about the potential authors, including tracts written by Hamilton and Madison, and used this to support the attribution of works. Their study enjoyed considerable attention and interest, appearing in *Time* in 1964 and attracting a formidable number of citations and related studies, including critiques, a proportion of which are undoubtedly justified; still, this study stands as an early example of the use of probabilistic methods in textual analysis.

The automated analysis of text was too useful for its business potential to be ignored for long. In 1958, an article in the *IBM Journal* (Hans Peter, 1958) described the use of data processing machines for auto-abstracting and auto-encoding textual documents. The author, Hans Peter Luhn, was a senior research engineer and computer scientist at IBM. He foresaw that the "sheer bulk" of literature of interest to science, industry and government, combined with the trend for increasing specialisation and divisionalisation, would become a formidable barrier to the flow of information. The proposed solution was a *business intelligence system*. Such a system would be capable of ingesting textual data, automatically generating descriptive metadata and summary information, and disseminating the information according to topic and user history. The system would be able to identify and retrieve information of relevance to a given task, and share it intelligently with the people who needed it most.

Business intelligence was originally data led, but the prevalence of information held in unstructured documents meant that the importance of textual analysis became very evident. Brachman et al. (1993) describe an area of research that makes use of data mining to search through corporate databases and extract useful information such as customer behaviour. They define this area as *data archaeology* – a polite term, given that some refer to leftover customer data as *digital dandruff*. Brachman et al. describe data archaeology as an iterative task requiring frequent human intervention, supported using appropriate tools. To access unstructured data such as full-text fields, some sort of natural-language processing approach became a requirement. As there is a direct financial motivation to improving one's understanding of the behaviour of customers, potential customers and one's own brand, business intelligence became a well-developed and well-funded field. Many commercial packages and providers are in existence today.

Text mining as a modern discipline is very seldom driven by the same imperatives that we attribute to personalities such as Bacon. Nowadays the choice of use case is overwhelmingly driven by the imperatives of business, government and research, and the methods used are generally based in the realm of the scientific. Even so, text mining is often employed in an attempt to see through dense or copious text to see the bones that lie beneath, whether it is the information carried by the text, or incidental information about the writer.

Sometimes, texts are also analysed for purposes related to law enforcement: to track, trace and understand contacts between among individuals, organisations and ideologies. Such uses rely on the principle first articulated by the pioneering forensic scientist Edmond Locard, "every contact leaves a trace". Locard's exchange principle applies to the search for evidence, information showing that an interaction has occurred. Originally, the envisaged transfer of material between individuals – perpetrator and victim, or criminal and accomplice – was expected to involve physical evidence, such as mud, hair or dust. Nowadays, such trace contact may be explored via digital forensics, such as mining log files (Lim, 2006). Locard's own writings provide insight into his past; he was fascinated by Arthur Conan Doyle's detective, Sherlock Holmes, to whom he referred in his own writings.

In response, Winthrop-Young (2012) proposes that humanity be renamed *Homo vestigia faciens*, or "Man, the trace-maker", who is, in Winthrop-Young's words, "a being defined by inscription surfaces, recording devices and storage facilities able to capture far more of its signs and traces than it is willing to divulge". Just as the extant remnants of the past determine the limits of our knowledge of Homer, Sappho or Shakespeare, so too do the traces left behind by the general public govern what is understood of individuals and of our past interactions with one another. Our society and interactions leave traces on every level from the local to the macroscopic. The same characteristics that make textual interaction a useful resource for the anthropologist, sociologist or linguist also make such data sets useful for market surveillance (Netzer et al., 2012) and, indeed, for the purposes of national surveillance.

1.2 THE READING ROBOT

The world in which we live is increasingly defined by information generation, transmission, sharing and consumption. For social media users, the transmission of information is the heartbeat of the social world. For businesses e-mails are sent, decisions made and documented, complaints and compliments received, reports are written and accounts are kept. A press release pops up on the newswire and is picked up by seven newspapers before anybody notices that it's an old story that first appeared in the press three years ago. Media reports detailing proposed changes to the law send thousands to air their opinion on government and pressure group websites. A coffee-fuelled graduate student in New Orleans trawls through a heap of journals looking for information of relevance to include in her literature review. A Somerset pensioner looks through his home directory for the poem sent by his granddaughter.

On any scale from the microcosm of the individual to the macrocosm of society, we are all to a greater or lesser extent vulnerable to the challenges associated with information management: our time is limited. We cannot know what we do not have time to read. By and large, we implicitly depend upon others to filter and summarise available information for us, so that data filtration has become a social function. Scholarly communications, for example, are subject to the workings of the peer-review process. The everyday information we encounter is filtered by convenience and availability, the information transmission characteristics of real-world social networks and online scale-free networks, and by the choices of traditional media organisations.

An obvious intervention suggests itself. Rather than relying on time and effort donated by human actors, could we not assign the problems of understanding and summarising text to a computer? The computer, after all, will neither tire nor lose interest. A correctly specified machine can attend to hundreds of thousands of simultaneous interactions on social media, e-mail lists or blogs. Unlike the tired graduate student, the computer can access papers in milliseconds and index them according to a given data model in the blink of an eye. A system with access to full historical databases of news would have been able to identify the duplicated story and save face for tired news editors across the world. In practice, many such systems are already in place today.

Text mining, the generation of new knowledge from bodies of text, is potentially a transformative technology. Text mining has the power and potential to enrich information and knowledge management processes. Using computational power to analyse texts means that the exploration of large amounts of text is no longer subject to the whims, limitations or biases of the human reader or annotator. That said, we are instead subject to the whims, limitations and biases of the system. In the words of Douglas Adams, "We are not home and dry: We could not even be said to be home and vigorously towelling ourselves off".

A key difficulty in the automated analysis of text is the complexity of the problem. The texts on which we wish to work are not *structured texts*, as they lack the "explicit semantics typically required for applications to interpret the information as intended by the human author or required by the end-user application" (Oasis, 2005). Unstructured texts are defined by OASIS (ibid) as the "direct product of human communication". In general, making use of these texts will require us to retrofit some level of structure into the text – to identify any available clues, guess at appropriate semantics, and to make a reasoned judgement as to the accuracy of our guess.

Computational tools for text mining are now effective enough and easy enough to use that they are applied in many real-world scenarios. Some are business focused, such as business intelligence and customer relationship management. Some are government focused, such as national security. Others are research focused. Text mining has a particularly high research profile in areas such as biochemistry and the life sciences, where there is an extremely extensive literature containing extensive and detailed coverage of innumerable observations. This resource benefits greatly from the availability of text mining-based systems. Because systematic literature review is so common and widely used in this area, there is an immediate business use case for tools that facilitate and simplify the literature review process.

This first chapter aims to give a brief introduction to text and its more generalised parent, data mining, as research areas. In so doing, this chapter aims to place into context the topics covered throughout the book.

1.3 FROM DATA TO TEXT MINING

Data Mining (noun): "Torturing data until it confesses ... and if you torture it enough, it will confess to anything"

Jeff Jonas, IBM

Text mining as a stand-alone discipline is typically traced back to data mining. Data mining itself is a child of the late 1980s and early 1990s (Coenen, 2011), during which time it grew from its parent disciplines – machine learning, databasing, data warehousing and knowledge discovery – into a subject in its own right. It covers a series of tools and methodologies designed to identify interesting patterns in databases. Data mining is "the art of extracting information from data" (Tuffery, 2011). It is often separated from the general practices involved in data analysis; data mining specifically focuses on the identification of knowledge that was not previously known.

Whilst its name dates from the 1990s, the field of data mining inherits a rich heritage from the field of statistics. As Stéphane Tufféry demonstrates in *Data Mining and Statistics for Decision Making* (Tuffery, 2011, p. 645), the growth of the discipline was tied closely to the increasing scale of activity, speed of analytical tools and the availability of enabling technologies.

Many database-backed activities are not data mining problems. Straightforward access to data, such as "What is the surname of the person who lives at No. 7 Market Street, Towcester?" is not a data mining problem. It is simply a straightforward database query. Even variants that involve aggregate statistics, as in "What is the average age of the inhabitants of Market Street?" are straightforward queries asked of available data. Activities qualifying as applications of data mining may

- link multiple data sets.
- predict trends.
- make use of real-time data access.
- support decision making through development of robust models.

Data mining is capable both of confirmation or refutation of existing preconceptions and of the identification and expression of new rules and associations (Tuffery, 2011, p. 27). It is characteristically useful on data sets that are large or complex enough to be difficult to analyse manually. The traditional examples involve the mining of customer purchase data or financial behaviour: customers who like *a* are also likely to purchase *b*; clients who pay *n*% of their credit card bill monthly have a likelihood of *m*% of defaulting on a loan, and so forth. Other examples include medicine, insurance, customer retention, real-time stock-market activity management, infrastructural power-load forecasting and research within the biological sciences.

The subject of data mining research need not be straightforward examples of business data. Any data source can be used, including those typically associated with ubiquitous and wearable computing or the "internet of things":

- CMOS/CCD image sensors: data taken from photographs or videos, including real-time video, and processed accordingly, such as via image recognition algorithms.
- Microphones.
- Textual data from e-mails, documents, file systems, the social web and so forth.
- Motion sensors.
- Smart energy monitors, monitoring electrical use within dwellings.
- Thermal sensors in devices ranging from laptops to home thermostats.
- Accelerometers in tablets, phones and hard drives.
- Medical devices such as pulse and blood pressure monitors.

In practice, the output of the majority of these sensors is not readily available. In many scenarios the most convenient source of data is available in the form of unstructured text. For this reason, text mining methods have become increasingly popular as part of the broader data mining environment, alongside existing suites of data mining methodologies and tool sets.

1.4 DEFINITIONS OF TEXT MINING

The development of text mining as a child discipline of data mining, still itself a relatively nascent field in the early 2000s, gave a new face and branding to a series of ideas drawn from existing disciplines. The origin of text mining as a field is twofold. The name exists as a homage to data mining; it has been suggested (Hearst, 1999) that an appropriate name for text mining would be "text data mining", implying that text data mining is a variation on the general field of data mining and exists as a subfield of that more generic field. Text mining is defined by Tuffery (2011) as "the automatic processing of natural language text data available in reasonably large quantities in the form of computer files, with the aim of extracting and structuring their contents and themes, for the purposes of rapid (nonliterary) analysis, the discovery of hidden data, or automatic decision making". Tuffery specifically differentiates text mining from subjects such as stylometry, but views it as closely linked to quantitative linguistics. This definition is by no means universal: recent talk surrounding literary text mining, for example, identifies subtasks including stylometric analyses (Green, 2011), authorship attribution, stylistic analysis, and genre analysis (Plaisant et al., 2006).

Many definitions of text mining refer to the definition provided by Marti Hearst in her 1999 paper, "Untangling text data mining", which effectively differentiated text mining from its sibling discipline, information retrieval. The paper gives the impression of text mining as a young discipline seeking to differentiate itself from its disciplinary neighbours. Hearst proposes that many of the activities that are sometimes described as text data mining are more appropriately classified as information retrieval research. For Hearst, text data mining is, in essence, about discovery of new information within data sets. Finding patterns or trends within textual data is not, for Hearst, text data mining: rather, such activities are applications of computational linguistics. Finding nonnovel "nuggets" of information within textual data is not text data mining either; it is simply information retrieval. Following this definition, an application may be described as text data mining if and only if novel information is retrieved, information that tells us something about the world rather than simply telling us something about the textual data.

This definition gave rise to considerable discussion. In a clarifying article, Hearst (2003) provided the following definition: "the discovery by computer of new, previously unknown information, by automatically extracting information from different written resources [and] the linking together of [...] extracted information [...] to form new facts or new hypotheses, to be explored further by more conventional means of experimentation".

Text mining has enjoyed considerable interest in recent years. Very similar tools, techniques and methods are in use in the broader domain, meaning that a community of practice exists that extends beyond the groups taking part in activities strictly definable as text mining. As a result, the various disciplinary groups have tended to adopt and adapt the nomenclature for their own purposes, with the consequence of a certain amount of brand dilution.

Text mining has recently been described as including stylometry, document clustering and techniques drawn from information retrieval (Meyer et al., 2008). It has been variously defined as development of an understanding or summary of the topics covered in a text (Argamon et al., 2003), a vast field of theoretical approaches and methods that share only the single characteristic of selecting text as an input source (Meyer et al., 2008), and "analysing information to discover patterns[,] going beyond information access to further help users analyze and digest information and facilitate decision making" (Aggarwal and Zhai, 2012). Little wonder, therefore, that some (see, e.g. Benoit, 2002) have concluded that the situation is confusing and the terminology inconsistent. A usefully succinct summary definition, which encapsulates most of those given above, is provided by Kao and Poteet (2007), for whom text mining is the discovery and extraction of interesting, nontrivial knowledge from free or unstructured text.

In this book, we will discuss text mining in the strictest sense, as well as activity related to the broader definitions of text mining, text analytics, and sibling or parent disciplines such as information retrieval. We attempt to provide a broad overview of relevant technologies, areas of research and expertise and potential future directions, rather than adhering closely to a particular subfield or domain. Our aim is to provide the reader with an overview that enables them to better imagine the potential of technologies, tools and methods that enable them to work with text. Our hope is that open and interdisciplinary discussion will make it easier for researchers to introduce text mining into their projects, platforms and thinking in the future.

1.5 EXPLORING THE DISCIPLINARY NEIGHBOURHOOD

Hearst identifies links between text mining and corpus-based computational linguistics, an area that makes use of computational methodologies to identify patterns and similarities in the use of language. Text mining also, inevitably, enjoys close links to natural language processing (NLP), which is a broad area covering the use of computers to understand and manipulate natural language text or speech [in order] to do useful things (Chowdhury, 2003).

Surprisingly, linguistics and text mining sometimes appear to have relatively little in common. That is not to say that text mining does not make use of tool sets drawn from linguistics, such as part-of-speech taggers, tokenisers and so forth (see Chapter 2 for a discussion of tools commonly used in text mining). These tools are used in text mining when there are utilitarian reasons to do so; for example, cases in which the use of such tools improves the practical outcome of a process. In practice, text mining does not always require any significant level of understanding of natural language text. It is common to take approaches to text mining that do not assume this, making use of simpler representations of texts or extracting elements as required without considering their placement within the text.

A very simple example would be the extraction of dates, names and addresses from available unstructured text. It is possible that we do not even know much about the documents themselves, which could be anything from newspaper articles to parliamentary archives. We do not know a great deal about the sentence context in which the names are used. Even if all we really know is that these names, times and places have been mentioned together, we can still apply traditional data mining methods to build up new knowledge that can be drawn upon to further research about people, places and times.

Informally, this distinction could be compared to deep and shallow reading (Chaofeng, 2011; Yang and Zhang, 2011). This refers to the distinction between reading a text carefully and attentively in order to acquire a good understanding of its meaning, and scanning a text briefly and partially, looking for relevant keywords or interesting sections (Liu, 2005). Franco Moretti of Stanford's Literary Lab contributed a related term to the digital humanities (Moretti, 2000), "distant reading". This practice can be contrasted to the traditional literary practice of "close reading". In distant reading, in place of detailed study of individual texts, a set of texts are compiled into a corpus, which is then analysed as a whole. It is worth noting that a distinction is often drawn between deep and shallow NLP (Schäfer, 2007). Deep NLP, or DNLP, attempts to apply linguistic knowledge to the analysis of natural language. It is an attempt to look for the structural bones (the "deep structure") that lie beneath the words of a sentence; that is, to acquire an understanding of the meaning beneath the text. Shallow NLP usually applies some level of linguistic knowledge to the text, but takes a relatively minimalist approach, which is often blamed for error. Pragmatically, most computational NLP applications will apply shallow NLP; many will limit themselves to shallow reading techniques.

Improving or customising tool support for new usage areas is one area within which linguistics intersects closely with text mining and NLP. The availability of tools, background resources and training materials can pose a challenge to those looking to introduce text mining into their research practices. Some languages, notably at the time of writing English, various Romance languages such as French and Spanish, German and to some extent Russian, Arabic and Chinese, are well supported. Relatively limited support is available for certain other languages within a subset of text mining tools. Areas that are broadly monetised have many available resources on which to draw, such as the biomedical sciences, in which text mining is widely used. Other areas must rely on sparser tool sets, data sets and disciplinary traditions.

Text mining is also closely linked to information extraction and knowledge management, both methodologically and in the choice of goals and outcomes. Tool sets designed for text mining include filters that are designed to distill complex texts into simpler, more manageable texts. Text mining allows us to extract the information that matters to us, and combine it with other information sources to teach us new things about the world. Information extraction is therefore a useful source of the types of tool that power text mining. Information extraction (Stavrianou et al., 2007) attempts to extract structured data from unstructured texts. Knowledge management (Alavi and Leidner, 2001) explores the use of information systems to construct, share and apply knowledge, usually within specific organisations. To a great extent knowledge – broadly definable as information we know, believe or at any rate, accept – is stored and shared in human-readable form, which is to say, as natural language text. The aggregation and use of knowledge within an organisational context requires the extraction of information from heterogeneous sources: project reports, performance reviews, mailing lists.

Information retrieval and text mining are also closely linked, to the extent that it is sometimes difficult to clearly disambiguate between the two (Stavrianou et al., 2007). Both are grappling with a very similar basic problem: the interpretation and characterisation of texts that are only imperfectly understood. Both attempt to filter information for a certain purpose; in the case of information retrieval, the intention is to collect together the features that characterise each text, so that the text can be indexed and made available to users searching for that type of text. The analytical tools that enable information retrieval are also applicable for text mining purposes: identifying the subject of texts, for example, or calculating the similarities between documents, are problems that can be approached using methods drawn from information retrieval.

Machine learning and text mining are also closely linked. Machine learning as a field studies the question of "giving computers the ability to learn without being explicitly programmed" (Samuel, 1959), learning about a given application domain through the evaluation of data (Kovahi and Provost, 1998). Machine learning is generally statistical, and is very much in the tradition of the evidence-based approach to classification taken by in the 1960s by Mosteller and Wallace during their work on the authorship of the Federalist papers.

A machine learning approach provides a flexible alternative to more traditional rule-based systems, which were dominant for many years in the field of knowledge engineering (Sebastiani, 2002). Machine learning is extremely useful in many domains of computer science that deal with evaluation of user input, or sensor input in the broader sense. Machine learning methods are extremely good at finding ways to approximate human judgement of problems, using available examples to develop rules; because machine learning algorithms can test rule sets extremely quickly and in an automated manner, they are capable of iteratively building far better rules than a human would generate. Such methods are quite distinct from artificial intelligence: although the methods used are sometimes biologically inspired, machine learning does not attempt to faithfully replicate human perception or reasoning.

A further area that may be linked to text mining is human-computer interaction. Many subdisciplines, such as affective computing, have an analogue in text mining. Affective computing is the ability of a computer to pay attention to human emotion, the *affect* caused by an event, situation or communication (Picard and Healey, 1997). Use cases such as opinion mining and sentiment analysis owe a great deal to existing research in human-computer interaction (HCI). Human-computer interaction research focusing on affect may depend upon physiological signals, spoken language or nonverbal cues to identify the user's current emotional state. Text mining applications can form part of affective computing (see, e.g. Ptaszynski et al., 2009), and comprises one strand of many available to the researcher looking to characterise, understand, sense and respond to emotional response. Texts may also be scrutinised for clues as to the personality of the author (see for example Noecker et al., 2013).

Text mining has been described as an unusual area, enjoying a great deal of hype but very few practitioners (Hearst, 1999). There is truth in this description, even at the time of writing of this chapter, some 15 years later. Few individuals would describe themselves as "text miners". Yet text mining in the broader sense is a core technology that powers many recent developments.

The massive growth in the quantities of data now available to business, government and academia – as the result of a *data flood* (Lohr, 2012), *data deluge* (Hey and Trefethen, 2003) or an *explosion* (Villars et al, 2011) – is usually described in terms that bring to mind disaster or destruction. Text mining is one of the components that power the analytical machinery that, it is implied by contemporary rhetoric, will save us from drowning in the flood of data.

1.6 PREREQUISITES FOR TEXT MINING

Text mining is an inherently interdisciplinary process, involving collaboration between individuals with specialities ranging from the technical to the humanities. Text mining activity will almost invariably require a good information technology infrastructure. It is necessary to have adequate information systems, data management, backup functionality and so forth. The data sets involved can sometimes be very large. This also means that there will be problems and issues in scale. This may make it necessary to involve domain specialists such as high-performance computing engineers, computer scientists and database specialists.

Barriers to text mining include legal and ethical indications of text mining that potentially reduce its adoption in academia. It is not always possible to gain rights to perform text mining on information, particularly proprietary information or formally published information. Academic articles, for example, are often held behind restrictive licences that do not permit text mining. Because text mining has not historically been used in many of the fields that would find it useful today, there is no tradition for its use. Any researcher or practitioner looking to introduce its use into such a field is likely to have an uphill struggle. Questions have also been raised about the reproducibility of research results (see, e.g. Boyd and Crawford, 2012). This issue is particularly prominent in text mining, as it is not always possible to gain the rights or the data to reproduce a given experiment.

At times it is also difficult to characterise or establish access to the data set that has been used. Gaining access to the material used for text mining often involves advice and support from information specialists, and in many cases will involve working with information resellers to negotiate access to data. Text mining is still sufficiently uncommon that establishing access to data sets is not an automatic or routine process.

The citation of linguistic data sets (or *corpora*, standard data sets) is usually achieved by the use of citation to a paper that describes that data set (corpus), because there is no single clear and straightforward means to cite the data set itself. Even if the data set is clearly identifiable, it may not be possible to access it. It is not always possible to publish data sets. One example of this is the use of social network data scraped from the Internet. Whilst it is possible to collect data for a specific purpose, it is not possible to republish it without resolving extant rights issues, such as the consent of named individuals and the terms of service under which the data are collected. Issues such as this are becoming more evident as text mining moves into widespread use and remain problematic today. Legal and ethical issues relating to text mining are discussed in Chapters 3 and 4 of this book.

In practice, projects involving text mining almost always require expert input from individuals familiar with the domain of application. Such domain experts are invaluable resources, able to support the project on the development of requirements, practical deployment, testing, evaluation and exploitation of any results. As there are often very few resources or tools available for specific areas (such as natural languages), domain experts are frequently key to the production of these resources. For example, a group looking to perform text analysis on historical documents written in Latin or Greek will be able to benefit from the existing resources made available by the research community, but may well find that the existing tools do not suffice for their purposes. A domain expert can identify the shortcomings of existing approaches and provide information that will help the developers improve the performance of the tool set.

Some text mining projects involve a deeper understanding of natural language than others. Those that require more may benefit from input provided by trained linguists. This does not necessarily mean that a linguist should be involved with every text mining project, although it would tend to be advisable to involve expert knowledge from this domain if possible. The development of text mining tools, on the other hand, will almost invariably involve linguistic knowledge unless the language and scenarios of use are well understood and bear similarities with known scenarios.

Similarly, text mining projects may take various approaches to data collection. Manovich (2011) separates data collection into *deep* data, in which detailed data is collected about a few subjects (a few individuals or small groups), and *surface* data, in which a little information is collected about many subjects. Traditionally, surface data was of interest to quantitative fields and deep data of interest to qualitative researchers; a similar point is made by Boyd and Crawford (2012), who stress the value of "small data", data collected on modest scales. The deluge of Big Data rhetoric brings with it an increasing acceptance of the collection of large amounts of data about many subjects, and alongside it, an increasing risk of finding oneself methodologically out of one's depth. Although this problem is not specific to text mining, it is a phenomenon common to text mining projects. Depending on the aim of the project, text mining projects may need input from researchers in the quantitative social sciences, and perhaps also researchers who take various approaches to study of the subject matter.

1.7 LEARNING MINECRAFT: WHAT MAKES A TEXT MINER?

Perceptive readers will note that one group that has been ignored from this description so far is text miners themselves. This is perhaps because the text miner is the most difficult of these entities to characterise. As Hearst (1999) described, there is more discussion than deployment of text mining thus far. There is an acknowledged potential for the use of text mining in many disciplines and subject areas, but we have not yet reached the point at which the area has become a firmly established discipline in its own right. Text mining is therefore not an individual discipline, but rather one of many potential endpoints for information specialists, computer scientists, engineers and domain specialists. There is therefore no single profile for the text mining expert.

There is also no single education or educational specialism that optimally prepares the individual for working in this discipline. A number of relevant academic courses and resources, which approach the art and practice of text mining from various theoretical backgrounds – including the humanities, linguistics and computing – are listed in Appendix D of this book.

Perhaps the best way of characterising the text miner today is by saying that you (might) know them when you see them. If an individual finds him- or herself using tools and resources designed for text mining and NLP, gaining useful resources from text mining forums or books, or describing his or her experiences at conferences devoted to text mining, analytics, information gleaned from analysis of large bodies of text, and so forth, then that individual de facto works in the area.

Because of the confusion surrounding the terminology of text mining, it is somewhat unlikely that most individuals working in the area would define themselves as text mining practitioners; the term is opaque and conveys little in the absence of clarification, so is not widely used except where it forms part of a team brand or identity. The term is contentious, to say the least. From personal experience, its use polarises people: a number of respondents during the planning stages for the *Working with Text* workshop on which this work is based raised definitional questions: Which definition of text mining was meant? Did we have the strict definition in mind? Did specific activities fall into the category in question? We found that text mining professionals are far more likely to identify themselves primarily as working within one of the parent disciplines, such as computer science, information science, computational linguistics, knowledge management, data mining, and machine learning.

1.8 CONTEMPORARY ATTITUDES TO TEXT MINING

The intersecting technologies upon which text mining in built, NLP and various forms of textual analysis, can no longer be considered a niche application area. Automated analysis of text is simply too significant an area to be ignored entirely and has made its way into too many fields, particularly in research. Combined with the legislative developments of the last few years, such as the Hargreaves report, which sparked reform in UK copyright law in favour of text mining practice, it is clear that the environment is changing rapidly for those with an interest in this area. It is to be hoped that in the future it becomes more straightforward to introduce text mining into your workflow as a researcher or as an information professional.

We have mentioned that text mining often finds itself at odds with the requirements and preferences of the publisher. There is a widespread expectation according to Smit and Van de Graaf (2011) that text mining will become "easy enough for the average researcher to use"; Smit reports that over 60% of publishers agree with this forecast. However, the majority of publishers surveyed by Smit also expressed the belief that corporate customers were more likely to ask for access for text mining purposes, as 68% of publishers had received requests by corporate customers, whilst 51% had received requests for research purposes, for example, by academic or research groups.

The rise of data journalism means that there is an increasing acceptance of data-led visualisations used in support of public narratives or to support political argument. This is an area that continues to develop and continues to raise many questions, both methodological and in terms of the developing vocabulary of visualisation elements and visual rhetoric (Hullman and Diakopoulos, 2011).

Beyond the practical questions of data access and distribution, an ongoing process of exploration and development is taking place that attempts to explore the form that may be taken by a text-mining process, data set and representation, once it is situated within the boundaries of specific host disciplines. Ultimately, the problem at hand is one of scientific communication. Research communities making use of extracted information must have confidence in the data, and in their ability to use it confidently. Appropriate conventions may vary between disciplines; Kerr et al. (2013) describes the process of developing and evaluating visualisations for a digital humanities Big Data analysis problem.

1.9 CONCLUSIONS

Popular interest in the field of text mining continues to wax and wane with the relevance of the topic to other contemporary movements in the technology industry. The rapid growth in data curated by universities, business and industry provide a clear business case for text mining as a field: too much text is available for any one individual to read in a lifetime. Nonetheless, text mining remains a hard sell: the technologies are complex, often fragile, domain-specific and with a high start-up cost. The skill set required to engage in the subject is not easily found, even though it is increasingly true that text mining tools are designed to be accessible to developers without subject-specific skills.

Before text mining can be sold as a mainstream technology in many fields, "killer applications", compelling applications that will be considered a must-have within the domain, must begin to emerge. That text mining can provide insight and value in the right hands is not in question. Whether it is ready for deployment in unfamiliar contexts is a question that can only be answered through trial, error and the sharing of experience. Consequentially, we encourage readers to choose from the available tools – cloud-based, web-based or locally installed – and make their own experiments. If you are not a computer scientist, programmer or engineer you may find it most comfortable to work with someone who is more comfortable with these domains, but the skills you gain in doing so will be useful in a future that is, more than ever, concerned with the large-scale analysis of text and data.

REFERENCES

Aggarwal, C.C., Zhai, C., 2012. Mining Text Data. Springer Science & Business Media, New York, USA.

Alavi, M., Leidner, D.E., 2001. Review: knowledge management and knowledge management systems: conceptual foundations and research issues. MIS Q. 25, 107–136.

Argamon, S., Šarić, M., Stein, S.S., 2003. Style mining of electronic messages for multiple authorship discrimination: first results. In: Proceedings of the Ninth ACM SIGKDD International Conference on Knowledge Discovery and Data Mining. ACM, New York, pp. 475–480.

Baym, N., 1996. Delia Bacon, history's odd woman out. NEQ 69, 223–249. Retrieved 2014-02-01 from, http://www.english.illinois.edu/-people-/emeritus/baym/essays/delia_bacon.htm.

Benoit, G., 2002. Data mining. In: Cronin, B. (Ed.), Annual Review of Information Science and Technology (ARIST), vol. 36. Information Today for ASIST, Medford, NJ, pp. 265–310.

Boudin, C., 2011. Publius and the Petition: Doe v. Reed and the History of Anonymous Speech. Yale Law J. 120, 2140–2181.

Boyd, D., Crawford, K., 2012. Critical questions for big data: provocations for a cultural, technological, and scholarly phenomenon. Inf. Commun. Soc. 15 (5), 662–679.

Brachman, R.J., Selfridge, P.G., Terveen, L.G., Altman, B., Borgida, A., Halper, F., Kirk, T., Lazar, A., McGuinness, D.L., Resnick, L.A., 1993. Integrated support for data archaeology. Int. J. Intell. Cooperative Inf. Syst. 2 (2), 159–185.

Chaofeng, D., 2011. The study of shallow reading and deep reading in the age of electronic media [J]. Libr. J. 3, 003.

Chowdhury, G., 2003. Natural language processing. Annu. Rev. Inf. Sci. Technol. 37, 51–89. ISSN 0066–4200.

Coenen, F., 2011. Data mining: past, present and future. Knowl. Eng. Rev. 26 (1), 25–29.

Coleman, C.B., 1922. The Treatise of Lorenzo Valla on the Donation of Constantine: Text and Translation into English. Yale University Press.

Cronin, V., 2011. The Florentine Renaissance. Vintage Digital.

Gouglas, S., Rockwell, G., Smith, V., Hoosein, S., Quamen, H., 2013. Before the beginning: the formation of humanities computing as a discipline in Canada. Digital Stud./ Le champ numérique 3(1).

Green, H.E., 2011. Finding the canary for text mining: analysis of the use and users of MONK text mining research software. J. Chicago Colloquium on Digital Humanities and Comput. Sci. 1(3).

Hans Peter, L., 1958. A business intelligence system. IBM J. 3 (4), 314–319.

Hearst, M., 1999. Untangling text data mining. Retrieved 2013-01-02 from, http://people.ischool.berkeley.edu/~hearst/papers/acl99/acl99-tdm.html.

Hearst, M., 2003. What is text mining? Retrieved 2013-01-02 from, http://people.ischool.berkeley.edu/~hearst/text-mining.html.

Hey, A.J., Trefethen, A.E., 2003. The data deluge: an e-science perspective. Grid Computing: Making the Global Infrastructure a Reality. Wiley, pp. 809–824.

Hullman, J., Diakopoulos, N., 2011. Visualization rhetoric: framing effects in narrative visualization. IEEE Trans. Visual. Comput. Graphics 17 (12), 2231–2240.

Jockers, M.L., 2013. Macroanalysis: Digital Methods and Literary History. University of Illinois Press, Champaign, Illinois, USA.

Kao, A., Poteet, S.R., 2007. Natural Language Processing and Text Mining. Springer Science & Business Media, New York, USA.

Kerr, K., Hausman, B.L., Gad, S., Javen, W., 2013. Visualization and Rhetoric: Key Concerns for Utilizing Big Data in Humanities Research: A Case Study of Vaccination Discourses: 1918–1919. In Big Data, 2013 IEEE International Conference. IEEE, pp. 25–32.

Kovahi, R., Provost, F., 1998. Glossary of terms. Mach. Learn. 30, 271–274.

Lim, N., 2006. Crime investigation: a course in computer forensics. Commun. Assoc. Inf. Syst. 18 (1), 10.

Liu, Z., 2005. Reading behavior in the digital environment: changes in reading behavior over the past ten years. J. Doc. 61 (6), 700–712.

Lohr, S., 2012. The age of big data. New York Times, 11.

Manovich, L., 2011. Trending: the promises and the challenges of big social data.

Meyer, D., Hornik, K., Feinerer, I., 2008. Text mining infrastructure in R. J. Stat. Software 25 (5), 1–54.

Moretti, F., 2000. Conjectures on world literature. New Left Rev. 1, 54.

Netzer, O., Feldman, R., Goldenberg, J., Fresko, M., 2012. Mine your own business: market-structure surveillance through text mining. Marketing Sci. 31 (3), 521–543.

Noecker, J., Ryan, M., Juola, P., 2013. Psychological profiling through textual analysis. Literary Ling. Comput.

OASIS, 2005. UIMA specification. Retrieved 05-2014 from, https://www.oasis-open.org/committees/download.php/28492/uima-spec-wd-05.pdf.

Picard, R.W., Healey, J., 1997. Affective wearables. Personal Technologies 1 (4), 231–240.

Plaisant, C., Rose, J., Yu, B., Auvil, L., Kirschenbaum, M.G., Smith, M.N., Lord, G., 2006. Exploring erotics in Emily Dickinson's correspondence with text mining and visual interfaces. In: Proceedings of the 6th ACM/IEEE-CS Joint Conference on Digital Libraries. ACM, pp. 141–150.

Ptaszynski, M., Dybala, P., Shi, W., Rzepka, R., Araki, K., 2009. Towards context aware emotional intelligence in machines: computing contextual appropriateness of affective states. In Twenty-First International Joint Conference on Artificial Intelligence.

Rockwell, G., 2003. What is text analysis, really? Literary Ling. Comput. 18 (2), 209–219.

Samuel, A.L., 1959. Some studies in machine learning using the game of checkers. IBM J. Res. Dev. 3 (3), 210–229.

Schäfer, U., June 2007. Integrating Deep and Shallow Natural Language Processing Components – Representations and Hybrid Architectures. PhD dissertation. Faculty of Mathematics and Computer Science, Saarland University, Saarbrücken, Germany.

Sebastiani, F., 2002. Machine learning in automated text categorization. ACM Comput. Surv. (CSUR) 34 (1), 1–47.

Smit, E., Van de Graaf, M., 2011. Journal Article Mining, A research study into Practices, Policies, Plans… and Promises. Commissioned by the Publishing. Research Consortium by Eefke Smit and Maurits van de Graaf, Amsterdam May 2011. http://www.publishingresearch. net/documents/PRCSmitJAMreport20June2011VersionofRecord.pdf.

Stavrianou, A., Andritsos, P., Nicoloyannis, N., 2007. Overview and semantic issues of text mining. ACM Sigmod Rec. 36 (3), 23–34.

Tuffery, S., 2011. Data Mining and Statistics for Decision Making. John Wiley and Sons Ltd., Oxford, UK.

Villars, R.L., Olofson, C.W., Eastwood, M., 2011. Big Data: What It Is and Why You Should Care. White Paper IDC, Framingham, MA, USA.

Winter, T.N., 1999. Roberto Busa, sj, and the invention of the machine-generated concordance. Classical Bulletin, 75(1), 3.

Winthrop-Young, G., 2012. Hunting a whale of a state: Kittler and his terrorists. Cult. Politics 8 (3), 399–412.

Yang, C., Zhang, J.W., 2011. Deep choices in the era of shallow reading. J. Acad. Lib. Inf. Sci. 1, 004.

CHAPTER 2

A Day at Work (with Text): A Brief Introduction

E.L. Tonkin[*,†]
[*]Department of Digital Humanities, King's College London, London, UK
[†]Department of Electrical & Electronic Engineering, University of Bristol, Bristol, UK

2.1 INTRODUCTION

An individual who is convinced, or at least suspects, that performing some form of analysis on a textual data set may offer some value, may see the path ahead as a challenging hike. The rocky path that leads up the mountain of integrating text mining into one's own practice seems to present a visual illusion. This path appears far more daunting before one begins the ascent than ultimately proves to be the case. Climbing the foothills gives us some much-needed perspective and a far better view of the landscape. This perspective lets the traveller look back to where she began, as well as onward and upward into the mountain range.

The terminology of text mining can be confusing. As is often true in computer science, text mining (as well as natural language processing and to some extent corpus linguistics) has been conflated for purely utilitarian reasons. Some of the tools in the text miner's toolbox were first discussed at artificial intelligence or machine learning conferences, while the parentage of others owes much to database theory or web semantics. Some are informed by psychology or cognitive science. Some have little basis in theory, but earn their place by working well in practical use cases. Such a heritage implies a heterogeneous body of research, which in turn can bar the door to researchers and developers new to the field.

We suggest that those new to the field become actively and practically involved in working with text as soon as possible, leaving interdisciplinary struggles to a later date. Text mining applications are often interdisciplinary, involving domains such as biomedical sciences, business intelligence or machine learning. Like the mythological chimera, a given text analysis application may be powerful and polished, but looking closer, we see that it is a monstrous hybrid constructed using parts taken from many sources.

Working with Text
http://dx.doi.org/10.1016/B978-1-84334-749-1.00002-0

Disciplinary and terminological variation exists for good reason, sometimes historical or methodological, but it is worth noting that these questions are not key to practical involvement in working with text. Terminology sometimes varies because of the origins or training of researchers and developers working within a domain, and sometimes because of the approaches and methods that researchers or developers choose to apply. It is useful to put the challenges of interdisciplinary work aside initially and begin with the practical questions: What does it do, where are its limits, and what can it do for us?

There are sufficient practical barriers to getting started in working with text to place semantic disagreements at a low priority. Commercial tools are often (although by no means always) very expensive. The skill sets required to make use of noncommercial tool sets appear to be thin on the ground, and they superficially appear to be difficult to learn. The level of market penetration of text mining or analysis tool sets is reasonably low, meaning that it is often difficult or expensive to hire domain experts with demonstrable skills and experience in the area. Large-scale text mining projects involve a great deal of data processing, meaning that under some circumstances an infrastructural investment may be required. The apparent cost of entry into text mining is understandably viewed by many as excessively high, and the risks are viewed as considerable. The outcomes of text mining projects may come with caveats, as with data mining work in general, meaning that the findings are difficult or complex to interpret or reuse. Associated legal risks and rights issues are also potentially considerable and under some circumstances potentially untenable. In short, text mining is understood as specialist, expensive and complicated.

The first key message of this book is that it is possible to apply text mining cheaply and reasonably easily. Inexpensive or free tools are available for many common use cases. Many of the skills and knowledge available for text mining map well to skills drawn from other disciplines, and are therefore more likely to be present within a team than may be expected. While it is true that the performance of tools can be improved by domain-specific "tuning", for which specialist knowledge may be required, risk may be mitigated by applying text mining as an iterative process rather than a single step.

In this spirit and for simplicity, in this chapter we will refer to "text mining" as a broad general term, using an informal definition: "operations performed on a text or texts, with or without the involvement of supplementary materials, in order to extract a useful output". This is a pragmatic, and possibly rather lazy, stance in comparison with Hearst's view that "real" text mining must discover new information, rather than simply finding overall trends in textual data or extracting information (Hearst, 2003). It does, however, permit us to disentangle ourselves from definitional arguments, and it is arguably valid to take the view that technologies related to text mining, such as information extraction methods, are enabling technologies for text mining as well as being useful in their own right (see, e.g. Mooney and Bunescu, 2005).

In this chapter, we review the stages in developing a text mining project, identifying challenges and pitfalls and recommending approaches that may mitigate some of the potential pitfalls.

2.2 ENCOURAGING AN INTEREST IN TEXT MINING

In practical terms, introducing text mining into one's working practices often involves persuasion: demonstrating to one's supervisor, manager or funding agency that text mining has potential and is worth a try. This can be difficult for several reasons, including cost, availability of talent and the ability to envisage the likely outcome.

The costs of a full-scale project can be considerable. Small-scale pilot studies using readily available technologies, either commercially available services or off-the-shelf open-source frameworks or applications, can break this stalemate. There are risks associated with this approach; for example, there is a strong possibility that off-the-shelf technologies will initially lead to indifferent results, meaning that expectation management is key.

Text mining is often assumed to be a specialist technology that requires an unusual combination of skills. In fact, many skill sets are useful or desirable for a text mining team, including technical and computational skills, linguistic background, psychology, cognitive science, mathematics and statistics, and sociology. Expert (domain) knowledge of relevance to the domain of use, which often includes the humanities, is also beneficial. One cannot always choose a team when introducing text mining into an existing context, but it is useful to establish the connections between your expertise, that of your team and the skill sets required for your intended project.

There exist a large number of text mining tools and frameworks, which vary in usability, accessibility and configurability (see the listing of text mining applications in Appendix A). At one extreme are relatively inflexible but extremely accessible graphical interfaces; at the other, extremely flexible but relatively inaccessible scripting languages or compiled programming languages. If your team's skill set fits well with a popular text mining framework, then the argument for a pilot project is more easily made.

Of the stumbling blocks listed, the worst is the last. It is always difficult, especially with a technology as overhyped as text mining, to provide a realistic but compelling description of the potential benefits of the technology. It is far easier to "ride the hype", but the risks of this are significant, as the listener is predisposed to expect too much (or, if already disillusioned, to expect nothing at all). It is useful to seek out case studies that demonstrate the potential of the technology in the domain (or, if this is not possible, in a related domain) in as a calm and realistic a manner as possible.

2.3 LEGAL AND ETHICAL ASPECTS OF TEXT MINING

There are significant risks involved in text mining, as one might expect of a technology that promises to extract what we know, think and feel from the texts that we leave behind us. These are discussed in detail in Chapter 3 of this book. A detailed and practical set of best practices involved in responsible text mining are described in Chapter 4.

2.3.1 Activities

Adapting the activity list presented by Krallinger et al. (2008), we pick out the following areas:

1. Comparison of different methods and strategies on a standard task; that is, exploring different approaches to solving common problems on a standard data set.
2. Exploring the state of the art of a field; learning about text mining and developing one's understanding of the field.
3. Exploring the potential of available technologies to meet real-world needs: How can text mining best support the needs of your research field, business or application area?
4. Development of useful "gold standard" data collections for use in further activities and testing; in effect, packaging up your data for later experimentation.
5. Applying text mining to evaluate potential uses of data and the information that can be extracted from it, alongside any further data with which it can be linked or enriched.
6. Making available structured data extracted from unstructured text, thus encouraging interest in and reuse of the material.

There are undoubtedly others, including the use of text mining to support further specialist community, business or research needs.

2.3.2 Selecting or Compiling a Data Set or Corpus

In some cases, the choice of data set will be obvious (although supplementary resources may be less so). Projects may use:

- **Standard corpora**, used for benchmarking activities such as tool evaluation or to explore novel approaches to a standard problem. It is worth noting that the definition of data set is a lot broader than that of a corpus; a corpus is a specialised type of data set designed to fulfil a very specific research problem. Sinclair (2004) defines a corpus as "A corpus is a collection of pieces of language text in electronic form, selected according to external criteria to represent, as far as possible, a language or language variety as a source of data for linguistic research". For example, a corpus of language text might be designed to be representative of language typically used by English teenagers between 2005 and 2010 writing within the modality of SMS messages. Such a corpus would be calibrated to provide a statistically representative, accessible and appropriately annotated sample enabling research into this area.

    Standard corpora do not exist for every medium, topic or demographic, meaning that for many projects the use of a standard corpus is not realistic.

- In-house data sets, held by the organisation performing the text mining operation. These may sometimes be treated or viewed as **proprietary corpora**, which is to say, a locally held standard data set designed and selected as a representative sample. In many cases, far less formal methods are used to build and test software against in-house data sets.

- Out-of-copyright data sets, such as material available from Project Gutenberg (www.gutenberg.org). Many such resources exist and are of particular use for scholars in specific domains, such as the study of literature or specific themes in historical research. These data sets often display specific weaknesses that result from the digitisation and optical character recognition processes such as systematic error in recognition of specific characters or elements in fonts (e.g. ligatures, typographic combinations of letters that look pleasant, but cannot always be read), although in some cases, texts are corrected manually. The quality of such data sets should be assessed because errors in the text may cause problems during the text mining process.

- Appropriately licenced data, such as textual material drawn from Wikipedia, which is licenced under a Creative Commons licence that permits reuse and "remixing" of the data as long as certain stipulations are met (notably attribution)

- Material collected via an information retrieval process; retrieval of documents from a database, crawling the Web for relevant material, downloading material from social network resources such as Twitter or Tumblr via an application programming interface (API) and so on. This approach may lead to licencing issues, depending on the envisaged usage and republication of the data.

Those looking for an accessible overview of issues in corpus construction are referred to Bauer and Gaskell (2000). Issues of representativeness in corpus construction are discussed in Biber (1993). Rizzo (2010) provides a comprehensive and accessible guide to corpus compilation for the purpose of corpus linguistics.

2.3.3 Building a Data Set

The size of a text mining corpus may be determined by practicality, as in the case of the questioned authorship of the Federal Papers. Identifying authorship is commonly done by comparison of the questionable texts with material that is understood to be attributed to the various authors. In general, digitisation of material is an expensive task. Therefore, historical projects will commonly be limited to material that has already been digitised, unless the project is exceptionally well funded or the material is in the course of digitisation for an unrelated reason.

If, as is the case in some examples, the size of the data set is not greatly constrained by the availability of data – for example, in cases in which the corpus is extracted from material drawn from the Web or from social networks, such as positive and negative tweets on particular subjects – then it is at times difficult to know how long data collection should continue. Once again, practicality is one constraint forbidding an excessively large data set. Projects have finite lengths and funding, if the project is lucky enough to have received funding at all. Not only do common text mining tasks on large data sets often take a considerable amount of time but also, in many cases, the data set (or at least a subset) will require extensive preprocessing before text mining can begin. Evaluation of many text mining processes requires manual annotation of at least a subset of the sample data; this will be discussed later in this chapter.

In general, it is expected that larger corpora will be more representative (Saloot et al., 2014). There is logic to this: if a corpus were made available that provided every novel ever published in the English language, that corpus would be truly representative of novels published in English, since it would contain every member of the target set. Such a corpus is purely theoretical, however, because inevitably a large proportion of members of that data set have not made it into a copyright library, being either self-published or informally published, and hence it is not possible to gather all such resources in one place. To quote McEnery et al. (2006), "Unless you are studying a dead language or a highly specialised sub-language, sampling is unavoidable".

Bigger is not always better. As text mining approaches "Big Data", the volume of material increases the complexity and cost of the task, and it is not always clear that a larger volume of data will improve the outcome. There is a risk that assumptions are made about similarities between samples taken from different times or places. The text produced by individuals or groups tends to change over time, making each document a snapshot of current practice in a given place and time. One of the criticisms levelled at authorship studies of the Federalist Papers is the choice of materials selected for comparison (Rudman, 2012), some of which differ in creation date by some 20 years from the Federalist Papers themselves.

Saloot et al. (2014), citing Smith (1976), remark that the sheer size of the corpus is less important than the representativity of the sample. That is, the extent to which the corpus is representative of general practice depends on whether the corpus is randomly sampled, or whether the sampling method skews the sample toward a given part of the overall data set. In our previous example, for example, a set of books purchased from the Amazon best seller list biases the sample toward the most marketable examples of the genre. Saloot et al. separate the sampling method into three stages:

1. Define the target population.
2. Specify the sampling frame (i.e. the overall set from which samples will be selected).
3. Gather data according to the specified sampling technique.

Appropriate sampling techniques, as is broadly true in statistical studies, depend upon the aim of the study at hand. Probability sampling techniques are often used, such as

- Simple random sampling - random selection from the sampling frame.
- Systematic sampling - regularly distributed samples, such as "every second text in the sampling frame" or "every half an hour".
- Stratified sampling – dividing the population into groups, such as gender, age group or location, a random sample can then be drawn from each stratum.

Where only a proportion of the overall population is of relevance, nonprobability sampling techniques may be used, such as biased ("purposive") sampling techniques. Full coverage of these methods, as with probability sampling techniques, is out of the scope of this chapter. Some examples of nonprobability sampling techniques are

- Homogeneous sampling – choosing samples that are considered to be representative of the group in question (e.g. "18–24 year old, resident within 20 km of London and studying modern languages").
- Convenience sampling – choosing samples who are willing to take part in a research project.
- Snowball sampling – using the social network of people who have already taken part in a research project to identify other people who may also be willing to take part. See Rothenberg (1995) for discussion of sampling in social networks.
- Expert sampling – collecting samples from individuals considered to be domain experts.

For further information, see Kitchenham and Pfleeger (2002) for a discussion of populations and samples, Davies (2007) for an overview of study design and McEnery et al. (2006) for a review of representativeness and sampling in the specific case of linguistic corpora.

2.4 MANUAL ANNOTATION: PREPARING FOR EVALUATION

Collecting and preparing an appropriate data set is a lengthy process. Indeed, Ordonez and Chen (2012) suggest that it is generally the most time-consuming part of data mining projects. If the intention is to extract information from the data set for purely practical purposes, such as indexing or visualisation, under circumstances in which the completeness or accuracy of the outcome is not critical, this is less true. However, where the aim of the project is to perform research on the data set itself, it will often be necessary to ensure not only that the data set is representative but also that the outcomes of the text mining process pass evaluation.

Work that requires preparation of data sets for assessment usually fits into issues 1, 4 or 5 of the list of approaches to evaluation proposed by Krallinger et al. (2008): comparison of different methods or strategies on a given task, ability of a technology stack or stacks to meet real-world needs, or the development of gold standard data collections for further research or analysis. For each of these purposes, the quality of the outcome depends on the ability to compare the actual outcomes of a process against the expected outcome. Consequentially, it is common to manually **annotate** (add notes to) the data set or corpus to reflect the expected outcomes. Those who perform this work are referred to as **annotators** or **coders**.

Establishing the expected outcome – the right answer, or at any rate the most popular answer – for a given annotation problem is not always straightforward. The **consistency** of annotations is usually measured by evaluating the extent to which different people agree on the correct answer. This measure is known as **interannotator consistency** or **agreement**.

If a single data point is annotated by two different people, and the same response is given in both cases, then the interannotator consistency is 100%. Various approaches exist to calculate partial consistency: popular approaches include the use of **Krippendorff's Alpha**, a statistical measures of agreement usable for any number of annotators, **Cohen's Kappa**, **Scott's Pi**, or **Fleiss' Kappa**. A brief overview of these measures is given in Table 2.1. Joyce (2013) provides an accessible, critical overview of interindexer

Table 2.1 Interannotator reliability ratings

Measure	Number of annotators	Type of data	Comment
Krippendorff's alpha	Any number	Can handle various data types	Reliable, but difficult; often used in opinion retrieval and computational linguistics
Fleiss' kappa	Any number	Binary/ nominal categories	Commonly used in information retrieval research; generalises Scott's pi over any number of annotators
Average pairwise percentage agreement	Any number	Binary/ nominal categories	Intuitive, but does not compare against likelihood that the annotation is coded by chance
Weighted kappa	2	Permits the use of ordinal scales	See Fleiss (1981)
Cohen's kappa	2	Binary/ nominal categories	
Scott's pi	2	Binary/ nominal categories	
Percentage agreement	2	Binary/ nominal categories	

measures, while detailed discussion and evaluation may be found in Banerjee et al. (1999) and Fleenor et al. (1996).

In practice, the consistency of annotation varies greatly depending on the type of problem. According to Leech (2005), interannotator agreement approaching 100% is achievable for part-of-speech tagging problems. Sentiment analysis, on the other hand, is relatively subjective and complex to judge: the problem requires the annotator to provide their best estimate of the writer's viewpoint. Because two human beings are quite unlikely to agree about the sentiment conveyed by some pieces of texts, it is inevitable that measurements of interannotator reliability reflect this. Subjectivity classification tasks, according to Pang and Lee (2008, p. 20), may reveal a proportion of about 15% of annotations that annotators view as uncertain (and that are therefore difficult to classify with any consistency). Interannotator agreement on annotations that are not marked as uncertain is still high, although it does not approach the level of agreement found in less subjective problems.

Manual annotation of a corpus is potentially expensive and time-consuming, although a number of strategies exist that reduce the overall cost. One is to find sources that already contain annotations of relevance to your purpose. Another is to automate annotation, and then manually review the results, although there is some possibility that this may skew one's judgement. A third is to share the annotation task with a community. A means may be found by which annotation tasks can be worked into existing practice in a field; Yu (2013) describes an interface that permits researchers to manually correct automated judgements of citation sentiment; Google applies a similar approach in their machine translation software, inviting users to submit manual corrections.

Alternatively, should sufficient public interest exist in the subject at hand, it is also possible to build interfaces that support public involvement in annotation as an exercise in **citizen science** or **crowdsourcing**. Finally, it is also possible to make use of paid crowdsourcing platforms, such as Amazon's Mechanical Turk or Crowdflower (Kittur et al., 2008; Buhrmester et al., 2011; Paolacci et al., 2010).

2.4.1 Avoidance of Overfitting

Once an annotated corpus is available, researchers often split it randomly into a "training set" (a set used to support the development of a text mining application) and a "test set" (a set used to evaluate the performance of the completed application). This approach is known as **hold-out** evaluation. The optimal distribution between the training set and the independent test set depends on

(a) the characteristics of the service under evaluation and (b) the overall size of the data set; for the evaluation of predictive classification functionality on large data sets of greater than 100 items, the random allocation of two-thirds of the data for training and one-third of the data for testing purposes is found by Dobbin and Simon (2011) to be close to accurate.

The benefit of this operation should become clear when one considers the risk of **overfitting**: refining the model used to fit a training data set so precisely that it is no longer capable of dealing with any other examples. As a trivial example of extreme overfitting, consider an application intended to extract e-mail addresses from arbitrary text. The data set consists of the following:

Training set	Independent test set
Ben, researcher, ben@example.com Anna works at NOCORP: e-mail her at anna (at) [her-workplace].com	*Bob, bob at another-example.com, lives in London Rachel James: rachel@james.co.uk*

The simplest programme that can be written to print e-mail addresses taken from the training set is PRINT "ben@example.com anna@nocorp.com"

This programme is a liar: it is pretending to extract e-mail addresses, when in fact it is simply printing a string we prepared earlier. And yet it appears to work perfectly: when tested against the training set, this script gives exactly the expected response. However, when tested against the test set it is clear that it is overfitted to the training set, and works very poorly when evaluated against the test set. A better model is application of the heuristic (rule-of-thumb) "extract any substring string that contains an @, as this is an e-mail address", which correctly extracts 50% of the addresses from each set.

The use of training and independent test sets is not the sole possible approach, and may be infeasible in certain cases, notably cases in which the data set is not very large. In such cases, more sophisticated **cross-validation** (rotation estimation) methods may be used, such as *v-fold* cross-validation, which repeatedly split the data set into *v* multiple segments, in each case using *v* − *1* subsamples as a training set and the remaining sample as a test set. Another alternative is **leave-one-out** (jack-knife) sampling (Weiss and Kulikowski, 1991), although this approach is not recommended for very small samples. An overview is provided in Japkowicz and Shah (2011).

2.4.2 Characterising the Problem

With the exception of pure research, most people looking to implement a text mining solution are hoping for a particular type of outcome. Usually, the likely outcome is a service that can adequately support some sort of application. For example, "I am looking for an API that allows me to identify plagiarism in submitted coursework, so that I can make use of it within the University's virtual learning environment" combines a service and a scenario for the use of that service.

Requirements analysis in applications involving natural language processing or text mining does not differ greatly from the general case, with the important caveat that such applications are more likely than most to suffer from inflated user expectations and subsequent disillusionment.

A useful step in progressing from a data set to implementation of a text mining service over that data set is the use of **paper prototyping** methods.

In user interface design, rough designs are drawn on paper to give the design team and user group a cheap, easily alterable and user-accessible early prototype. These can be used as a useful resource on which to base discussion and initial development. Pen-and-paper prototyping methods are an important part of expressing a design to oneself, to one's team, to collaborating researchers or to potential users of the software.

Some of the many approaches to design and prototyping available to text mining are

- Worked examples, which help to express required functionality. In the case of text mining or natural language processing there are (at least) two systems to prototype back-to-back: the user interface – how the user experiences and interacts with the service – and the background service which performs the text mining functionality. It is the back-end system which benefits most from back-of-an-envelope worked examples.
- Methods such as paper prototyping provide a straightforward means of creating "lo-fi" mockups of interfaces and demonstrating workflows to users.
- In cases in which a previously untested approach is to be explored, meaning that there is little existing experience on which to build, design methods that are intended to support team members and users in conceptualising as-yet-nonexistent tools may also be useful. User-centred design processes are an important part of any such process, helping to characterise the user's skills, limitations, habits, context and views. There is no need to limit oneself to one mode of user engagement, however.

Other approaches, such as the use of design fiction methods to support speculative design, make use of narratives expressed through the medium of video or written text to convey ideas and support discussion or debate (Lukens and DiSalvo, 2012).

It is not unusual when building data analysis systems to leave user-facing interface design entirely out of the equation, viewing this side of things as an afterthought. This is understandable, in that it is difficult to establish the interface required before the characteristics and limitations of the service are understood. However, there are many reasons to take a user-centred design process.

As Yu (2013) states, tools designed for a given purpose should be designed with the involvement of potential users of the software. For example, a citation sentiment analysis tool (intended to establish whether an author's opinion of a cited paper is positive or negative) should be designed with the needs of researchers in mind, as researchers are the most likely end users of that software. According to Yu, this is not usually true. The outcome, that tools are designed without taking into account the behavioural patterns and literature review practices of researchers, may mean both that the tools in question do not support researcher needs effectively and (an equally important point) that the research community is less inclined to lend their support to the further development of the tool.

Another argument is purely pragmatic: if user involvement, experience and interface design are considered at an early stage, it becomes possible to establish the real constraints of the problem and hence the minimal features required of the text mining service. This is an important step in establishing the plausibility of the proposed outcome, which can often be estimated from existing examples or case studies, saving considerable expense in lost time and money. If it is known that a 60% or 75% accuracy on a given text mining problem can satisfy the minimal requirements for the proposed implementation, and that analogous projects on somewhat similar data sets have achieved 80% accuracy, it is reasonable to assess the project as feasible in principle and proceed to the prototyping stage. If, on the other hand, 99% accuracy is required, whilst the best accuracy ever achieved on similar projects is 64%, then further thought may be required before proceeding to the implementation phase. Interface prototyping and user testing can help to establish requirements at an early stage.

Detailed discussion of requirements analysis, interface design, and usability testing may be found in Sharp et al., 2011, Wiegers and Beatty (2013) and others.

2.4.3 Managing User Expectations

As we have mentioned elsewhere, text mining solutions often suffer from overhyped presentation and marketing, as do many applications of machine learning or artificial intelligence. The idea that a computer can perform an activity usually reserved to a literate human being, whilst impressive, tends to lead to an expectation that the computer understands the task as a human might. As we know, the computer programme is in fact merely an attempt to approximate the performance of a human on a given task, and is nothing like the complex cognitive system whose performance and capabilities it is attempting to emulate.

The errors made by a computer programme when faced with performing a task on natural language text, such as the errors made by speech-to-text recognition systems, or by predictive text functionality on mobile telephones, often appear bizarre or silly to end users. Because the end user's expectations of the system are high, these errors stand out more than they might with simpler systems. A video of a 2006 Windows Vista speech-to-text demo that went wrong led to a rash of articles in online magazines and journals, went viral and received millions of YouTube views, spread over several copies of the uploaded file. Thanks to the prevalence of the touchscreen mobile keyboard, various more or less obscene variants of the phrase "Damn You, Autocorrect" are websites, books, Twitter hashtags and memes. Automated translation, too, is funny, although sharing of poorly autotranslated signs found in shops and leisure centres has lost ground in recent years, in favour of the sometimes quirky output of automated closed-captioning software. Natural language processing errors are subjects for humour and comment to a far greater extent that most types of software error.

This observation might remind some of the phenomenon of the **uncanny valley** (Mori, 1970). This term refers to the observation that objects or representations of humans (such as robots or animated puppets) that make little attempt to be lifelike inspire a more positive response from viewers than objects or representations that try hard to be lifelike, but fail in small ways (Pollick, 2010). When a viewer sees human-like representations that are almost realistic, but have something about them that seems slightly wrong or unexpected, the viewer tends to find it odd, disconcerting or creepy: it is not quite a pleasant experience. We do not suggest that the underlying mechanisms are the same – they are not. In particular, the uncanny valley is attributed by some (Pollick, 2010) to a mismatch between perceptual cues. Nor do we suggest that the irritation felt by a user faced with a fallible predictive text mechanism can be directly compared to the viewer's sense that a puppet or android is "creepy". We are not usually repulsed by the types of poor-quality natural language processing software that we meet in everyday life: most such technology is not good enough for that. Instead, we laugh at it. Nonetheless, attempts by roboticists and filmmakers to explore and characterise the uncanny valley offer us a useful lesson: they show us that it is possible to engineer one's way out of the uncanny valley, to avoid the "almost-but-not-quite" zone of distrust or discontent. Likewise, it is possible for an engineer to work with users to manage user expectations and carefully design interfaces to minimise user frustration with systems that *almost-but-not-quite* do what the user hopes the system will achieve.

2.5 COMMON TEXT MINING TASKS

Once the goals of the text mining activity are known, it is useful to explore the feasibility of those goals. A starting point is the identification of tools that are likely to achieve some part of the outcome that the developer or researcher envisages.

It is often true that no single tool exists that is capable of meeting the project requirements. In text mining, as in many fields that work with complex data to achieve a given outcome, it is generally true that multiple tools must be chained together to solve a problem. This is commonly envisaged and implemented as a sequence of filters through which text is passed, each of which annotate the text with additional information. Where text mining tools are chained together, this is often referred to as a **pipeline** through which the text is passed.

In some cases, where very specific tasks or innovative tasks are envisaged, it is quite possible for no existing tools or combination of tools to be available that can support the development of an envisaged implementation. In the majority of cases, however, tasks will fall broadly into one of the known application areas for text mining technologies.

The following section sets out several of the most common application areas in text mining, alongside brief examples of their use.

2.6 BASIC CORPUS ANALYSIS

2.6.1 Evaluating Frequency of Word and Term Use

One of the simplest possible metrics for corpus analysis is also one of the best known: evaluation of the frequency of occurrence of words. Despite the simplicity of this metric, frequency-sorted word lists remain useful tools. Multiword terms (phrases) are often preferred for indexing purposes, as this improves the specificity of the indexing vocabulary (Jacquemin, 2001); single-word terms may be polysemous (carry multiple meanings). The popularity of word frequency as a tool is also approached by a related statistic: the cooccurrence of two or more linguistic elements (such as words) (Gries, 2008, 2010).

2.6.2 Identifying Characteristic Words or Terms

Gries (2008) notes that as a single statistic, frequency of occurrence can mislead. It is often useful to explore the distribution of term use. Concretely, a word that is often used in a specific discipline but seldom used in others is a specialised term, relevant to students of that discipline, yet if we looked at nothing but overall word frequency, we would think the term of little importance in general. Hence, linguists often apply methods of calculating **dispersion**, which is to say, measurements of the amount of variation in a corpus or data set. An overview of dispersion measures used in linguistics is given in Gries (2008).

A venerable rule of thumb for terminology extraction, originating in the domain of information retrieval, is the use of the TF/IDF measure (Jones, 1972; Salton et al., 1975). This measures the **term frequency** of a given term in a certain document against the **inverse document frequency**, which is essentially an estimate of the rarity of the term across an entire data set .Inverse document frequency is calculated as the logarithm of the number of documents in the corpus, divided by the number of documents. The fewer the number of documents the term appears in, the larger the TF/IDF measure. Witschel (2005) suggests that a similar approach can be taken to the selection of characteristic terms in a given field.

2.7 PREPROCESSING A TEXT

It is often useful to preprocess a text in various ways. The preferred method of preprocessing depends on the type of document. On a common-sense level, we understand that different types of documents have different characteristics. For example, most novel-length documents can be segmented into chapters, sections, paragraphs or sentences. Newspapers carry news stories and editorials, straplines, headlines, advertisements and letters to the editor. A set of pages extracted from a web forum may contain forum-specific navigational elements, forum headings and subtitles. These pages also contain a number of forum posts, each of which can be separated into poster identifier and nickname, title, the body of the posting and the signature.

Identification of interesting document content is a domain-specific problem, in that researchers studying the comparative evaluation of menu systems might make the opposite choices to researchers evaluating forum postings. Still, some generalisations can usefully be made about material which is irrelevant to the content of the page itself or which is likely to be judged uninteresting. Material which is standard across an entire website (menus, adverts, templates and copyright information), is sometimes referred to as **boilerplate**. Kohlschütter et al. (2010) conclude that this material typically is not related to the main content, and recommend its removal on the basis that the retention of such irrelevant material may reduce search precision.

Boilerplate removal is an easy problem for human beings, particularly if the reader is fluent in the language. For computers, it is more difficult to detect page layout templates reliably. Kohlschütter et al. (2010) identifies several approaches, mostly based around the use of machine learning methods such as *n*-gram or conditional random field-based classifiers. Several text mining platforms provide boilerplate removal functionality, such as the **boilerpipe** plugin made available to users of GATE (NACTEM's General Architecture for Text Mining; see Appendix A).

Even a simple text file that contains no templating information will generally display the most common structures found in texts, such as paragraphs and sentences. **Segmentation** of a text into its component elements (topic, word or sentence boundary detection) is a language-specific problem, as different languages take different approaches to formatting texts. Chinese, for example, is often written without spaces between words (Stanford, 2014). Particular types of text also raise specific challenges, such as reported speech in short fiction: "We'll use apostrophes in place of speech marks", decided S. M.E.R.S.H., "because that will make it a little harder for this segmentation algorithm to identify where our speech begins and ends". Abbreviations, too, can cause difficulties: consider the sentence "Jane wrote approx. 12 papers". Text segmentation is a core function of text analysis applications.

The segmentation process requires text to be **tokenised**, which is to say that the terms within the text are separated into individual tokens. A well-behaved tokeniser will correctly identify and treat terms such as "We'll", "S.M.E.R.S.H." and "approx." as individual tokens, and will recognise that the punctuation used in these tokens is not indicative of sentence boundaries in this particular case. Many mature tokenisation approaches and implementations exist for English and for various other languages.

Because the effectiveness of the sentence or word tokenising process depends on correctly identifying the language in use, one additional preprocessing step involves the application of a **language detection** algorithm, to identify the language or languages in use in a given text.

2.8 EXTRACTING FEATURES FROM A TEXT

Text analysis begins with characterisation of a text – conversion into a representation that can usefully support the goals of the application area (Pang and Lee, 2008). Sometimes the conversion model is very simple. Here, we demonstrate several simple conversions that can be applied to text.

We will use a tongue twister as our sample sentence: "How much wood would a woodchuck chuck if a woodchuck could chuck wood?"

We might apply the *bag of words* model, which depends on the general idea that a text is made up of a sequence of words and that the order of these words is immaterial. Our sample sentence contains two uses of the single words "wood", "chuck", "a" and "woodchuck", and the single words "how", "much", "would", "if" and "could". This set of counted terms is the *feature vector* extracted from this sentence. In this context, the "vector" is a list of words, alongside a count of term frequency (the number of times each term appears in the text).

In the terminology of natural language processing, single words ("terms") are also referred to as "**unigrams**". It is also possible to extract features that involve multiple words. In the terminology of the field, these are referred to as multiword terms (phrases), or as "higher order *n*-grams", which is to say, "collections of words with a length (order) greater than one". If we decided to extract **bigrams** (i.e. features of two words in combination), we would find ourselves with the following feature vector of bigrams, all of which appear once in the sentence: "how much", "much wood", "wood would", "would a", "a woodchuck", "woodchuck chuck", "chuck if", "if a", "a woodchuck", "woodchuck could", "could chuck" and "chuck wood"

It is sometimes desirable to **stem** text, which is to say, reducing terms to their common root (Lovins, 1968; Porter, 1980). For example, "yellowing", "yellower", "yellowed" and "yellowest" are all reduced to the common root term, "yellow". The practicality of stemming algorithms is disputed for specific information retrieval tasks, particularly in English: nonetheless, the approach is frequently used in text mining tasks. A related task is that of **lemmatisation**, establishing the canonical (dictionary) form of a given word or set of words. Given a word and a sentence context, usually represented by part of speech tags (e.g. "noun" or "verb"), a lemmatiser is designed to identify the dictionary form of the word given. For example, the adjective "best" may be lemmatised to "good".

Both stemming and lemmatisation have the useful effect of **dimensional reduction**: that is, at the expense of reducing the amount of detail, we have reduced the number of words in our data set (Hotho et al., 2005). This can be reduced further using **stopword filtering**. Filtering reduces the number of words ("dimensions") in our data set, and can have various positive effects. A data set containing fewer words is more compact – it takes up less storage space. A leaner data set may also be more efficient. If we can store only the features that are of interest to us, there is no need to retain irrelevant information. It would be time-consuming and wasteful to process the unnecessary data. Worse, the presence of useless features in our data set may impair overall accuracy.

The use of a **stop list** is common in many fields of natural language processing (Frantzi et al, 2000). Stop lists contain a set of stopwords, which are destined to be removed from a text at some point during processing. When building a search index, for example, common words such as "and" or "very" may be ignored on the basis that they do not contain useful information (or, specifically, that their retention reduces the precision of the service; see "Evaluation", later in this chapter). A list of stopwords may be compiled to support a terminology extraction process within a given domain, but is unlikely to transfer well across domains.

As an example, the term "very high frequency radio" is useful in domains including electrical engineering, telecom engineering, marine engineering and radio telemetry. It is the formal International Telecommunication Union (ITU) designation for radio waves from 30 to 300 MHz. If the term "very" were applied as a stopword, the text would be misidentified as referring to "high frequency radio", which is the ITU designation for the 3-30 MHz frequency range. Hence, the use of a heuristic intended to improve the precision of terminology in one domain can significantly impair precision when applied to another.

2.9 INFORMATION EXTRACTION

2.9.1 Terminology Extraction

A very common problem in information extraction, terminology extraction (also known as terminology mining or key phrase extraction) attempts to identify and extract terms from a document. This may be useful for automated indexing, in the sense of building up an index of terms contained within a certain document, or to support the creation of a glossary, dictionary or thesaurus (Witschel, 2005). Terminology extraction is also a useful first step for corpus-driven ontology design, building up a structured hierarchy of concepts based on terms drawn from a set of texts (Gillam and Tariq, 2004; Gillam et al., 2005): a detailed discussion of this process may be found in Buitelaar and Cimiano (2007). The extraction of a set of "feature vectors", terms that describe a text for machine learning purposes, is also useful for automated clustering or classification of texts (Witschel, 2005). That is, short but descriptive extracted terms can provide useful clues as to what a text is about, which can then be used to work out the relations between the texts contained in the data set.

Terminology extraction overlaps functionally with named entity recognition (see below) under some circumstances. Named entity recognition additionally attempts to categorise terms. That is, terminology extraction may identify the terms "Barack Obama" and "House of Representatives", but named entity recognition will identify the former as a person and the latter as an organisation.

The most popular approaches to terminology extraction depend on syntactic features, as identified using a part-of-speech tagger (Paaß, 2011). Target types of term (Frantzi et al, 2000) include
- Noun phrases, which are groups of words that are used as nouns. These include one or more nouns, as well as any modifiers. In the phrase "We met *the current prime minister*", for example, the italicised terms act as a noun phrase. Technical terms are often noun phrases (Witschel, 2005; Arppe, 1995).
- Adjectival phrases, which are groups of words that are used as an adjective, describing a noun or pronoun. "The minister's briefcase was *bilious green*".
- Verb phrases (verbal phrases): a verb and its dependents: "Jones used an algorithm *to predict motion*".

In practice, tuning a terminology extractor has a domain-specific component, exemplified by the problems of (a) expected term length in that domain and (b) which terms to filter out, using for example a stop list. Informally, Frantzi et al. observe that multiword terms in science and technology tend toward greater length than those used in the arts and humanities.

2.9.2 Named Entity Recognition (NER)

This term, coined in 1996 by Grishman and Sundheim, refers to methods that permit the extraction of structured information from unstructured text. Nadeau and Sekine (2007) trace the literature behind this approach back to a paper presented in 1991 by Lisa F. Rau at the Seventh IEEE Conference on Artificial Intelligence Applications. In the mid 1990s, the purpose of this activity was described as **message understanding**, a type of problem in which texts are examined for information about events and activities, which is then extracted and aggregated.

Decomposing the message understanding problem into stages, one might take the following approach:

1. Identify interesting "entities" (names, numbers, dates and so on) within the text.
2. Classify those entities (i.e. "New Line Cinema" is an industry body; "Jamie Oliver" is a chef; "$1.6 bn" expresses a number of dollars).
3. Explore the links between these entities: given the text "New Line Cinema made $1.6 bn in the opening weekend of their new Jamie Oliver biopic", establish that an industry body made a certain profit from a movie about a certain chef.

Step 3 is not included within named entity recognition; it is a broader problem in the area of information extraction. Named entity recognition is often applied as one step in a longer text mining process, or *pipeline*.

Named entity recognition formally refers to extraction of a subset of "interesting entities": entities "for which one or many rigid designators [stand] for the referent" (Nadeau and Sekine, 2007). That is, *London, Ford Motor Company* and *Doctor Who* are all named entities. In practice, the term now refers to types of proper names (persons, locations and organisations) and temporal and numerical expressions such as dates, times and prices. The reader is referred to Nadeau and Sekine (2007) for an extensive and readable discussion of technical approaches to named entity recognition.

A number of potential pitfalls exist in named entity recognition:

- Issues of **ambiguity**; for example, entities can legitimately be classified in multiple ways. "Betty Crocker" is a trademark of General Mills and hence appears as part of a product name, but Betty is also a living trademark, which is to say that she is assigned an image and a personality and has been portrayed by actresses on radio and television. Even a human volunteer, when faced with the phrase "I went with Betty Crocker", might need to look at the broader context when deciding whether a persona, a foodstuff or an enterprise is meant.

- The **type, genre** or **domain** of the text: named-entity recognition is very accurate under optimal circumstances, but reduces rapidly in accuracy where the text displays nonoptimal characteristics. Nadeau and Sekine (2007) report that systems designed for one domain were found by Poibeau and Kosseim (2001) to reduce by between 20% and 40% in popular measures of performance (precision and recall) when tested on other types of text.
- Capitalisation and punctuation, or the lack of either, can confuse entity recognition. A system presented with the text "In Middle Manchester" may, depending on the approach used to implement the system, conclude either that Manchester is referenced, that Middle Manchester (in Nova Scotia) is referenced, or that "In Middle Manchester" is a place.

2.9.3 Entity Disambiguation

Knowing that the author of a certain text is "Smith, John" is useful, but it leaves open significant opportunities for ambiguity or error, as the name is shared by over 25,000 Americans (Hartman, 2013). Although most names occur less frequently, it is still common for researchers to find that they are not the only person working under the same forename and surname in their discipline, field or even department. The question, then, when a certain named entity is identified, is: To which individual of that name does this information refer?

There exist a variety of approaches to the general problem of named entity disambiguation, some of which require a structured knowledge base containing lists of entities, and some of which do not (Dredze et al, 2010).

2.9.4 Relationship Extraction and Coreference Resolution

Coreference resolution attempts to establish which extracted entity references return to the same entity. For example, consider the paragraph, "I gave the money to Eddie Jones. I knew he'd do the right thing. Eddie's a good guy." *Eddie Jones, he* and *Eddie* all refer to the same entity. Coreference resolution groups these references together, ascertaining that they all belong to the same entity.

This is often implemented as a rule-based system, at least in part. A simple rule-based coreference system uses information such as string matching and comparison, alongside heuristics such as *multiple references to the same string in a single document belong to the same entity* and *pronouns such as "he" can be assumed to refer to the last entity referenced* (Weiss et al, 2010). Rule-based approaches may be used alongside machine learning-based information extraction systems; for examples of such an implementation see Weiss et al., pp. 130–131.

Similarly, **relationship extraction** (also known as relation extraction) attempts to identify and extract relationships between entities. Looking at the first sentence of our previous example, applying an appropriate relationship extraction method will enable us to extract the fact that there exists a relationship *give* between the first-person narrator of the story and the named entity, *Eddie Jones.*

There exist various approaches to relationship extraction, of which Bach and Badaskar (2007) provide a useful summary. These include supervised binary classification approaches (which is to say, machine learning approaches that are trained using training data to give yes/no answers); semi-supervised approaches, which require a smaller training set; and an approach that attempts to learn more complex relations. In practice, relationship extraction pipelines often involve a combination of methods, such as the use of a machine learning-based classifier to mark up texts, followed by the application of heuristic rule sets over the annotated text to associate the identified entities.

2.9.5 Fact Extraction

Many of the most impressive uses of text mining today involve the extraction of facts from unstructured text. That is, given a piece of text that contains a number of assertions, such as "*The Red Sox took advantage of several errors in pitching to score seven runs in last Wednesday's game against the Kansas City Royals. The Sox surrendered just two runs at the bottom of the fifth*", a fact extraction system focused on baseball scores may identify the teams in question, the date of the game and the overall score. The reader may, given the previous sections, have some thoughts as to how this may be accomplished – the use of named entity recognition, extraction of relevant patterns and the use of coreference resolution, for example – and indeed the architecture of an information extraction system will generally make use of all of these elements (Turmo et al., 2006).

An early example of fact extraction is the extraction of current news items from press releases (Andersen et al., 1992). Another is the extraction of information characterising the relation between particular medicines and specific symptoms or outcomes, as used in the biomedical domain (Thompson et al., 2009). Whilst fact extraction is ordinarily domain-specific, some impressive recent examples (such as IBM Watson) make use of cross-domain fact extraction, with the caveat that the information is used for a closely constrained purpose; in the case of IBM Watson, the information is used to improve the machine's performance as a contestant on a specific game show, *Jeopardy* (Ferrucci, 2012). Implementations of technologies such as **automated question answering** typically make heavy use of fact extraction (Fan et al, 2006).

2.9.6 Temporal Information Extraction

Alongside the extraction of information about events comes the need to extract information about event timings (Ling and Weld, 2010). A number of parsers have been implemented and tested to identify and extract event and time expressions (see Ling and Weld, 2010; Mani, 2004). The aim of these systems is to anchor extracted events in time, enabling the information to be used for various purposes, such as sophisticated question answering ("In what year did the Red Sox most recently win the World Series?") and information summarisation, placing events from a number of different sources into a single time line or narrative.

2.9.7 Automated Geotagging or Geoindexing of Text

The automated extraction of location information is often combined with the use of databases of geographical information. This enables extracted location information to be enhanced with data from a knowledge base. Geocoding existing data sources can provide opportunities for data mining, and is consequently used to analyse patterns of crime (Ratcliffe, 2004), incidence of cancer (Rushton et al., 2006), and many other applications. When used alongside real-time data streams, such as social media streams or weblogs, geocoding has been successfully used alongside predictive analytics methods to track epidemics (Ji et al., 2012; Sugumaran and Voss, 2012; Nagar et al., 2014) and earthquakes (Earle et al., 2012).

2.10 APPLICATIONS OF INDEXING AND METADATA EXTRACTION

Indexing and metadata extraction is a very common and broad use case, particularly in library and information science. Examples of this type of activity include

- **Automated indexing**, extraction of structured information from a large document set for the purpose of indexing that document set; that is, to build an index for later search and retrieval. The material extracted is often taken from an **ontology** or **standard vocabulary** – place names, people, or subject descriptions (often referred to as **subject headings**, these are a controlled list of terms or phrases used to classify materials). Automated indexing clearly relates closely to terminology extraction and named entity recognition.

- **Automated classification** makes use of available information (such as automatically extracted index terms) to identify candidate classifications for documents within a document set, to cluster documents together, and so on. Classification of documents is sometimes also called **document filtering**, on the assumption that large numbers of incoming documents are filtered into appropriate sections; Sebastianini (2002) gives the example of a newsfeed containing stories about many topics, which must be filtered to ensure that the news agency's customers receive only the information of interest to them.

- **Automated extraction** of common document elements, such as the extraction of titles and abstracts from academic texts (document meta-data), or **automated metadata generation**. Such technologies are closely associated with automated indexing, as both may extract information from documents that is usually used for search and retrieval. However, automated metadata generation may include metadata that is not directly present within the material indexed, but is generated by reference to document features.

- **Concept linking** (Fan et al., 2006) enables documents to be linked by the concepts to which they refer, with advantages for the interface. For example, this permits information system users to browse between related documents.

- **Topic tracking** (Fan et al., 2006) supports information system users in tracking topics of interest to them.

- **Topic modelling** (Blei, 2012) attempts to extract and annotate large sets of documents with thematic information. A common approach to this is latent Dirichlet allocation, which makes the following assumptions: (1) each document refers to multiple topics, and (2) statistical analysis of terms used in each document can indicate the topic areas referenced by that document.

2.11 EXTRACTION OF SUBJECTIVE VIEWS

2.11.1 Opinion Mining

The extraction of subjective views from a text, rather than objective fact, is known as opinion mining – that is, in the words of Pang and Lee (2008), to find out what other people think; to seek out and understand the opinions of others. Opinion mining exists in contrast to more traditional approaches that focus on fact-based analysis, and is an important approach for many business intelligence applications.

A popular application of opinion mining is the aggregation and summarisation of user reviews, such as product or service reviews. Pang and Lee quote a 2004 statistic from the Pew Internet and American Life Project, which found that 30% of American adults had provided online comments or product reviews. However, it is worth noting that the majority of published opinions are written by a small proportion of Internet users. Ofcom found in a 2014 study that 56% of UK Internet users often read user reviews, whilst just one in ten regularly write them.

Subjective opinions might be taken from movie review websites: "*This movie was a lot of fun*", or "*It's well worth watching but they should have cut it to less than two hours*".

2.11.2 Sentiment Analysis

Sentiment analysis is a specific subtask within the broad area of opinion mining; in short, the classification of texts according to the emotion that the text appears to convey. Sentiment analysis typically classifies texts according to positive, negative and neutral classifications; so that "*This movie is great!*" is classified as positive, while "*This movie was too long and I got bored half way through*" is classified as negative. Opinion mining and sentiment analysis tools, depending on the implementation, often suffer from a few key problems. In particular:

- It is not always clear which of the people or things referenced within a given text are liked or disliked: "*The movie had some decent acting but I can't forgive the use of Papyrus font for the end credits*".
- Sarcasm is difficult to detect (Liu, 2012): "*Great movie – nearly as much fun as watching paint dry*".

Outcomes from a sentiment analysis process may be used to improve recommendation systems; for example, by identifying and reranking contentious products to detect controversy and disagreement (Wang and Cardie, 2014). This is potentially a useful ability in automated summarisation tasks, where a range of viewpoints may exist. In the field of social computing, sentiment analysis is envisaged to be useful in supporting collaborative work.

Some of the limitations of sentiment analysis arise from the source material. People are more likely to express positive than negative feelings in social environments (Guerra et al., 2014; Jordan et al., 2011), and are more likely to express extreme than average feelings (Guerra et al., 2014; Dellarocas and Narayan, 2006).

2.12 BUILD, CUSTOMISE OR APPLY? CHOOSING AN APPROPRIATE IMPLEMENTATION

Text mining tools are typically evaluated against certain sample tasks or corpora. It is ordinarily true that the performance of tools against novel corpora cannot easily be predicted. Certain heuristics (rules-of-thumb) generally apply, although with limited accuracy. Ordinarily, tools that function well within a given application area can be expected to function acceptably within similar application areas. Application areas themselves may vary on a number of axes, including but not limited to the language used, the level of formality of the written text, the subject area of the text and the stylistic conventions of the venue.

For example, tools that perform well on scientific papers in one discipline are reasonably likely to function well on scientific papers in a closely related discipline. Similarly, tools that function well on informal writing taken from a mailing list may provide acceptable performance when tested on informal writing taken from a web forum. Samples of text drawn from platforms that require characteristics such as brevity of expression and impose limitations on length, such as Twitter, online chat or SMS, may be expected to enjoy comparable characteristics, thus permitting many tools developed for one platform to be used on material drawn from others.

However, this heuristic is solely indicative. A recent comparative study of Twitter, online chat and SMS (Hu et al., 2013) shows that Twitter users produce relatively standard and formal language than users of SMS and online chat, and is therefore "closer to traditional written language than to speech-like mediums" (Hu et al., 2013). Furthermore, it is suggested by Hu et al. that tweets act to shape opinion on existing content rather than presenting new information. The style used by Twitter users is "linguistically unique".

So while one might try to draw conclusions on the basis of similar message formats or even from personal experience, our intuition sometimes fails us. We can make predictions, but the best way to establish the performance of likely candidate tools is to test them and see.

2.13 EVALUATION

Once a text analysis pipeline is built and results have been generated, it is useful to begin a phase of evaluation. Evaluation is often taken to refer to accuracy, as measured by precision and recall, although there are several other dimensions both to the evaluation of a service or tool designed to perform text mining, and the evaluation of any outcomes of data-led experiments. Evaluation of experimental outcomes is not discussed here, as there exist many excellent resources on experimental design and evaluation in the various domains likely to make use of text mining.

2.13.1 Evaluating Accuracy: Precision, Recall and F-measure

These measures are extremely useful and commonplace (Powers, 2011). Consider a text mining pipeline intended to annotate all references to politicians in a news corpus. The text mining pipeline appears capable of high levels of accuracy. When exploring the output, you remark that anything that it identifies as a reference to a politician almost always turns out to be a reference to a politician. That is, the **false positive** rate (also known as type I error) is extremely low. However, on close investigation it turns out that whilst it seldom misclassifies entities as politicians, it often fails to notice when politicians are mentioned. Consequentially, the **false negative** (type II error) rate of the system is quite high.

Precision refers to the number of instances that our classifier correctly predicted; because it is usually right when it identifies an entity as a politician, the precision of the classifier is quite high. Precision in this instance is calculated by dividing the number of entities correctly identified as politicians with the overall number of entities identified as politicians. The precision of our fictitious political text mining pipeline is excellent.

Recall, also known as sensitivity in some areas, such as machine learning and psychology (Powers, 2011), refers to the proportion of instances that our classifier successfully identified, compared with the overall number of instances that it should have identified. It is calculated by dividing the number of instances successfully identified by the sum of the number of true positives and the number of false negatives. The recall of our imaginary politician filter is known to be poor.

Specificity refers to the ability of a test to avoid false alarms, and is derived from the false positive rate. The higher the number of false positives (individuals who are not politicians, in our test, who are incorrectly identified as politicians), the lower the specificity of the test. It is calculated by dividing the number of true negatives by the number of entities that formally should have been identified as true negatives (true negatives plus false positives).

The **F-measure** (also known as F1-score or F-score) is one of several single-number measures proposed to describe the performance of classifiers.

Alongside these quantities, it is sometimes useful to make use of analytical methods drawn from machine learning, such as **ROC analysis** – visualisation of what is known as the receiver operator characteristics of a classifier. This explores the interplay between the false positive rate and the true positive rate. For a basic binary (true-false) classifier in which 50% of the correct answers are "true" and 50% are "false", the ROC curve will be a straight line across the graph. Plotting the behaviour of a ROC curve shows how well the classifier performs, by comparison to a "classifier" that classifies according to random chance.

2.13.2 Process Cost in Resources, Time and Processing Resources

Text analysis methods can be resource-intensive and consequentially slow. As a consequence, when implemented as part of a broader infrastructure, text analysis stages can act as a bottleneck limiting the quantity of data that can be processed. Whilst it is true that, either through optimisation or through the use of infrastructural developments such as cloud computing (see Appendix A), it is often possible to increase the speed of existing pipelines, it is also useful to consider the efficiency of text mining processes. If a fast process is nearly as accurate as a very slow process, and does not seriously reduce the efficacy of the overall system, then it may be preferable to make use of the fast, less accurate process.

2.13.3 Fit with User Requirements and Expectations

If a service is intended for practical uses, usability evaluation is also to be recommended. A successful service does not necessarily imply that the system will fulfil the intended application use case; nor does the failure to fulfil a use case necessarily mean that the service cannot be used for other purposes.

2.13.4 Contextualisation of Results

In the first chapter of this book, we discussed the *other* type of significance; not the statistical significance of a correlation, but the importance ascribed by scholars to the characteristics of important texts. Linguists are often interested in the characteristics of text *qua* text: the text itself is the subject of linguistic study. For many researchers, text is a convenient data source of the type that in climate research would be referred to as a **proxy**: an indirect indicator used to develop a better understanding of the phenomenon under study. As glaciologists collect and analyse ice cores to study historical trends in atmospheric change, so researchers collect and analyse data to study debate, opinion and reaction to events.

The analysis of text can represent a telescope focused on the past or into the lives of others, and is therefore viewed as a powerful tool; it can be motivated by academic interest, patriotism, the need to exploit much larger quantities of data than any individual can process, business interest, curiosity or simply an interest in answering questions that, it may appear, cannot be answered any other way.

If a text mining pipeline were a telescope, however, and natural language processing were the science of optics, it would by no means encompass everything that is done in the field of astronomy. The subjects covered in many text mining applications (history, authorship, opinion, society and social change, the dynamics of information dissemination and so forth) are the subjects of a great many disciplines. One interviewee for this book recommended that every team that makes use of text mining to study contemporary texts should include a sociologist. In text mining, there is strength in interdisciplinary collaboration.

Yet this leaves us with unresolved questions. In the digital humanities, a famously interdisciplinary subject, a recent bibliographic study found less indication of collaboration (as measured by coauthorship) than might be expected. The cause of this discrepancy is unclear; perhaps each researcher publishes in his or her own discipline, perhaps engineers are simply thanked in the acknowledgement section of each publication, or perhaps engineers do not publish at all. We do not know, but we may suspect that stitching together the output of multiple disciplines – combining quantitative and qualitative studies, for example – is a nontrivial problem. Although the outcome may be a stronger study than might be achieved by a combination of quantitative and qualitative methods than by either family of approaches alone, aggressively interdisciplinary research is fraught with difficulties in funding, in publication and in presentation of the work. Nonetheless, interdisciplinary involvement is often an underutilised approach in evaluating studies.

In plain terms, as well as talking to technologists, engineers and specialists in natural language processing, it is useful to talk to people working within the subject area of your research, to discuss and compare findings and methods, and to collaborate where possible.

2.14 THE ROLE OF VISUALISATION IN TEXT MINING

Text mining does not require visualisation to be effective. Nonetheless, these tools are often a useful component of text mining projects (Don et al., 2007). Visualisation tools and techniques are useful multipurpose tools, which can support various processes within data-driven projects. Examples include supporting users in the analysis of large quantities of textual material, presentation of the outcomes of performance evaluation processes in tools, components or pipelines, or the publication of data sets derived from a text mining project. Visualisation platforms may be as simple as graphical spread-sheet packages or as complex as full programming languages.

All of these examples have a common goal: to help people think – either about the data, or about real-world phenomena that underlay the data. Purchase et al. (2008, p. 58) summarise information visualisation as the use of "computer graphics and interaction to assist humans in solving problems". Such problems may include the making of discoveries, decisions, or explanations (Plaisant, 2005) about patterns (e.g. temporal or geographical trends), groups or individuals. Information visualisation is, for this reason, sometimes referred to as "visual data mining" (Plaisant, 2005).

Formally, information visualisation has been defined by Card et al. (1999) as "the use of computer-supported, interactive, visual representations of abstract data to amplify cognition". Information visualisation makes available representations of data, which may be as simple as maps, charts, time lines and networks, or may equally involve less commonplace approaches designed specifically for given tasks or contexts. These representations transform complex data into relatively accessible forms; rather than being faced with raw numbers, percentages or lists, the user can explore the information visually.

It is worth noting that this amplification of cognition is not necessarily restricted to individuals: groups may collaborate in exploring a data set. Information visualisation may be designed to support individual work, group work or both. It is one thing for an individual to come to an understanding of a data set, and to be able to represent the information to his or her own satisfaction; it is quite another to share this understanding with domain experts in their own or other specialities. Visualisation provides an opportunity to share findings in an accessible manner, opening up opportunities to talk about data. Asynchronous collaboration can be supported using shared visualisation and discussion systems (Danis et al., 2008); it is suggested that visualisations can provide useful resources from which to spark a conversation.

Ultimately, visual representations of data sets rely on the capabilities of the human visual system (Kerren et al., 2008). Human visual processing offers several key strengths that make visual data representation a powerful approach. The working memory limits the human ability to explore and compare data points. Visualisations offer the ability to view large amounts of information in a single, rapidly searchable, location, and to rapidly seek through and compare large numbers of data points, reducing dependency on recall (the ability to remember and compare with what has been read before). The perceptual system is also able to process some attributes of visualisations in parallel, and to use features such as spatial grouping or similarity in size, colour, and so forth, to infer properties such as proximity or similarity between items. The designer of an information visualisation system is tasked with building visual representations that effectively employ the strengths of human visual perception (Card et al, 1999).

The success of a visualisation is in its ability to support a cognitive process, coming to an understanding of a data set, rather than its beauty or apparent professionalism. A visualisation should offer an aid to perception, a useful frame of reference through which to view the data and to support review and discussion process. Stasko (2013) describes the purposes of visualisation as "more than just answering a specific question", containing as it does the entire process of investigative analysis, helping "us to learn about, develop awareness of, and generate trust in the data, its domain, and its context".

Alongside the increasing popularity of visualisation technologies, an increased recognition and support for data visualisation is developing, fuelled by the growing prevalence of data visualisations, literacy in their use and interest, feedback and further development of visualisation tools and methodologies. Evaluation of the effectiveness of visualisations, however, has lagged behind. Because of the complexity of the processes that a given visualisation is designed to support, evaluation of a visualisation is "extremely difficult" (Stasko, 2013). Stasko identifies two proposed approaches: insight-based evaluation (Saraiya et al., 2005) and case study evaluation (Shneiderman and Plaisant, 2006).

Despite the difficulties, evaluation is important. As we have seen, a poorly designed visualisation that does not make good use of the strengths of human perception may present usability issues. Even a well-designed visualisation may present difficulties under certain circumstances. For example, commentators in the digital humanities have drawn attention to the possibility that visualisations may mislead the user. Where data is uncertain, visualisations may confer a false sense of certainty. For example, Drucker (2011) criticises geographic visualisations as "naturalised [and hence] unquestioned representations", whilst Bodenhammer, 2008 (in Stokes, 2011) suggests that maps "carry the impression of certainty".

A very large number of visualisation tools exist, some of which are packaged alongside text or data mining software and some of which are distributed separately. This chapter cannot hope to cover anything more than a small subset of tools, including a few designed for general purpose visualisation and a few designed primarily to support geographical information visualisation tasks.

2.15 VISUALISATION TOOLS AND FRAMEWORKS

A selection of visualisation packages and frameworks are listed in Appendix C. Many of these visualisation tools depend on technologies adapted for the Web, such as JavaScript and HTML 5. Designers seeking to use web-based visualisation tools that rely on JavaScript may wish to familiarise themselves with an appropriate JavaScript framework, such as the JQuery library or a similar alternative. The use of a JavaScript framework to perform simple tasks such as accessing data often means that less "housekeeping" code must be written, resulting in fewer bugs and shorter code.

The use of web-based visualisation technologies confers a number of useful advantages, such as the ability to publish results to the Web, the opportunity to make use of interactive or dynamic elements and to apply methods drawn from animation or film to grasp and retain attention, or to present a compelling narrative. Disbenefits correspondingly include the practical limitations of web technologies in a print publication format. Although some electronic formats such as EPUB and PDF provide a mechanism for embedding some profiles of dynamic visualisation, in general publication-ready formats cannot support interactive elements. It is sometimes useful to consider both print and live publication modalities when designing visualisations.

It is worth noting that the compatibility of web-based visualisation libraries with various devices and browsers may vary. For example, old browsers may not display information as expected, if at all. Additionally, interaction design decisions that work well on a laptop with a touchpad or an external mouse may be difficult or impossible to use as intended on a touchscreen tablet. It is advisable to test visualisations on a broad variety of devices if they are intended for use by the general public.

2.16 CONCLUSIONS

Text mining exists at the intersection of artificial intelligence, machine learning, statistics, database design and linguistics. As such, it can appear forbiddingly inaccessible. As we have discussed in this chapter, however, there is no single "magic" technology; there are only large numbers of individual functions that, combined into an appropriate pipeline, can produce impressive and useful results.

These technologies – information extraction, opinion extraction, automated indexing and classification, sentiment analysis, characterisation and comparison of texts, and others – hold significant potential to enable new avenues of research in many domains and to facilitate common tasks in others. For business users, text mining holds potential to support existing tasks and enable new approaches to engaging with customers and making use of available knowledge.

Despite the promise of these technologies, there are practical and ethical risks. Overselling of technology is followed by disillusionment and disinterest, so we must be cautious to promise no more than the technology can provide. Certain technologies and solutions can become extremely expensive, so it is important to cautiously explore and evaluate options.

Finally, the looming spectre of unethical use of a technology understandably leads us to reconsider our own intentions, lest we violate the mission statement that Google made famous: "Don't be evil". Text mining has received considerable positive and negative comment over the last few years, ranging from the partially realised promise of the semantic web to the application of computational tools to facilitate surveillance – the collection and interpretation of the "digital dandruff" that web users leave behind. If we choose to climb this mountain, it is our responsibility to ensure that we take the right path and that we are considerate to our fellow hikers on the trail.

REFERENCES

Andersen, P.M., Hayes, P.J., Huettner, A.K., Schmandt, L.M., Nirenburg, I.B., Weinstein, S.P., 1992. Automatic extraction of facts from press releases to generate news stories. In: Proceedings of the Third Conference on Applied Natural Language Processing (ANLC '92). Association for Computational Linguistics, Stroudsburg, PA, USA, pp. 170–177. http://dx.doi.org/10.3115/974499.974531.

Arppe, A., 1995. In: Term Extraction from Unrestricted Text. NODALIDA-95, Helsinki.

Bach, N., Badaskar, S., 2007. A review of relation extraction. In: Literature Review for Language and Statistics II. http://www.cs.cmu.edu/~nbach/papers/A-survey-on-Relation-Extraction.pdf.

Banerjee, M., Capozzoli, M., McSweeney, L., Sinha, D., 1999. Beyond kappa: a review of interrater agreement measures. Can. J. Stat. 27 (1), 3–23.

Bauer, M., Gaskell, G., 2000. Qualitative Researching with Text, Image and Sound: A Practical Handbook. Sage, London.

Biber, D., 1993. Representativeness in corpus design. Lit. Linguist. Comput. 8 (4), 243–257.

Blei, D.M., 2012. Probabilistic topic models. Commun. ACM 55 (4), 77–84. http://dx.doi.org/10.1145/2133806.2133826.

Bodenhamer, D., 2008. History and GIS: implications for the discipline. In: Knowles, A. (Ed.), first ed., In: Placing History: How Maps, Spatial Data, and GIS are Changing Historical Scholarship, ESRI Press, Redlands Calif.

Buhrmester, M., Kwang, T., Gosling, S.D., 2011. Amazon's mechanical turk: a new source of inexpensive, yet high-quality, data? Perspect. Psychol. Sci. 6 (1), 3–5. http://dx.doi.org/10.1177/1745691610393980 (cit. on p. 187).

Buitelaar, P., Cimiano, P., 2007. Bridging the gap from text to knowledge. selected contributions in ontology learning and population from text. https://gate.ac.uk/sale/olp-book/Book_Final.pdf.

Card, S.K., Mackinlay, J.D., Shneiderman, B., 1999. Readings in Information Visualization: Using Vision to Think. Morgan Kaufmann Publishers Inc. Chapter 1, pp. 1–34.

Danis, C.M., Viegas, F.B., Wattenberg, M., Kriss, J., 2008. In: Your Place or Mine?: Visualization as a Community Component, Proc. of ACM CHI '08, April 2008.

Davies, M.B., 2007. Doing a Successful Research Project: Using Qualitative or Quantitative Methods. Palgrave Macmillan, Basingstoke, UK.

Dellarocas, C., Narayan, R., 2006. A statistical measure of a population's propensity to engage in post-purchase online word-of-mouth. Stat. Sci. 21 (2), 277–285.

Dobbin, K.K., Simon, R.M., 2011. Optimally splitting cases for training and testing high dimensional classifiers. BMC Med. Genomics 4, 31.

Don, A., Zheleva, E., Gregory, M., Tarkan, S., Auvil, L., Clement, T., Plaisant, C., 2007. Discovering interesting usage patterns in text collections: integrating text mining with visualization. In: Proceedings of The Sixteenth Acm Conference on Conference on Information and Knowledge Management. ACM, New York, NY, USA, pp. 213–222.

Dredze, M., McNamee, P., Rao, D., Gerber, A., Finin, T., 2010. Entity disambiguation for knowledge base population. In: Proceedings of Conference on Computational Linguistics (COLING).

Drucker, J., 2011. Humanities Approaches to Graphical Display. 5.001 (2011): n. pag. Web. 12 Mar 2011.

Earle, P.S., Bowden, D.C., Guy, M., 2012. Twitter earthquake detection: earthquake monitoring in a social world. Ann. Geophys. 54 (6), 688–707.

Fan, W., Wallace, L., Rich, S., Zhang, Z., 2006. Tapping the power of text mining. Commun. ACM 49 (9), 76–82.

Ferrucci, D.A., 2012. Introduction to "this is watson". IBM J. Res. Dev. 56 (3.4), 1–15.

Fleenor, J.W., Fleenor, J.B., Grossnickle, W.F., 1996. Interrater reliability and agreement of performance ratings: a methodological comparison. J. Bus. Psychol. 10 (3), 367–380.

Fleiss, J.L., 1981. Statistical Methods for Rates and Proportions, second ed. Wiley, New York.

Frantzi, K., Ananiadou, S., Mima, H., 2000. Automatic recognition of multi-word terms: the C-value/NC-value method. Int. J. Digit. Libr. 3 (2), 115–130.

Gillam, L., Tariq, M., 2004. Ontology via terminology? In: Proceedings of Workshop on Terminology, Ontology and Knowledge Representation (Termino 2004), Lyon, France.

Gillam, L., Tariq, M., Ahmad, K., 2005. Terminology and the construction of ontology. John Benjamins Publishing Company. Terminology 11, 55–81.

Gries, S.T., 2008. Dispersions and adjusted frequencies in corpora. Inter. J. Corpus Linguistics 13 (4), 403–437.

Gries, S.T., 2010. Useful statistics for corpus linguistics. In: A Mosaic of Corpus Linguistics: Selected Approaches. Peter lang, Frankfurt, Germany. 269–291.

Guerra, P.C., Meira Jr., W., Cardie, C., 2014. Sentiment analysis on evolving social streams: how self-report imbalances can help. In: Proceedings of the 7th ACM International Conference on Web Search and Data Mining. ACM, pp. 443–452.

Hartman, L., 2013. John Smith: why don't more Americans have this most common name? http://www.slate.com/articles/life/slate_labs/2013/11/john_smith_why_don_t_more_americans_have_this_most_common_name.html.

Hearst, M., 2003. What is text mining. SIMS, UC, Berkeley.

Hotho, A., Nürnberger, A., Paaß, G., 2005. A Brief Survey of Text Mining. LDV Forum - GLDV Journal for Computational Linguistics and Language Technology 20(1), 19–62.

Hu, Y., Talamadupula, K., Kambhampati, S., 2013. Dude, srsly?: the surprisingly formal nature of twitter's language. In: Proceedings of ICWSM, 2013.

Jacquemin, C., 2001. Spotting and Discovering Terms through Natural Language Processing. MIT Press, Cambridge, MA.

Japkowicz, N., Shah, M., 2011. Evaluating Learning Algorithms: A Classification Perspective. Cambridge University Press, New York, NY, USA.

Ji, X., Chun, S.A., Geller, J., 2012. Epidemic outbreak and spread detection system based on twitter data. In: Health Information Science. Springer, Berlin, Heidelberg, pp. 152–163.

Jones, K.S., 1972. A statistical interpretation of term specificity and its application in retrieval. J. Doc. 28 (1), 11–21. http://dx.doi.org/10.1108/eb026526.

Jordan, A.H., Monin, B., Dweck, C.S., Lovett, B.J., John, O.P., Gross, J.J., 2011. Misery has more company than people think: underestimating the prevalence of others' negative emotions. Pers. Soc. Psychol. Bull. 37 (1), 120–135.

Joyce, M., 2013. Picking the best intercoder reliability statistic for your digital activism content analysis. Retrieved 04-2014 from http://digital-activism.org/2013/05/picking-the-best-intercoder-reliability-statistic-for-your-digital-activism-content-analysis/.

Kerren, J., Stasko, T., Fekete, J., North, C. (Eds.), 2008. Theoretical foundations of Information Visualization. In: Lecture Notes in Computer Science, 4950. Springer-Verlag, Berlin, Heidelberg, pp. 46–64. http://dx.doi.org/10.1007/978-3-540-70956-5_3.

Kitchenham, B., Pfleeger, S.L., 2002. Principles of survey research: part 5: populations and samples. ACM SIGSOFT Soft. Eng. Notes 27 (5), 17–20.

Kittur, A., Chi, E.H., Suh, B., 2008. Crowdsourcing user studies with mechanical turk. In: Proceedings of the SIGCHI Conference on Human Factors in Computing Systems. (Florence, Italy). CHI '08. ACM, New York, NY, USA, ISBN: 978-1-60558-011-1, pp. 453–456. http://dx.doi.org/10.1145/1357054.1357127 (cit. on p. 187).

Kohlschütter, C., Fankhauser, P., Nejdl, W., 2010. Boilerplate detection using shallow text features. In: Proceedings of the Third ACM International Conference on Web Search and Data Mining (WSDM '10). ACM, New York, NY, USA, pp. 441–450. http://dx.doi.org/10.1145/1718487.1718542.

Krallinger, M., Morgan, A., Smith, L., Leitner, F., Tanabe, L., Wilbur, J., Hirschman, L., Valencia, A., 2008. Evaluation of text-mining systems for biology: overview of the second biocreative community challenge. Genome Biol. 9 (Suppl. 2), S1. PMCID: PMC2559980.

Leech, G., 2005. Adding linguistic annotation. In: Wynne, M. (Ed.), Developing Linguistic Corpora: A Guide to Good Practice. Oxbow Books, Oxford, pp. 17–29. Chapter 3.

Ling, X., Weld, D.S., 2010. Temporal information extraction. In: AAAI.

Liu, B., 2012. Sentiment analysis and opinion mining. Synthesis Lectures on Human Language Technologies 5 (1), 1–167.

Lovins, J., 1968. Development of a stemming algorithm. Mechanical Translation and Computational Linguistics 1, 22–31.

Lukens, J., DiSalvo, C., 2012. Speculative design and technological fluency. Inter. J. Media and Learning 3 (4), 23–40.

Mani, I., 2004. Recent developments in temporal information extraction. In: Proceedings of the International Conference on Recent Advances in Natural Language Processing (RANLP'03), pp. 45–60.

McEnery, T., Xiao, R., Tono, Y., 2006. Corpus-Based Language Studies. Routledge, London.

Mooney, R.J., Bunescu, R., 2005. Mining knowledge from text using information extraction. SIGKDD Explor. 7 (1), 3–10.

Mori, M., 1970/2012. The uncanny valley (K. F. MacDorman & N. Kageki, Trans.). IEEE Robotics & Automation Magazine 19 (2), 98–100. http://dx.doi.org/10.1109/MRA.2012.2192811. See also, http://spectrum.ieee.org/automaton/robotics/humanoids/an-uncanny-mind-masahiro-mori-on-the-uncanny-valley.

Nadeau, D., Sekine, S., 2007. A survey of named entity recognition and classification. Lingvist. Invest. 30 (1), 3–26 (24).

Nagar, R., Yuan, Q., Freifeld, C.C., Santillana, M., Nojima, A., Chunara, R., Brownstein, J.S., 2014. A case study of the New York city 2012–2013 influenza season with daily geocoded twitter data from temporal and spatiotemporal perspectives. J. Med. Internet Res. 16 (10), e236.

Ofcom. Adults' media use and attitudes report 2014. http://stakeholders.ofcom.org.uk/market-data-research/other/research-publications/adults/adults-media-lit-14/.

Ordonez, C., Chen, Z., 2012. Horizontal aggregations in SQL to prepare data sets for data mining analysis. IEEE Trans. Knowl. Data Eng. 24 (4), 678–691.

Paaß, G., 2011. Document classification, information retrieval, text and web mining. In: Mehler, A., Romary, L. (Eds.), Handbook of Technical Communication. De Gruyter, Mouton, Berlin, Germany, pp. 141–188.

Pang, B., Lee, L., 2008. Opinion mining and sentiment analysis. Foundations and Trends in Information Retrieval 2 (1–2), 1–135.

Paolacci, G., Chandler, J., Ipeirotis, P.G., 2010. Running experiments on amazon mechanical turk. Judgm. Decis. Mak. 5 (5), 411–419. http://journal.sjdm.org/10/10630a/jdm10630a.html. ISSN: 1920–2975 (cit. on p. 187).

Plaisant, C., 2005. Information visualization and the challenge of universal usability. In: Dykes, J., et al., (Eds.), Exploring Geovisualization. Elsevier, Amsterdam, pp. 53–82.

Poibeau, T., Kosseim, L., 2001. Proper name extraction from non-journalistic texts. In: Daelemans, W., Sima'an, K., Veenstra, J., Zavrel, J. (Eds.), Language and Computers, Computational Linguistics in the Netherlands 2000, pp. 144–157(14).

Pollick, F.E., 2010. In search of the uncanny valley. In: Daras, P., Ibarra, O.M. (Eds.), User Centric Media. Springer, Berlin, Heidelberg, pp. 69–78.

Porter, M., 1980. An algorithm for suffix stripping. Program 14 (3), 130–137.

Powers, D.M.W., 2011. Evaluation: from precision, r ecall and f-measurue to ROC, informedness, markedness and correlation. J. Mach. Learn. Technol. 2 (1), 37–63.

Purchase, H.C., Andrienko, N., Jankun-Kelly, T.J., Ward, M., 2008. Theoretical Foundations of Information Visualization. In information Visualization: Human-Centered Issues and Perspectives, A.

Ratcliffe, J.H., 2004. Geocoding crime and a first estimate of a minimum acceptable hit rate. Int. J. Geogr. Inf. Sci. 18 (1), 61–72.

Rau, L.F., 1991. Extracting company names from text. In: Proc. Conference on Artificial Intelligence Applications of IEEE.

Rizzo, C.R., 2010. Getting on with corpus compilation: from theory to practice. ESP World 1 (27), 1–23.

Rothenberg, R.B., 1995. Commentary: sampling in social networks. Connections 18, 105–111.

Rudman, J., 2012. The twelve disputed 'Federalist' papers: a case for collaboration. Proceedings Digital Humanities 2012, 353–356.

Rushton, G., Armstrong, M.P., Gittler, J., Greene, B.R., Pavlik, C.E., West, M.M., Zimmerman, D.L., 2006. Geocoding in cancer research: a review. Am. J. Prev. Med. 30 (2), S16–S24.

Salton, G., Wong, A., Yang, C.S., 1975. A vector space model for automatic indexing. Communications of the ACM 18 (11), 613–620.

Saloot, M.A., Idris, N., Mahmud, R., 2014. An architecture for Malay Tweet normalization. Inform. Process. Manag. 50 (5), 621–633. ISSN 0306-4573. http://dx.doi.org/10.1016/j.ipm.2014.04.009.

Saraiya, P., et al., 2005. An insight-based methodology for evaluating bioinformatics visualizations. IEEE Trans. Vis. Comput. Graph. 11 (4), 443–456.

Sebastiani, F., 2002. Machine learning in automated text categorization. ACM Comput. Surv. 34 (1), 1–47.

Sharp, H., Rogers, Y., Preece, J., 2011. Interaction Design: Beyond Human-Computer Interaction, third ed. John Wiley & Sons, ISBN: 9780470665763.

Shneiderman, B., Plaisant, C., 2006. Strategies for evaluating information visualization tools: multi-dimensional in-depth long-term case studies. BELIV 2006, 1–7.

Sinclair, J., 2004. Intuition and annotation – the discussion continues. In: Aijmer, K., Altenberg, B. (Eds.), Advances in Corpus Linguistics. Papers from the 23rd International Conference on English Language Research on Computerized Corpora (ICAME 23). Rodopi, Amsterdam/New York.

Smith, T.M.F., 1976. The foundations of survey sampling: a review. J. Roy. Stat. Soc. A 139 (2), 183–204. http://dx.doi.org/10.2307/2345174 Wiley.

Stanford, 2014. Stanford Word Segmenter. http://nlp.stanford.edu/software/segmenter.shtml.

Stasko, J., 2013. The Value of Visualisation for Exploring and Understanding Data.Sicsa Summer School on Big Data InfoVis.

Stokes, N.H., 2011. A study in digital geospatial history. A Master's Paper for the M.S. in L.S. Degree.

Sugumaran, R., Voss, J., 2012. Real-time spatio-temporal analysis of west nile virus using twitter data. In: Proceedings of the 3rd International Conference on Computing for Geospatial Research and Applications. ACM, p. 39.

Thompson, P., Iqbal, S.A., McNaught, J., Ananiadou, S., 2009. Construction of an annotated corpus to support biomedical information extraction. BMC Bioinf. 10 (1), 349.

Turmo, J., Ageno, A., Català, N., 2006. Adaptive information extraction. ACM Computing Surveys (CSUR) 38 (2), 4.

Wang, L., Cardie, C., 2014. A Piece of my mind: a sentiment analysis approach for online dispute detection. In: Proceedings of the 52nd Annual Meeting of the Association for Computational Linguistics, 2, pp. 693–699.

Weiss, S.M., Indurkhya, N., Zhang, T., 2010. Fundamentals of Predictive Text Mining. Springer Science & Business Media.

Weiss, S.M., Kulikowski, C.A., 1991. Computer Systems that Learn: Classification and Prediction Methods from Statistics, Neural Nets, Machine Learning, and Expert Systems. Morgan Kaufmann Publishers Inc., San Francisco, CA, USA.

Wiegers, K., Beatty, J., 2013. Software Requirements, third ed. Microsoft Press, Redmond, WA, ISBN: 978-0-7356-7966-5.

Witschel, H.F., 2005. Terminology extraction and automatic indexing. In: Terminology and Knowledge Engineering (TKE).

Yu, B., 2013. Automated citation sentiment analysis: what can we learn from biomedical researchers. Proc. Am. Soc. Inform. Sci. Technol. 50 (1), 1–9. PDF 10.1002/meet.14505001084.

CHAPTER 3

If You Find Yourself in a Hole, *Stop Digging*: Legal and Ethical Issues of Text/Data Mining in Research

A. Charlesworth*, E.L. Tonkin[†,‡]
*University of Bristol Law School, Bristol, UK
[†]Department of Digital Humanities, King's College London, London, UK
[‡]Department of Electrical & Electronic Engineering, Univeristy of Bristol, Bristol, UK

3.1 INTRODUCTION

A professor in computer science, while discussing new data mining techniques that could potentially unmask interesting information points affecting individuals or groups from within vast data sets of interaction data (e.g., internet search terms), pronounces himself amazed at the leeway that the law permits him when analysing data relating to individuals, or their activities, in ways that he himself would consider to be "intrusive".

A report prepared for the UK government on intellectual property calls for copyright law to be amended to permit copyright works held in databases, or otherwise aggregated, to be data mined en masse by researchers to generate useful information, without the need to seek the individual copyright holders' permission.

A postgraduate researcher presenting a paper at a conference describes collecting and mining the conversations on Islamic chatrooms seeking words that might indicate extremist conversations, without either informing or gaining the consent of the participants, on the grounds that the conversations are "in the public domain".

These activities, all real-life examples, have implications for the ways that our current legal system addresses (or fails to address) the opportunities and risks of data mining in particular contexts, but at the same time they also pose questions about the rational and proportionate application of existing ethical premises in research.

3.1.1 The Relationship Between Law and Ethics

The nature of law and ethics is such that they are inextricably intertwined, but it is important to recognise that while their rationales and objectives may

Working with Text
http://dx.doi.org/10.1016/B978-1-84334-749-1.00003-2
61

overlap, they often differ significantly. For example, the understandings underpinning research ethics may be described thusly:

> In broad terms, ethical standards in research seek actively and explicitly to do three things. First, to protect the rights and legitimate interests of research participants (e.g. by normally requiring informed consent). Second, to create trust in both researchers and research outcomes (e.g. by endorsing or rejecting practices affecting the actual or perceived reliability or trustworthiness of research data). Finally, to preserve the research environment (e.g. by seeking to prevent practices which might restrict future access to research participants or reduce the effectiveness of future research). Alongside these aims, an additional consideration ... will undoubtedly be protection of the researcher's reputation, and that of their institution, against allegations of unethical or unlawful behaviour. (Charlesworth, 2012, p. 88)

While legal rules may address similar issues and concerns, their underlying rationales may differ, and the approaches taken may fail to mirror or indeed, consciously sacrifice, ethical principles on utilitarian and/or pragmatic grounds:

> By contrast, general laws, like the UK's data protection law, are designed to regulate broader spheres of human activity. In consequence, the impact of such laws upon academic (and commercial) research practices is likely to be a relatively minor consideration for legislators and regulators. While a law may appear to seek to address broadly similar goals to ethical standards (e.g. protecting the rights and legitimate interests of individuals, including research participants), its drafters are unlikely to be particularly sensitive to its compatibility with established ethical research processes, or the practicalities of research. (Charlesworth, 2012, p. 88)

Such differences are reflected in our examples above. In the first and third examples, the research being carried out may not trigger a UK legal rule, in this case the Data Protection Act 1998, because the law applies to the processing of data about identifiable living individuals. Research using data that is properly anonymised does not meet this criterion, and thus will fall outside the sphere of regulation. However, an ethical review body, such as an Institutional Review Board (IRB) or Research Ethics Committee (REC) might find the analysis of data sets of human interactions, being a form of human subject research, problematic on ethical grounds without provision of additional protections by the researchers for both individuals and communities involved, whether individuals are clearly identified or not. Equally, the covert observation of individuals, such as the recording of chat room and discussion group interactions, without the informed consent of those participating or, if informed consent is not sought, then demonstrable measures to reduce any risk of harm to research subjects, would also be likely to be deprecated.

In the second example, the law involved, the Copyright Designs and Patents Act 1988 (CDPA, 1988), as originally drafted, effectively prioritised the economic right of individual copyright holders to control the uses of their work above the social good of permitting the extraction of potentially valuable information from an aggregate of their combined works. While promoting a potential public good over a possible economic interest might in itself perhaps be considered to be ethical, UK law requires explicit provision for limiting rightsholders' intellectual property rights in this fashion. As such, until 1 June 2014 any engaging in unauthorised or unlicensed data mining of copyright works would have infringed upon the rights granted exclusively to rightsholders by law, permitting them to bring a legal action against an infringer. There was also a further hurdle to negotiate: where works were aggregated by rightsholders, or by a third party such as a database provider, data mining of those resources could also be explicitly barred by the contract or terms of service between the rightsholder/database provider and the researcher or the entity through which they accessed the service.

This chapter will explore and expand upon these and related issues, and consider, firstly, how researchers might plausibly develop and structure the application of data mining techniques in the light of current legal requirements and ethical practices; and, secondly, examine the case for legal reform and review of what is considered accepted ethical practice. The latter discussion is not specifically seeking to legitimize particular instances of data mining, but rather to consider how researchers might aim, as a "community", to develop an effective and proportionate ethical framework for utilising data mining in research, and how that might in turn influence legal regulation of the area. Such an approach has been utilised with some success in the area of Internet research by the Association of Internet Researchers (AoIR) who have produced two reports to assist Internet researchers in making ethical decisions in their research (AoIR, 2002, 2012).

3.1.2 Law, Technology and Change

It is a modern-day truism that the cautious speed with which the law adapts to change means that its applicability to new technologies and new social practices facilitated by, or developing from, those technologies is often unclear or unexplored. There are many reasons for this apparent inertia; for example, legislators may be unwilling to act where

- there is insufficient information/evidence that legislation is required, or about the appropriate factors to be considered when amending existing laws or creating new ones;

- there is a risk that legislating at an early stage might hamper the development of a technology, impede useful applications of a technology, or create other unintended negative consequences;
- there is a risk of creating "technology specific" legislation, when "technology neutral" legislation would be more appropriate to a particular technological field;
- the creation, or amendment of, legislation to address a new technology may undo an existing social consensus, be opposed by a significant interest group or groups, or unduly advantage or disadvantage particular groups;
- it is unclear whether legislating at a national level will conflict with a country's bilateral, regional or multilateral international obligations and understandings; and
- there is a view that the issue would best be addressed by national courts interpreting existing legislation or, in the United Kingdom, utilising common law principles.

Equally, the courts may be unwilling to act where

- existing legislation or common law principles cannot readily be interpreted/stretched to cover new technologies or new social practices; and
- there is a view that by seeking to address an uncertainty or lacunae in the law, they might be seen to be usurping the role of the legislature to determine policy issues.

Sometimes these factors may lead to legal gridlock, for example, in the development of UK privacy law. Here, despite repeated calls from government-convened committees (e.g., Calcutt, 1993) and from the courts (e.g., Kaye v Robertson, 1991) that Parliament should consider enacting a right to privacy, Parliament held to the view that legislation was unnecessary (e.g., HM Government, 1995) or that the courts could be left to address the issue (e.g., House of Commons, 2003). A solution began to emerge only after Parliament passed the Human Rights Act 1998 which, by incorporating the European Convention on Human Rights into UK law, required the courts to work out how to give effect to Art.8 ECHR on the right of privacy (e.g., Campbell v Mirror Group Newspapers Ltd., 2004).

Thus, it can be seen that navigating the considerations behind decisions whether or not to create, amend or interpret laws so as to address the consequences of technological advances, will rarely be a simple matter.

3.2 KEY LEGAL ISSUES IN DATA MINING

The two main questions that are often raised in relation to the legality of academic data mining are "Can I utilise data sets that are created by a third party?" and "Can I utilise data sets that contain data about third parties?" This section will seek to address those initial questions, but also to raise and discuss a third relevant question: "When mining data sets for information, how should I treat the outputs/information I have acquired?"

3.2.1 Data as Property

Professor Hargreaves (2011), in his UK government-commissioned report *Digital Opportunity: A Review of Intellectual Property and Growth* (hereafter *Hargreaves*) took particular aim at what he perceived as ways in which UK copyright law blocked new technologies, with specific reference to text and data mining (p. 41). Some idea of the rate at which these technologies had developed might be gauged by the fact that the previous UK government-commissioned report, the *Gowers Review of Intellectual Property* (2006) a mere 5 years earlier, covered much of the same ground, yet made no mention of text or data mining. The points *Hargreaves* raised would chime with a range of researchers:

- while copyright was not specifically aimed at regulating developments in technology, it was capable of being used to "block or permit developments or applications of technology" (p. 46);
- text and data mining of copyright works required the carrying out of acts requiring the permission of copyright holders (e.g., digitising, copying) which might be difficult or impossible to obtain, particularly if the works in question were "orphan works" where the copyright holder could not be identified (p. 47);
- even where researchers or their institutions had purchased access to digitised archives of works, they could be prevented from using those archives for text and data mining by terms in the copyright licence/access contract (p. 48);
- no exception existed in UK copyright law to permit text and data mining, even under the noncommercial research fair dealing provisions – CDPA, 1988, ss 29–30 (p. 48).

This was certainly the experience of at least one university Ph.D. researcher, known to the author, who had attempted to test data mining tools on a journal database to which their university carried a subscription. When the database provider noticed that the tool was being run, they restricted the entire institutional access to the database, claiming that access to the database did not include the right to run automated data mining tools, and suggesting that permission to do so would be conditional upon the institution purchasing a further licence permitting data mining.

Hargreaves suggested that the United Kingdom should, at a minimum, provide a copyright exception permitting text/data mining in a noncommercial research context that should also preclude contractual terms seeking to set it aside (pp. 47–48), and that the United Kingdom should seek to influence change in copyright law at the EU level that would permit text/data mining in a commercial research context (p. 48). The key argument put forward for such changes was that technologies such as text/data mining did not utilise the underlying creative and expressive purpose of the work – and were thus a "nonconsumptive use".

To put it another way, if a student downloads a journal article from a database to which their university subscribes, to read it, they are utilising the work in the way in which it was intended to be used; a "consumptive use". There is copying, and this copying for a consumptive purpose would breach the copyright holder's rights unless it was licenced. If a student uses a data mining tool to download and search multiple articles, there is also copying, but the copying is simply to allow the software to analyse the documents; the software does not treat the work as a work, but rather as a storage medium for information. In the words of an engineer on another large text mining project (Google Books) "we're not scanning all those books to be read by people. We're scanning them to be read by Artificial Intelligence" (Dyson, 2005, cited in Borghi and Karapapa (2011)).

This type of distinction, and some of its consequences, are analysed in greater detail by Borghi and Karapapa (2011) in the context of the Google Books litigation (Author's Guild, Inc. v Google, Inc., 2013). They suggest that it might be helpful to consider the scenario not just in terms of "use of" a work, but rather in terms of "use of" and "use on" a work; reading a journal article is "use of" a work, automated processing of it is "use on" a work. In the latter case, and particularly in the context of mass digitisation, the work might be viewed simply as a container of data that is processed not as the expression of an idea by its creator, but as a set of information upon which software-based algorithms can be run (pp. 44–45). This does not fit comfortably into the copyright paradigm of ways of dealing with copies of works; the dissemination and the use of copies. However, Borghi and Karapapa are not arguing that all "use on" a work, where "works are not used as works but as data" should fall outside copyright protection. They suggest that "use on" a work to facilitate "use of" a work (e.g., automatic processing for indexing and search) should be treated as noninfringing (p. 51). However, they argue that when uses on works become substitutive, or totally irrelevant, to uses of works (i.e., automated processing for computational analysis and for data mining), the justification for denying an author the right to restrict use is perhaps weaker, because such use on works involves a degree of content appropriation that trespasses upon the very purpose of creating a work.

As such, Borghi and Karapapa's analysis appears to suggest that legislative moves to permit text/data mining, like those suggested by *Hargreaves*, whilst clarifying the legal position, and potentially releasing valuable information and correlations from "orphan work" limbo, might at the same time unduly strip rights of control from authors (and indirectly, rightholders to whom the authors' rights have been assigned), by permitting uses of a work in ways that the author did not intend (i.e., potentially not as a work at all). In contrast, the US District Court's eventual ruling in November 2013 in *Author's Guild, Inc. v Google, Inc.* took a more pragmatic view, holding that Google's use of the works, including "a type of research referred to as 'data mining' or 'text mining'" was "fair use" under US copyright law:

> Google Books provides significant public benefits. It advances the progress of the arts and sciences, while maintaining respectful consideration for the rights of authors and other creative individuals, and without adversely impacting the rights of copyright holders. (p. 26)

3.2.1.1 Data Mining and Utilitarian Copyright Perspectives

The position in the US courts at the time of writing (subject to the appeal of the judgement in *Author's Guild, Inc. v Google, Inc.* pending before the US Court of Appeals for the Second Circuit) is, of course, centred firmly in US copyright law's "fair use" provisions, which are considerably more wide ranging than the "fair dealing" defences under the UK CDPA, 1988. However, the UK government responded favourably to *Hargreaves* (HM Government, 2011), and legislation The Copyright and Rights in Performances (Research, Education, Libraries and Archives) Regulations (2014), which implements *Hargreaves* proposals for an exception to copyright to permit text/data mining in a noncommercial research context, and forbid contractual provisions seeking to overcome that exception, came into force on 1 June 2014, amending s.29 CDPA, 1988 as follows:

s.29 Research and private study.

(1)Fair dealing with a work for the purposes of research for a non-commercial purpose does not infringe any copyright in the work provided that it is accompanied by a sufficient acknowledgement.

(1B)No acknowledgement is required in connection with fair dealing for the purposes mentioned in subsection (1) where this would be impossible for reasons of practicality or otherwise.

[...]

(4B) To the extent that a term of a contract purports to prevent or restrict the doing of any act which, by virtue of this section, would not infringe copyright, that term is unenforceable.

29A Copies for text and data analysis for noncommercial research

(1) *The making of a copy of a work by a person who has lawful access to the work does not infringe copyright in the work provided that*
   (a) *the copy is made in order that a person who has lawful access to the work may carry out a computational analysis of anything recorded in the work for the sole purpose of research for a noncommercial purpose, and*
   (b) *the copy is accompanied by a sufficient acknowledgement (unless this would be impossible for reasons of practicality or otherwise).*

(2) *Where a copy of a work has been made under this section, copyright in the work is infringed if*
   (a) *the copy is transferred to any other person, except where the transfer is authorised by the copyright owner, or*
   (b) *the copy is used for any purpose other than that mentioned in subsection (1)(a), except where the use is authorised by the copyright owner.*

(3) *If a copy made under this section is subsequently dealt with*
   (a) *it is to be treated as an infringing copy for the purposes of that dealing, and*
   (b) *if that dealing infringes copyright, it is to be treated as an infringing copy for all subsequent purposes.*

(4) *In subsection (3) "dealt with" means sold or let for hire, or offered or exposed for sale or hire.*

(5) *To the extent that a term of a contract purports to prevent or restrict the making of a copy which, by virtue of this section, would not infringe copyright, that term is "unenforceable".*

As such, subject to the conditions in s.29–29A, it is possible to copy and text/data mine copyrighted works for noncommercial purposes without breaching copyright, and this defence cannot be excluded by contract. While this is clearly not as extensive an ability to copy and subject to computational analysis and text/data mining as appears to be presently the case in the United States, it will make it easier for many researchers to develop, test and utilise text/data mining tools without fear of inadvertently infringing copyright or breaching a contract with a rights holder or supplier of works.

It is likely, of course, to lead to some debate about the scope of noncommercial purposes and whether certain types of research carried out in conjunction with, or sponsored by, commercial organisations might fall outside the defence. Contemporary university research increasingly crosses the line between commercial and noncommercial research, often on the same project or line of research and, in the sciences, the distinction has become increasingly difficult to realistically maintain. Ideally, the exception will be broadened in the future to encompass at least some commercial data or text mining uses, not least because researchers in academic institutions and commercial organisations often utilise the same major databases or libraries. Maintaining the difference between commercial and noncommercial use may thus result in unnecessary duplication of effort to obtain the same or similar information. However, the main barrier to achieving change for commercial research lies in Art.5(3) *Directive 2001/29/EC on the harmonisation of certain aspects of copyright and related rights in the information society*, which by providing a closed list of the exceptions to, or limitations on, right holders' exclusive reproduction rights that member states can provide, signally restricts the United Kingdom's room for independent manoeuvre.

Looking to the future, it may be that if the US approach to computational analysis and text/data mining as being an acceptable form of fair use survives legal challenge, that there will be increasing competitive pressure on the European Union to broaden the scope of its exceptions or limitations. Whether the civil law jurisdictions, which have traditionally been more protective of authors' rights, on a personality right basis (i.e., that the author's rights are not just premised on protecting their economic rights, but on the fact that they have put something of their personality into the work) are willing to accede to a utilitarian perspective of "public good" on this matter without a struggle remains to be seen. The willingness of French authors and publishers to strike a deal with Google over digitisation of their works in 2012 suggests this might be a possibility, although that deal came at some financial cost to Google.

Other questions may arise with regard to competition – a key element of opposition to Google's Google Book Search Settlement Agreement was the fear that it would give Google too much market power in digitisation and computational analysis – and with the possibility of the use of technical protection measures (TPM) by database providers and others to limit computational analysis and text/data mining, as this is not explicitly excluded in the new legislation. In the United Kingdom such action would probably fall under s.296ZE CDPA, 1988, which allows a person prevented from carrying out a permitted act in relation to a work (except computer programs) to issue a notice of complaint to the secretary of state (s.296ZE(2)), and for the secretary of state to direct the owner or exclusive licensee of that copyright work to make available to the complainant the means of carrying out the permitted act to the extent necessary to so benefit from it (s.296ZE (3)). However, to date, actual use of this section appears to have been minimal; it was criticised by the Gowers Review for being ineffective (Gowers, 2006, p. 71), and an Intellectual Property Office response to a Freedom of Information Act request in 2010 indicated that, while it had received 10 complaints, the IPO considered that none contained sufficient information to warrant forwarding them to the secretary of state.

3.2.2 Data as Personally Identifying Information (PII)

The mass collection and storage of data relating to individuals or personally identifiable information (PII), in particular, by government and commercial entities, has been the subject of controversy for decades, whether in paper form (Wheeler, 1969) or in automated systems (Warner and Stone, 1970; Miller, 1971). However, the lack of coordination between disparate data holdings, and the extent to which the potential pace of collection outstripped the computational capacity of organisations to address it in other than relatively structured automated processes, provided significant barriers to large-scale automated processing operations that could provide the correlations and insights that contemporary "Big Data" processing can now generate.

Examples of these barriers could be found in the lack of data connectivity in, and between, government departmental data holdings (e.g., between databases of taxation data and benefit data), or in the failure of the US authorities to piece together the dispersed information known to its intelligence and law enforcement agencies about the activities of terrorist suspects prior to 9/11. The latter example was responsible for an upsurge of interest in data sharing and data mining that initially led to the development of the US Total Information Awareness project (Cohen, 2010), then later, after the apparent demise of that program, the development of the rather less high-profile, but no less ambitious programs brought to light prior to, and during, the recent Edward Snowden revelations, such as PRISM (Berghel, 2013).

The legal response to the expansion of collection, storage and processing of PII since the 1970s has often been the introduction of national legislation designed to minimise the risks to individuals arising out of misuse of data that relates to them. In some jurisdictions, like the EU member states, this takes the form of an overarching data protection regime; in others (e.g., the United States), there is no overarching regime, but rather a series of state and federal laws addressing particular areas of activity. National legislation can often trace its roots to international data protection/data privacy principles, such as those contained in the OECD Guidelines on the Protection of Privacy and Transborder Flows of Personal Data (OECD, 1980, 2013).

The OECD Guidelines set out a series of basic principles:

- Collection Limitation – there should be limits to the collection of PII, it should be obtained by lawfully and fairly and, ideally, with the knowledge/consent of the data subject.

- Data Quality – PII should be relevant to the purposes for which it is to be used, and should be accurate, complete and up-to-date enough for those purposes.

- Purpose Specification – purposes for which PII are collected should be specified at the time of data collection. Subsequent use should be limited to those purposes or such others compatible with those purposes and specified on each change of purpose.

- Use Limitation – PII should not be disclosed, made available or otherwise used for unspecified purposes except with data subject consent or by authority of law.

- Security Safeguards – PII should be protected by reasonable security safeguards against such risks as loss or unauthorised access, destruction, use, modification or disclosure of data.

- Openness – data subjects should be able to establish the existence and nature of PII, and the main purposes of its use, and the identity and location of the data controller.

- Individual Participation – an individual should be able to be informed by a data controller whether it holds PII relating to him or her; to have the PII communicated to him or her in meaningful form and reasonable time and at reasonable cost; to be informed if the PII will not be communicated and to be able to challenge that denial, where the PII is not lawfully held to have it erased, rectified, completed or amended.

- Accountability – a data controller should be accountable for complying with measures that give effect to the other principles.

These principles, in essence, underlie the EU Data Protection Directive 1995 and its national implementations, such as the UK Data Protection Act 1998 (see further, Carey, 2009).

However, when one examines the aggregation and automatic analysis of "Big Data" and popular perceptions of how such technology may be utilised (e.g., Mayer-Schonberger and Cukier, 2013), it becomes clear that there are potentially some fundamental incompatibilities between those established principles for handling PII, and the ways in which PII might be processed and even generated in the course of text/data mining (Table 3.1).

As such, it can be seen that the premises underlying the current European legal regime may fit uncomfortably with some of the techniques and possible outcomes of automated analysis of large data collections.

3.2.2.1 Text/Data Mining and Accountability

It is no secret that the EU data protection regime is in need of reform, not least because its regulatory techniques are increasingly ineffective at addressing contemporary technical developments (Charlesworth and Pearson, 2013; Gutwirth et al., 2014). The EU Commission has proposed a new draft

Table 3.1 Potential incompatibilities between the OECD data privacy principles and automated analysis of collections of data potentially containing PII

Principle	Automated analysis of data sets
Collection limitation	The larger the data collection, the better the potential for identifying interesting correlations
Data quality	"Messy data" is fine, it's not clear what is relevant until its analysed, and even inaccurate or incomplete data can be useful
Purpose specification	Data may have been collected for a particular purpose, but analysis may indicate further unrelated and previously unknown, but valuable, purposes. Data as collected may not be obviously PII, but analysis of it may identify individuals
Use limitation	There may be value in sharing and aggregating data that may not be apparent at the time of collection
Security safeguards	It may be unclear what security issues, if any, arise from a particular collection of data or its analysis
Openness	Where data is collected and analysed, it may not be obvious that it is PII, and even in circumstances where it is, the researcher may have no way of informing the data subject of its use
Individual participation	Data that is anonymous may still be utilised in ways that can cause risk/harm to an individual
Accountability	How and when might a researcher to be held accountable and for what?

Data Protection Regulation that seeks to address some of the key weaknesses that have been identified over the last 20 years. At the time of writing, this document is slowly making its way through the EU legislative process. If it is passed (which is not a certainty), the draft DP Regulation will automatically become part of member state law; unlike the current DP Directive, it will not require national laws to implement it.

The draft regulation, as currently constituted, will make some significant changes to the data privacy regime in the European Union. A key element of the draft regulation is the attempt to reduce "red tape" (e.g., registration/ notification by data controllers), but with a concomitant increase in the importance placed on the notion of the "accountability" of data controllers. The commission's intention appears to be that the updated data protection regime would seek to rely less upon the bureaucratic mechanisms of the DP Directive, but rather place greater responsibility upon data controller and processors to ensure that they have the necessary policies and procedures in place to meet the requirements of the regulation; that is, the effective protection of the personal data of data subjects. In the words of the "Paris Project" of privacy regulators and privacy professionals, such accountability would entail

> ... a demonstrable acknowledgement and assumption of responsibility for having in place appropriate policies and procedures, and promotion of good practices that include correction and remediation for failures and misconduct. It is a concept that has governance and ethical dimensions. It envisages an infrastructure that fosters responsible decision-making, engenders answerability, enhances transparency and considers liability. It encompasses expectations that organisations will report, explain and be answerable for the consequences of decisions about the protection of data. Accountability promotes implementation of practical mechanisms whereby legal requirements and guidance are translated into effective protection for data. (Centre for Information Policy Leadership, 2010, p. 2)

The implication of the foregoing is that there is going to be an increased requirement for researchers conducting automated analysis of data collections to consider whether

- the data, as collected, is likely to contain PII, or if processing the data, including combining data collections, might lead to PII being generated as a result of the nature of the analysis;
- the PII that might be processed is of a type that could pose a particular risk for data subjects if it is disclosed;
- the research processes and the security used to protect the PII are appropriate in the context of the research being undertaken; and

• publication of research outputs will not disclose PII in breach of the rights of data subjects under DP law.

From the perspective of researchers, if the draft regulation is implemented in its current form, it may permit a more flexible approach to the handling of PII in research contexts. This would counter some of the criticism of the impact upon research of the existing data protection regime. This criticism suggests that research institutions, in attempting to limit any perceived legal liability, have created increasingly formalised/legalistic, and often centralised, institutional oversight mechanisms, which demonstrate compliance with data protection rule sets that are designed for nonresearch contexts . Such approaches may unnecessarily hamper both academic research that is in the public interest, and carries minimal risk to research participants (if suitable care is taken by researchers); and research that creates a significant risk to participants, but one that is publicly justifiable (e.g., exposure of wrongdoing) (Erdos, 2011, 2012; Charlesworth, 2012).

Refocusing upon developing mechanisms for accountability could, by reducing institutional reliance on "box-ticking" approaches to data protection in research, foster a subsidiarity approach to protection of PII in research, by returning the responsibility for determining the appropriate accountability processes for particular research contexts to researchers working in those fields. This would also potentially alter the role of institutional bodies, such as research ethics committees, from one of ensuring strict conformity with often unnecessarily strict data protection rule sets (e.g., institutional gatekeeping) to one that could provide education and advice on appropriate protection in particular research contexts.

This is not to say, however, that such an approach would be welcomed by all researchers. A "tick box" approach to legal/ethical issues may be constraining in some research contexts, but for others it has the advantage of short-circuiting discussion that might throw up awkward questions. For example, in the data mining context, a "tick box" data protection question that asks "Will you be processing personal data?" for a project analysing search terms input to a particular search engine, might plausibly be answered in the negative – the project is, on its face, simply processing search terms. However, if whilst processing those terms, personal data might be created by data triangulation (as AOL discovered in 2006) then the answer becomes more complicated than Yes or No. A researcher asked to consider the potential risks of their research as regards third-party PII, how serious those risks are, whether the research justifies running those risks, and whether a research methodology could be used that reduces or removes those risks, will undoubtedly be better prepared for being held accountable, but they are going to have to spend more time and effort on the process and be prepared to justify their reasoning.

3.2.3 *Primum non Nocere*: Some Thoughts on False Positives, Patternicity and Liability

On the blog "Spurious Correlations", Tyler Vigen demonstrates, via a series of humorous examples such as the "link" between "total revenue generated by US games arcades" and the "number of US computer science doctorates awarded", the hazards of forgetting the scientific/statistical rule that "correlation does not imply causation" (Viglen, 2014). Mistakenly believing there to be patterns or linkages in data where there are none, which Shermers dubs "patternicity" (in statistics, a type I error), or mistakenly believing there are no patterns or linkages when they in fact exist dubbed "apatternicity" (in statistics, a type II error) are, he suggests, the result of the inability of a built-in human "pattern recognition" mechanism to handle sophisticated contexts/information (Shermers, 2011). This tendency toward "patternit-city" or "apatternicity" appears in contexts as varied as the "gambler's fallacy" and conspiracy theories, and its potential for creating or supporting misapprehensions when dealing with probabilities arising from research data is a matter that both researchers, and those relying upon the outputs of third-party research, neglect to account for at their peril.

Text mining and data mining would seem to provide a great deal of potential for inadvertent or deliberate misinterpretation of data. Take, for example, a total information awareness-like program that aims to mine data extracted from a range of travel-related transaction databases (e.g., airline passenger manifests, railway ticket websites, etc.), to attempt to identify suspicious patterns of travel behaviour that can be linked to named individuals. From the start this system suffers from a major problem: as unique IDs, names are terribly poor. There are frequent duplicates: an American named James Smith has over 38,000 contemporary namesakes, whilst Michael, Robert and David Smith enjoy over 30,000 each (Hartman, 2013). A system that cannot effectively differentiate between individuals with the same name, in concert with human users who cannot (perhaps because the system does not flag it), or choose not to (perhaps because the negative consequences do not fall on them), take into account the possibility of errors, is inevitably going to cause difficulties for some of those individuals. For example, in 2004, US Senator Ted Kennedy, a highly recognisable public figure, was repeatedly stopped and questioned at US airports, apparently because "Edward Kennedy" was used as an alias by a suspected terrorist on the US Department of Homeland Security watch list (Goo, 2004).

Named entity disambiguation (entity linking) attempts to figure out the identity referred to by a given instance of a given name. This is error-prone even in a closely constrained context, such as "researchers who publish in the field of computational linguistics". Where less contextual information is involved, named entity disambiguation becomes nothing more than well-informed guesswork. An international or cross-cultural data set confuses the issue further as a result of transliteration, internationalisation and cultural variation in data representation. An insufficiently sensitive algorithm will be confused into failing to link entities that should be referenced. An excessively sensitive algorithm will result in false positives.

This is fairly unimportant when the intention is to develop a bibliographic network: accidentally linking a legal academic to a medical researcher's research output is unlikely to result in long-term career damage, even if it does increase their spam e-mails (Elsevier's own Cite Alert is endearingly incapable of distinguishing A. Charlesworth, Bristol Law School, from A. Charlesworth, Nottingham Clinical Research Group). A system intended to support national security is facing higher stakes and an entirely different risk analysis.

As well as false positives and false negatives, those working in text mining, classification or machine learning often talk about *precision* and *recall*. Imagine that researchers are exploring a haystack looking for needles, but they find that the haystack also contains a large number of pins. They use a haystack mining algorithm to try to identify instances of needles, which results in a sample of sharp pointy things. *Precision* is defined as the number of needles in their sample of sharp pointy things, divided by the total number of sharp pointy things in their sample. *Recall* is defined as the number of needles in their sample of sharp pointy things, divided by the total number of needles in the haystack.

The researchers may choose to tune their sampling method for maximising the number of sharp pointy things returned, if they believe that it does no harm to accidentally misclassify pins as needles in a few cases, or they may choose to optimise precision at the expense of recall. In large, noisy data sets (as in the example of web search engines) precision matters a lot, whilst recall is somewhat academic when there are 128,000,000 search results to choose from. If, on the other hand, researchers are looking for a very small group of very valuable needles (potential terrorists in a chat room, for example, recalling our third example), they may wish to tune the system to greater sensitivity in recall at the expense of precision. If researchers choose to make this adjustment, a responsible system designer should ensure that the implications of a match are clearly signposted to the user of the system.

It is challenging to express the practical implications of matches in which the system has low confidence. People tend to find that probabilities are difficult to visualise or understand. Consider the example of a classification function, correct 99% of the time and intended to identify that the individual is suffering from a specific disease that will hit 1 person in 10,000. This example commonly appears in explanations of Bayesian reasoning (commonsense probability) for beginners (Hoffrage et al., 2000), as an example of a situation in which probabilities offered by the medical profession tend to mislead the general public. Ninety-nine percent sounds like an excellent estimate: if an individual is classified by an algorithm that is 99% accurate as suffering from a particular disease, then should we not have confidence in the result? The answer to this question is "no": we should not, at this stage, have confidence in the result. The probability of an accurate classification in general is not the interesting part of the problem for us. The more important point is whether we are likely to have been *falsely classified* as suffering from this disease, and probability theory tells us that even with a classification function that is 99% accurate, the chances are over 92% that this classification represents a *false positive* (see further, Azad, 2007).

It is commonplace for researchers to develop and benchmark classifiers with little information about the eventual context(s) of use. Consequentially, it is often up to the tertiary researcher or developer to figure out the practical implementations of the use of classifiers, and to decide for themselves how to express those insights to the user. This leads us to the place where science meets art in text mining: making and expressing assumptions and then coping with their consequences.

3.2.3.1 *The Road to Hell May Be Paved With … Risky (but Often Necessary) Assumptions*

Assumptions enable activity and activity enables evaluation. There is, therefore, nothing wrong with operating on the basis of assumptions, *provided that these are in turn recognised and evaluated*. Examples of the types of assumptions that may be made in academic research in text and data mining (and their downsides) include:

- Proxy indicators are (more or less) stable and reliable. Text mining (Hearst, 1999) tends to rely on a combination of the extraction of reasonably well-structured information – dates, addresses, patent numbers, email addresses, Twitter IDs – and feature extraction from "unstructured" text, such as terms taken from the body of a tweet or email or the text within an article. Examples of the article-of-faith assumptions underlying common operations are:

o *Bibliographic references are positive indicators of impact.* Admittedly, the text surrounding the citation may be of the form "Our approach, unlike the poorly-functioning methodology described by Smith (2010) ..." but ordinarily it is assumed that this happens only rarely and is therefore not statistically significant.

o *People who use certain terms are using them for the obvious reasons.* Seeking to identify the start of a flu epidemic on Twitter, a researcher scans Twitter for features such as the word "flu" and relevant terms (such as the symptoms of flu). The work is reported in national media. The story is discussed on Twitter. Immediately thereafter, the flu detection algorithm falsely detects the start of an epidemic.

In short, as Shaw (2012) puts it "All mathematical models of language are wrong. Nevertheless they may be useful".

• Cultural invariance (aka "users are interchangeable"). It is sometimes assumed (or at any rate hoped) that filters trained on the judgement of a small group of 18–25 year old North Americans (that is, undergraduate and postgraduate students) will perform adequately when applied to unrelated groups in other locales (Kroes, 2010). This assumption has a long history in academic research, being criticized as "the science of the behavior of sophomores" as early as 1946 (McNemar, 1946, p. 333).

• Temporal invariance. It is sometimes assumed (or hoped) that filters trained in the past will perform adequately in the present. To quote Weiss et al., "... over relatively short time horizons, we assume that new documents are similar to old documents or that events will unfold in a similar way ... Because the sample may change over time, we can expect somewhat worse results in the future". (Weiss et al., 2005, p. 77).

• Domain expertise is desirable. In practice, subject specialists performing classification tasks carry with them the expectations, vocabulary and views of that domain; these are employed when interpreting texts (Banasiewicz, 2013, p. 103). However, these expectations, vocabulary and views, being domain specific, may not match those of the target groups.

• Data sets are usually balanced. Classifiers are biased against types of data that appear only rarely and are therefore said to be subject to *class imbalance* (see Zhuang et al., 2012).

- Classification is easy to perform and to replicate. In practice, several people asked to annotate a document will quite probably disagree (that is, interannotator consistency will be low). This problem plagues sentiment analysis in particular (Libermann, 2012).
- In Internet-based research, what is retweeted frequently is true; or, put informally, the provenance of the information is somewhere between poor and nonexistent... but let's not concentrate on that, let's emphasise the huge sample size.

As noted at the start of this section, in experimental contexts, there may be good reasons for researchers to include assumptions, even "risky" assumptions in their research methodologies. The danger, both legal and ethical, lies in circumstances where those assumptions are either not recognised or ignored, and their potential consequences for the validity or reliability of the research outputs are not suitably adjusted for in the research, or their details are included as part of the research output. As in other fields, the pressure to publish may lead researchers to either de-emphasize or ignore the effect of assumptions made during their research that might potentially be seen to undercut potentially high-profile outputs. Clearly such action would be ethically unsound, and where funding or promotion was forthcoming as a result of a researcher knowingly publishing misleading outputs, funders and employers might consider the matter to cross the line from unethical into unlawful (e.g., fraudulent behaviour).

3.2.3.2 You Call it a "Failure Mode", I Call it "Possible Grounds for Legal Action"

Once the assumptions made in a particular research project have been identified and evaluated, the researcher may also need to address other methodological hazards before significant weight (including, for example, public policy actions or inactions that may carry legal consequences) can be given to the research outputs. Key methodological "failure modes" or reasons why outputs may be unreliable despite initially appearing sound include:

- Overfitting. As in traditional machine learning, when training an algorithm against a series of examples, a high level of accuracy in evaluation is viewed as desirable. In the interest of pushing up accuracy, especially with a relatively small and noisy data set, the temptation is to keep training the model until accuracy reaches a suitably high number. The problem is that a model with extremely high accuracy in training may then not work well at all on another data set. Overfitting is a well-understood phenomenon and can be avoided; this is a case in which robust evaluation methods can forewarn and forearm the user (Leinweber, 2007).

- Selection bias. Some level of selection bias is probably unavoidable in many text mining applications. After all, a corpus of complaint letters is largely made up of letters written by those who are temperamentally predisposed to writing and sending complaints by post, which is likely to be a small subset of the larger group of people who, if asked, would say that they had something to complain about. Sometimes selection bias results from pragmatic necessities, as in the example of the evaluation-by-student phenomenon described above. Collection of source materials is therefore often subject to some form of selection bias. In some cases it is possible to mitigate or avoid selection bias when selecting test data or test participants; in others it suffices to acknowledge that the bias exists.
- Cherry-picking. Selection bias in reporting. It is not uncommon for projects to result in a dozen uninteresting results and a single interesting finding. Does this mean that the interesting finding is accurate, or is it simply an overfitted model that hasn't been proven wrong... yet? (Rudman, 2003).
- Confirmation bias. Researchers with a specific question in mind are motivated to define and carry out experiments to explore that question. Researchers with a specific answer in mind are cognitively primed to pick out data that seems to support that conclusion; that is, they tend to exhibit confirmation bias (see Nickerson, 1998; Jonas et al., 2001). Good experimental design can help to quantify and mitigate this phenomenon, as can judicious use of statistical methods. Nonetheless, this is commonly seen in the text mining literature – perhaps because it is easier to justify funding for the ability to detect interesting groups on a social network than to justify funding for exploratory analysis of a network that may, or may not, contain interesting groups.

As with the use of assumptions, it is possible to either counter the misleading effects of methodology failures, or at least to make clear the fact that they may exist, so that other researchers, developers and nonexperts seeking to develop, or to utilise, the research can determine the weight they give to those research outcomes. This, of course, requires researchers to both undertake an honest assessment of the effect of their assumptions and potential weaknesses in research methodology prior to publication, and in the normal course of events, to allow their research methodology and research outputs to be subject to external scrutiny and peer review, in good time (and, ideally, before calling a press conference about the research outcomes).

This is particularly important in areas of research that may touch upon controversial public policy subject matter, such as terrorism or climate change. Here, proponents of a particular viewpoint may seek to promote research outputs favourable to that viewpoint without knowing about or averting to relevant assumptions made by researchers, or potential methodological weaknesses in a particular research study. Without careful presentation by researchers, such "appropriation" of research outputs may serve to bring both the researcher and his or her field of research into disrepute. Additionally, if third parties suffer detriment as a result of flawed research being used to make public policy decisions, then those affected might have grounds not just for complaint about the research, but also for seeking legal redress and recompense.

3.3 ETHICS

Over the last 20 years UK academic research that involves human beings as subjects (where "research subject" is defined increasingly broadly) has become increasingly subject to ethical review. As noted in Section 3.1.1, much ethical research practice tends to assume that researchers will not deliberately break the law, even if the purpose of the research undertaken is to highlight or demonstrate that a particular law is flawed. However, simply abiding by the law may, by itself, be considered by discipline-based research communities as insufficient to meet their ethical requirements.

Particular difficulties arise where research communities in different disciplines diverge on what criteria need to be met to demonstrate ethical research. Attempts at "ethical transplants" from one academic discipline to another that do not take account of different research methodologies and contexts may arguably place barriers in the way of valuable research; not only fail to address, but actively disguise, ethical dilemmas of epistemology and methodology; and engender hostility toward ethical review processes generally (Charlesworth, 2012). For example, the UK Economic and Social Research Council's Framework for Research Ethics (ESRC, 2010) has been criticised for imposing a "medical and psychological model" unsuited to many forms of social sciences qualitative research (e.g., Hammersley, 2006; Hammersley and Traianou, 2012).

Despite the spread of a medical and psychological-premised "one-size-fits-all" research ethics approach amongst institutions, there remains scope for academic research communities to develop and defend their own discipline-specific research ethics framework drawing on general ethical principles, but applying these in a context-sensitive fashion. Working from a plausible discipline-specific model provides a much better basis for resistance to "ethical transplants" from, or "ethical colonisation" by, other disciplines. However, this requires a level of disciplinary introspection and engagement with research ethics theory and practice that, to date, appears largely absent from the text/data mining literature, which appears to concentrate largely on legal compliance, and less upon wider social impacts. While there are papers that urge greater engagement with ethical issues, these appear both fairly rudimentary and few and far between (e.g., van Wel and Royakkers, 2004; Seltzer, 2005; Wahlstrom et al., 2006; Payne and Landry, 2012), and there appears to have been little enthusiasm for cross-disciplinary discussion of potential ethical issues and dilemmas (and how these might be appropriately addressed) arising from their work, on the part of those engaging in data/text mining in information and computer sciences. This is unfortunate, for as Wahlstrom et al. note, in relation to their argument that researchers interested in the integrity of their work should be able to follow relevant well documented and clearly defined ethical guidelines that address not just practical matters (e.g., data collection, storage and retention), but also the sociological influence of their research results:

> While computer scientists' understanding of their work provides them with the capacity to argue on the work's behalf, it does not provide the capacity to estimate the work's social impact. Only a combination of suitably qualified individuals, historical information and a comprehensive understanding of the emerging technology can adequately provide such an estimate.

3.3.1 A Research Ethics Framework for Data/Text Mining

On a positive note, anyone setting out to develop research ethics guidance for academic data/text mining research will not be starting in an information vacuum. There is a huge literature on research ethics generally, with commentaries on the value of considering cross-disciplinary ethics discussions (e.g., Richardson and McMullan, 2007), and a considerable amount of relevant discussion drawn from long-standing debates relating to ethics issues in Internet-based research, such as when informed consent for data collection/mining might be expected, and how it might be implemented (e.g., Solberg, 2010; Zimmer, 2010). Many of the core ethical principles and questions will be similar to those that form the basis for guidelines in other disciplines (e.g., AoIR, 2002; SLSA, 2009) although their relative importance to data/text mining may vary according to both the research context and variables such as the risk to research subjects. In addition, the discussion in Section 3.2.1

and 3.2.2 above suggests some areas of law/ethics that may be specifically relevant to the legitimate and ethical collection and mining of data/text, whilst the discussion in Section 3.2.3 suggests some specific ethical issues (with possible legal implications) that might need to be considered with regard to methodology and presentation of research outputs.

The following list of questions or considerations are suggested as a starting point for consideration of the legal/ethical issues that might arise from a text/data mining project:

- Are human participants involved in the research? Are those individuals involved as research subjects (as understood in medicine and the social sciences), or are they involved as authors of materials that will be mined? What ethically significant risks might individuals involved as research subjects be exposed to as participants in the research? How does the researcher expect the benefits of the research to outweigh any such risks to the research subjects?

- Where individuals are involved as research subjects, how and when will the researcher seek to obtain their consent? How will the researcher ensure that their consent is based on full knowledge of all material matters including the purpose of the research, funding sources and intentions regarding dissemination? If informed consent is not to be sought, what is the rationale for this decision? If informed consent is not to be sought, what alternative mechanisms will be used to protect the rights and interests of the research subjects against identified risks?

- Does the data set to be mined involve the PII of identifiable individuals? Do the methodology and data handling processes envisaged meet the requirements of local legislation governing use of PII? Has adequate consideration been given to anonymity, privacy, confidentiality and data protection?

- From where was the data set to be mined obtained? Are there any ethical/cultural expectations raised by the venue(s) (or participants) from which the data set was obtained that should be considered?

- Are there any legal conditions placed on the use of information or works in the data set? Are there ethical/cultural expectations on the part of those whose information or works form part of the data set? Does the research impact upon any moral or intellectual property rights held by third parties in the data set? How have these expectations and rights been addressed?

- What is the researcher's purpose for obtaining the data set to be mined? What research outputs are they seeking to generate? What was the purpose for which the material in the data set was originally produced / collected? Is this compatible with the researcher's research objectives/ intended outputs? What is the effect on the quality and appropriateness of the data set for the research if its content was generated for purposes other than the research purpose?

- How reliable/complete is the data set the researcher is seeking to mine? Is the content of the data set fixed or changing and is the research replicable?
- Does the researcher or their research team have adequate domain knowledge? Will known knowledge/capacity limitations be assessed, documented and written up with the research outcomes?
- What assumptions will be built into the methodology for the research? What are the implications of those assumptions and will they be documented and written up with the research outcomes?
- What are the methodological risks of the research? How will the results obtained be assessed for statistical significance?
- Will the methodology, assumptions used and any knowledge/capacity limitations identified be made available alongside the data set as part of the peer-review process?
- To what use might the research outputs be put by the researchers or by third parties? What risks might arise for research subjects, or other parties as a result of those uses? If the research is funded research, or consultancy, how will the researcher seek to maintain its intellectual and ethical integrity and ensure that their limitations and those of the research data produced are made clear both in submitting tenders and in publishing results?

3.4 CONCLUSIONS: WORKING ON THE BORDERS OF LAW AND ETHICS

Even if one is left unmoved by the hyperbole generated about the subject over the last decade, primarily in the commercial sector, the potential importance of data/text mining in unlocking interesting and economically valuable information from a range of data sources remains clear. The fact that the UK government has been persuaded that a defence to copyright infringement for noncommercial data/text mining should be incorporated into UK law provides compelling evidence of the expectation that freeing innovation in this area of research will ultimately bring about social and commercial dividends. The proposed changes to the EU data protection regime should also enable researchers to more effectively and efficiently address the balance between proportionate privacy protection and effective data utilisation. However, both these developments require researchers to think carefully about the structuring of their future research, as failure to be seen to be adequately protecting the interests of authors, publishers, data subjects and research participants when carrying out data/text mining is likely to lead to future calls for the (re)imposition of legal controls.

From an ethical perspective, the field currently appears underserved in terms of a community-developed framework of ethical guidance for researchers. This may be because disciplines such as computer science are still adjusting to the ongoing ethical review developments in UK universities. However, it is suggested that it would be prudent to observe the difficulties that other disciplines (e.g., the social sciences) have faced when ethical review regimes have been imposed on them from above, either by their institutions or by funders like the ESRC, without those regimes being tailored toward discipline-specific research environment/contexts. Developing a discipline-specific set of ethical guidelines may thus go some way to providing individual researchers with the support necessary to persuade institutional ethics review bodies that they are capable of meeting institutional requirements for legal and ethical compliance, without being forced into a procrustean institutional ethical process.

REFERENCES

AoIR, 2002. Ethical Decision-making and Internet Research: Recommendations from the AoIR Ethics Working Committee, November 2002. Available at: http://aoir.org/reports/ethics.pdf.

AoIR, 2012. Ethical Decision-making and Internet Research 2.0: Recommendations from the AoIR Ethics Working Committee. Available at: http://aoir.org/reports/ethics2.pdf.

Authors Guild, Inc. v. Google, Inc., 2013. 954 F.Supp.2d 282 (S.D.N.Y. November 14, 2013).

Azad, K., 2007. An Intuitive (and Short) Explanation of Bayes' Theorem. Available at: http://betterexplained.com/articles/an-intuitive-and-short-explanation-of-bayes-theorem/ (website – accessed 24/09/14).

Banasiewicz, A.D., 2013. Marketing Database Analytics: Transforming Data for Competitive Advantage. Routledge, New York.

Berghel, H., 2013. Through the PRISM darkly. Computer 46 (7), 86–90.

Borghi, M., Karapapa, S., 2011. Non-display uses of copyright works: Google books and beyond. Queen Mary J. Intellect. Prop. 1 (1), 21–52.

Calcutt, D., 1993. Review of Press Self-Regulation (Cmd 2135). HMSO, London.

Campbell v Mirror Group Newspapers Ltd, 2004. UKHL 22.

Carey, P., 2009. Data Protection: A Practical Guide to UK and EU Law, third ed. OUP, Oxford.

CDPA, 1988. Copyright, Designs and Patents Act 1988 c.48 (as amended) Available at: http://www.legislation.gov.uk/ukpga/1988/48/contents.

Centre for Information Policy Leadership, 2010. Demonstrating and Measuring Account-ability: A Discussion Document. Centre for Information Policy Leadership, Washington, DC. Available at: http://www.huntonfiles.com/files/webupload/CIPL_Accountability_Phase_II_Paris_Project.PDF.

Charlesworth, A., 2012. Data protection, freedom of information and ethical review com-mittees: policies, practicalities and dilemmas. Inform. Commun. Soc. 15 (1), 85–103.

Charlesworth, A., Pearson, S., 2013. Developing accountability-based solutions for data pri-vacy in the cloud. Innov.: Eur. J. Soc. Sci. Res. 26 (1–2), 7–35.

Cohen, E.D., 2010. Mass Surveillance and State Control: The Total Information Awareness Project. Palgrave Macmillan, Basingstoke, UK.

Dyson, G., 2005. Turing's Cathedral. A Visit to Google on the Occasion of the 60th Anniversary of John von Neumann's Proposal for a Digital Computer, 24 October 2005. Available at: http://www.edge.org/3rd_culture/dyson05/dyson05_index.html.

Erdos, D., 2011. Systematically handicapped? Social research in the data protection frame-work. Inform. Commun. Technol. Law 20 (2), 83–101.

Erdos, D., 2012. Constructing the Labyrinth: the impact of data protection on the develop-ment of 'ethical' regulation in social science. Inform. Commun. Soc. 15 (1), 104–123.

ESRC, 2010. Available at: http://www.esrc.ac.uk/funding/guidance-for-applicants/research-ethics/.

Goo, S.K., 2004. Sen. Kennedy flagged by no-fly list. Washington Post (Friday, August 20, 2004): A01

Gutwirth, S., Leenes, R., de Hert, P. (Eds.), 2014. Reforming European Data Protection Law. Springer, New York.

Hammersley, M., 2006. Are ethics committees ethical? Qualitative Res. (2). [Online] Available at: http://www.cardiff.ac.uk/socsi/qualiti/QualitativeResearcher/QR_Issue2_06.pdf.

Hammersley, M., Traianou, A., 2012. Ethics in Qualitative Research: Controversies and Contexts. Sage, London.

Hargreaves, I., 2011. Digital opportunity: a review of intellectual property and, growth, May 2011 (Hargreaves report). Available at: http://www.ipo.gov.uk/ipreview-finalreport.pdf.

Hartman, L., 2013. Why aren't there more John Smiths in the U.S.? Slate, 3 November 2013. Available at: http://www.slate.com/articles/life/slate_labs/2013/11/john_smith_why_don_t_more_americans_have_this_most_common_name.html.

Hearst, M.A., 1999. Untangling text data mining. In: ACL '99 Proceedings of the 37th Annual Meeting of the Association for Computational Linguistics on Computational Linguistics' pp. 3–10.

HM Government, 1995. The Government's Response to the House of Commons National Select Committee – Privacy and Media Intrusion (Cmd 2918). HMSO, London.

HM Government, 2011. The Government Response to the Hargreaves Review of Intellectual Property and Growth, August 2011. Available at: http://www.ipo.gov.uk/ipresponse-full.pdf.

HM Treasury, 2006. Gowers review of intellectual property, December 2006 (Gowers report). Available at: https://www.gov.uk/government/publications/gowers-review-of-intellectual-property.

Hoffrage, U., Lindsey, S., Hertwig, R., Gigerenzer, G., 2000. Communicating statistical information. Science 290 (5500), 2261–2262.

House of Commons, 2003. Privacy and Media Intrusion: Fifth Report of Session 2002–03 Culture, Media and Sport Committee, HC 458-I. TSO, London.

Jonas, E., Schulz-Hardt, S., Frey, D., Thelen, N., 2001. Confirmation bias in sequential information search after preliminary decisions: an expansion of dissonance theoretical research on selective exposure to information. J. Pers. Soc. Psychol. 80 (4), 557–571.

Kaye v Robertson, 1991. FSR 62.

Kroes, J., 2010. CS Students and their Bias in HCI Evaluation Tasks. In: Proceedings of 13th Twente Student Conference on IT, June 21, 2010. Available at: http://referaat.cs.utwente.nl/conference/13/paper/7200/cs-students-and-their-bias-in-hci-evaluation-tasks.pdf.

Leinweber, D., 2007. Stupid data miner tricks: overfitting the S&P 500. J. Invest. 16 (1), 15–22.

Libermann, M., 2012. Automatic measurement of media bias. Language Log, Available at: http://languagelog.ldc.upenn.edu/nll/?p=3759 (blog – accessed 24/09/14).

Mayer-Schonberger, V., Cukier, K., 2013. Big Data: A Revolution That Will Transform How We Live Work and Think. John Murray, London.

McNemar, Q., 1946. Opinion attitude methodology. Psychol. Bull. 43 (4), 289–374.

Miller, A.R., 1971. The Assault on Privacy: Computers, Data Banks and Dossiers. University of Michigan Press, Ann Arbor.

Nickerson, R.S., 1998. Confirmation bias: a ubiquitous phenomenon in many guises. Rev. Gen. Psychol. 2 (2), 175–220.

OECD, 1980. Guidelines on the Protection of Privacy and Transborder Flows of Personal Data. Available at: http://www.oecd.org/internet/ieconomy/oecdguidelinesontheprotectionofprivacyandtransborderflowsofpersonaldata.htm.

OECD, 2013. Guidelines on the Protection of Privacy and Transborder Flows of Personal Data. Available at: http://www.oecd.org/sti/ieconomy/privacy.htm#newguidelines.

Payne, D., Landry, B.J.L., 2012. A composite strategy for the legal and ethical use of data mining. Int. J. Manage. Knowl. Learn. 1 (1), 27–43.

Richardson, S., McMullan, M., 2007. Research ethics in the UK: what can sociology learn from health? Sociology 41 (6), 1115–1132.

Rudman, J., 2003. Cherry picking in nontraditional authorship attribution studies. Chance 16 (2), 26–32.

Seltzer, W., 2005. The promise and pitfalls of data mining: ethical issues. In: Proceedings of the American Statistical Association, Section on Government Statistics. American Statistical Association, Alexandria, VA, pp. 1441–1445.

Shaw, R., 2012. Text-mining as a Research Tool in the Humanities and Social Sciences. Available at: https://aeshin.org/textmining/ (website – accessed 24/09/14).

Shermers, M., 2011. The Believing Brain. Times Books, New York.

SLSA, 2009. Statement of Principles of Ethical Research Practice, January 2009. http://www.slsa.ac.uk/index.php/ethics-statement.

Solberg, L.B., 2010. Data mining on Facebook: a free space for researchers or an IRB nightmare. Univ. Illinois J. Law, Technol. Policy. 311.

The Copyright and Rights in Performances (Research, Education, Libraries and Archives) Regulations, 2014 (No. 1372/2014). Available at: http://www.legislation.gov.uk/uksi/2014/1372/contents/made.

van Wel, L., Royakkers, L., 2004. Ethical issues in web data mining. Ethics Inf. Technol. 6, 129–140.

Viglen, T., 2014. Spurious Correlations. Available at: http://www.tylervigen.com/ (website – accessed 24/09/14).

Wahlstrom, K., Roddick, J.F., Sarre, R., Estivill-Castro, V., deVries, D., 2006. On the ethical and legal implications of data mining. Technical report SIE-06-001, School of Informatics and Engineering, Flinders University, Adelaide, Australia.

Warner, M., Stone, M., 1970. The Data Bank Society: Organizations, Computers, and Social Freedom. Allen & Unwin, London.

Weiss, S.M., Indurkhya, N., Zhang, T., Damerau, F., 2005. Text Mining: Predictive Methods for Analyzing Unstructured Information. Springer, New York.

Wheeler, S., 1969. On Record: Files and Dossiers in American Life. Russell Sage Foundation, New York.

Zhuang, L., Gan, M., Dai, H., 2012. Improving reliability of unbalanced text mining by reducing performance bias. In: Dai, H., Liu, J., Smirnov, E. (Eds.), Reliable Knowledge Discovery. Springer, New York, pp. 259–268.

Zimmer, M., 2010. "But the data is already public": on the ethics of research in Facebook. Ethics Inf. Technol. 12 (4), 313–325.

CHAPTER 4

Responsible Content Mining

J. Molloy*, M. Haeussler†, P. Murray-Rust*, C. Oppenheim‡
*University of Cambridge, Cambridge, UK
†University of California, Santa Cruz, CA, USA
‡Queensland University, Brisbane, Australia

4.1 INTRODUCTION TO CONTENT MINING

Content mining refers to automated searching, indexing and analysis of the digital scholarly literature by software. Typically this would involve searching for particular objects to extract, for example, chemical structures, particular types of images, mathematical formulae, data sets or accession numbers for specific databases. At other times, the aim is to use natural language processing to understand the structure of an article and create semantic links to other content. This chapter aims to provide a practical introduction to responsible use of content mining technologies. Such practical advice was highlighted as necessary in the JISC report "The value and benefits of text mining to UK further and higher education" (McDonald et al., 2012):

> Recommendation 5: Advice and guidance should be developed to help researchers get started with text mining. This should include: when permission is needed; what to request; how best to explain intended work and how to describe the benefits to research and copyright owners.

We aim to address the points above alongside technical guidance on choosing and configuring software for content mining that will behave responsibly on the web and in tracking licensing and attributions throughout a text mining project (Figure 4.1).

4.2 OBTAINING PERMISSION TO CONTENT MINE

Responsible content mining entails operating within the law; currently, the legality of applying content mining technology to published articles falls under three legal areas: copyright, database rights, and contract law. Permissions granted to universities and other research institutions under publisher licence agreements may deal with the right to view, download, text mine and publish the resulting analysis separately. Many researchers in the text mining community assert that "the right to read is the right to mine"

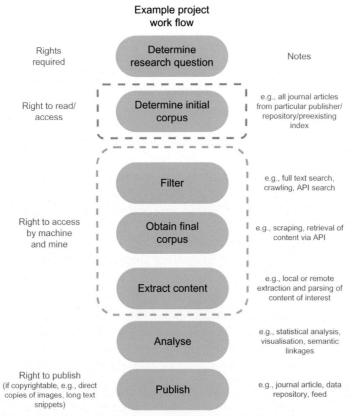

Figure 4.1 An exemplar workflow for a TDM project detailing the rights required at each stage and the type of activity undertaken.

(Murray-Rust et al., 2012), but until this right is confirmed by changes in publisher policies and/or by changes to legislation, text miners have no choice but to make individual approaches to obtain permissions, often on a publisher-by-publisher, if not journal-by-journal basis.

This time-consuming burden places huge restrictions on the availability of content to mine and on the time available to perform a mining-based study. For example, the Wellcome Trust found that it is illegal to mine 87% of articles in UK PubMedCentral, the UK's main medical research database (McDonald et al., 2012). It also calculated the cost of obtaining permissions to mine articles containing the word "malaria" in the title, which would total around £3000 of researcher time for the 187 journals covered. Moving to a full-text search for malaria would generate enough journal hits that making the relevant requests would take 60% of a working year

(McDonald et al., 2012). Researchers such as Max Hauseller and Casey Bergman have tracked their efforts at obtaining permissions for the text2genome project enabling automatic annotation of human genome regions with relevant papers, demonstrating the sheer volume of contacts that must be made across journals and time taken, with 27 positive responses since 2009 from a total of 46 requests.[1] It is therefore not surprising that the vast majority of text mining studies undertaken so far have been based on open access materials. However, inevitably, this means that such studies are limited, as in all subject areas there will be either a significant minority, or even a majority of texts that are behind paywalls and subject to licence permissions.

The following section explains to the potential content miner how the law applies to content mining, maps the current landscape of publisher policies and offers practical guidance on requesting permissions for mining.

4.2.1 Copyright Law as Applied to Content Mining

Copyright protects the creative expression of intellectual output and in general, prohibits copying, publicly distributing, and/or adapting the original without the permission of the copyright holder. Small amounts of data are not generally considered a creative expression, and so are not protected by copyright, although in the EU and in the US, collections of data where there is clear evidence of creativity, for example, in the fact that the collection of data involved has involved decision making on what is to be included and what is not, are protected by copyright. Databases are discussed further in Section 4.2.2.

The Agreement on Trade Related Aspects of Intellectual Property Rights (TRIPS, 1994), Article 9(2) states:

Copyright protection shall extend to expressions and not to ideas, procedures, methods of operation or mathematical concepts as such.

Copyright does not apply to single words or short sentences, but anything from a long sentence to an entire article or book will be subject to copyright. The original owner of the copyright is the author unless the work was created as part of their employee duties, when the default legal position is that the employer owns the copyright. However, by custom and practice, most universities and public sector research institutes do not enforce their rights, and leave the copyright with the researchers. Private sector research bodies, such as the R&D Departments in pharmaceutical industries, are less likely to be so generous. However, typically, when submitting

---

[1] Available at: http://text.soe.ucsc.edu/progress.html, accessed 18 September 2014.

outputs to a publisher, the original copyright owner agrees to assign their copyright to the publisher (i.e., to pass over ownership). At that point the researcher has no further say in how the publisher chooses to exercise the copyright, and indeed, may find that they themselves are unable to access their own outputs without permission. Not all publishers require such assignments, and even those that do will often back down when challenged by the researcher who has submitted the manuscript and will be content with a licence to publish, leaving the ownership with the researcher. But it is often difficult to ascertain this fact amongst a publisher's electronic offerings.

To undertake content mining, copying and/or adaption and/or digitisation of the original work is required. These initial acts, even if that copy is never made public, is a potential infringement of copyright. Infringement takes place whenever a third party (i.e., not the copyright owner) copies, or adapts all or a "substantial part" of a copyright work without express permission. "Substantial part" means "what is important in the work", and arguably any content mining activity will involve a substantial part of the original work. Incidentally, the fact that large scholarly publishers own the rights to the vast majority of the materials on their services means they can carry out text and data mining on a large scale.

To review the implications for potential content miners: the acts involved in content mining involve potential copyright infringement. The only way one can be sure that one is not infringing copyright is *either* if the copyright owner has given explicit or implicit permission for third parties to copy, *or* if the actions fall under an exception to copyright. Exceptions to copyright are to be found in all countries' copyright laws, but differ in detail. In essence they say that certain actions will never infringe copyright, as long as the ground rules imposed by law are followed; that is, there is no need to ask for permission to undertake these actions. Bear in mind that any exception relates to the country where the copying is taking place. Thus, for example, the fact that the materials to be mined are owned by a US corporation but are maintained in Canada is irrelevant. What is relevant is where the instruction to carry out the mining comes from. Thus, there may be exceptions to copyright that will lessen or remove copyright issues in your jurisdiction:

1. Copyright exemptions for content mining (Japan, UK since Oct 2014)
   This is the most important of the exceptions. Japan was until 2014 the only country with a copyright exception specifically for content

mining purposes, which is a provision in Article 47 of The Japan Copyright Act (McDonald et al., 2012):

For the purpose of information analysis ("information analysis" means to extract information, concerned with languages, sounds, images or other elements constituting such information, from many works or other such information, and to make a comparison, a classification or other statistical analysis of such information; the same shall apply hereinafter in this Article) by using a computer, it shall be permissible to make recording on a memory, or to make adaptation (including a recording of a derivative work created by such adaptation), of a work, to the extent deemed necessary.

The UK government implemented a change in its law (The Copyright and Rights in Performances (Research, Education, Libraries and Archives) Regulations 2014, 2012), for non-commercial content mining from October 2014 following the recommendations of the Hargreaves Report (Hargreaves, 2011). The change in the law makes text and data mining permissible without going through any bureaucracy or paying any fees for those with "lawful access" to the original materials, as long as the mining is for a "non-commercial purpose". In practice, lawful access means a licence of some kind, either paid for, for example, access via a university subscription or free, for example, via Creative Commons licensing. Importantly, the new UK legislation makes any contractual term that purports to restrict one's ability to take advantage of the new exception null and void.

In addition to explicit copyright exemptions, some Nordic countries have laws that facilitate text mining through university libraries (LACA, 2011).

2. Fair use clauses (US and Israel)

The "fair use" exception in the US is generally considered sufficient to allow for content mining, although researchers may be reluctant to test the law, which is not well defined for these activities. The difference between "fair use" in the US and "fair dealing" in the UK is that the US law does not specify the purpose of the copying, whereas fair dealing is very specific. This means that whilst fair use appears to be generous, one can only be certain by testing a case in court—and indeed, the US is famous for the number of court cases that do test the limits of fair use in various circumstances.

In terms of digitisation and TDM, there is limited case law but notable recent developments include the American Author's Guild vs

Hathi Trust,[2] who had created a searchable digital library for universities and research libraries (Kishor, 2014). The presiding U.S. District Judge Harold Baer decided that this did fall under fair use:

I cannot imagine a definition of fair use that would not encompass the transformative uses made by Defendants' MDP and would require that I terminate this invaluable contribution to the progress of science and cultivation of the arts that at the same time effectuates the ideals espoused by the Americans with Disabilities Act.

This verdict was upheld by the second circuit on appeal.[3] No court cases directly concerning academic content mining are known to the authors.

3. Non commercial research (EU)

In addition to the specific exception for text mining, EU member states permit copying for noncommercial research or private study. Whilst not explicitly including content mining in the broad definition involved, the legislation may be sufficiently broadly worded that researchers in EU member states may wish to consider undertaking content mining on the basis of their exception.

At the time of going to press, Eire was considering introducing a similar mining exception to that of the UK, and at the same time, the European Union itself was thinking about the possibility of introducing a directive on the topic. If passed, which would be a lengthy process, this would impose an obligation on all EU member states to introduce similar legislation in their national copyright laws. The chances of such an exception being adopted by the World Intellectual Property Organisation, the UN special agency with responsibility for copyright laws worldwide, in the foreseeable future are very low.

To conclude on exceptions, checking local copyright law and considering collaborating with partners in countries with more permissive copyright laws is strongly recommended.

The extent to which the results of content mining analysis are protectable under copyright is a grey area; the majority of outputs will be facts or reconstructions of data, for example, chemical structures will be rerendered rather than a direct copy of the publisher's image being republished. However, in some cases one may wish to republish images or excerpts of text, in which case further consideration of copyright implications will be necessary.

---

[2] Authors Guild, Inc. v. HathiTrust, 902 F. Supp. 2d 445 – Dist. Court, SD New York, 2012
[3] Authors Guild, Inc. v. HathiTrust, Case No. 12-4547-cv (2d Cir. 2014)

4.2.2 Database Rights as Applied to Content Mining

In Europe, the 1996 EU Database Directive (Directive 96/9/EC, 1996) grants so-called sui generis rights to those who make a substantial investment in a database through collecting, verifying or presenting the contents. This results in a somewhat complex set of rights associated with collections of data. Copyright, with all the rules associated with it as explained above, applies to a database only if there is sufficient creativity involved in the presentation or arrangement of the data collection. Quite separately, database rights apply if the substantial investment described above has been expended. Note that "collecting" does NOT mean "creating from scratch", but rather "collecting from somewhere else". Thus, if someone undertakes a series of experiments to find the melting points of compounds that have never been synthesised before, that collection of data, counterintuitively, will not enjoy database rights. But if the person had scanned the literature and collected a set of melting point data from a variety of sources, that collection would enjoy database rights. Note that an EU-based database is perfectly capable of enjoying both copyright and database rights. As copyright is a much stronger right than database rights in terms of length of protection and the rights conferred upon the owner, if a database does enjoy both copyright and database rights, then the database rights protection can be ignored by both owner and users. Finally, a very few databases enjoy no protection at all if they are not subject to either copyright or database rights.

In the case where the database only has database rights, extraction or reuse of the entire collection or a substantial subset would require permission. Continuous extraction and reuse of database components, for example, running a continuous query via an API to extract updated records, also requires permission. The copyright exceptions described in Section 4.2.1 do not apply to a database, which only has database rights.

It should be noted that individual items of data do not enjoy any protection at all and can be reproduced freely.

4.2.3 Contractual Restrictions on Content Mining

As has been already noted, in the absence of the use of an appropriate exception to copyright, the only way a content miner can lawfully undertake his or her research is by getting permission to do so from the copyright owner. In some cases, for example, open-access materials, the Creative Commons licence permits, at no charge, content mining subject to certain conditions, depending on the particular Creative Commons licence adopted. Details of these licence terms can be found at the Creative Commons website.[4]

---

[4] Available at:http://creativecommons.org/licenses/, accessed on 18 September 2014.

In the case of scholarly content available from a commercial supplier on a subscription basis, charges will usually be made unless mining permissions are bundled into the subscription already, and there will be strict conditions to follow. Restrictions placed on subscribers to content via publisher licence agreements are usually restrictive, with many, for example, banning the use of all automated search and index software (Table 4.1). However, most open-access publishers have permissive policies in terms of use of their sites for text mining in addition to permissive licensing (Table 4.2).

Since the changes to UK copyright law, certain publishers, including Elsevier, have announced their willingness to let researchers undertake text mining of their materials so long as the researcher uses an API developed by the publisher and so long as the researcher signs a contract that defines what they can do in terms of mining and what they can do with the results. Such a contractual term can be ignored under the new law, but what if, despite that, the publisher restricts the ability of the researcher to content mine, for example, by deliberately slowing the mining procedure for those who haven't signed up? UK copyright law includes a provision for making a complaint about technical restrictions preventing a bona fide user from enjoying an exception to copyright, but the complaints procedure is extremely convoluted and is hardly used for that reason.

Unfortunately, some user licence agreements are specific to institutions and may not be available online, so one would need to check with one's institutional library if permission has already been granted before approaching publishers individually. To add to the complications, the publisher may not own the copyright to every item in its collection, and not all publishers have developed clear content mining policies, and so may take a long time to respond to a request for permission to mine.

It may therefore be worth considering collaborating with researchers at institutions with more permissive licences, or with researchers based in countries with clear exceptions for content mining embedded into their copyright law.

4.2.4 Practical Advice for Obtaining Permissions

Where permission does need to be obtained from the copyright owner, the following points are worth considering:

1. Obtaining individual permissions from relevant publishers is a time-consuming and often unsuccessful process.

Table 4.1 Permissions for machine access to content in licensing agreements from a selection of major "traditional" publishers and where applicable whether that access is provided via publisher API only. Correct as of 18 September 2014

Publisher	Mining explicitly prohibited?	API Only?	Quote from standard licence agreement
ACS	Yes	NA	Grantee acknowledges that ACS may prevent Grantee, its Authorized Users and Other Users from using, implementing, or authorizing use of any computerized or automated tool or application to search, index, test, or otherwise obtain information from ACS Products (including without limitation any "spidering" or web crawler application) that has a detrimental impact on the use of the services under this Agreement[a]
BMJ	Unclear	NA	Systematic downloading is prohibited[b]
Elsevier	No	Yes	Researchers can text mine subscribed content on ScienceDirect for non-commercial purposes, via the ScienceDirect API's. Text and data mining enabling clauses for non-commercial purposes will be included in all new ScienceDirect subscription agreements and upon renewal for existing customers. Librarians interested in adding the TDM clause to their existing agreement prior to renewal are able to request a simple contract e-amendment via their Elsevier Account Manager[c]
JSTOR	Yes	Yes[d]	Institutions and users may not: (d) undertake any activity such as the use of computer programs that automatically download or export Content, commonly known as web robots, spiders, crawlers, wanderers or accelerators that may interfere with, disrupt or otherwise burden the JSTOR server(s) or any third-party server(s) being used or accessed in connection with JSTOR[e]
Nature	Yes	NA	1) Author deposited manuscripts: Users may view, print, copy, download and text and data-mine the content in such documents, for the purposes of academic research, subject always to the full conditions of use. 2) NPG Material: the Licensee warrants that it will not:... (j) make mass, automated or systematic extractions from or hard copy storage of the Licensed Material[f]
OUP	Yes	NA	The Licensee and Authorised Users may not: 2.3.2 systematically make printed or electronic copies of multiple portions of the Licensed Work(s) for any purpose[g]
Royal Society	No	No	The Licensee may: Use Text and Data Mining (TDM) technologies to derive information from the Licensed Materials meaning: Download, extract and index information from the Licensed Materials to which the Authorized User has access under this License. Where required, mount, load and integrate the results on a server used for the Authorized User's text-mining system and

Continued

Table 4.1 Permissions for machine access to content in licensing agreements from a selection of major "traditional" publishers and where applicable whether that access is provided via publisher API only. Correct as of 18 September 2014—cont'd

Publisher	Mining explicitly prohibited?	API Only?	Quote from standard licence agreement
			evaluate and interpret the Text and Data Mining Output for access and use by Authorized Users. The Authorized User shall ensure compliance with Publisher's Usage policies. Text and data mining may be undertaken on either locally loaded Licensed Materials or as mutually agreed. Electronic copies of the Licensed Materials may be locally stored for this purpose only during the lifetime of any TDM project[h]
Springer	No	No	Individual researchers are encouraged to download subscription and open access content for TDM purposes directly from the SpringerLink platform. No registration or API key is required. Full-text content can be accessed easily and programmatically at friendly URLs based on the content's Digital Object Identifier (DOI)[i]
Taylor and Francis	Yes	NA	Licensee must not: 8.3.2 use automated retrieval devices (such as so called web robots, wanderers, crawlers, spiders or similar devices)[j]
Wiley–Blackwell	Unclear	NA	Except as provided above or in any applicable Open Access License(s), Authorized Users may not copy, distribute, transmit or otherwise reproduce, sell or resell material from Electronic Products (s); store such material in any form or medium in a retrieval system; download and/or store an entire issue of a Electronic Product or its equivalent; or transmit such material, directly or indirectly, for use in any paid service such as document delivery or list serve, or for use by any information brokerage or for systematic distribution, whether or not for commercial or non-profit use or for a fee or free of charge[k]

[a] Available at: http://pubs.acs.org/userimages/ContentEditor/1367593694540/ACS_Institutional_Access_Agreement_Academic.pdf.

[b] Available at: http://www.bmj.com/company/single-institution-license/.

[c] Available at: http://www.elsevier.com/about/policies/content-mining-policies.

[d] Data mining for research is available only via a JSTOR provided user interface with fixed tools, not an API. Available at: http://about.jstor.org/service/data-for-research.

[e] Available at: http://www.jstor.org/page/info/about/policies/terms.jsp.

[f] Available at: http://www.nature.com/libraries/site_licenses/license_agreements.html.

[g] Available at: http://www.oxfordjournals.org/en/help/inststitelicence.pdf.

[h] Available at: http://royalsocietypublishing.org/text-data-mining and http://royalsocietypublishing.org/text-data-mining.

[i] Available at: http://www.springer.com/gb/rights-permissions/springer-s-text-and-data-mining-policy/29056.

[j] Available at: http://www.tandf.co.uk/libsite/pdf/licensingInfo/TermsAndConditions.pdf.

[k] Available at: http://onlinelibrary.wiley.com/termsAndConditions.

Table 4.2 Permissions for machine access to content in licensing agreements from a selection of major open-access publishers and where applicable whether that access is provided via publisher API only. Correct as of 18 September 2014

Publisher	Mining explicitly prohibited?	API Only?
Biomed Central	No[a]	No
eLife	No[b]	No
F1000 Research	No[c]	No
Hindawi	No[d]	No
PLOS	No[e]	No

[a] Available at: http://www.biomedcentral.com/about/datamining.
[b] Available at: http://elifesciences.org/terms-and-conditions-of-use.
[c] Available at: http://f1000research.com/about/legal/termsandconditions.
[d] Available at: http://www.hindawi.com/corpus/.
[e] Available at: http://blogs.plos.org/opens/2014/03/09/best-practice-enabling-content-mining/.

2. Services are in development to streamline the process, for example, in the UK, an interesting initiative called The Copyright Hub[5] was launched in summer 2013 to streamline licence permission requests. However, progress on the Hub has been painfully slow, very few copyright owners are connected to it, and content mining does not appear to have been considered as a possible use of copyright materials.

3. We recommend that any agreement with a publisher to content mine should only permit restrictions on the amount of, or speed of content download that are "in the reasonable opinion of the publisher" necessary to protect its commercial interests and technical performance. It should not restrict the licensee to use the publisher's API, but should permit any reasonably efficient API to undertake the work. If the publisher refuses to negotiate on these points, the researcher should seriously consider alternative approaches.

4. Open-access content that is licensed as CC-BY-NC or an equivalent, or a more permissive licence can be used without risk of copyright infringement but might still fall under contractual agreements with regard to reasonable restrictions on the use of publisher servers and download of materials.

5. Explaining your intended work well may increase the chance of permission being granted.

[5] Available at: http://www.copyrighthub.co.uk/get-permission, accessed on 18 September 2014.

Case Studies: Obtaining Permission for Text Mining
Text-mining at the University of British Columbia

Heather Piwowar wanted programmatic access to Elsevier journals for her research on how scientists use, reuse and cite data. During 2012 she extensively documented her attempt to gain permission, which started with a Tweet that got picked up by Elsevier's Director of Universal Access and went on to involve meetings with six Elsevier employees and Piwowar's institutional librarians (Piwowar, 2012a). Permission was eventually granted for the purposes of:

- direct analysis for research;
- selection of excerpts for citizen science;
- calculating statistics on the usage of research objects for open dissemination in research tools (Piwowar, 2012b).

Importantly, this agreement was made available for others to read unlike many subscription publisher terms of agreement which are subject to non-disclosure agreements. Initially permission was granted only for Piwowar's research but this was soon extended to cover the whole university. While a success in several respects, Piwowar considers this process to be unscaleable across the many hundreds of research projects which could benefit from access to the literature for text mining. In addition Elsevier is only one of many publishers with content that could strengthen data citation research results.

Piwowar advises researchers to talk to librarians at their institutions to find out about license terms and conditions and the process for their negotiation. She also encourages librarians to take a pro-active stance on negotiating for text mining rights and providing researchers with information and training on its potential (SPARC, 2012).

text2genome project

Maximilian Haeussler, Casey Bergman and the text2genome project have documented their progress[a] in obtaining permission to mine full-text articles to annotate the UCSC Genome Browser with links out to relevant publications. So far 27 positive responses have been received from a total of 46 requests since 2009 and crawling is underway on the available corpus. Bergman reports that:

> it takes six months to two years per publisher to get a final written agreement to mine and release extracted content, and often when pushed these deals fall through on the issue of releasing extracted content (SPARC, 2012).

The documentation of approaches made to publishers includes copies of default end user license agreements and UCSC library agreements where available. Interestingly, in at least one case the library license agreement allows text mining but permission has still been refused. This demonstrates the importance of checking permissions but also the extent to which copyright exemptions as enacted in the UK and Japan can save researchers valuable time in a process which is currently fraught with uncertainty and requires extensive communication and follow-up with individual publishers.

[a]Available at: http://text.soe.ucsc.edu/progress.html, accessed 18 September 2014.

4.3 RESPONSIBLE CRAWLING

The rest of this chapter assumes that the content miner has legal permission to mine for the purposes of their research and now discusses the resposibilities of exercising your right to mine.

4.3.1 Understanding the Impact of Crawling

Gathering content for the purposes of content mining requires finding and copying articles and other content of interest on the web. The software agent performing this task is known as a crawler and will visit a list of seed URLs, followed by additional URLs harvested during the crawling process; for example, all those on a journal issue's contents page. It is important that web crawling is perfomed ethically to minimise any costs, disruption and privacy or security concerns (reviewed in (Thelwall and Stuart, 2006)).

Crawlers can send multiple requests per second to the same server and potentially download large files, particularly if the content of interest is in PDF format. It is therefore not surprising that publishers are concerned about the potential impact of uninhibited crawling activities on the performance of their servers, which already deal with multiple requests from subscribers. Crawlers require considerable bandwidth and poorly written crawlers even more so, which is one of several reasons that some publishers, such as Elsevier, attempt to require content miners to use their own approved APIs, as well as imposing maxima on what may be downloaded. Download speed should not be a major problem for big international publishers, who have to deal with dozens of requests per second during the whole year. Smaller publishers, for whom one single crawler can affect the performance of the website, have more of a problem.

Another issue is the access logs that publishers keep for libraries. For each subscription and journal, the librarians can find out from the publisher how many articles were accessed by users and in which journals. A crawler that retrieves all articles from a journal can significantly alter the access statistics. We suggest that anyone wishing to content mine use a defined useragent string in all HTTP requests such that publishers can distinguish crawlers from normal requests.

The "useragent" of a web request is the name of the internet browser that is transmitted when a page is requested from a web server. An example is "Mozilla/5.0 (iPad; U)" for a web request from an IPad. Google's crawlers are usually excluded from any access logs, as they can be identified by IP address or their "useragent". We suggest using a useragent string that clearly indicates that the web request comes from a crawler like "GoogleBot" or "TDMCrawler" and adding in parenthesis contact information of a person that can stop the crawler in case problems occur.

There exists a robots exclusion protocol, which indicates which parts of a web server must not be accessed by crawlers, but as publishers want their content to be indexed by search engines such as Google, these are most often not implemented.

Crawling OA Content: Journal Perspectives

As an OA publisher we are certainly happy for people to use our published content for text mining purposes. As you mentioned, there is some concern about the load that this may place on our web servers, so we are in the process of setting up an FTP site where researchers will be able to download the XMLs of all of our published articles for text mining purposes, which should help reduce the load on our servers. Practically speaking, the impact of text mining on our servers has not yet become a problem, and I'm sure that the load from search engine spiders is a lot higher than from researchers trying to text mine our content. Also, given that we host all of published articles using Amazon's Simple Storage Service (S3) my guess is that it would take quite a few researchers doing text mining on our content at the same time to cause any real problems.

Paul Peters, Head of Business Development, Hindawi Publishing Corporation (McDonald et al., 2012)

We haven't had any problem with server load performance from robots text mining the journal sites. Previously, there were occasions that site performance would degrade from what appeared to be out-of-control scripts hitting a single article.

In that case, we would block the IP of the script. But since we implemented the new software, we haven't seen this problem come up. There are no restrictions for text mining our content other than respecting the crawl-delay in robots.txt (currently set to 30 seconds) and fetching content from one journal at a time.

Public Library of Science (PLOS) (McDonald et al., 2012)

4.3.2 Respecting Crawler Limits

Publishers will often impose crawling limits to protect their technological infrastructure and presently these can extend to complete blocks on any crawling software (Table 4.3). Going above crawling limits is likely to lead to publisher action to block your IP address and potentially cut off institutional access if they feel the service is being abused. In most cases, delays of 10-20 s between two consecutive requests should be sufficient to avoid overloading the publisher's web server. Respecting current crawler limits is severely limiting to text miners, as they are typically set low to discourage such usage of their content.

4.3.3 Choosing and Configuring Crawler Software

Writing code that respects crawler limits but remains on a site without causing problems for the server is challenging. There are existing pieces of

Table 4.3 Example crawler limits for a range of publishers from which UCSC has obtained permission to text mine or which allow crawling by default (e.g., open-access publishers PLOS, Biomed Central and eLife) and have published limits.

Publisher or platform	Crawler restrictions	Reference
Highwire	Weekday 10 s between requests, Weekend 5 s. No crawling during US East Coast work hours.	UCSC
Wiley	1 s. IP address needs to be authorised by publisher	UCSC
Elsevier	Need to sign license and go through Elsevier ConSyn. 20 s between requests	UCSC
Springer	Require FTP access and 20 s between requests	UCSC
PLOS	30 s between requests	Neylon (2014)
Biomed Central	1 s between requests	Neylon (2014)
eLife	10 s between requests	Neylon (2014)

software and we recommend that new text miners make use of these before attempting to write their own crawler code. Often publishers will block the IP address of crawlers that place too high a load on their servers so the following guidelines should be followed for responsible crawling and mining.

1. E-mail each publisher to notify it of the proposed crawling activity, including the crawler IP address and the date(s) and time(s) when crawling is most likely to take place.
2. Attempt, wherever possible, to crawl publisher websites outside the working hours of the publisher time zone.
3. Keep delays to 10-20 s between requests.
4. Set the useragent to TDMCrawler, adding contact and project information.

4.4 PUBLICATION OF RESULTS

Publishing the results of a content mining project requires decisions regarding the availability, presentation and format of the mined data. As per all research outputs, the limitations of your methods should be described and potential error rates presented.

4.4.1 Access and Licensing

Many research funders now mandate, or are introducing requirements for open publication of research data, and it is considered good practice to store the output of your analysis publicly using recognised repositories or other storage with persistent identifiers and distributed copies, ideally adhering to guidelines such as the Panton Principles for Open Data in Science (Murray-Rust et al., 2010). Data licensing is a complex area, but it is generally considered that as facts are not copyrightable and there can be legal interoperability issues between differently licensed data sets, a copyright waiver or public domain licence such as the CC0 waiver[6] or the Public Domain Dedication License[7] are most appropriate for scientific data.

One area where text mining may raise copyright problems is where one wishes to publish verbatim results, either because this is the unit of data you are interested in or it is necessary for contextualisation or illustrative

---

[6] Available at: http://creativecommons.org/publicdomain/zero/1.0/, accessed on 18 September 2014.
[7] Available at: http://opendatacommons.org/licenses/pddl/, accessed on 18 September 2014.

purposes. In this case, we recommend publishing no more than around 200 words in the case of text, although it must be stressed that what is considered to be copying outside what the country's copyright law limits for an exception for research to apply varies from case to case, and so there is no set number of words that are "safe". For this reason, it is safest to discuss the matter with the copyright owner(s) of the original works that had been mined before submitting the results of your mining activity for publication.

If a publisher takes issue with your publication of content derived from mining their articles, it is helpful to provide a contact address and notice and take down procedure clearly stated on your website or repository entry and to document their objections and obtain legal advice where possible. The Jorum notice and takedown policy,[8] which is available under a Creative Commons licence that can be edited to suit your requirements, is recommended.

4.4.2 Downstream Use

The majority of the end user licence agreements, which allow content mining and the copyright exemptions proposed exceptions adopted by the UK government apply only to non-commercial research, despite several arguments for not making this distinction (Hagedorn et al., 2011; Klimpel, 2012). It is unclear as to what extent "noncommercial" applies to typical downstream uses of the data arising from academic mining projects. In the UK, the Intellectual Property Office, the government agency responsible for handling copyright law, understandably refuses to give an opinion on the matter, as this is something for courts to decide. There has been some research on what the general population defines as noncommercial (e.g., Creative Commons (2008)) but confusion remains (Klimpel, 2012).

Some downstream activities, such as making money from the sales of reports of the work, are clearly "commercial", but others, such as using the results in a lecture to students, are unlikely to be. What is important to note is that the restriction to noncommercial refers to the researcher's plans at the time of copying. Thus, if completely unexpected, a commercially valuable result is obtained, there is not a problem with the original mining activity. If, on the other hand, it could reasonably be surmised that something commercially valuable would result, then the mining activity will be deemed to have been "commercial".

---

[8] Available at: http://www.jorum.ac.uk/policies/jorum-notice-and-takedown-policy, accessed on 18 September 2014.

4.5 CITATION AND ACKNOWLEDGEMENT

Responsible use of text mining technology includes citing the articles and data sets mined as per community norms for reuse of scholarship. This raises considerable technical issues in the text mining workflow as to how to record each source and maintain the association of mined content to source throughout the analysis, especially as some mined resources may not be used in the analysis.

There are no current established norms for citation in content mining projects and it is clear that applying the norms of lower throughput scholarship, where an article may reference the work of 100 other works or less, will in many cases be unpragmatic and extremely technically challenging in the face of thousands of potential sources.

Ironically, many tools that allow better tracking of articles and data sets as well as the generation of alternative metrics rely on programmatic access to the literature themselves (Piwowar, 2012a). We encourage all potential content miners to explore their options for attribution and where possible to assist the research community in building tools for this purpose.

4.6 PROPOSED BEST PRACTISE GUIDELINES FOR CONTENT MINING

We present a list of principles to which we hope both text miners and publishers can subscribe, ensuring that both parties are able to make use of text mining technology to conduct fruitful research without detriment to content providers. We hope that increased uptake of content mining through greater clarity of the rights of researchers (The right to read is the right to mine) and their responsibilities undertaking these analyses (The Content Mine) help unlock the potential of content mining as a technique to discover more about the world by using the knowledge we have already accumulated in the scholarly literature to its full potential.

Responsible Content Mining Code
1. **Don't break the law**
    (a) Honour copyright as you understand it and consult about current interpretations in your jurisdiction.
    (b) If there is no copyright exemption for content mining in your country, consult your institutional librarians for the terms of your

licensing contracts with publishers that do not explicitly permit mining.

(c) Be aware of additional legal permissions required for mining with intended commercial use of results.

2. Don't break servers or services

(a) Set acceptable delays between each crawl.

(b) Try not to recrawl and use public repositories of crawled or submitted materials where they exist and allow this.

(c) Avoid corrupting content in the crawling process.

3. Be visible and polite

(a) Use a defined useragent string in all HTTP requests that clearly identifies you as a crawler and provide contact details.

(b) If you are using any subscription material inform your library and the publisher of your proposed crawling.

4. Work with other content miners

(a) Consult publicly online about current good practice before starting.

(b) Use de facto standard tools (only write your own if there's a gap).

5. Give credit where credit is due

(a) Credit original producers of mined research outputs whenever possible, as per community norms for the reuse of scholarship.

The Right to Read is the Right to Mine

Principle 1: Right of legitimate accessors to mine

We assert that there is no legal, ethical or moral reason to refuse to allow legitimate accessors of research content (OA or otherwise) to use machines to analyse the published output of the research community. Researchers expect to access and process the full content of the research literature with their computer programs and should be able to use their machines as they use their eyes. The right to read is the right to mine

Principle 2: Lightweight processing terms and conditions

Mining by legitimate subscribers should not be prohibited by contractual or other legal barriers. Publishers should add clarifying language in their subscription agreements that content is available for information mining by download or by remote access. Where access is through researcher-provided tools, no further cost should be required. Publishers should always explain to subscribers in countries that have implemented an exception to copyright for text and data mining that this exception exists, and should also ensure that in those countries they will not attempt to sidestep the exception by adding terms or conditions, or technical barriers, to restrict what subscribers are entitled to do under the law. Users and providers should encourage machine-processing.

Principle 3: Technical restrictions

Bona fide content mining should not be restricted by unreasonable or unjustified technical restrictions imposed by publisher servers.

Principle 4: Agree what is commercial and what is noncommercial

Publishers should make clear by means of use cases linked to their licences as what sorts of downstream activities they reasonably consider to be commercial, and what activities they consider to be noncommercial.

Principle 5: Use of mining results

Researchers can and will publish facts and excerpts that they discover by reading and processing documents. They expect to disseminate and aggregate statistical results as facts and context text as fair use excerpts, openly and with no restrictions other than attribution. Publisher efforts to claim rights in the results of mining further retard the advancement of science by making those results less available to the research community. Such claims should be prohibited. Facts don't belong to anyone.

REFERENCES

Creative Commons, 2008. Defining 'noncommercial': a study of how the online population understands 'noncommercial use'. Creative Commons Wiki.

Directive 96/9/EC, 1996. Directive 96/9/ec of the European Parliament and of the Council of 11 March 1996 on the Legal Protection of Databases. http://eur-lex.europa.eu/LexUriServ/LexUriServ.do?uri=CELEX:31996L0009:EN:HTML, accessed: 18 Sep 2014.

Hagedorn, G., Mietchen, D., Morris, R.A., Agosti, D., Penev, L., Berendsohn, W.G., et al., 2011. Creative commons licenses and the non-commercial condition: Implications for the re-use of biodiversity information. ZooKeys (150), 127.

Hargreaves, I., 2011. Digital opportunity: a review of intellectual property and growth. An independent report.

Kishor, P., 2014. Legal implications of text and data mining (tdm). In: Presented at Open Knowledge Festival 2014, Berlin, 15–17 July 2014. https://upload.wikimedia.org/wikipedia/commons/1/15/LegalImplicationsofTextandDataMining%28TDM%29.pdf

Klimpel, P., 2012. Consequences, risks, and side-effects of the license module non-commercial–nc. http://openglam.org/files/2013/01/iRights_CC-NC_Guide_English.pdf.

LACA, March 2011. Independent review of intellectual property and growth response by LACA: the libraries and archives copyright alliance. http://www.ipo.gov.uk/ipreview-c4e-sub-libraries.pdf.

McDonald, D., McNicoll, I., Weir, G., Reimer, T., Redfearn, J., Jacobs, N., et al., 2012. The value and benefits of text mining. Technical Report of Jisc. https://www.jisc.ac.uk/reports/value-and-benefits-of-text-mining.

Murray-Rust, P., Molloy, J., Cabell, D., 2012. Open content mining. In: The First Open-Forum Academy Conference Proceedings, pp. 57–64.

Murray-Rust, P., Neylon, C., Pollock, R., Wilbanks, J., 2010. Panton principles: principles for open data in science. Panton Principles.

Neylon, C., 2014. Best practice in enabling content mining. http://blogs.plos.org/opens/2014/03/09/best-practice-enabling-content-mining/.

Piwowar, H., 2012a. Data citation and text mining. http://researchremix.wordpress.com/2012/04/19/data-citation-text-mining/. accessed: 18 Sep 2014.

Piwowar, H., 2012b. Elsevier agrees ubc researchers can text-mine for citizen science, research tools. http://researchremix.wordpress.com/2012/04/17/elsevier-agrees/. accessed: 18 Sep 2014.

SPARC, 2012. Pushing the frontier of access for text mining: A conversation with Heather Piwowar on one researcher's attempt to break new ground. http://www.sparc.arl.org/news/pushing-frontier-access-text-mining-conversationheather-piwowar-one-researcher%E2%80%99s-attempt-break, accessed: 18 Sep 2014.

The Copyright and Rights in Performances (Research, Education, Libraries and Archives) Regulations 2014, 2014. No. 1372. Regulation 3, http://www.legislation.gov.uk/uksi/2014/1372/regulation/3/made.

Thelwall, M., Stuart, D., 2006. Web crawling ethics revisited: Cost, privacy, and denial of service. J. Amer. Soc. Informat. Sci. Tech. 57 (13), 1771–1779.

TRIPS, 1994. http://www.wto.org/english/docse/legale/legale.htm#TRIPs, accessed: 18 Sep 2014.

CHAPTER 5

Text Mining for Semantic Search in Europe PubMed Central Labs

W.J. Black*, A. Rowley*, M. Miwa[†], J. McNaught*, S. Ananiadou*
*University of Manchester, Manchester, UK
[†]University of Manchester and Toyota Technological Institute

5.1 INTRODUCTION

Europe PubMed Central (Europe PMC), sponsored collectively by 26 major funders[1] of biological and medical research, and dedicated to the promotion of open access to scientific literature, provides a literature search service that has been enhanced by text mining. As part of that service, Europe PMC Labs provides a platform for prototype services that use text mining in innovative ways, providing semantically guided search. This chapter describes the *EvidenceFinder* application, which provides passage retrieval of facts by generating questions from basic search terms. As well as introducing the search user interfaces, we explain the genesis of the service from text mining applied to the whole corpus (at date of writing) of 3 million full-text research articles, and review several related advanced search tools.

EvidenceFinder is a search aid, designed for use in the context of a full-text retrieval service, which automatically suggests questions on the basis of what has been entered in the search engine's query field. Figure 5.1 illustrates this in action. When searching the *EvidenceFinder*-augmented search engine for the Europe PMC repository of full-text scientific papers, a user who typed the query *MDM2* would be presented with a set of suggested questions such as those in Table 5.1, at the same time as the first page of full-text search results is displayed. In Table 5.2 we show some of the range of expressions in the text that can be retrieved by selecting the question *What binds to MDM2?* The variety of syntactic structures in the examples serves to illustrate why a sophisticated text analysis involving full parsing is needed to underpin the application. The suggested questions are automatically generated by the system, from a prior analysis of the entire corpus, which involves:

(i) named entity analysis to locate expressions denoting genes/proteins, metabolites, diseases, drugs, and terms denoting biological or medical processes in either verbal or nominal variant forms;

[1] http://europepmc.org/Funders/

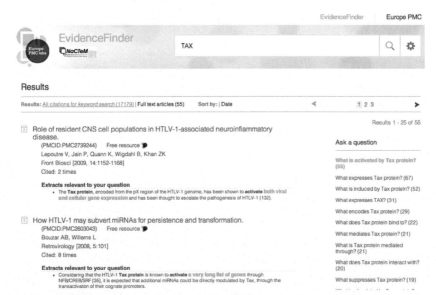

Figure 5.1 EvidenceFinder in Europe PMC Labs after selecting a question proposed by the application.

Table 5.1 Top 10 suggested questions corresponding to the query *MDM2*

Question	Doc. freq.
What binds to MDM2?	34
What interacts with MDM2?	31
What affects MDM2?	15
What changes in MDM2?	10
What is regulated by MDM2?	9
What is involved in MDM2?	8
What is inhibited by MDM2?	8
What is induced by MDM2?	7
What differs in MDM2?	7
What complexes with MDM2?	7

(ii)   fully parsing all sentences in the text collection having a biological process term and at least one named entity;

(iii) extracting the *logical* subject, verb and object of all parses in which the verb is in the BioLexicon (Thompson et al., 2011) and the subject or object (SVO) contains a named entity as a constituent, and saving this, paired with the chunk-level analysis of the corresponding clause within its sentence context, as the index entry;

Table 5.2 A sample of document clauses matching the question *What binds to MDM2?*

- When **bound** to **MDM2**, *p53* becomes ubiquitinated and targeted for proteasome-mediated degradation.
- In addition to p53, *a number of other proapoptotic proteins* are known to **bind** to <u>the N terminus of **MDM2**</u> and …
- *The Ser and Thr mutant peptides*, which are more helical in the CD data (Figure 5.2), have much higher entropic benefits when **binding** to **MDM2**.
- *The N-terminal ends of the peptides* are largely unstructured when **bound** to **MDM2**.
- In the cytosol *p53* **binds** to **mdm2** and is rapidly degraded.
- In this study, we found that *Met11 of MIP* was important for **binding** to **MDM2**.
- Consequently, we identified MIP as *an optimized peptide sequence* for **bindin**g to **MDM2** from all possible sequences.

Note: **bold** – expression matching the verb or object of the question; *slanted* – expression marked as answering the Wh-question; <u>underline</u> – expression identified by the parser as the syntactic subject or object, in which <u>the **entity** named in the question</u> is a constituent.

(iv) normalizing the named entity expressions to eliminate spurious duplication in search;

(v) augmenting the searchable index with subexpressions and variants.

EvidenceFinder is a question-suggesting system that offers passage retrieval and is deployed as a service on a full document collection scale, where it is the full text of the documents and not just their abstracts that is indexed. It is designed not as an alternative to a full-text retrieval system, but as an auxiliary search gadget for those occasions when the questions it suggests promise to satisfy the user's information need more directly than paging through the relevance-ranked or recency-ranked list of document metadata and downloading and reading selected articles.

The larger system in which *EvidenceFinder* is embedded supports metadata queries, as its users are often interested in locating articles by specific authors or from particular journals. *EvidenceFinder* comes into play when the query terms are not qualified to indicate a metadata search, and we will henceforward refer to this type of query as a *full-text query*.

What *EvidenceFinder* does with a full-text query is to look up its index of parsed facts for instances where one or more words from the query occur as the filler of a subject or object slot in a triple[2] that represents a clause, or sometimes a predication within a complex noun phrase.

[2] Not to be confused with an element in a triple store.

It returns a ranked list of matches where the predicate in the triple is paired with the query term in its subject or object role and the document frequency of the triple. The entities in complementary roles (e.g., subject where the query term was an object and vice versa) are not listed individually in this intermediate search result.

For presentation of these fact search results to the user, a formulation as a question has been chosen, as the easiest way to summarise each set of facts, which have a predicate and one argument in common, but a spread of values for the other argument.

Choosing one of the suggested questions, a user next obtains a paginated list of matching documents, each with sentence-sized passages containing the text in which an "answer" to the "question" occurs. The quotation marks are used deliberately here, to reinforce the point that the questions are not those of the user, but suggested by the system.

A final service that *EvidenceFinder* provides is when the user is viewing a single document from the search results, they can elect to see the set of indexed fact-annotated sentences from the article, each one hyperlinked to a new query shown in English in a form such as *"Find other articles in which* named-entity *is said to* verb" as a tool tip.

5.2 PREVIOUS WORK

EvidenceFinder's technical foundations are text mining combined with full-text retrieval, but it has little more than this in common with natural language question-answering as normally understood, as user-entered queries are neither parsed nor evaluated as natural language questions. The indexing contribution to *EvidenceFinder*'s functionality is broadly very similar to that in MEDIE (Miyao et al., 2006; Ohta et al., 2006), although the user interface is very different. Another deployed application that offers somewhat similar functionality to *EvidenceFinder* is *Quertle* (Coppernoll-Blach, 2011), but it differs in the way and extent to which it proposes queries.

5.2.1 Biomedical Text Mining

Text mining refers to activities where data mining takes place on collections where the raw data is expressed as natural language text. There are alternative methods for undertaking text mining, but a typical approach is to apply information extraction techniques to the individual documents in a collection to populate a database.

Information extraction is a selective semantic analysis of the text, biased toward the types of conceptual entity (Srinivasan et al., 2002), relationship and fact (Ananiadou et al., 2010) that are salient in a specific field of discourse. In biology and medicine, these include genes and proteins, diseases, chemicals and drugs, amongst others.

These fields are particularly well-served by online reference materials about those conceptual entities. It is an established practice for literature services in these fields to provide cross-references to the databases, and vice versa for the databases to cite the literature sources backing up assertions about the entities.

5.2.2 Applications of Text Mining in Search Engines

Having associated semantic descriptions with text spans in a document collection, there are multiple ways of exploiting this for the benefit of the user of a search engine.

Linked Data

Minimally, semantic annotations can be displayed either within or beside a retrieved article's metadata. If the annotations go beyond merely classifying text spans according to the class of entity they denote, and associate them with database identifiers, then text mining has helped to create a valuable linked data resource (Hoffmann, 2007; Vanteru et al., 2008; McEntyre et al., 2011).

Semantic Metadata Search

Semantic annotations can be themselves searchable, so that the query PROTEIN:cat (indicating semantic restriction to the named entity of type protein) retrieved far fewer matches (13,226) than the corresponding full-text query cat (109,913—including hits about felines and scanners) in the Kleio semantic search engine (Nobata et al., 2008) of MEDLINE® content.

Faceting and Clustering

From the user's point of view, a full-text search often produces a very large result set. For example, at the time of writing the query "*diabetes*" produces a result set of 396,658 abstracts in PubMed, ordered by recency, or optionally, by relevance.

Various techniques exist to show the user ways in which the result set can be broken down into smaller sets.

Faceting shows the distribution of a result set among subsets sharing metadata attributes and values, and is now a very popular tool in e-commerce, where product and service descriptions have, like bibliographic records, a mixture of simple and textual attribute values. Nobata et al. (2008) demonstrates the use of facets generated by indexing in 16 semantic categories in addition to supplied metadata such as publication type and MESH headings. Three advantages of facet navigation of search results are that the semantic classification can be browsed, its quantitative distribution is visible at the outset, and the results breakdown is exhaustive of the main result set. These characteristics make facet search valuable for the conduct of a systematic review of a field of enquiry. Facta (Tsuruoka et al., 2008) displays six columns of classified named entity instances ranked according to strength of association with the query term—this is equivalent to a facet-based query analysis where all the facets are open simultaneously.

Clustering of search results (Osinski and Weiss, 2005) can be produced on the basis of unsupervised algorithms that assign indicative labels to sets of lexically similar documents, but is only practical for a subset of the largest result sets.

Fact and Passage Retrieval

In information extraction, semantic annotations that classify text spans according to the conceptual classes to which their referents belong are considered a step toward analysis of the factual content of the text. Alternative approaches to this task are to treat the problem as fully parsing and semantically interpreting the text, or filling a template representation of facts of specific salience in the current domain.

There are several search engines for protein interactions and biological entity relations, including iHOP (Hoffmann and Valencia, 2005), PIE (Sun et al., 2008), MEDIE (Miyao et al., 2006), Chilibot (Chen and Sharp, 2004) and BIOSMILE (Dai et al., 2008).

MEDIE provides semantic search interfaces for semantic analyses including predicate–argument structures by Enju (Miyao et al., 2009) and biomedical events by EventMine (Miwa et al., 2010). The Enju parser produces syntactic and semantic analyses of texts in the linguistic grammar formalism HPSG (Head-driven Phrase Structure Grammar), and combining Enju with a dependency grammar-based parser GDep (Sagae and Tsujii, 2007), EventMine extracts events represented as a deep semantic structure.

Passage retrieval, from the user perspective, is the provision of extracts from full text that are most relevant to the current query, as an alternative or a prelude to the full text. Whilst there are many techniques for passage retrieval that do not depend on parsing of factoids (Mengle and Goharian, 2009;

Otterbacher et al., 2009; Chen et al., 2011), sentence passages are the natural result of a fact retrieval system that is based on mapping indexable facts to their textual context.

Normalisation and Query Expansion

One of the practical concerns of semantics is the two way mapping between words and senses, where the same concept may have multiple synonyms.

Applied to information retrieval, word sense disambiguation would be valuable in removing ambiguity when analysing texts to produce links to ontologies, but is not currently capable of the reliability needed for full automation. However, by putting the human in the loop, at query time, word–sense mappings can be deployed to suggest alternative synonyms that may be added to a query to improve recall without the danger of adding annotations that are erroneous assertions.

Apart from genuine natural language synonyms, technical discourse abounds with complex terms that may be orthographically rendered in many variants. Examples are singular/plural, use of hyphenation, punctuation, spelling variation and so on. Popular query engines handle some of these sources of variation, in the way that lexical analysis is used in indexing and query processing, but analysis for lexical variation and acronym/abbreviation expansion (Okazaki and Ananiadou, 2006) as part of an information extraction pipeline can benefit IR systems.

Question Suggestion

Query suggestion (Xu et al., 2011) is a commonplace feature of web search engines, whose extensive user base makes it easy to accumulate web logs in which to search for super terms of the user's query and present them in a *suggest-box* version of the standard query input field.

5.3 DESIGN AND IMPLEMENTATION

5.3.1 Motivation for EvidenceFinder's Design

The goal of the work reported here was to complement the Europe PMC search service with innovative search aids based on text mining. The initial idea was to provide a similar functionality to MEDIE (Miyao et al., 2006; Ohta et al., 2006) (Figure 5.2) in which queries are entered in a three-field form, with captions subject, verb and object (henceforward SVO) and the system responds with extracted passages in one of three formats: title+bibliographic metadata+matching sentence with highlighting; title+abstract

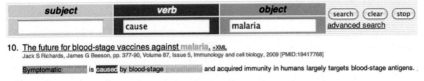

Figure 5.2 Input and extract from output of MEDIE.

```
809 9852 sentence id="s1535" parse_status="success"
9809 9851 cons id="c76744" cat="S" xcat="" head="c76746" sem_head="c76746" schema="mod_head"
lex_head="t35995"
9809 9816 cons id="c76745" cat="ADVP" xcat="" head="t35992" sem_head="t35992"
lex_head="t35992"
9809 9816 tok id="t35992" cat="ADV" pos="RB" base="however" lexentry="[&lt;ADVP&gt;]V"
pred="adj_arg1" arg1="c76746"
9816 9851 cons id="c76746" cat="S" xcat="" head="c76748" sem_head="c76748" schema="mod_head"
lex_head="t35995"
9816 9817 cons id="c76747" cat="PN" xcat="" head="t35993" sem_head="t35993"
lex_head="t35993"
9816 9817 tok id="t35993" cat="PN" pos="," base="-comma-" lexentry="[&lt;COMMA&gt;]V"
pred="punct_arg1" arg1="c76748"
9818 9851 cons id="c76748" cat="S" xcat="" head="c76751" sem_head="c76751"
schema="subj_head" lex_head="t35995"
9818 9824 cons id="c76749" cat="NP" xcat="" head="c76750" sem_head="c76750"
schema="empty_spec_head" lex_head="t35994"
9818 9824 cons id="c76750" cat="NX" xcat="" head="t35994" sem_head="t35994"
lex_head="t35994"
9818 9824 tok id="t35994" cat="N" pos="NN" base="vegf-e" lexentry="[D&lt;N.3sg&gt;]_1xm"
pred="noun_arg0"
...
```

Figure 5.3 Part of the Enju parse tree of "However, VEGF-E binds only to VEGFR-2." in standoff annotation.

with highlighting; tabular format with columns for subject, verb, object and highlighted sentence extract. MEDIE retrieves matching facts and text snippets directly from an index of full parses, such as that shown in Figure 5.3, by interpretation of expressions in the GCL query language (Masuda and Tsujii, 2008), which allows the advanced user to formulate arbitrarily complex queries targeting facts expressed in complex and/or compound sentences. The queries are executed against an ordered search of the parse trees, most recent documents first, and results are returned one at a time (albeit very quickly).

Although MEDIE is an inspiration for *EvidenceFinder*, it cannot be used directly as the back end, because its index is based on PubMed abstracts, whereas the principal data collection for Europe PMC is the full-text article collection. In addition to designing our own indexing analysis pipeline, the nature of the user interface was also reconsidered.

Firstly, we excluded any requirement to cater for advanced usage in terms of complex queries, from which it followed that no purpose would be served by retaining the full detail of the parse tree in the searchable index, in place of a simpler abstraction of the core of a fact.

Secondly, among interested parties consulted about the design, a strongly expressed view was that users would be put off by an input form with more than one text entry field, and by linguistic terminology appearing as labels. Instead, we chose to design a style of interface that would be like query suggestion, faceting or clustering, in that the user should be prompted with the types of fact available in relation to their own query terms.

What counts as an indexable fact for *EvidenceFinder* is a predication that can be extracted from the parse tree where the following two conditions are met:

1. The predicate (whether it be a verb or a nominal derived form) is one of those from the BioLexicon, where the verbs are those used to express processes in molecular biology, for example, "bind", "activate" and "phosphorylate". In practice these verbs also include some rather generic ones, such as "cause", "increase" and "demonstrate".
2. The subject, direct object, indirect object, or object marked by a preposition is a named entity.

5.3.2 Index Design and Implementation

Clearly, the real sentences of scientific articles are much more complex and varied in structure than the *man bites dog* SVO pattern. However, the way this is used in MEDIE shows that it is a useful level of abstraction, in that it is often useful to count as matches those cases where a named entity occurs not as an entire subject or object, but as a constituent of a longer phrase that occupies that syntactic role. Table 5.2 already showed how that works in the context of *EvidenceFinder*.

For the logical and concrete design of the index for *EvidenceFinder*, we considered two alternatives before settling on the current design.

Firstly, we created a Solr index in which a "document" was an individual fact within a sentence with fields for the subject, direct, indirect and prepositional phrase objects where appropriate, and the sentence snippet with HTML markup to show the constituents according to a colour code. To make this work, we had to conduct multiple facet queries on a generate and test basis, which was fast enough until the server ran out of cache memory, when performance degraded severely.

Secondly, mindful that different verbs have different sentence frames and are not all transitive with a subject and a single object, we created a relational database schema in which one row represented a sentence argument. When we completed initial work on the question generation algorithm, it became apparent that we were rarely able to instantiate templates that had more than two arguments, and we finally settled on the simpler representation, also in a relational table, that a fact is represented as a row with columns for the subject, verb and object, for the respective semantic categories of these constituents, and for the marked up sentence for user consumption.

Matching query terms to fact triples cannot be purely literal, and so there is an additional search index table. This table contains in addition to full subject and object slot fillers, subsequences of those strings when they comprise multiple words. In this way, a query such as "diabetes" can be mapped to facts where the subject or object is a longer phrase such as "diabetes mellitus", "Type II diabetes mellitus", "adult-onset diabetes mellitus", or many others. Because these tables have to be joined at query processing time, we use a symbolic (i.e., unique number) representation of named entity expressions for efficiency, and hence a symbol table of named entities.

5.3.3 Parsing Full Papers to Support Fact Retrieval

The MEDIE event recognition workflow takes as input an XML file that includes article titles and texts, and produces biomolecular events mentioned in the texts.

The workflow invokes the following modules: a sentence splitter, a named entity recogniser, two syntactic parsers, and an event structure recogniser. The sentence splitter detects sentence boundaries in a text chunk using machine learning techniques. The named entity recogniser detects text spans that mention named entities in a sentence. The two syntactic parsers, Enju (Miyao et al., 2009) and GDep (Sagae and Tsujii, 2007), perform syntactic analysis of the sentence. The event structure recogniser EventMine (Miwa et al., 2010) extracts biomolecular events related to the named entities in a sentence using the syntactic analyses.

The MEDIE workflow software was provided to us by its developers as a starting point for the implementation of the *EvidenceFinder* indexing workflow, and it was adapted in the following ways: the named entity recogniser was substituted by one of our own, NeMine (Sasaki et al., 2008); only one parser, Enju, was used; and the event structure recogniser was replaced by a parse extraction component that extracts SVO representations from the standoff representation of the parse tree, which is illustrated in Figure 5.3.

Collection-Scale Processing

This is facilitated by a workflow system *GXP make* (Taura et al., 2010). GXP make supports automatic distribution of tasks in a workflow described with GNU Makefile, supporting heterogeneous log-in systems (e.g., SSH, TORQUE, Sun Grid Engine), fault tolerant re-execution based on analyses of task dependency in Makefile, and others.

Using GXP make, 1.8 million articles were fully analysed by our adapted workflow in 90,000 processor core hours in a high-performance cluster; that is, at a rate of 20 full papers per hour.

Updating Workflow

The indexing of documents for *EvidenceFinder* is now done using the pipeline shown in Figure 5.4, whereas the collection-scale processing described in the previous section invoked Enju unconditionally on all texts immediately after sentence splitting.

Newly issued, revised or withdrawn documents are identified as having a time stamp more recent than the date of last update, and are downloaded and analysed using a large cluster of computers at EMBL-EBI, and the final results uploaded to where *EvidenceFinder*'s web services are hosted. This workflow is now carried out daily.

5.3.4 Query Processing

Users may invoke *EvidenceFinder* by using a web user interface that is almost identical in appearance to the one that they would use to search Europe PMC normally, and so it provides the same functionality, providing ranked lists of articles that match the chosen search terms. Whenever the search terms contain no metadata qualifiers, they are additionally input to *EvidenceFinder*'s query processing, which results in a list of questions that appears to the right of the search results display, above a similar auxiliary output labelled "popular content sets".

Mapping from Queries to Questions

The search term from the user interface is first tokenised and plurals reduced to singular, then words from a general stop list and from a list of verbs are

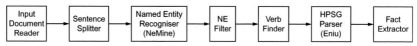

Figure 5.4 EvidenceFinder analysis and indexing workflow.

removed. The remaining search terms have all subsequences generated and these are matched with the search index, producing a set of named entity symbols joined with the fact table. If any two or more word terms are matched, their subterms are not considered separately. The result set is grouped by document ID to produce the document frequency of each question that will be generated, and the resulting list is ranked in order of the question document frequency.

During development of *EvidenceFinder*, user engagement was undertaken to assist with design (see Section 5.4.3), and this feedback was used in developing refinements to the question generation process.

Generating Grammatically Correct Questions

Generated questions generally take one of the forms below (or their negated variants):

* What *verbs* (*preposition*) *named_entity*?
* What does *named_entity verb*?

The first form occurs when the named entity (from the user's query) occurs in an object position, and the second when it is the subject of a sentence. In both cases, the template applies correctly only to transitive verbs. Where a preposition occurs with a named entity in object position, its grammatical appropriateness has been filtered by reference to syntactic frames in the Bio-Lexicon at the indexing stage.

One type of syntactic infelicity that we now eliminate is where the verb is intransitive. In these cases, there is no question to answer, and they are simply now suppressed. (Named entities as the subject of an intransitive verb may convey information, but cannot be transformed into a *wh*-question.)

Other special cases treated with additional templates include those

* where the verb's subject is human, the form *Who or what … * is generated;
* where the verb is bi-transitive, for example,
  - when the verb is *play*, the direct object *a role* is inserted;
  - when the verb is *cause* and the object preposition is *in*, a direct object *some phenomenon* has been omitted from the index; these questions are suppressed;
* where the verb takes a descriptive theme, the question starts "How" instead of "What";
* where the subject or object is a personal pronoun, the question is suppressed.

Generating Questions that Make Scientific Sense

Users and collaborators used this form of words to express the difference between generated questions they found to be semantically coherent and those that were semantically incoherent, although they were not always able to tell us which these were.

The largest category of questions that did not make scientific sense that we induced from examples were cases where the verb was in a set including *demonstrate, identify, describe, show* and *replicate*, which we associate with description of activities in the methods section of an article. These typically have an uninformative subject and a complex object, and we now suppress them altogether. The perception of questions not making scientific sense has improved as we dealt better with the syntactic special cases.

Nonetheless, there are cases where because of the indexing policy whereby we match subjects or objects that contain named entities as a proper subphrase, some questions systematically fail literally to make sense.

A case in point would be where the verb is *cause* or another whose object is conceptually a phenomenon rather than an entity. Whereas *What causes disease ?* is conceptually coherent, *What causes* protein/chemical *?* is strictly not, and would need to be understood as a simplification about causation of some process involving an entity or quantitative change in it. Currently questions in the simplified form are retained due to the importance of causal relationships, although future work is planned on using a richer representation of complex processes, and correspondingly more appropriately structured questions.

Generating Questions that are not too Similar

The parse extraction process, operating as it does on the level of syntactic deep structure, based on the logical rather than grammatical subject and object of a clause, already normalises many alternative syntactic forms to a canonical one. Nevertheless, it is still possible for *EvidenceFinder* to generate questions that appear to be very similar, because of the similarity of meaning of either the verb or the phrases in subject or object position.

Users might consider the second and third questions in Table 5.1 to be close together in meaning, and hence prefer to see the questions somehow combined. An experiment in clustering the verb and object combinations is under way, but the generation of generalised questions corresponding to the clusters is not yet resolved.

A further cause of multiple similar questions being generated was where the verb denotes a reflexive relationship (i.e., *is associated with*). A set of such verbs was identified and all relevant occurrences reduced to a canonical form.

Term variation is responsible for much apparent duplication of questions. Some of this variation is due to spelling and other orthographical variants, such as differences in the use of hyphens and apostrophes (e.g., diseases named after someone). Many of these sources of localised variation would be dealt with in a typical search engine, but among ones that often are not, we also deal appropriately with British and American spelling variation and with apostrophes.

For many biomedical entities and concepts, synonymous forms exist, and it is not always possible to distinguish between additional words that serve to subclassify a concept from those that are modifying the term in a particular context of use or those that are alternative names in apposition. More work is needed on deploying reference resources and heuristics to help group equivalent entity names together.

The perception that some questions might duplicate others is the single characteristic of *EvidenceFinder* that has drawn the most criticism from users, and if their information need would be best served by finding all article passages that match a question, they need to understand that the "similar" questions index disjoint subsets of documents. Hence this aspect of *EvidenceFinder*'s behaviour is the one that requires most attention.

5.3.5 Integration with Full-Text Query Service

The *EvidenceFinder* service is a distributed web application, using web services to access indexes held in geographically separate locations. The user interface is a version of the standard Europe PMC search engine with minor modifications, principally the provision of a "gadget" that displays and allows the selection of generated questions, and the additional tab that shows analysed sentential extracts from full text when a document summary is being viewed, as well as handling additional callbacks.

The *question generation* web service method returns a list of question objects, each comprising an English question, a "formal" question and a frequency. The server limits the number of questions to 20, although as many as 2,000 can sometimes be generated in response to a given query.

The *question selection* method returns a paginated list of bibliographic records indexed by a formal question, each containing HTML marked-up passages for each distinct sentence in the document matching the question. This method subcontracts to a preexisting web service co-located with the bibliographic data for the main full-text search engine.

The *all document facts* method returns all the indexed sentence passages for a selected article. Each of these contains the HTML marked-up sentence, as well as the subject, verb and object, and an English rendition of a request for similar sentence passages to be retrieved using the question selection method.

5.4 PERFORMANCE AND CRITIQUE

5.4.1 Response Times and Throughput

One important criterion for *EvidenceFinder* is that response times should be quick. Part of the response time is due to user interface and network components of the configuration, but the key component is the method, encapsulated in a web service, that takes a query and returns a set of questions. This has been tested using JMeter with queries selected at random from a set obtained from Europe PMC logs in late 2010.

The first column in Table 5.3, which summarises results of these tests, shows the number of simultaneous users, and next the number of test queries invoked. The remaining columns show the mean and spread of question generation times, and finally the throughput of queries per second obtainable from the setup, which was 2 load-balanced servers sharing the same database instance.

The mean response times and throughput show that the questions can usually be generated quickly enough in real time, although the occasional

Table 5.3 Question generation times and throughput in a selection of JMeter tests of the web service with no query↦question cache

Users	Calls	Query times (ms)				Thro'put qu's/s
		Mean	Min	Max	SD	
1	10	175	5	1607	477.42	5.7
10	10	28	4	1599	158.04	54.0
20	10	30	4	1720	169.75	82.1
50	10	55	4	3503	329.84	109.3
1	50	44	3	1595	221.67	22.1
10	50	36	3	2454	219.82	108.2
20	50	86	3	591	300.72	122.0
50	50	173	3	17665	1461.18	111.0

longer response times are less satisfactory. The response times are proportional to the number of named entity index entries (variants) of query subterms, and the number of entries in the fact table matched by each of those. The longer response times are almost all associated with common disease terms such as "diabetes", "heart disease", "breast cancer", which can match as many as one-fourth of the documents in the collection as full-text queries.

The query↦question mappings can be cached in the system, to reduce the response time for the longer queries toward the mean response time. However, the question document frequency needs to be recomputed whenever new documents are indexed, which occurs daily at present.

5.4.2 Degree of Success in Question Generation

When no questions can be suggested for a user query, a message "No questions available" appears. Clearly, a quality criterion for the service ought to be that this occurs as infrequently as possible, although in any search engine, some searches will produce no result, and when the questions are generated, they appear relevant to the query terms from which they were derived. Table 5.4 summarises tests carried out with the same collection of queries as used for the throughput tests, and shows that overall, 79% of the 100 test queries resulted in a set of questions being generated. Analysing the 21 cases where this did not happen, we noted that among the 9 one-word queries, 5 were off-topic for a biomedical resource, and 3 were lab or medical procedures, a category of named entity that we do not currently index. Among the 7 two-word cases, 5 were the names of species, either disease vectors or medicinally useful plants. This is a category of named entity that we plan to add to the analysis in the near future. One of the two-word and one of the three-word queries failed to match because of lexical analysis—a plural

Table 5.4 Results of sample analysis of question generation outcome and relevance, by query word count and overall

Words	Freq.	Generated	Relevant	Irrel.
1	31	23	23	0
2	25	19	9	10
3	18	14	7	7
4	15	14	7	7
5	4	4	3	1
6	5	4	2	2
8	1	1	1	0
Overall	100	79	52	27

word that was not the head of the phrase was not reduced to singular. In both these cases, the amended query succeeded.

The last column of Table 5.4 counts the question sets in which the questions did not relate well to the original query, and taken as a proportion of the total generated queries, constitutes a measure of error rate. Analysing the cases in question, they occur because the criteria for matching multiword queries to the named entity search index are too lax. Of the 17 "irrelevant" question sets generated from two- and three-word queries, 8 were in error because one of the two words was matched and being an adjective, readily combines with other specific terms, for example. This suggests that by making the matching criteria for multiword query terms to the named entity index stricter, using minimal linguistic information, we can significantly reduce the overall question generation error rate.

5.4.3 User Feedback and Analysis of Question Usefulness

Two focus groups were conducted at earlier stages in the development of *EvidenceFinder* with a total of 20 habitual PubMed users who were given a structured introduction to both Europe PMC and to *EvidenceFinder* as it then was. At the end of the main development phase of the *EvidenceFinder*, an in-depth evaluation was conducted, in which 8 subjects, all graduate students or life science researchers, carried out queries that were motivated by their own research, and recorded their observations on all the questions generated in response to them.

Early Focus Groups

Participants were divided between some who thought that *EvidenceFinder* would only occasionally be a useful adjunct to their normal use of a bibliographic retrieval service and others who were pleased with the early prototype of the question suggestion feature and passage retrieval capabilities. Of the more detailed constructive criticisms given to the developers, the three most frequently cited were that some of the questions did not appear to be grammatically well-formed, that others, whilst grammatical, did not make scientific sense, and finally, that some of the questions appeared to duplicate others. We have already discussed ways in which the implementation has been amended to ameliorate those general perceptions.

In-Depth Evaluation

This evaluation was carried out independently of the developers of *EvidenceFinder*, and testers were individually briefed before the test task and asked to evaluate the relevance of both the questions generated by *EvidenceFinder* as well as the subsequent articles and evidence derived in relation to particular search terms. For each search term used, up to eight questions were either scored for relevance to the original query or marked as redundant or repeat questions. Following this, up to six of the most relevant questions generated for a single query were selected by the tester and used to extract evidence and scored for relevance to the original query. Follow-up interviews were conducted to capture additional feedback, including site layout/feel.

In the question evaluation,

- Overall, 85% of search term queries successfully generated a question; 15% of queries resulted in no questions being generated.
- 40% of questions were graded as "acceptable" or "good" in terms of relevance, 40% of questions were considered "irrelevant"; 20% of questions were rated as too similar to other questions generated by that query.
- Searches for proteins (e.g., names of proteins) were most likely to generate good questions according to our testers.
- Broad search terms or terms involving multiple words were least successful at generating suitable questions (e.g., acronyms such as "DSPS" or "atomic force microscopy").

In the evidence passage retrieval evaluation,

- Users rated 74% of the evidence passages retrieved by relevant questions as "satisfactory" or "good"; 26% of the evidence retrieved was considered to be poor.
- The yield of good quality evidence depended on the number of articles available for a particular search term and the appropriateness or quality of that search term.
- Specialist search terms in some research areas yielded good results in terms of the relevance of extracted evidence; conversely broad search terms and those found in multiple areas of research extracted a high number of articles considered to be irrelevant to the original query.

Comparing these data with those in Table 5.4, the proportion of "relevant" generated questions is higher, which suggests that in use by a user population who are well versed in the scope of the document collection, as opposed to a set of queries collected randomly from Europe PMC users, the perceived quality of system-suggested questions is encouraging.

5.5 CONCLUSIONS

The *EvidenceFinder* is a practical demonstration of a search aid that helps locate passages from the full text of scientific articles in the fields of molecular biology and medicine. A simplified representation of a clause (or nominalised proposition) referenced to the document sentence in which it occurred is the unit of indexation. The index is produced by filtering the output of parsing sentences from the full-text document collection. Users are enabled to retrieve these factoids by a question suggestion mechanism, which we have demonstrated to be efficient enough in normal operation to be invoked on demand. User trials have provided feedback that the service does often provide fast access to passages that help very quick decisions about the relevance of individual articles to a research question. They also indicate that although there are various ways that generated question quality can be improved, it is already an effective search aid for some information needs.

5.6 AVAILABILITY

EvidenceFinder can be accessed at http://labs.europepmc.org. Europe PMC Labs is being developed into an open platform in which third-party text mining pipelines can be applied to the Europe PMC full-text collection, or the open-access subset of documents within the collection.

REFERENCES

Ananiadou, S., Pyysalo, S., Tsujii, J., Kell, D.B., 2010. Event extraction for systems biology by text mining the literature. Trends Biotechnol. 28 (7), 381–390. http://dx.doi.org/10.1016/j.tibtech.2010.04.005.

Chen, H., Sharp, B., 2004. Content-rich biological network constructed by mining PubMed abstracts. BMC Bioinformatics 5 (1), 147. http://dx.doi.org/10.1186/1471-2105-5-147.

Chen, R., Lin, H., Yang, Z., 2011. Passage retrieval based hidden knowledge discovery from biomedical literature. Expert Syst. Appl. 38 (8), 9958–9964. http://dx.doi.org/10.1016/j.eswa.2011.02.034.

Coppernoll-Blach, P., 2011. Quertle: The conceptual relationships alternative search engine for PubMed (review). J. Med. Libr. Assoc. 99, 176–177.

Dai, H.J., Huang, C.H., Lin, R.T.K., Tsai, R.T.H., Hsu, W.L., 2008. BIOSMILE web search: a web application for annotating biomedical entities and relations. Nucl. Acids Res. 36 (Suppl. 2), W390–W398.

Hoffmann, R., 2007. Using the iHOP information resource to mine the biomedical literature on genes, proteins, and chemical compounds. Curr. Protoc. Bioinformat. http://dx.doi.org/10.1002/0471250953.bi0116s20. Chapter 1, Unit 1.16.

Hoffmann, R., Valencia, A., 2005. Implementing the iHOP concept for navigation of biomedical literature. Bioinformatics 21 (Suppl. 2), 252–258.

Masuda, K., Tsujii, J., 2008. Nested region algebra extended with variables for tag-annotated text search. In: Proceedings of CIKM'08, pp. 1349–1350.

McEntyre, J.R., Ananiadou, S., Andrews, S., Black, W.J., Boulderstone, R., Buttery, P., et al., 2011. UKPMC: a full text article resource for the life sciences. Nucl. Acids Res. 39 (Database issue), D58–D65. http://dx.doi.org/10.1093/nar/gkq1063.

Mengle, S., Goharian, N., 2009. Passage detection using text classification. Journal of the Association for Information Science and Technology 60 (4), 814–825. http://dx.doi.org/10.1002/asi.21025.

Miwa, M., Sætre, R., Kim, J.D., Tsujii, J., 2010. Event extraction with complex event classification using rich features. Journal of Bioinformatics and Computational Biology 8 (1), 131–146. http://dx.doi.org/10.1142/S0219720010004586.

Miyao, Y., Ohta, T., Masuda, K., Tsuruoka, Y., Yoshida, K., Ninomiya, T., et al., 2006. Semantic Retrieval for the Accurate Identification of Relational Concepts in Massive Textbases. In: Proc. COLING-ACL 2006, Sydney, Australia, pp. 1017–1024.

Miyao, Y., Sagae, K., Sætre, R., Matsuzaki, T., Tsujii, J., 2009. Evaluating contributions of natural language parsers to protein-protein interaction extraction. Bioinformatics 25 (3), 394–400.

Nobata, C., Cotter, P., Okazaki, N., Rea, B., Sasaki, Y., Tsuruoka, Y., et al., 2008. Kleio: a knowledge-enriched information retrieval system for biology. In: Proc. 31st Annual International ACM SIGIR Conference on Research and Development in Information Retrieval, SIGIR '08. ACM, New York, pp. 787–788. URL, http://doi.acm.org/10.1145/1390334.1390504.

Ohta, T., Miyao, Y., Ninomiya, T., Tsuruoka, Y., Yakushiji, A., Masuda, K., et al., 2006. An intelligent search engine and GUI-based efficient MEDLINE search tool based on deep syntactic parsing. In: Proc. COLING/ACL 2006 Interactive Presentation Sessions, pp. 17–20.

Okazaki, N., Ananiadou, S., 2006. Building an abbreviation dictionary using a term recognition approach. Bioinformatics 22 (24), 3089–3095. http://dx.doi.org/10.1093/bioinformatics/btl534.

Osinski, S., Weiss, D., 2005. A concept-driven algorithm for clustering search results. IEEE Intell. Syst. 20 (3), 48–54.

Otterbacher, J., Erkan, G., Radev, D.R., 2009. Biased LexRank: Passage retrieval using random walks with question-based priors. Informat. Process. Manage. 45 (1), 42–54. http://dx.doi.org/10.1016/j.ipm.2008.06.004.

Sagae, K., Tsujii, J., 2007. Dependency parsing and domain adaptation with LR models and parser ensembles. In: Proc. of the CoNLL Shared Task Session of EMNLP-CoNLL 2007. ACL, Prague, Czech Republic, pp. 1044–1050.

Sasaki, Y., Tsuruoka, Y., McNaught, J., Ananiadou, S., 2008. How to make the most of NE dictionaries in statistical NER. BMC Bioinformatics 9 (Suppl. 11), S5.

Srinivasan, S., Rindflesch, T.C., Hole, W.T., Aronson, A.R., Mork, J.G., 2002. Finding UMLS metathesaurus concepts in MEDLINE. In: Proc. AMIA Symp, pp. 727–731.

Sun, K., Shin, S.Y., Lee, I.H., Kim, S.J., Sriram, R., Zhang, B.T., 2008. Pie: an online prediction system for protein–protein interactions from text. Nucl. Acids Res. 36, W411–W415.

Taura, K., Matsuzaki, T., Miwa, M., Kamoshida, Y., Yokoyama, D., Dun, N., et al., 2010. Design and implementation of GXP Make – a workflow system based on Make. IEEE International Conference on e-Science, 214–221. doi: http://doi.ieeecomputersociety.org/10.1109/eScience.2010.43.

Thompson, P., McNaught, J., Montemagni, S., Calzolari, N., del Gratta, R., Lee, V., et al., 2011. The BioLexicon: a large-scale terminological resource for biomedical text mining. BMC Bioinformatics 12, 397. http://dx.doi.org/10.1186/1471-2105-12-397.

Tsuruoka, Y., Tsujii, J., Ananiadou, S., 2008. Facta: a text search engine for finding associated biomedical concepts. Bioinformatics 24 (21), 2559–2560. http://dx.doi.org/10.1093/bioinformatics/btn469.

Vanteru, B.C., Shaik, J.S., Yeasin, M., 2008. Semantically linking and browsing PubMed abstracts with gene ontology. BMC Genomics 9 (Suppl. 1), S10. http://dx.doi.org/10.1186/1471-2164-9-S1-S10.

Xu, Z., Luo, X., Yu, J., Xu, W., 2011. Mining Web search engines for query suggestion. Concurr. Comput. Pract. Experi. 23 (10), 1101–1113. http://dx.doi.org/10.1002/cpe.1689.

APPENDIX: RESOURCES USED FOR INDEXING

The verb dictionary is provided by the BioLexicon (Thompson et al., 2011), a corpus-based study of usage in biomedicine. The named entity lists are taken from the following specialised dictionaries:

Protein and gene names:
BioThesaurus
http://pir.georgetown.edu/pirwww/iprolink/biothesaurus.shtml
Genia Corpus
http://www.nactem.ac.uk/genia/genia-corpus

Metabolites:
Human Metabolome Database (HMDB)
http://www.hmdb.ca/

Drug names:
DrugBank http://www.drugbank.ca/

Disease names:
Unified Medical Language System (UMLS)
http://www.nlm.nih.gov/research/umls/

CHAPTER 6

Extracting Information from Social Media with GATE

K. Bontcheva*, L. Derczynski*
*University of Sheffield, Sheffield, UK

6.1 INTRODUCTION

In recent years, social media – and microblogging in particular – have established themselves as high-value, high-volume content, which organisations increasingly wish to analyse automatically. For instance, the widely popular Twitter microblogging platform has around 288 million active users, posting over 500 million tweets a day,[1] and has the fastest growing network in terms of active usage.[2]

Researchers have therefore started to study the problem of mining social media content automatically. The focus of this chapter is on information extraction, but other hotly researched topics include opinion mining (Maynard et al., 2012), summarisation (Rout et al., 2013a), and visual analytics and user and community modeling (Bontcheva and Rout, 2014). It is relevant in many application contexts, including knowledge management, competitor intelligence, customer relation management, eBusiness, eScience, eHealth and eGovernment.

Information extraction from social media content has only recently become an active research topic, following early experiments that showed this genre to be extremely challenging for state-of-the-art algorithms. For instance, named entity recognition methods typically have 85–90% accuracy on longer texts, but 30–50% on tweets (Ritter et al., 2011; Liu et al., 2012).

The aim of this chapter is to provide a thorough analysis of the problems and to describe the most recent GATE algorithms, specifically developed for extracting information from social media content. Comparisons against other state-of-the-art research on this topic are also made. These new GATE

---

[1] See http://news.cnet.com/8301-1023_3-57541566-93/report-twitter-hits-half-a-billion-tweets-a-day/.

[2] See http://globalwebindex.net/thinking/social-platforms-gwi-8-update-decline-of-local-social-media-platforms/.

Working with Text
http://dx.doi.org/10.1016/B978-1-84334-749-1.00006-8

components have now been bundled together, to form the new TwitIE IE pipeline, made available as a GATE plugin.

As the chapter progresses, the information extraction tasks and algorithms become progressively more complex and, consequently, more error-prone. For instance, on longer, well-formed content, tokenisation and part of speech (POS) tagging are typically performed with 95–98% accuracy, entity recognition between 90% and 95%, and even less for parsing. Genre adaptation is also a major issue, and again performance on tweets varies more widely as the tasks become more complex.

Consequently, there is a trade-off between the sophistication of the linguistic analysis and its accuracy, especially on unseen, noisier types of text. As a result, it is advisable, as an integral part of system development, to carry out rigorous quantitative evaluation against a gold standard data set. It is through such experiments that it is possible to establish the usefulness of each of the text mining processing steps. GATE offers a wide range of evaluation tools described in detail in Cunningham et al. (2002, 2011a).

On large data sets, computational complexity and implementation efficiency would also need to be considered. To address this challenge, the GATE family has been extended recently with GATECloud (see Section 6.3.3 for details).

The rest of the chapter is structured as follows. Section 6.2 discusses the characteristics of social media content, which make it particularly challenging for state-of-the-art text mining algorithms. Next, Section 6.3 introduces briefly the GATE family of text mining tools. As the focus of this chapter is primarily on information extraction (IE) methods, Section 6.4 provides a brief overview of IE and differentiates it from information retrieval. Next, Section 6.5 discusses in detail IE from social media and introduces the TwitIE pipeline of reusable GATE components for extracting information from social media content. The chapter concludes with a brief discussion on outstanding challenges and future work.

6.2 SOCIAL MEDIA STREAMS: CHARACTERISTICS, CHALLENGES AND OPPORTUNITIES

Social media sites allow users to connect with each other for the purpose of sharing content (e.g., web links, photos, videos), experiences, professional information and online socialising with friends. Users create posts or status updates and social media sites circulate these to the user's social network. The key difference from traditional web pages is that users are not just passive information consumers, but many are also prolific content creators.

Social media can be categorised on a spectrum, based on the type of connection between users, how the information is shared, and how users interact with the media streams:

- Interest-graph media (Ravikant and Rifkin, 2010), such as Twitter, encourage users to form connections with others based on shared interests, regardless of whether they know the other person in real life. Connections do not always need to be reciprocated. Shared information comes in the form of a stream of messages in reverse chronological order.

- Social networking sites (SNS) encourage users to connect with people they have real-life relationships with. Facebook, for example, provides a way for people to share information, as well as comment on each other's posts. Typically, short contributions are shared, outlining current events in users' lives or linking to something on the Internet that users think their friends might enjoy. These status updates are combined into a time-ordered stream for each user to read.

- Professional networking services (PNS), such as LinkedIn, aim to provide an introductions service in the context of work, where connecting to a person implies that you vouch for that person to a certain extent, and would recommend them as a work contact for others. Typically, professional information is shared and PNS tend to attract older professionals (Skeels and Grudin, 2009).

- Content sharing and discussion services, such as blogs, video sharing (e.g., YouTube, Vimeo), slide sharing (e.g., SlideShare), and user discussion/review forums (e.g., CNET). Blogs usually contain longer contributions. Readers might comment on these contributions, and some blog sites create a time stream of blog articles for followers to read. Many blog sites also advertise automatically new blog posts through their users' Facebook and Twitter accounts.

These different kinds of social media, coupled with their complex characteristics, make text mining extremely challenging. State-of-the-art natural language processing algorithms have been developed primarily on news articles and other carefully written, long web content (Bontcheva and Cunningham, 2011). In contrast, most social media streams (e.g., tweets, Facebook messages) are strongly interconnected, temporal, noisy, short, and full of slang, leading to severely degraded results.[3]

---

[3] For instance, named entity recognition methods typically have 85–90% accuracy on news but only 50% on tweets (Liu et al., 2011; Ritter et al., 2011).

These challenging social media characteristics are also opportunities for the development of new text mining approaches, which are better suited to media streams:

Short messages (microtexts): Twitter and most Facebook messages are very short (140 characters for tweets). Many semantic-based methods reviewed below supplement these with extra information and context coming from embedded URLs and hashtags.[4] For instance, Abel et al. (2011) augment tweets by linking them to contemporaneous news articles, whereas Mendes et al. (2010) exploit online hashtag glossaries to augment tweets.

Noisy content: Social media content often has unusual spelling (e.g., 2moro), irregular capitalisation (e.g., all capital or all lowercase letters), emoticons (e.g., :-P), and idiosyncratic abbreviations (e.g., ROFL, ZOMG). Spelling and capitalisation normalisation methods have been developed (Han and Baldwin, 2011), coupled with studies of location-based linguistic variations in shortening styles in microtexts (Gouws et al., 2011). Emoticons are used as strong sentiment indicators in opinion mining algorithms (see, e.g., Pak and Paroubek (2010)).

Conversational: This content has very conversational linguistic style, including ubiquitous use of slang and swear words. Moreover, microblog services like Twitter hide conversations amongst the stream of tweets and to fully interpret the meaning of a reply tweet it is often necessary to process it together with the preceding tweets in the conversation. In many cases, however, detecting conversational threads automatically is far from trivial, as threads can branch and more participants join.

Temporal: In addition to linguistic analysis, social media content lends itself to analysis along temporal lines, which is a relatively underresearched problem. Addressing the temporal dimension of social media is a prerequisite for much-needed models of conflicting and consensual information, as well as for modeling change in user interests. Moreover, temporal modeling can be combined with opinion mining, to examine the volatility of attitudes toward topics over time.

Social context is crucial for the correct interpretation of social media content. Semantic-based methods need to make use of social context (e.g., who is the user connected to, how frequently they interact), to

---

[4] A recently study of 1.1 million tweets has found that 26% of English tweets contain a URL, 16.6% – a hashtag, and 54.8% contain a user name mention (Carter et al., 2013)

derive automatically semantic models of social networks, measure user authority, cluster similar users into groups, as well as model trust and strength of connection.

User generated: Because users produce as well as consume social media content, there is a rich source of explicit and implicit information about the user; for example, demographics (gender, location, age, etc.), interests, opinions. The challenge here is that in some cases, user-generated content is relatively small, so corpus-based statistical methods cannot be applied successfully.

Multilingual: Social media content is strongly multilingual. For instance, less than 50% of tweets are in English, with Japanese, Spanish, Portuguese and German also featuring prominently (Carter et al., 2013). Unfortunately, semantic technology methods have so far mostly focused on English, while low-overhead adaptation to new languages still remains an open issue. Automatic language identification (Carter et al., 2013; Baldwin and Lui, 2010) is an important first step, allowing applications to first separate social media in language clusters, which can then be processed using different algorithms.

6.3 THE GATE FAMILY OF TEXT MINING TOOLS: AN OVERVIEW

The GATE family of open-source text mining tools has grown over the years to include a desktop application for researchers developing new algorithms, a collaborative workflow-based web application, an annotation indexing and retrieval server, a Java library, an architecture and a process. To summarise, GATE comprises:

- **GATE Developer**: An integrated development environment (IDE) for language processing components, which is bundled with a widely used information extraction (Cunningham et al., 2002) system and a diverse set of several hundred other plugins (Cunningham et al., 2013).
- **GATE Cloud** (Tablan et al., 2013): A cloud computing solution for hosted large-scale text processing.
- **GATE Teamware** (Bontcheva et al., 2013): A collaborative environment for large-scale manual semantic annotation projects built around a workflow engine and a heavily optimised back end service infrastructure.
- A multiparadigm index server, **GATE Mímir** (Cunningham et al., 2011b), which can be used to index and search over text, annotations, semantic schemas (ontologies), and semantic metadata (instances),

allowing queries that arbitrarily mix full text, structural, linguistic and semantic constraints and that can scale to terabytes of text.

- A framework, **GATE Embedded**: An object library optimised for inclusion in diverse applications giving access to all the services used by GATE Developer and others.
- An architecture: A high-level organisational picture of language processing software composition.
- A process for the creation of robust and maintainable NLP applications.

Note that GATE Developer and Embedded are bundled together, and in early distributions were referred to just as "GATE".

6.3.1 GATE Developer

GATE Developer is a specialist integrated development environment (IDE) for language engineering R&D. It is analogous to systems like Eclipse or Netbeans for programmers, or Mathematica or SPSS for mathematics or statistics work. The system performs tasks such as:

- Visualisation and editing of domain-specific data structures associated with text: annotation graphs, ontologies, terminologies, syntax trees, and so forth.
- Constructing applications from sets of components (or plugins).
- Measurement, evaluation and benchmarking of automatic systems relative to *gold standard* data produced by human beings, or to previous runs of variants of experimental setups.

A sophisticated graphical user interface provides access to the models of the GATE architecture and particular instantiations of that architecture.

Figure 6.1 displays a tweet, where the tweet text and JSON tweet metadata are imported as document content. The central pane shows a version of the source text from which formatting markup has been removed (and converted into arcs in an annotation graph associated with the document). The left pane details resources loaded in the system, including any application being used to annotate the text (e.g., TwitIE, see below) and the documents under analysis. The right pane lists the annotation types that exist in the document. Annotations are organised in annotation sets and here the "Original markups" set is shown, where the JSON fields are used to create different annotations. For example, a description annotation is created, which covers the text from the user profile ("The latest stories..."); a text annotation covers the tweet text ("Police sorry for..."), etc.

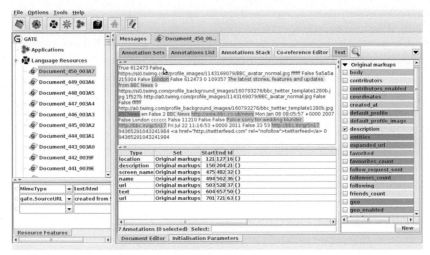

Figure 6.1 The GATE developer interface.

The central pane highlights the selected annotation types and there is also an optional annotations list table underneath, which shows more details on each annotation, including its start and end character offset, any features contained, and so on.

6.3.2 GATE Embedded

Underlying GATE Developer (and most of the rest of the GATE family tools) is an object-oriented Java framework called GATE Embedded. Some of the architectural principles that we adopted when developing the framework are as follows:

- *Neutrality*: The framework tries hard to be nonprescriptive and theory neutral. This is a strength because it means that no approach to language processing that users favour is excluded, but it is also a weakness because more restricted and specialised tools can capture more abstractions about their target domains.

- *Reuse*: We minimise the impact of that weakness by emphasising reuse and interoperation with related systems, and avoid reimplementation wherever possible. Thus GATE provides diverse XML support, integration with the OWLIM semantic repository (Kiryakov, 2006), the Weka machine learning library (Witten and Frank, 1999), the

Lingpipe[5] and OpenNLP[6] language analysis pipelines, the SVM Lite library (Li et al., 2009) and many others (see (Cunningham et al., 2011a)).

- *Componentisation*: Almost everything in GATE is modelled as a component, and the various component sets are all user extendable. This means that all the functions of the system can be swapped out, extended or replaced by users and developers with specific needs.
- *Multiple usage modes*: Almost all operations are available both from API (GATE Embedded) and UI (GATE Developer). A common process is to develop and test using the IDE and then embed in the target environment using the Java library. In both cases exactly the same underlying framework is in operation.

The set of plugins that are integrated with GATE is called CREOLE, a Collection of REusable Objects for Language Engineering. Components are defined as Java Beans bundled with XML configuration, and the overheads imposed by the model are very small (the minimal component comprises a few lines of Java code plus a few lines of XML). Components can be packaged in the same way as other Java libraries and can be loaded over the network via a URL.

GATE Embedded encapsulates a number of modular APIs for text processing, which cover functions including

- persistence, visualisation and editing;
- a finite state transduction language (JAPE, a java annotation patterns Engine (Cunningham et al., 2000));
- extraction of training instances for machine learning (ML – methods for automated abstraction of pattern recognition models from data, see, e.g., Carbonell et al. (1983))
- pluggable ML implementations (e.g., Weka (Witten and Frank, 1999), support vector machines (Li et al., 2009), etc.);
- components for language analysis, for example, parsers, taggers and stemmers for various languages;
- a very widely used information extraction system (ANNIE) that has been evaluated in comparative events including MUC, TREC, ACE, DUC, Pascal, NTCIR and so on (Gaizauskas et al., 1995; Voorhees and Harman, 1999; Iwayama et al., 2005; Li et al., 2005, 2007);
- indexing and search tools (including Lucene, Google and Yahoo plugins);
- a simple API for RDF, OWL and linked data.

---

[5] http://alias-i.com/lingpipe/
[6] http://opennlp.apache.org/

The modularity of the library and the low level of commitment imposed on its clients has proven flexible enough to prosper for more than a decade since the release of version 2 (the first Java version).

6.3.3 GATE Cloud

`GATECloud.net` (Tablan et al., 2013) is a web-based platform that deploys GATE analysis pipelines and GATE server products on Amazon EC2 (Elastic Compute Cloud – a popular cloud computing platform). GATE annotation pipelines provide a PaaS (platform as a service (Geelan, 2009)) arrangement: software produced using GATE Developer/Embedded can be trivially scaled up to large data volumes. In this way GATE Teamware and Mímir on the cloud provide a SaaS (software as a service) arrangement where responsibility for installation and administration are removed from the end user.

GATE Cloud is based on a **parallel** execution engine of automatic annotation processes (using pooling and model sharing to minimise the load on individual nodes) and **distributed** execution of the parallel engine (Tablan et al., 2013). Its characteristics include

- **scalability**: auto-scaling of processor swarms dependent on loading;
- **flexibility**: user-visible parameters configure system behaviour, select the GATE application being executed, the input protocol used for reading documents, the output protocol used for exporting the resulting annotations, and so on;
- **robustness**: jobs run unattended over large data sets using a parallelisation system that has been extensively tested and profiled.

In general, making optimal use of virtual IaaS infrastructures for data-intensive NLP again comes with a significant overhead; for example, having to learn the intricacies of Amazon's APIs for the elastic compute cloud and simple storage services. An added complication is that not all NLP algorithms are actually implementable in the MapReduce paradigm; for example, those requiring a shared global state.

Therefore, the GATECloud platform was designed as an open cloud platform that can run existing NLP algorithms on large data sets, as well as algorithms already adapted to Hadoop. Cloud infrastructural issues are dealt with by the GATECloud platform, completely transparently to the user, including load balancing, efficient data upload and storage, deployment on the virtual machines, security, fault tolerance, and resource usage.

6.4 INFORMATION EXTRACTION: AN OVERVIEW

Information extraction (IE) is a technology based on analysing natural language to extract snippets of information. For example, when extracting information about companies, key information to be identified would be the company address, contact phone, fax numbers, e-mail address, products and services, members of the board of directors and so on.

The process takes texts (and sometimes speech) as input and produces fixed-format data as output. This data may be used directly for display to users, or may be stored in a database or spreadsheet for later analysis, or may be used for indexing purposes in information retrieval (IR) applications such as Internet search engines like Google.

IE is quite different from IR:

- An IR system finds relevant texts and presents them to the user.
- An IE application analyses texts and presents only the specific information from them that the user is interested in.

The main tasks carried out during information extraction are

- named entity recognition, which consists on the identification and classification of different types of names in text;
- coreference resolution, which is the task of deciding if two linguistic expressions refer to the same entity in the discourse;
- relation extraction, which identifies relations between entities in text.

Information extraction usually employs the following natural language processing components: part-of-speech (POS) taggers, morphological analyser, named entity recognisers, full (or shallow) parsing and semantic interpretation. Generic versions of these linguistic processors are available in GATE (Cunningham et al., 2002), although some require adaptation to social media.

There are two main classes of approaches to information extraction:

1. Rule-based systems that are built by language engineers, who design lexicons and rules for extraction.
2. Machine learning systems that are trained to perform one or more of the IE tasks. Learning systems are given either an annotated training corpus (i.e., supervised machine learning) or unannotated corpus together with a small number of seed examples (i.e., unsupervised or lightly supervised methods).

The advantages of rule-based approaches are that they do not require training data to create (although a small gold standard is needed for evaluation) and harness human intuition and domain knowledge. Depending on the lexical and syntactic regularity of the target domain, rule creation ranges from extremely fast (when few, clear patterns exist) to rather time-consuming (if more ambiguities are present). Depending on the system design, some changes in requirements may be hard to accommodate. Because rule-based systems tend to require at least basic language processing skills, they are sometimes perceived as more expensive to create.

In comparison, machine learning approaches typically require at least some human-annotated training data, in order to reach good accuracy. While the cost per individual annotator is lower than the cost of language engineers, given the size of data needed, often more than one or two annotators are required. This raises the problem of interannotator agreement (or consistency), as the accuracy of the learnt models can be affected significantly by noisy, contradictory training data. However, getting training annotators to agree on their labels is again dependent on the complexity of the target annotations and could in itself be rather time-consuming. Another potential problem could arise if the semantic annotation requirements change after the training data has been annotated, as this may require substantial reannotation.

To summarise, both types of approaches have advantages and drawbacks and the choice of which one is more appropriate for a given application depends on the target domain, the complexity of the semantic annotations (including the size of the ontology), and the availability of trained human annotators and/or language engineers. Last but not least, there is no reason why one cannot have a hybrid approach, which uses both rules and machine learning.

6.5 IE FROM SOCIAL MEDIA WITH GATE

GATE comes prepackaged with the ANNIE general purpose IE pipeline. ANNIE consists of the following main processing resources: tokeniser, sentence splitter, POS tagger, gazetteer lists, finite state transducer (based on GATE's built-in regular expressions over annotations language (Cunningham et al., 2002)), orthomatcher and coreference resolver. The resources communicate via GATE's annotation API (Cunningham et al., 2002), which is a directed graph of arcs bearing arbitrary feature/value data, and nodes rooting this data into document content (in this case text).

The ANNIE components can be used individually or coupled together with new modules in order to create new applications. For example, we reuse the ANNIE sentence splitter and name gazetteers unmodified on social media content, but retrain and adapt other components to the specifics of this genre.

Adaptation to the specifics of the social media genre is required, to address the genre-specific challenges discussed in Section 6.2. General purpose linguistic tools such as POS taggers and entity recognisers do particularly badly on such texts (see Sections 6.5.4 and 6.5.6, respectively).

Therefore, we have developed TwitIE – a customisation of ANNIE, specific to social media content, which we have currently tested most extensively on microblog messages. The latter content is both readily available as a large public stream and also is the most challenging to process with generic IE tools, due to the shortness, noisy nature, and prevalence of slang and Twitter-specific conventions.

Figure 6.2 shows the TwitIE pipeline and its components. TwitIE is distributed as a plugin in GATE, which needs to be loaded for these processing resources to appear in GATE Developer. Components reused from ANNIE without any modification are shown in blue, whereas the red ones are new and specific to social media.

The first step is language identification, which is discussed next (Section 6.5.1), followed by the TwitIE tokeniser (Section 6.5.2).

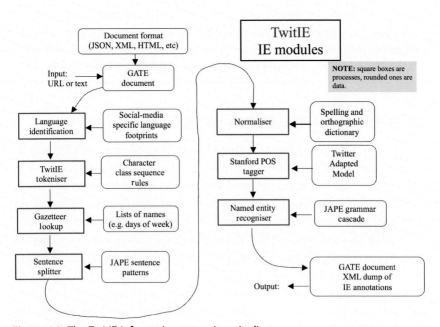

Figure 6.2 The TwitIE information extraction pipeline.

The **gazetteer** consists of lists such as cities, organisations, days of the week, and so on. It not only consists of entities, but also of names of useful *indicators*, such as typical company designators (e.g., "Ltd."), titles, and so forth. The gazetteer lists are compiled into finite state machines, which can match text tokens. TwitIE reuses the ANNIE gazetteer lists, at present, without any modification.

The **sentence splitter** is a cascade of finite-state transducers, which segments text into sentences. This module is required for the POS tagger. Again, at present, the ANNIE sentence splitter is reused without modification, although when processing tweets, it is also possible to just use the text of the tweet as one sentence, without further analysis.

The normaliser, the adapted POS tagger, and named entity recognition are discussed in detail in Sections 6.5.3, 6.5.4 and 6.5.6, respectively.

We have also included a section on stemming and morphological analysis in GATE (Section 6.5.5), as these can be useful in some applications. By default they are not included in the TwitIE pipeline, but can easily be added, if required.

6.5.1 Language Identification

It is critical to determine the language in which a document is written, to know which tools to apply. The *language identification* task is thus typically performed before other linguistic processing, having as its goal to output a language suggestion given some unprocessed text. We consider two types of approach: n-gram frequency-based and n-gram information gain-based.

Both approaches include an implicit tokenisation step, though this is speculative and does not inform later processes in the GATE TwitIE pipeline. TextCat (Cavnar and Trenkle, 1994) relies on n-gram frequency models to discriminate between languages, relying on token sequences that are strong language differentiators. The information gain-based langid.py (Lui and Baldwin, 2012) uses n-grams to learn a multinomial event model, with a feature selection process designed to cope with variations of expression between text domains. They have both been adapted for microblog text, using human-annotated data from Twitter. The TextCat adaptation (Carter et al., 2013) works on a limited set of languages; the langid.py adaptation (Preotiuc-Pietro et al., 2012) on 97 languages.

We evaluated four system runs on the ILPS TextCat microblog evaluation data set.[7] Results are given in Table 6.1, with the Twitter-specific

---

[7] http://ilps.science.uva.nl/resources/twitterlid.

Table 6.1 Language classification accuracy on the ILPS data set for systems before and after adaptation to the microblog genre

System	Overall accuracy	English	Dutch	French	German	Spanish
TextCat	89.5%	88.4%	90.2%	86.2%	94.6%	88.0%
langid	89.5%	92.5%	89.1%	89.4%	94.3%	83.0%
TextCat (-twitter)	**97.4%**	**99.4%**	**97.6%**	**95.2%**	**98.6%**	**96.2%**
langid (-twitter)	87.7%	88.7%	88.8%	88.0%	92.5%	81.6%

versions marked "-twitter". It should be noted that the adapted version of TextCat has a slightly easier task than langid.py does, as it expects only five language choices, whereas the adapted langid.py is choosing labels from a set of 97 languages. The latter assigned a language outside the five available to 6.3% of tweets in the evaluation set. Why the adapted langid.py performed worse than the generic version is not clear; the results are quite close for some languages, and so if an approximate 6% improvement could be made in these cases, the Twitter-adapted version would be better.

The results below demonstrate that language identification is harder on tweets than longer texts. Nevertheless, it has reasonable accuracy, which can be used to inform choices of later tools, without introducing too many errors.

Given the above much higher results, only the adapted TextCat is distributed as part of the GATE TwitIE plugin. Due to the shortness of tweets, it makes the assumption that each tweet is written in only one language. The choice of languages used for categorisation is specified through a configuration file, supplied as an initialisation parameter.

Figure 6.3 shows three tweets, one English, one German and one French. TwitIE TextCat was used to assign automatically the lang feature to the tweet text (denoted by the Tweet annotation).

Given a collection of tweets in a new language, it is possible to train TwitIE TextCat to support that new language as well. This is done by using the Fingerprint Generation PR, included in the `Language_Identification` GATE Plugin (Cunningham et al., 2011a). It builds a new fingerprint from a corpus of documents.

Reliable tweet language identification allows us to only process those tweets written in English with the TwitIE English POS tagger and named entity recogniser. GATE also provides POS tagging and named entity recognition in French and German, so it is possible to process tweets differently, dependent upon the language they are written in. This is achieved by

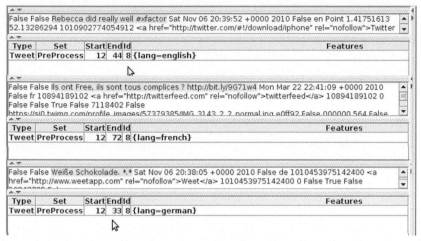

Figure 6.3 Example tweets annotated by TextCat.

making the execution of these components conditional on the respective tweet being in English, German, or French, by using a conditional corpus pipeline (Cunningham et al., 2011a).

6.5.2 Tokenisation

Tokenisation is the task of splitting the input text into very simple units, called tokens. Tokenisation is a required step in any linguistic processing application, because more complex algorithms typically work on tokens as their input, rather than using the raw text. Consequently, it is important to use a high-quality tokeniser, as errors are likely to affect the results of all subsequent NLP algorithms.

Different languages require different tokenisers, with some easier than others (Mcnamee and Mayfield, 2004). Even punctuation use can differ between languages for the microblog genre, in which "smileys" (comprised of extended sequences of punctuation symbols) are prevalent.

Commonly distinguished types of tokens are numbers, symbols (e.g., $, %), punctuation and words of different kinds (e.g., uppercase, lowercase, mixed case). Tokenising well-written text is generally reliable and reusable, as it tends to be domain-independent. One widely used tokeniser for English is bundled in the open-source ANNIE system in GATE (Cunningham et al., 2002).

However, such general purpose tokenisers need to be adapted to work correctly on social media, to handle specific tokens like URLs, hashtags (e.g., #nlproc), user mentions in microblogs (e.g., @GateAcUk), special abbreviations (e.g., RT, ROFL), and emoticons. A study of 1.1 million tweets established that 26% of English tweets have a URL, 16.6% – a hashtag, and 54.8% – a user name mention (Carter et al., 2013). Therefore, tokenising these accurately is very important.

To take one tweet as an example:

```
#WiredBizCon #nike vp said when @Apple saw what
http://nikeplus.com did, #SteveJobs was like wow I didn't
expect this at all.
```

One option is to tokenise on white space alone, but this does not work that well for hashtags and @mentions. In our example, if we have #nike and @Apple as one token each, this will make their recognition as company names harder, because the named entity recognition algorithm will need to look at subtoken level. Similarly, tokenising on white space and punctuation characters does not work well, because in that case URLs get separated in more than one token (e.g., http, nikeplus), as are emoticons and e-mail addresses.

Therefore, the TwitIE tokeniser in GATE is an adaptation of the ANNIE English tokeniser. It follows Ritter's tokenisation scheme (Ritter et al., 2011). More specifically, it treats abbreviations (e.g., RT, ROFL) and URLs as one token each. Hashtags and user mentions are two tokens (i.e., # and nike in the above example) plus a separate annotation HashTag covering both. Capitalisation is preserved, but an orthography feature is added: all caps, lowercase, mixCase. Lowercasing and emoticons are optionally done in separate modules, as they are not always needed. Consequently, tokenisation is faster and more generic, as well as more tailored to the needs of named entity recognition.

In terms of implementation, the TwitIE tokeniser relies on a set of regular expression rules which are then compiled into a finite-state machine. This differs from most other tokenisers in that it maximises efficiency by doing only very light processing, and enabling greater flexibility by placing the burden of deeper processing on the grammar rules, which are more adaptable. For example, there is a specialised set of rules for recognising the hashtags and user mentions.

To evaluate the benefit from making adaptations to microblog and social media content, we compare the TwitIE tokeniser against the general purpose ANNIE tokeniser in GATE (Cunningham et al., 2002) on Ritter's

Table 6.2 Tokeniser performance on sample microblog text

Approach	Precision	Recall	F1
ANNIE Tokeniser	90%	72%	80%
TwitIE Tokeniser	**98%**	**94%**	**96%**

tweet data set (Ritter et al., 2011). Performance was measured in terms of precision and recall, as well as F1 measure, and is given in Table 6.2.

The original tokeniser performed poorly, reaching an F1 of only 80% (near 100% is typical), and with many errors around punctuation and Twitter-specific entities. This is too weak to accurately inform later tasks. Smileys cause some trouble for tokenisers, many of which do not occur in the training data. Orthographic errors are also rife in this genre, an analysis of which can be found in Foster et al. (2011). Aside from smileys and typos, the low performance of a conventional tokeniser such as this is mostly due to differing tokenisation rules regarding user names and Twitter-specific content.

6.5.3 Normalisation

Noisy environments such as microblog text pose challenges to existing tools, being rich in previously unseen tokens, elision of words, and unusual grammar. Normalisation is commonly proposed as a solution for overcoming or reducing linguistic noise (Sproat et al., 2001). The task is generally approached in two stages: first, the identification of orthographic errors in an input discourse, and second, the correction of these errors.

Example 6.1 shows an original microblog message, including a variety of errors, and the postnormalisation repaired version.

Example 6.1 Source text: *@DORSEY33 lol aw . i thought u was talkin bout another time . nd i dnt see u either !*

Normalised text: *@DORSEY33 lol aww . I thought you was talking about another time . And I didn't see you either !*

As can be seen, not all the errors can be corrected (*was* ought to be *were*, for example) and some genre-specific slang remains – thought not in a particularly ambiguous sense or grammatically crucial place. Note the frequent shortening of words in messages entered by users, possibly attributable to both their effort to minimise the energy cost of communication and also out of habit of fitting within the tight message length limits typical of the genre.

Normalisation approaches are typically based on a correction list, edit distance based, cluster-based, or a mixture of these, with hybrid approaches common. They often include a dictionary of known correctly spelled terms, and refer to in-vocabulary (IV) and out-of-vocabulary (OOV) terms with respect to this dictionary.

One common source of errors on social media content is variation of spelling of proper names, which in turn impacts the accuracy of named entity recognition. Therefore, resources have been developed to capture the many variations on spellings seen for given entities. For example, JRC-Names (Steinberger et al., 2011) is a list-based collection of name variations for many entities, coupled with an algorithm for matching target words to a given entity. An integration of JRC-Names into GATE is currently ongoing.

Dictionary-based approaches can be used to repair errors on all kinds of words, not just named entities; for example, Han et al. (2012) construct a general purpose spelling correction dictionary for microblogs. This achieves state-of-the-art performance on both the detection of misspelled words and also applying the right correction.

The TwitIE normaliser is currently a combination of a generic spelling correction dictionary and a spelling correction DICTIONARY specific to

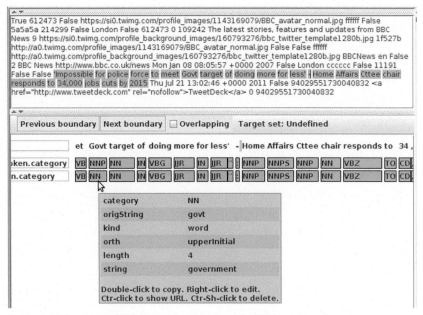

Figure 6.4 Comparing POS tagger output: a normalisation example.

social media. The latter contains entries such as "2moro" and "brb", similar to Han et al. (2012). Figure 6.4 shows an example output from normalisation, where the abbreviation "Govt" has been normalised to government.

Instead of a fixed list of variations, it is also possible to use a heuristic to suggest correct spellings. Both, text edit distance and phonetic distance can be used to find candidate matches for words identified as misspelled. Han and Baldwin (2011) achieved good corrections in many cases by using a combination of Levenshtein distance and double-metaphone distance between known words and words identified as incorrectly entered. We experimented also with this normalisation approach in TwitIE, with mixed success. Namely, this method has higher recall – more wrong words can be corrected by the resource – but lower precision, in that some corrections are wrong. A detailed error analysis and evaluation of dictionary-based versus heuristic normalisation is presented in Derczynski et al. (2013).

6.5.4 Part of Speech Tagging

Part of speech (POS) tagging is concerned with tagging words with their part of speech, by taking into account the word itself, as well as the context in which it appears. A key part of this task is the tag set used and the distinctions that it makes. The main categories are verb, noun, adjective, adverb, preposition, and so on. However, tag sets tend to be much more specific; for example, distinguishing between singular and plural nouns. One commonly used tag set is the Penn Treebank one (referred to as PTB) (Marcus et al., 1994).

In terms of approaches, researchers have achieved excellent results with hidden Markov models, rule-based approaches, maximum entropy, and many other methods. GATE's English POS tagger (Hepple, 2000) is a modified version of the Brill transformational rule-based tagger (Brill, 1992), which produces a POS tag as an annotation on each word or symbol, using the Penn treebank tag set. The tagger uses a default lexicon and ruleset (the result of training on a large corpus taken from *The Wall Street Journal*). Both of these can be modified manually if necessary.

Later, Toutanova et al. (2003) introduced the Stanford POS tagger, trained on newswire texts. It has sophisticated feature generation, especially for unknown words, and a highly configurable re-trainable engine. This is generally thought to represent the current state of the art for news texts and is also integrated in GATE. Models using the PTB set are available for both these taggers.

The accuracy of these general purpose English POS taggers is typically excellent (97-98%) on texts similar to those on which the taggers have been trained (mostly news articles). However, they are not suitable for microblogs and other short, noisy social media content, where their accuracy declines to 70–75% (Derczynski et al., 2013).

Thus the TwitIE application in GATE now contains an adapted model for the Stanford POS tagger, trained on PTB-tagged tweets. Extra tag labels have been added for retweets, URLs, hashtags and user mentions. The Stanford POS tagger was retrained (Derczynski et al., 2013) using some hand-annotated tweets (Ritter et al., 2011), the NPS IRC corpus (Forsyth and Martell, 2007), and news texts (*The Wall Street Journal* part of the Penn treebank (Marcus et al., 1994)). The resulting model achieves 83.14% POS tagging accuracy, which is still below the 97% achieved on news content.

The most common mistakes (just over 27%) arise from words that are common in general, but do not occur in the training data, indicating a need for a larger training POS-tagged corpus of social media content. Another 27% of errors arise from slang words, which are ubiquitous in social media content and are also often misspelled (e.g., *LUVZ*, *HELLA* and *2night*) and another 8% from typos. Many of these can be addressed using normalisation (see Section 6.5.3). Close to 9% of errors arise from tokenisation mistakes (e.g., joined words). Lastly, 9% of errors are words to which a label may be reliably assigned automatically, including URLs, hash tags, retweets and smileys, which we now pre-tag automatically with regular expressions and lookup lists.

Another frequently made mistake is tagging a proper noun (NN/NNP) – an observation also made by Ritter et al. (2011). Therefore, we use GATE's ANNIE gazetteer lists of personal first names and cities (Cunningham et al., 2002) and, in addition, a manually constructed list of unambiguous corporation and website names frequently mentioned in the training data (e.g., *YouTube*, *Toyota*).

Therefore, by combining normalisation, gazetteer name lookup, and regular expression-based tagging of Twitter-specific POS tags, we achieve performance improvement from 83.14% accuracy to 86.93%. By generating additional 1.5M training tokens from automatically annotated tweets using two preexisting POS taggers (namely (Ritter et al., 2011; Gimpel et al., 2011)), we improve further the performance of the Twitter-adapted Stanford POS tagger to 90.54% token accuracy. For further details on the evaluation see Derczynski et al. (2013).

The Twitter-tailored Stanford POS tagger is part of the GATE TwitIE plugin. It is distributed with the specially trained model discussed above. To ensure the best possible performance, it needs to be run after the TwitIE tokeniser and normaliser. Because it is currently trained only on English content, it should only be run on tweets identified as English by the TwitIE language identifier.

Figure 6.4 shows an example tweet, which has been tagged both without normalisation (upper row of POS tags) and with tweet normalisation (the lower row of POS tags). The word "Govt" is normalised to government, which is then tagged correctly as NN, instead of NNP.

6.5.5 Stemming and Morphological Analysis

Another set of useful low-level processing components are stemmers and morphological analysers. Stemmers produce the stem form of each word, for example, "driving" and "drivers" have the stem "drive", whereas morphological analysis tends to produce the root/lemma forms of the words and their affixes, for example, "drive" and "driver" for the above examples, with affixes "ing" and "s", respectively.

GATE provides a wrapper for the widely used, open-source Snowball stemmers, which cover 11 European languages (Danish, Dutch, English, Finnish, French, German, Italian, Norwegian, Portuguese, Russian, Spanish and Swedish) and makes them straightforward to combine with the other low-level linguistic components. The stemmers are rule-based (Porter, 1980) and easy to modify, following the suffix-stripping approach of Porter.

The English morphological analyser in GATE is also rule-based, with the rule language supporting rules and variables that can be used in regular expressions in the rules. POS tags can taken into account if desired, depending on a configuration parameter.

6.5.6 Named Entity Recognition

Named entity recognition (NER) is difficult on user-generated content in general, and in the microblog genre specifically, because of the reduced amount of contextual information in short messages and a lack of curation of content by third parties (e.g., that done by editors for newswire). In this section, we examine how the ANNIE NER component from GATE (Cunningham et al., 2002) performs in comparison to a Twitter-specific approach, on a corpus of 2 400 tweets comprising 34,000 tokens (Ritter et al., 2011). Namely, we compare here against Ritter et al. (2011), who take

Table 6.3 Named entity recognition performance

System	Precision	Recall	F1
ANNIE	47%	**83%**	60%
TwitIE	77%	**83%**	**80%**
Ritter	73%	49%	59%

a pipeline approach, performing first tokenisation and PoS tagging before using topic models to find named entities. For an in-depth comparison against other approaches (including Stanford NER (Finkel et al., 2005)) and error analysis, see Derczynski et al. (2013).

Results are given in Table 6.3. We did not consider percent-type entity annotations in these evaluations because there were so few (3 in the whole corpus) and they were all annotated correctly.

In the first experiment, we compared the default ANNIE pipeline against our TwitIE pipeline, and found an absolute Precision increase of 30% – mainly with respect to date, Organisation and in particular person. Recall remained identical after TwitIE's customised tokenisation, normalisation, and POS tagging, which led to an increase of 20% in F1. Note that we did not consider the Twitter-specific UserID annotation as a person annotation, as these were all 100% correct. Because the regular ANNIE does not consider these, there were many false positive Person annotations as part of UserIDs.

Both ANNIE and TwitIE currently use the same named entity recognition grammars, so part of our ongoing research is now on adapting these to social media. As we can see microblog domain adaptation is critical to good NER. Thanks to adaptation in the earlier components in TwitIE, we demonstrate a +30% absolute precision and +20% absolute F1 performance increase. However, compared against state-of-the-art NER performance on longer news content, an overall F1 score of 80% leaves significant amounts of missed annotations and generates false positives.

6.6 CONCLUSION AND FUTURE WORK

This chapter discussed the problem of extracting information from social media content and presented a number of state-of-the-art open-source GATE tools, comprising the TwitIE IE pipeline. As can be seen from the evaluation results reported here, even though significant inroads have been made into this challenging problem, there is still a significant gap in accuracy, when compared against performance on news texts, mostly due to insufficient linguistic context and lack of training data. Next we discussed how further improvements can be made.

One source of additional context is the geospatial information present in social media. A notable proportion comes explicitly geotagged (Sadilek et al., 2012), and studies suggest that it is possible to infer the geolocations of about half of the remaining such content (Rout et al., 2013b). Social media also has at least a creation time as temporal context. None of this explicit and implicit spatiotemporal (ST) metadata is currently exploited by the methods discussed above, which is one promising avenue for future work. Our ongoing work here is on evaluating and adapting the TIMEN approach (Llorens et al., 2012) to social media content.

A second key major open issue is lack of sufficient amounts of training and evaluation gold standard corpora of social media content. For example, there are fewer than 10,000 tweets hand-annotated with named entities, which hampers the development of high-performance machine learning algorithms. Crowdsourcing has recently emerged as a promising method for creating shared evaluation data sets (Sabou et al., 2012). Adapting these efforts to the specifics of creating large-scale training and evaluation corpora is the second key focus of future work on TwitIE.

ACKNOWLEDGEMENTS

This work was supported by funding from the Engineering and Physical Sciences Research Council (grants EP/I004327/1 and EP/K017896/1) and by the EU-funded FP7 TrendMiner[8] project.

REFERENCES

Abel, F., Gao, Q., Houben, G.J., Tao, K., 2011. Semantic enrichment of Twitter posts for user profile construction on the social web. In: ESWC, 2, pp. 375–389.

Baldwin, T., Lui, M., 2010. Language identification: The long and the short of the matter. In: Human Language Technologies: The 2010 Annual Conference of the North American Chapter of the Association for Computational Linguistics, Los Angeles, CA, pp. 229–237.

Bontcheva, K., Cunningham, H., 2011. Semantic annotation and retrieval: Manual, semi-automatic and automatic generation. In: Domingue, J., Fensel, D., Hendler, J.A. (Eds.), Handbook of Semantic Web Technologies. Springer, New York.

Bontcheva, K., Cunningham, H., Roberts, I., Roberts, A., Tablan, V., Aswani, N., et al., 2013. Gate teamware, a web-based, collaborative text annotation framework. Language Resources and Evaluation 47 (4).

Bontcheva, K., Rout, D., 2014. Making sense of social media through semantics: A survey, Semantic Web – Interoperability, Usability, Applicability 5 (50), 373–403.

---

[8] http://www.trendminer-project.eu/

Brill, E., 1992. A simple rule-based part-of-speech tagger. In: Proceedings of the Third Conference on Applied Natural Language Processing. Trento, Italy.

Carbonell, J., Michalski, R., Mitchell, T., 1983. An overview of machine learning. In: Carbonell, J., Michalski, R., Mitchell, T. (Eds.), Machine Learning: An Artificial Intelligence Approach. Tioga Pub. Co., Palo Alto, CA, pp. 3–23

Carter, S., Weerkamp, W., Tsagkias, E., 2013. Microblog language identification: Overcoming the limitations of short, unedited and idiomatic text. Language Resources and Evaluation Journal 47 (1), 195–215.

Cavnar, W., Trenkle, J., 1994. N-gram-based text categorization. In: Proceedings of the Annual Symposium on Document Analysis and Information Retrieval, pp. 161–175.

Cunningham, H., Maynard, D., Bontcheva, K., Tablan, V., 2002. Gate: an architecture for development of robust hlt applications. In: Proceedings of the 40th Annual Meeting on Association for Computational Linguistics, 712 July 2002, ACL 02. Association for Computational Linguistics, Stroudsburg, PA, USA, pp. 168–175.

Cunningham, H., Maynard, D., Bontcheva, K., Tablan, V., Aswani, N., Roberts, I., Gorrell, G., Funk, A., Roberts, A., Damljanovic, D., Heitz, T., Greenwood, M., Saggion, H., Petrak, J., Peters, W., 2011. Text processing with GATE (version 6). http://www.amazon.com/gp/product/0956599311?keywords=Bontcheva&qid=1444125689&ref_=sr_1_1&sr=8-1.

Cunningham, H., Maynard, D., Tablan, V., 2000. JAPE: a Java Annotation Patterns Engine (Second Edition). Research Memorandum CS-00-10, Department of Computer Science University of Sheffield, Sheffield, UK.

Cunningham, H., Tablan, V., Roberts, A., Bontcheva, K., 2013. Getting more out of biomedical documents with gate's full lifecycle open source text analytics. PLoS Comput. Biol. 9 (2), e1002854.

Cunningham, H., Tablan, V., Roberts, I., Greenwood, M.A., Aswani, N., 2011. Information extraction and semantic annotation for multi-paradigm information management. In: Lupu, M., Mayer, K., Tait, J., Trippe, A.J. (Eds.), Current Challenges in Patent Information Retrieval. In: The Information Retrieval Series, vol.29. Springer, Berlin, Heidelberg, pp. 307–327.

Derczynski, L., Maynard, D., Aswani, N., Bontcheva, K., 2013. Microblog-genre noise and impact on semantic annotation accuracy. In: Proceedings of the 24th ACM Conference on Hypertext and Social Media. ACM.

Finkel, J., Grenager, T., Manning, C., 2005. Incorporating non-local information into information extraction systems by Gibbs sampling. In: Proceedings of the 43rd Annual Meeting on Association for Computational Linguistics, Association for Computational Linguistics, pp. 363–370.

Forsyth, E., Martell, C., 2007. Lexical and discourse analysis of online chat dialog. In: International Conference on Semantic Computing. IEEE, pp. 19–26.

Foster, J., Çetinoglu, O., Wagner, J., Le Roux, J., Hogan, S., Nivre, J., et al., 2011. #hardtoparse: Pos tagging and parsing the twitterverse. In: Proceedings of the AAAI Workshop On Analyzing Microtext, pp. 20–25.

Gaizauskas, R., Wakao, T., Humphreys, K., Cunningham, H., Wilks, Y., 1995. Description of the LaSIE system as used for MUC-6. In: Proceedings of the Sixth Message Understanding Conference (MUC-6), 6–8 November. Morgan Kaufmann, California, pp. 207–220.

Geelan, J., 2009. Twenty-one experts define cloud computing, [online], SYS-CON Media Inc., http://virtualization.sys-con.com/node/612375.

Gimpel, K., Schneider, N., O'Connor, B., Das, D., Mills, D., Eisenstein, J., Heilman, M., Yogatama, D., Flanigan, J., Smith, N., 2011. Part-of-speech tagging for twitter: annotation, features, and experiments. In: Proceedings of the 49th Annual Meeting of the Association for Computational Linguistics: Human Language Technologies. ACL, pp. 42–47.

Gouws, S., Metzler, D., Cai, C., Hovy, E., 2011. Contextual bearing on linguistic variation in social media. In: Proceedings of the Workshop on Languages in Social Media, LSM '11, pp. 20–29.

Han, B., Baldwin, T., 2011. Lexical normalisation of short text messages: makn sens a #twitter. In: Proceedings of the 49th Annual Meeting of the Association for Computational Linguistics: Human Language Technologies. HLT'11, pp. 368–378.

Han, B., Cook, P., Baldwin, T., 2012. Automatically constructing a normalisation dictionary for microblogs. In: Proceedings of the conference on Empirical Methods in Natural Language Processing, ACL, pp. 421–432.

Hepple, M., 2000. Independence and commitment: Assumptions for rapid training and execution of rule-based part-of-speech taggers. In: Proceedings of the 38th Annual Meeting of the Association for Computational Linguistics, Hong Kong.

Iwayama, M., Fujii, A., Kando, N., 2005. Overview of classification subtask at NTCIR-5 patent retrieval task. In: Proceedings of the Fifth NTCIR Workshop Meeting on Evaluation of Information Access Technologies: Information Retrieval, Question Answering and Cross-lingual Information Access, 6–9 December, pp. 278–286.

Kiryakov, A., 2006. OWLIM: balancing between scalable repository and light-weight reasoner. In: Proceedings of the 15th International World Wide Web Conference (WWW2006), 23–26 May, 2010. Edinburgh, Scotland.

Li, Y., Bontcheva, K., Cunningham, H., 2005. SVM based learning system for information extraction. In: Winkler, J., Niranjan, M., Lawerence, N. (Eds.), Deterministic and Statistical Methods in Machine Learning. In: Lecture Notes in Computer Science, vol. 3635. Springer Verlag, Sheffield, UK, pp. 319–339. First International Workshop, 7-10 September, 2004.

Li, Y., Bontcheva, K., Cunningham, H., 2007. Cost sensitive evaluation measures for f-term patent classification. In: The First International Workshop on Evaluating Information Access (EVIA 2007), 15 May, Tokyo, Japan, pp. 44–53.

Li, Y., Bontcheva, K., Cunningham, H., 2009. Adapting SVM for data sparseness and imbalance: A case study on information extraction. Natural Lang. Eng. 15 (2), 241–271.

Liu, X., Zhang, S., Wei, F., Zhou, M., 2011. Recognizing named entities in tweets. In: Proceedings of the 49th Annual Meeting of the Association for Computational Linguistics: Human Language Technologies, pp. 359–367.

Liu, X., Zhou, M., Wei, F., Fu, Z., Zhou, X., 2012. Joint inference of named entity recognition and normalization for tweets. In: Proceedings of the Association for Computational Linguistics, pp. 526–535.

Llorens, H., Derczynski, L., Gaizauskas, R.J., Saquete, E., 2012. Timen: An open temporal expression normalisation resource. In: Proceedings of the Eighth International Conference on Language Resources and Evaluation (LREC), Istanbul, Turkey, pp. 3044–3051.

Lui, M., Baldwin, T., 2012. langid. py: An off-the-shelf language identification tool. In: Proceedings of the 50th Annual Meeting of the Association for Computational Linguistics (ACL 2012). Demo Session, Jeju, Republic of Korea.

Marcus, M.P., Santorini, B., Marcinkiewicz, M.A., 1994. Building a large annotated corpus of English: The Penn Treebank. Comput. Linguist. 19 (2), 313–330.

Maynard, D., Bontcheva, K., Rout, D., 2012. Challenges in developing opinion mining tools for social media. In: Proceedings of @NLP can u tag #usergeneratedcontent?! Workshop at LREC 2012, Turkey.

Mcnamee, P., Mayfield, J., 2004. Character n-gram tokenization for European language text retrieval. Informat. Retriev. 7 (1), 73–97.

Mendes, P.N., Passant, A., Kapanipathi, P., Sheth, A.P., 2010. Linked open social signals. In: Proceedings of the 2010 IEEE/WIC/ACM International Conference on Web Intelligence and Intelligent Agent Technology, WI-IAT '10. IEEE Computer Society, Washington, DC, USA, pp. 224–231.

Pak, A., Paroubek, P., 2010. Twitter based system: Using twitter for disambiguating sentiment ambiguous adjectives. In: Proceedings of the 5th International Workshop on Semantic Evaluation, pp. 436–439.

Porter, M., 1980. An algorithm for suffix stripping. Program 14 (3), 130–137.

Preotiuc-Pietro, D., Samangooei, S., Cohn, T., Gibbins, N., Niranjan, M., 2012. Trendminer: An architecture for real time analysis of social media text. In: Proceedings of the workshop on Real-Time Analysis and Mining of Social Streams.

Ravikant, N., Rifkin, A., 2010. Why twitter is massively undervalued compared to Facebook. URL http://techcrunch.com/2010/10/16/why-twitter-is-massively-undervalued-compared-to-facebook/ TechCrunch.

Ritter, A., Clark, S., Mausam, Etzioni O., 2011. Named entity recognition in tweets: An experimental study. In: Proc. of Empirical Methods for Natural Language Processing (EMNLP), Edinburgh, UK.

Rout, D., Bontcheva, K., Hepple, M., 2013. Reliably evaluating summaries of twitter timelines. In: Proceedings of the AAAI Symposium on Analyzing Microtext.

Rout, D., Preotiuc-Pietro, D., Bontcheva, K., Cohn, T., 2013. Where's @wally? a classification approach to geolocating users based on their social ties. In: Proceedings of the 24th ACM Conference on Hypertext and Social Media.

Sabou, M., Bontcheva, K., Scharl, A., 2012. Crowdsourcing research opportunities: Lessons from natural language processing. In: 12th International Conference on Knowledge Management and Knowledge Technologies (I-KNOW), pp. 17–24.

Sadilek, A., Kautz, H., Silenzio, V., 2012. Modeling spread of disease from social interactions. In: International AAAI Conference on Weblogs and Social Media (ICWSM). AAAI, pp. 322–329.

Skeels, M.M., Grudin, J., 2009. When social networks cross boundaries: A case study of workplace use of Facebook and LinkedIn. In: Proceedings of the ACM 2009 international conference on Supporting group work. GROUP09. ACM, New York, USA, pp. 95–104.

Sproat, R., Black, A., Chen, S., Kumar, S., Ostendorf, M., Richards, C., 2001. Normalization of non-standard words. Comput. Speech Lang. 15 (3), 287–333.

Steinberger, R., Pouliquen, B., Kabadjov, M., Belyaeva, J., van der Goot, E., 2011. JRC-names: A freely available, highly multilingual named entity resource. In: Proceedings of the 8th International Conference in Recent Advances in Natural Language Processing, pp. 104–110.

Tablan, V., Roberts, I., Cunningham, H., Bontcheva, K., 2013. Gatecloud.net: a platform for large-scale, open-source text processing on the cloud. Phil. Trans. R. Soc. A 371 (1983), 20120071.

Toutanova, K., Klein, D., Manning, C.D., Singer, Y., 2003. Feature-rich part-of-speech tagging with a cyclic dependency network. In: Proceedings of the 2003 Conference of the North American Chapter of the Association for Computational Linguistics on Human Language Technology, NAACL '03, pp. 173–180.

Voorhees, E.M., Harman, D., 1999. Overview of the eighth Text REtrieval Conference (TREC-8). In: The Eighth Text REtrieval Conference (TREC-8), 16–19 November 1999, National Institute of Standards and Technology (NIST), pp. 1–24.

Witten, I.H., Frank, E., 1999. Data Mining: Practical Machine Learning Tools and Techniques with Java Implementations. The Morgan Kaufmann Series in Data Management Systems. Morgan Kaufmann, San Francisco, CA.

CHAPTER 7

Newton: Building an Authority-Driven Company Tagging and Resolution System

M. Thomas*, H. Bretz*, T. Vacek*, B. Hachey[†], S. Singh*, F. Schilder*

*Thomson Reuters, NYC, NY, USA
[†]University of Sydney, Sydney, Australia

7.1 INTRODUCTION

The Newton tagging and resolution system was developed to tag company mentions in text and resolve them against an authority file of 32,000 companies. Given a stream of input documents, the system needs to identify and resolve not only unambiguous company names (e.g., *Chesapeake Energy*), but it also has to recognise that some company names can be ambiguous, as in the following example sentence[1]:

> *Despite the example of Chesapeake Energy, whose high-cost natural gas wells in the Northeast became unprofitable with falling prices, the continued strength of oil is pushing Occidental to keep investing.*

Short ambiguous company names have to be resolved correctly if used in a company sense. *Occidental* in (7.1), for example, refers to the *Occidental Petroleum Corporation*, but it would not, if used in a different context, such as *Occidental College*.

The Newton system was designed and developed with these challenges in mind and incorporated into a larger production system for text processing. The requirements for this production system were twofold: (a) the tagging and resolution system deployed on a customer machine needs to run sufficiently fast, (b) the tagging and resolution needs to be done with acceptable accuracy. The range of acceptable precision and recall values depend on the respective use case, but often range between 0.7 and 0.9.

---

[1] There are three companies in our authority file that may be referred to by *Northeast*: Northeast Community Bancorp, Inc., Northeast Pharmaceutical Group, Co., and Northeast Digital Networks, Inc.

We addressed these requirements by utilising the UIMA framework[2] and by solving the quality problem via a two-stage tagging and resolution approach. As a first step, a look-up tagger extracts all potential company mentions including short ambiguous ones (e.g., "United" or "Occidental"). This step identifies possible mentions and generates candidate entities for resolution. The second step consists of a classifier that simultaneously models whether the mention is correct and which candidate entity is the best resolution.

Conventional approaches to entity tagging and subsequently resolution to a unique identifier fail for this use case because the pipeline model propagates errors. Even if tagging and resolution have an f-value of 0.8, the highest performance for the sequential pipeline would be 0.64. Moreover, the underlying authority file is subject to change. The company tagger would have to be retrained every time the authority changed.

The need for a different approach also developed after testing off-the-shelf company taggers (Finkel et al., 2005) on a variety of news websites others than Reuters news including social media sites that report on companies as well. The performance of such taggers that showed high-quality tagging on well-established data sets such as MUC-5 (Sundheim and Chinchor, 1993) and CONLL 2003 (Tjong Kim Sang and De Meulder, 2003) degraded quickly.

In addition to meeting these research objectives, the development of the Newton system had to overcome specific enterprise and general software development challenges:

- create a general text mining framework;
- overcome noisy alternative names;
- obtain training data;
- identify duplicates in authority (e.g., subsidiaries, multiple listings);
- be prepared for possible changes in the company authority;
- develop a company tagging and resolution pipeline with state-of-the-art performance;
- track performance and alert developers both of commits that break the build and commits that hurt performance;
- manage development across a team of six people.

In our solution, we addressed all the above concerns. In particular, we leverage UIMA to develop a general framework for easy reuse of the various software components.

We evaluated the quality of the Newton system by carrying out experiments on the Reuters News Archive (RNA). We trained on automatically

---

[2] http://uima.apache.org/.

annotated annotations (i.e., silver data) obtained by projecting metadata into 70k RNA stories. On a held-out test set, our mention detection obtains high precision of 0.89 with recall of 0.76. Resolution precision and recall is very high at 0.94/0.95.

Finally, the overall performance of the system was tracked by a Hudson build server generating nightly builds that resulted in entries in a database. Quick checks after each commit also ensured that feature changes or other changes did not decrease the overall performance and if they occur, they can be tracked and the code changes can be identified.

7.2 RELATED WORK

Much work with named entities has focused on mention detection – identifying textual references to, for example, people, organisations, locations (Lin and Wu, 2009; Turian et al., 2010). However, entities can have multiple names and names can refer to multiple underlying entities. Resolution grounds mentions to an identifier corresponding to the underlying entity (Dozier and Haschart, 2000; Benjelloun et al., 2009).

Recently, Wikipedia has driven entity linking research – resolving to encyclopedia articles about named entities (Cucerzan, 2007; Ji et al., 2011; Hachey et al., 2013). However, the commonly adopted stepwise approach (mention detection followed by resolution) ignores the interdependence of the two tasks, resulting in error propagation. We model mentions and resolution simultaneously in an authority-driven approach of lookup followed by classification.

Several authors take a similar approach for the task of Wikification – linking both to entity pages and to general concept pages (Milne and Witten, 2008; Kulkarni et al., 2009). All eschew conventional named entity recognition in favor of an authority-driven approach like ours. However, Wikipedia is much richer than our authority, having detailed encyclopedic text, categorisation structure, as well as rich interarticle linking. Both mining and linking approaches take advantage of these features.

The approaches most like ours are found in the biomedical informatics literature. The BioCreative challenges include a series of gene normalisation tasks (Hirschman et al., 2005; Morgan et al., 2008; Lu et al., 2011). These differ in that the goal is to return the set identifiers corresponding to the mentioned genes and proteins in a document, not the mentions themselves. But, the gene authority database is identical to our company database – a set of entities with corresponding identifiers and name variations. Furthermore, the most successful participants use an authority-driven approach like ours but also leverage inter-entity relationships (Hakenberg et al., 2007).

Several production-ready tools for named entity recognition are freely available (Curran and Clark, 2003; Finkel et al., 2005; Carpenter, 2007; McCallum et al., 2009; Ratinov and Roth, 2009), and many companies now provide software or services (e.g., Identifinder, OpenCalais, Extrativ, Alchemy). To our knowledge, however, no paper describes the corresponding development and deployment processes for mention detection and resolution as we do here.

We also describe an architecture for development and performance tracking. This builds a reusable software framework on the general-purpose UIMA (Ferrucci and Lally, 2004) and ClearTK (Ogren et al., 2009) tools. Clarke et al. (2012) describe an architecture for text processing pipelines, but focus on reusability of intermediate stages of computation in complex NLP pipelines. Our performance-tracking infrastructure complements a continuous integration server that runs unit tests on each commit. It provides a way for our team to quickly pinpoint code that causes changes in accuracy on our development data sets.

One of the main challenges of our problem setting is overcoming the lack of a rich authority like Wikipedia. We derive text context from a large collection of text documents, leveraging company identifiers in metadata creating large amounts of silver data. The approach, in particular, is related to bootstrapping information extraction from metadata (Canisius and Sporleder, 2007; Wu et al., 2008; Yao et al., 2010). We are not aware of similar work for deriving precise names from a noisy authority, nor for cleaning and weighting alternative names.

7.3 SYSTEM OVERVIEW

We utilised the Apache UIMA™ framework for defining the overall pipeline (Ferrucci and Lally, 2004). UIMA was developed by IBM and is now an open-source Apache project.[3] It was also used by IBM for building the question answering system Watson (Ferrucci, 2012). The following section describes the overall concepts behind UIMA. The section also discusses clearTK (Ogren et al., 2009), the UIMA-based toolkit for rapidly developing statistical natural language (NLP) components, and introduces the recently developed utility component called uimaFIT that allows a researcher in text mining to quickly put together an information extraction pipeline.

---

[3] http://uima.apache.org/.

The next section describes the overall system architecture of the NEWTON system starting with the overall text mining framework we created to maximise reuse of various components. The last section provides more details on the actual Newton pipeline explaining how the different components of the pipeline work together.

7.3.1 UIMA, ClearTK, uimaFIT

The unstructured information management applications (UIMA) framework is an Apache-licenced open-source framework for analyzing large amounts of unstructured data to extract information such as entities (e.g., persons, companies) and relations holding between these entities.

UIMA was designed to increase reusability of natural language (NLP) components such as sentence splitters, POS taggers or named entity taggers. To facilitate the combination of different so-called analysis engines (AEs) a data structure was introduced that allows us to carry commonly shared annotations between such engines. The common annotation structure (CAS) stores annotations that were added to a text by an AE. A news text, for example, is first tokenised and all tokens are identified by their character offset and this information is stored in the CAS and can be easily accessed by all subsequent AEs.

Figure 7.1 describes how annotations are organised in the CAS referring to the mention of a name and also to the unique entity (i.e., Fred Center).

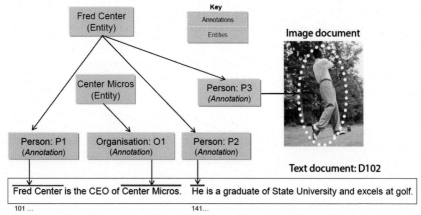

Figure 7.1 The CAS contains the text and the respective annotations.

In addition to references to the text mention, UIMA is also capable of integrating other media types such as pictures.[4]

Other NLP components that were developed outside of UIMA can also easily be wrapped by translating the respective data structure (e.g., array of strings) into the CAS annotation. Many components are available as a wrapper or have been developed within UIMA.[5]

The UIMA framework originally did not offer much support for NLP and in particular machine learning-based classifiers. The development of ClearTK[6] changed this shortcoming and allowed the rapid development of classifiers and sequence taggers based on commonly used machine learning packages such as Mallet (McCallum, 2002), OpenNLP,[7] libsvm (Chang and Lin, 2011) and others.

Finally, the uimaFIT package makes the usage of UIMA very straight forward by offering many utility classes that are frequently used in the UIMA pipeline development (e.g., creating a pipeline, subiterating through annotation span given an annotation).

7.3.2 The Text Mining Framework

To manage a large text mining system, a certain infrastructure has to be in place. Ideally, many components used in the system should be reused or made reusable for other future systems. To meet this challenge of using previously developed code efficiently and developing new pipelines rapidly, we created a multilayered project with the Maven[8] build tool separating different subprojects.

This section also describes the architecture of the pipeline in more detail and how the different components interact with each other.

The framework infrastructure is set up to maintain reusability of different components developed and to provide support to different text mining tasks. The framework is a set of modules that have components that can be plugged together to form a pipeline that does the required processing for a task. The framework has the following modules:

[4] For more information, see the UIMA documentation available at http://uima.apache.org/d/uimaj-2.4.0/index.html.
[5] http://uima.apache.org/sandbox.html#uima-addons-annotators, http://u-compare.org/components/index.html.
[6] http://code.google.com/p/cleartk/.
[7] http://opennlp.apache.org/index.html.
[8] http://maven.apache.org/.

Type Systems This module contains all the different type systems that can be used with the UIMA pipeline. These are data structures that define the annotations created by UIMA analysis engines.

Data This module contains different types of data. The data can be raw or gold annotated. This is accessible by other modules and can be used for pipeline development and testing. This also contains some tools that can be used to preprocess any data before it can be used by any pipeline.

Utilities This module contains a variety of utility classes that are shared by different modules in the framework.

IO Components To read and write from a CAS (the data structure the UIMA pipeline uses to store the document and any output of components that should be passed along) special readers and writers are required. This module contains the different implementations that can handle different document types and output different types as required. These components can be mixed and matched and used by different pipelines as needed.

Tokenisers and Sentence Splitters Most of our pipelines work with sentences and tokens as their starting point. This module contains different implementations for sentence splitting and word tokenisation.

Feature Engineering This module contains a wide variety of feature extractors. The feature extractors follow the ClearTK framework's methodology for creating features. This gives the extractors the needed flexibility to be used in different feature generation scenarios.

Sequence Classifiers This contains a set of ClearTK-based classifier implementations that can be used in different sequence tagging and classification problems. The classifier's feature sets are configurable by means of a Spring configuration. This enables the implementation to switch out features with relative ease and be adapted to different problems. The classifier algorithms can also be switched out by configuration. which is possible by virtue of it conforming to ClearTK framework's conventions. Each implementation available here can use a variety of statistical methods to train and classify (e.g., Maximum Entropy, LIBSVM, Mallet, OpenNLP).

Coreference After extracting entities, some pipelines require a way to group mentions of the same entity. This module contains different algorithms that would do that and components that use them.

Entity Resolution This module contains algorithms and implementations that would resolve entities found in a document to a given target.

Salience After entities are detected, there may be a need to identify whether the entity is salient to the document at hand. The different approaches in this module implements a saliency classifier that identifies whether a company mentioned in an article is salient or not. Salient companies are identified if the main topic of the article is about such a company. Reporting companies or companies mentioned only in passing are of low saliency. This module is an example of a different text mining problem that, however, is not inside of the scope of this chapter.

Pipelines This module enables the construction of different pipelines using components from the other modules. The different modules can be selected and plugged together to perform a sequence of processes on a document to obtain the desired output.

One of the pipelines in this overall framework is the Newton pipeline. The following section describes in more detail how the Newton pipeline is integrated into a separate production system.

7.3.3 Newton System Design

The Newton system plugs into a bigger product that processes news articles from a variety of sources (see Figure 7.2). Unlike most entity extraction

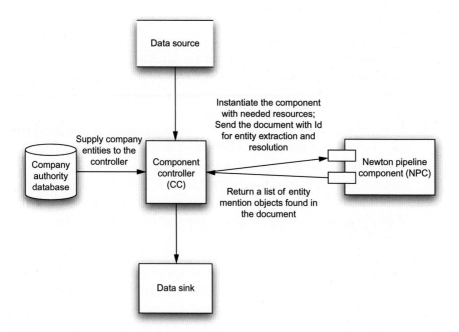

Figure 7.2 Newton pipeline embedded in production system.

systems, the process is driven by the authority database – a set of 32,000 frequently mentioned companies. This data is proprietary, but the authority-driven approach we describe generalises similar problem settings.

Each entry in the authority comprises an identifier, a set of canonical names, and a set of synonyms. The canonical name is the name by which the company is known as (e.g., *International Business Machines*). A synonym (or alternative name) is a name variation by which the company can be referred to in different news articles (e.g., *IBM*). The task at hand is to identify and resolve mentions of these companies in the news articles that are run through the system.

The Newton pipeline uses Apache UIMA – ClearTK to combine the different components that are needed to accomplish the task. The components have a shared resource that is built by consuming the authority. There are different types of resources that are compiled from the authority. These resources are used for feature generation during classification and sequence tagging. First step before creating the pipeline is initialising these shared resources. After the resources are created the pipeline is initialised. The pipeline when run in full production mode has the following components:

Tokeniser splits the text into tokens.

Sentence Splitter identifies sentence boundaries.

Lookup tagger tags all word sequences in the authority.

Company Classifier classifies each company candidate against a set of possible candidates whether the company ID is correct or not. The scores of multiple candidates are ranked and the highest-ranked company ID is linked to the company annotation.

Company Reannotator tags alternative names in the same article, if a company is at least once identified in the the same article.

The production system also requires the Newton pipeline to be paused and reloaded with an updated or changed authority. In addition, the load of the system may vary and the Newton system needs to be able to adapt to a higher number of documents if necessary.

The Newton pipeline is composed of components as described in Figure 7.3. Each component in the pipeline applies its particular set of algorithms to the document to create the required annotations for subsequent components.

The sentence splitter and Tokeniser regex-based implementations identify sentence boundaries and token boundaries. The sentence splitter finds sentence boundaries and adds sentence annotations to the CAS. The Tokeniser finds each word in the document and adds it as a token to the CAS.

The next component is the lookup tagger. The input to this component are the tokens and sentences created by the tokeniser component. The lookup

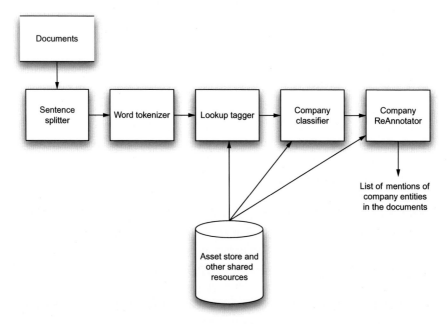

Figure 7.3 The Newton pipeline.

tagger finds all possible sequences based on word maps (i.e., word to IDs) built up using the authority. This aims at high recall at the cost of precision. The idea is to identify all possible sequences that could be a company mention. In addition it also finds the possible candidate entities each mention could resolve to in the authority. If the lookup tagger found a mention, it will have a set of candidate entities. For more details see Section 7.4.1.

Once all possible mentions are identified, the document is run through the company classifier. The company classifier is developed within the ClearTK framework. It can be set to use a variety of statistical methods to train and classify. In this case an SVM classifier was chosen. Because of the flexibility in the framework, the machine learning algorithm can be easily switched out to be a maximum entropy model or logistic regression model or any other algorithm that fits with the ClearTK framework by means of changing the configuration. The classifier determines whether any given mention detected by the lookup tagger is actually a company mention or not. The classifier does this by linking it to an ID and deciding whether a given string (e.g., IBM) is linked to an ID or not. The classifier has a feature configuration based on which it trains a model and classifies. The feature configuration is set up as a Spring configuration. The advantage of using the Spring framework is that the pipeline can be run with different feature sets without changing the component code. More details are provided in Section 7.4.2.

Any mention that was not classified as a company mention is kept in the CAS because the reannotator AE may decide to resolve it to an ID, if it is an alternative name of a company already identified by the company classifier. The reannotator goes through all the resolved Company mentions in the document and consults the authority resources to find other name variations of the resolved company in the authority. After these other names are compiled, it iterates through the mentions that were not classified as company mentions by the classifier and checks whether the mention belongs to the alternate names possible for other entities found in the document. If there are any company mentions found that have not been linked to the company, those get resolved to the company for which the mention is a name. The others get removed as a mention in the document. This step helps to improve the recall without sacrificing the precision of the classifier.

Once the process is completed, all the mentions are returned with the ID for the company name a mention is referring to and the character offsets of the mention in the document.

The following section describes our approach and experimental results.

7.4 LEARNING COMPANY NAME LINKS

This section focusses on the core of the Newton system: the tagging and resolution of company names from a set of 32,000 companies. Our approach starts with a lookup tagger that tries to capture all possible mentions of companies in the text with reasonable precision. To make sure only actual companies are tagged and also linked to the correct ID, we employ a classifier that learns whether a string is actually the respective company.

We evaluate our approach on automatically generated silver data we created from the Reuters News Archive by generating 70k documents for training and 30k documents for testing. Our results show high precision and recall scores for the tagging (0.89/0.76) and the actual resolution (0.94/0.95). The combined score of the actual system results in 0.84 precision and 0.72 recall.[9]

7.4.1 Company Name Lookup

The lookup tagger, given a set of company names derived from the authority, identifies all the possible matches in the input text. At this stage, we aim for

---

[9] See formal definition of these metrics in Section 7.4.4.3.

high-recall, but not necessarily high-precision tagging so that the subsequent classifier can examine each tag and determine if it is actually a targeted company. The matching process is word-based and more flexible than the hash table- or trie-based look up where it requires the exact match of the company name to be in the authority. This approach is advantageous for the desired high-recall approach because the company's short name or nickname is often used instead of the official name, and it is not possible to anticipate all variations of company names that might appear in the input.

The authority file should contain all the company names and their IDs that uniquely identify them. Additionally, it should contain as many name variations as possible, especially when they look completely different (e.g., IBM and International Business Machine). The variations belonging to the same company should have the same ID (e.g., IBM and International Business Machine should refer to the same ID). Company suffix variations, such as Corp., LTD., Inc., are automatically generated, so it is not necessary to list suffix variations in the authority file (Microsoft Corporation covers Microsoft and Microsoft Corp.)

As part of initialisation, the lookup tagger reads the authority file, normalises the names (capitalisation, stopword removal, etc.) and stores them in two maps. One map contains unique words that appear as the first word of a company as the key, and the value is a list of companies that have this word as a first word in their name. The other map contains unique words that appears as the rest of the company names as the key, and sets of their corresponding companies as the value.

When processing an input text, we first identify possible company names by capitalisation. Consider the following text.

> A year after Occidental Petroleum Corporation announced it was cutting drilling in the Bakken over high costs, that looks like a token protest. Despite the example of Chesapeake Energy, whose high-cost natural gas wells in the Northeast became unprofitable with falling prices, the continued strength of oil is pushing Occidental to keep investing.

For simplicity's sake, let's assume our authority file contains only the companies described in Table 7.1.

Derived from the simplified authority in Table 7.1, the first word map can be constructed, as described in Table 7.2.

The text is split into sentences and sentences are split into tokens. For each sentence, we examine each token, starting from the left, and see if the token can possibly be a first word of a company name by checking (1) if there is at least one capital letter in the word, and (2) if the word is

Table 7.1 A simplified authority of companies and the respective IDs

Occidental Petroleum Corporation	ID1
Occidental Petroleum	ID1
Chesapeake Energy	ID2
Chesapeake Gold Corporation	ID3
Northeast Community Bancorp, INC.	ID4
Northeast Pharmaceutical Group, Co.	ID5
Northeast Digital Networks, Inc.	ID6

Table 7.2 The one word map for the simplified authority

Occidental	ID1
Chesapeake	ID2,ID3
Northeast	ID4,ID5,ID6

in the first-word map. Once a word that satisfies these two conditions is found, we try to identify the end boundary of the company name. We check each subsequent words to see (1) if the the token contains at least one capital letter, (2) the word is found in the rest-of-the-words map, (3) there is at least one company in the set of the companies containing the word (obtained from the rest-of-the-words map) that is common to the previous company set. As soon as one of the three conditions fails, we consider it as the end of the company name. For a detailed algorithm, see the pseudo code described in algorithm 1.

From capitalisation, we identify the following word groups are possible matches:

- Occidental Petroleum Corporation
- Bakken
- Despite
- Chesapeake Energy
- Northeast
- Occidental

"Bakken" and "Despite" are dropped because they are not in the first-word map. The word groups listed in Table 7.3 are marked as potential companies with their candidate company IDs. They are sent to the classifier.

Table 7.3 The set of word sequences that are company candidates

Occidental Petroleum Corporation	ID1
Chesapeake Energy	ID2
Northeast	ID4,ID5,ID6
Occidental	ID1

Broadly speaking, the problem of linking a test document D to a set of entities $\mathcal{E}$ can be viewed as $|D| \times |\mathcal{E}|$ (nonindependent) decisions; that is, for each token in the document and for each company in the corpus, decide if there is a link. The task of the lookup tagger is to merge decisions over individual words into a single decision over a string and to apply simple, human-generated rules to identify and remove decisions that have extremely low probability. The reduced set of possible links are represented as mention-company candidates, which identify a string in the document that possibly refers to a specific company. These pairs can be viewed as a first-pass entity linking, and from this perspective we are seeking perfect recall with less concern for precision.

Data: Tokenised input sentence S
Result: Company annotations with their candidate resolutions
initialisation;
while *Not at the end of the sentence* **do**
> **while** *Not the end of the sentence* **do**
>> **if** *Word in the current position is contained in the first word map* **then**
>>> Mark the current position as the beginning position;
>>> Keep the values (a set of companies that has this word as the first word);
>>> Increment the word position;
>>> Exit the loop;
>> **else**
>>> Increment the word position;
>> **end**
> **end**
> **if** *Company first word is found in the above loop* **then**
>> **while** *Not the end of the sentence and the word at the current position contains at least one capital letter* **do**
>>> Get the set of the companies that contain this word;
>>> Take the intersection between this and the previous company set;
>>> **if** *At least one company is in the intersection* **then**
>>>> Increment the word position;
>>> **else**
>>>> Mark the previous position as the end position;
>>>> Keep the previous company set as the candidate pool;
>>>> Exit the loop;
>>> **end**
>> **end**
> **else**
>> Mark the previous position as the end position;
>> Keep the previous company set as the candidate pool;
>> Exit the loop;
> **end**
end

Algorithm 1 Lookup Algorithm Pseudocode.

7.4.2 Company Classification

The company candidate classification step is a machine learning approach to deciding whether the mention-company candidates produced by the lookup tagger are true or not. That is, we wish to answer the question, *Is a given string (in context) a mention of a given company?* The question can be viewed as a binary classification problem. Moreover, the question can be formulated as the conjunction of two further questions:

1. Is the given string (in context) a mention of an organisation?
2. Assuming the previous, is the given company the referent of the mention?

Note that (1) is the named entity recognition (NER) problem, which has been studied previously (e.g., Liao and Veeramachaneni (2009) describes a NER product developed by this organisation). The Newton system attempts to answer these two questions jointly rather than independently. To illustrate the appeal of the joint approach, note that some strings unambiguously refer to a company, such as "Walmart". In these cases, high confidence for the second question implies the first question. For strings like "Apple", we must lean heavily on the first question to distinguish the famous technology company from the fruit and the singer. Most strings are somewhere in the middle, with moderate evidence for both questions. Therefore, to answer the main question we must balance our confidence for each of the secondary questions. Our approach is to generate features for each of the secondary questions and use machine learning to do the balancing. However, we make a special exception for the "Walmart" example; any mention-company candidate that matches the pregenerated precise names list is accepted straightaway, bypassing the machine learning step.

Unfortunately, it is an oversimplification to present the company classification step as a binary classification problem. In this application, the number of company candidates for a particular mention string is data-dependent. Because at most one of the mention-candidate pairs can be true, whereas the lookup tagger can generate multiple pairs, the distribution of true versus false patterns is not defined, and the problem seems to violate the first principles of machine learning. The solution is to divide the problem into two steps:

1. Which candidate is the best candidate for the mention string? (ranking)
2. Is the best candidate good enough to be a match? (classification)

The application is novel in the sense that a single model accomplishes both steps. The model is primarily a classifier, with the ranking derived from the classifier's relative confidence on the candidates for the same mention. Nevertheless, we have to train and tune the classifier with the dual role in mind.

We use a linear support vector machine (SVM) classifier, as implemented in LIBLINEAR (Fan et al., 2008). While SVM is one of many possible choices for binary classification, the method is particularly attractive in this case for having theoretical error bounds that are independent of the dimension of the input (Vapnik, 1999), for having a way to control the tradeoff between precision and recall by unequal misclassification costs, and for giving confidence scores based on the normal distance from a test point to the decision boundary. All of these qualities are useful for the application. The feature space is very large as it includes n-gram and bag-of-words features, so the dimension-independent error bound is beneficial. Unequal misclassification costs empirically improved system performance. Of course, the ranking aspect of the task requires confidence scores.[10]

The features used in the classifier can be divided into two groups, corresponding to the two questions (at the beginning of the section) that jointly determined whether a mention-company candidate was true. The first group, to determine whether a string is a mention of a company at all, consists in features similar to those used in the NER problem. These are summarised briefly in Table 7.4. The second group of features, to determine whether a specific company is a match, are not only summarised in Table 7.4 but also discussed in more detail below.

The linking features represent the evidence that the mention string – assuming it refers to some company – in fact refers to a specific company. We assume that the linking problem can be divided into one of two cases:

1. Companies that are not common knowledge (the tail). For these we expect at least one mention in the document that is lexically close to the official name of the company.

2. Well-known companies that may be referred to with a large number of short forms and synonyms and without use of the official name anywhere in the document (the head).

There are linking features for each case. Beginning with the second case, the feature *alt_name_prob* gives the scaled joint probability (MAP) of the mention string appearing in Reuters News Archive as a mention and referring to the candidate company. This feature is intended to help the classifier identify mentions that are inherently ambiguous but have an overwhelmingly unambiguous referent in common usage. For instance, the string "United" overwhelmingly refers to the airline in common usage. In addition, the

---

[10] While there are a number of proposed methods to estimate the class conditional probability $\Pr(y|x)$ for SVM such as Wu et al. (2003), we simply use the normal distance.

Table 7.4 List of features for company classification

NER features	
Ngram	Binary: Ngrams of candidate mention and preceding and following context
Bag	Binary: Bag of words (n=5) of preceding and following context
Covered	Binary: exact text of covered text by candidate mention
max_case_ratio	Ratio between word starting with an uppercase and lowercase character, take the maximum value of all the words covered by mention
word shape	Binary: Word shape of preceding and following words (e.g., sequence of uppercase or lowercase characters)
ORG_Any_Token	Binary: Is any token of the mention tagged as an organisation entity by standard NER system (Liao and Veeramachaneni, 2009)? Repeated for person & location
ORG_Contained	Binary: Is the entire mention string contained in an organisation entity tagged by standard NER system? Repeated for person & location
Linking features	
alt_name_prob	Probability of mention string referring to candidate in RNA
contextSimilarity	Cosine sim between document with mention and RNA documents with a candidate mention
cosine	Cosine/TFIDF sim between mention and name list match
cosine_bin	Series of binary features for membership in integer bin of log cosine value
cosine_sd	Binary: Is candidate's cosine score a high outlier among all the candidates for the mention?
cosine_mean	Mean cosine score of all the candidates
cosine_max	Max cosine score among all the candidates
candidate_sd	Binary: Is candidate's cosine score close to the max of all the candidates?
is_unique_outlier	Binary: Does the candidate have the highest cosine score and no other candidate is within one standard deviation?
levenshtein	Normalised Levenshtein (edit) distance between mention string and name list match
levenshtein_sd	Binary: Is Levenshtein score an outlier among all candidates?
levenshtein_mean	Mean Levenshtein score among all candidates
is_one_word	Binary: Is the mention string one word?
mention_length	Character length of mention string
candidate_length	Character length of name list match
candidate_num	Number of candidates
candidate_num_bin	Series of binary features for membership in integer bin of log candidate_num

contextSimilarity feature attempts to quantify evidence for the candidate in terms of the semantic context. For instance, the existence of the string "flight" in proximity to "United" is strong evidence that the latter string refers to the well-known airline. The context words are mined from known mentions of the candidate in RNA, and the feature value is the cosine similarity with an 80-character window on each side of the mention.

The remaining features are for the first case, when the task is to identify a reference that is similar to the official (or full) name of the company. These features attempt to quantify how good the mention string matches the alternative name as a lexical match. In many cases, the mention string matches the full name exactly. In other cases, however, the difference is merely a word like "Inc." or "LP", so the system must be robust to inexact mentions. One approach is cosine/tfidf and the other is Levenshtein distance. These features are passed to the classifier as a raw number and as binary features indicating membership in logarithmically spaced bins. The feature *is_one_word* is an indicator for whether the mention string is a single token.

There are also several candidate-pool features, which arise from the observation that the distribution of the cosine feature over the candidate companies for a mention is informative. In particular, when one candidate is a strong outlier and the rest have less significant values, such a distribution is evidence that the mention string unambiguously refers to the outlier candidate. The feature *cosine_sd* indicates whether a candidate's cosine value is one standard deviation above the mean over the candidate pool – in other words, an outlier. The feature *candidate_sd* indicates whether a candidate is within one standard deviation of the highest candidate in the pool; this is designed to measure if a candidate is close to the highest candidate. The feature *is_unique_outlier* indicates whether the given candidate has the highest cosine score among all candidates and no other candidate is within one standard deviation. Finally, the number of candidates is given to the classifier, both as a number and as indicators for logarithmically spaced bins, as well as the mean and max cosine score over the candidate pool.

Any features that are not binary are standardised over the training data. The standardising transformation is memorised and applied to new data at classification time.

Finally, remember that exceptions are made for mention–company candidates that match a pregenerated precise names list. The precise name list contains unambiguous name–identifier pairs. We filter based on three types of ambiguity: (1) name can refer to more than one entity in the target universe, (2) name can refer to an entity outside of the target universe, and (3) name is a common word or phrase.

The first is addressed by removing any alternative name associated to more than one entity in our authority. We also remove short names (length <4). The second is addressed by removing person names found in Wikipedia article titles and redirects. The third is addressed by removing names that appear in WordNet (Fellbaum, 2005).

The original authority has 300,281 names. The process above removes 18,987 ambiguous names. Finally, we manually add back some names that got removed even though they are not ambiguous and are very likely to refer to a single entity (e.g., IBM, Facebook).

7.4.3 Training the Classifier

As previously noted, the classifier serves the dual role of classification and ranking, and the dual role must be accounted for when training. The goal is to learn a model with higher confidence for better candidates, and thus the model can serve both as a ranker and as a classifier. We noted that, for a given mention, an arbitrary number of false mention-candidate pairs can be generated, but at most one of these will be true. When generating training data for the classifier, only the candidate with the highest cosine score is made into a training sample (which is then labeled as either true or false according to ground truth). Note that all of the NER features and all the candidate-pool linking features are the same for every candidate. Including more than one candidate for a mention would imply that the classifier could not learn to discriminate on those features as the training data would be inherently inseparable in that subspace.

The training examples are highly biased to the negative class; that is, most string-candidate pairs identified by the lookup tagger are false. To balance precision and recall, the misclassification cost for the SVM must be weighted to be higher for positive examples. This weight and the SVM misclassification penalty are chosen by cross-validation.

7.4.4 Evaluation

We carried out a host of different experiments with data from the Reuters News archive. Results show that the tagging and linking can be carried out at an overall precision of 0.84 and recall of 0.72. Our experiments also show that more data improve the overall test results.

7.4.4.1 Data

We obtain 2.5 million articles from the Reuters News Achieve and randomly sampled 100k documents. The articles were stripped of any additional meta information and only the headline and the body text were extracted. Training and test data was generated following these transformation steps. Note that no manual review was performed and that all data was automatically generated. However, precise metadata added to the documents by Reuters editors was heavily utilised:

- Given a list of unambiguous long company names containing company specific suffixes (e.g., *Corp*) a list of precise company names was compiled.
- From the authority the list of Reuters Instrument Codes (RICs) were added to the list of precise names (e.g., TRI.N is the RIC for Thomson Reuters at the New York Stock Exchange).
- All articles that contain a precise name are tagged with the respective ID, resulting in a tuple of documents and the list of organisations that have a precise name mentioned in it.
- Given the list of alternative names for each company, tag all such occurrences in the respective article. If an article, for example, mentions *Apple Inc*, then tag also all occurrences of *Apple* as well.
- Produce an output file with these annotations and the respective ID for training, keeping apart one portion of the silver data for testing.

7.4.4.2 Experiments

We trained various sets of the training data with an SVM classifier and recorded precision, recall and f-values for the held-out test set. An instance in our training set was a word sequence detected by the lookup tagger and the outcome label was set to true, if there was an ID detected while generating the silver data. This was the case if there was either an unambiguous company name (e.g., *Microsoft*) or when there was a RIC mentioned in the text. If such a link did not exist, the instance will be marked as false indicating that there is no link.

Note that there is a chance of noise introduction given the way the silver training data is generated. Noise may be introduced, if a company name is tagged by the lookup tagger, but not found in the silver data, or if companies are wrongly annotated in the silver data (e.g., alternative name is too common such as *United*). However, the number of times this can happen is relatively small because the silver data is based on the RIC mentions that are added by human editors.

Given the training data, we trained a model with the LIBLINEAR package (Fan et al., 2008). We used LIBLINEAR because it allows us to process lots of data more efficiently than the LIBSVM package.[11]

---

[11] See http://www.csie.ntu.edu.tw/~cjlin/liblinear/ for more information.

7.4.4.3 Results

The generated model for the binary classifier was used to test on a held-out test set of 30k documents. To see the impact of more data on the overall performance we incrementally increased the size of the training set starting with 1k documents.

The performance was recorded with the standard metrics precision, recall and f-score[12] :

$$\text{Precision} = \frac{\text{TP}}{\text{TP} + \text{FP}}, \ \text{Recall} = \frac{\text{TP}}{\text{TP} + \text{FN}}, \ \text{F-score} = 2 \times \frac{\text{Precision} \times \text{Recall}}{(\text{Precision} + \text{Recall})}$$

Table 7.5 summarises the results for the sequence of training experiments we carried out. A small data set already showed reasonable performance with overall precision and recall of 0.82 and 0.69. Precision and recall, however, increase with more data, although slowly, as indicated by Figure 7.4.

7.5 SYSTEM DEVELOPMENT

This section describes the various means we employed to keep the system in a stable state during development with several researchers and developers working on the same code base. Similar to a typical software development project, unit tests were employed to ensure that the system builds after every code change. However, the text mining components require functional tests on different levels and have to be tuned toward the nature of a text mining system that often entails experimenting with various new features. Moreover, the end-to-end performance in terms of precision and recall needs to be monitored and recorded. A unit test would be more of a hindrance here because the experiments with the classifier presupposes a certain flexibility, but at the same time past experiments need to be reproducible as well.

7.5.1 Feature Consistency Testing

This section provides details on how we ensured the correctness and consistency of the features generated.

Throughout the development cycle, it is crucial to ensure the consistency in the feature generation. The generated feature values should change only when we intend them to, and accidental changes should be avoided at all cost because they could cause serious adverse effects on

---

[12] TP, true positives; FP, false positives; FN, false negatives.

Table 7.5 Results for training on RNA training data/testing on RNA test data

	#docs	#entities	#TPs	P	R	F	P	R	F	P	R	F
1	1000	8208	3772	0.87	0.73	0.80	0.94	0.95	0.94	0.82	0.69	0.75
2	2000	16222	7254	0.87	0.74	0.80	0.94	0.95	0.94	0.82	0.70	0.75
3	5000	41697	19812	0.88	0.73	0.80	0.95	0.95	0.95	0.83	0.70	0.76
4	10000	83737	39532	0.89	0.74	0.81	0.95	0.95	0.95	0.84	0.70	0.77
5	15000	125210	58857	0.89	0.75	0.81	0.95	0.95	0.95	0.84	0.71	0.77
6	20000	167970	78681	0.88	0.75	0.81	0.94	0.95	0.95	0.83	0.71	0.77
7	30000	253488	118882	0.89	0.76	0.82	0.94	0.95	0.94	0.83	0.72	0.77
8	40000	338568	158873	0.89	0.76	0.82	0.94	0.95	0.94	0.83	0.72	0.77
9	50000	425576	199619	0.89	0.76	0.82	0.94	0.95	0.94	0.84	0.72	0.78
10	60000	510254	239347	0.89	0.77	0.82	0.94	0.95	0.94	0.84	0.73	0.78
11	70000	595649	279279	0.89	0.76	0.82	0.94	0.95	0.94	0.84	0.72	0.78

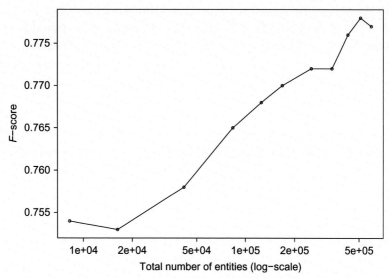

Figure 7.4 Increase of training data (log-scale) increases overall F-score.

the performance. To be able to detect accidental changes as early as possible, we automated the consistency checking using the Hudson continuous integration system. We wrote a test to generate features for a set of input text and compare against the expected output (see Figure 7.5). The test fails if the generated features do not match the baseline (rounding errors are allowed). The Hudson build ensures that a test is run after each change submitted to the source control system, and if the output is different

```
@Test
public void newtonAnnotatorFeatureGeneratorBaselineTest() throws Exception {
    String testDirName = "src/test/resources/data/newtonTest/LookupTaggerTest";    //Where input file is
    String[] suffixArr = {".ann"};
    CollectionReader testFileReader = BratReaderUtils.createBratReader(testDirName, suffixArr);
    AnalysisEngineDescription lookupTagger = GallifreyComponentCreator.createLookupTaggerDescriptor();
    AnalysisEngineDescription dexterAnnotator = GallifreyComponentCreator.createDexterAnnotatorDescriptor(dexterConfigFile,
        dexterModelFile);
    AnalysisEngineDescription newtonAE = GallifreyComponentCreator.createNewtonAnnotatorDescriptorForBaseline(
        outputDir, true, "");

    SimplePipeline.runPipeline(
        testFileReader,
        AnalysisEngineFactory.createPrimitiveDescription(TextTokenizer.class, NewtonDataGenerator.TYPE_SYSTEM_DESCRIPTION),
        lookupTagger,
        dexterAnnotator,
        newtonAE
    );

    String baselineFile = "src/test/resources/data/newtonTest/newtonAnnotatorTest/baseline_training-data.mallet";
    String newFile = "ben/output/training-data.mallet";

    FeatureGenerationTest featureGenerationTest = new FeatureGenerationTest();
    boolean isBaselineMatched = featureGenerationTest.compareTwoTrainingFiles(baselineFile, newFile);

    if(!isBaselineMatched)
    {
        String fullBaselineFilePathInPerforce="//depot/mainline/Gallifrey/gallifrey-pipelines/gallifrey-evaluationUtils/"+baselineFile;
        updateBaselineFileInPerforce(baselineFile,newFile,fullBaselineFilePathInPerforce);
    }

    Assert.assertTrue("New Feature vector doesn't match with the baseline feature vector. See standard output for details", isBaselineMatched);
}
```

Figure 7.5 Code example for the feature consistency test.

from the previously recorded baseline, it sends out an e-mail notification with a list of features affected. Then, the developer who submitted the change is responsible for reviewing the feature changes. Sometimes the changes are intentional and valid, for example, due to new features, bug fixes, the modification or deletion of existing features, and so on. In such cases, the changes should affect only the targeted set of features, and it should not affect other features. Once the new feature values are validated, they become the new baseline.

There are cases where the feature values are not consistent even without code change (e.g., When a README file is added, when the documentation is added but no actual code changes). This is usually caused due to inconsistencies caused by nondeterminism such as indeterministic sorting order or threading race condition. That randomness can exist without being caught by the consistency tests for a long time because they rarely reproduce. So we periodically ran stress tests on multiple machines to make sure that given the same snapshot of the code and input data, the output should always be the same. Of course, it is not guaranteed that these stress tests will expose those inconsistencies, so it is a good idea to code review and search for possible hideout of randomness in addition.

As the same code for feature generation is used for training and classifying, checking the generated features catches most of the bugs that may be introduced. This is a very effective way to speed up the development process because:

- When the feature does not change, we have high confidence that the code change does not have an inadvertent effect, allowing aggressive modification of the code.
- When feature values change, we know what exact change caused the inconsistency, significantly reducing the debugging and troubleshooting time.

Feature consistency checking has a different purpose than regression tests, which keeps track of the performance. It ensures the overall consistency of the system rather than the quality of the output.

7.5.2 Performance Tracker

The development of a complex text mining system often involves several researchers and developers working simultaneously on the same code base. Software development patterns will not be enough if the output of a complex pipeline may be affected by multiple modules of the entire system.

A change in the lookup tagger, for example, would influence the training of the classifier and hence the overall performance. A feature extractor needs to produce always the same results. The training parameters for the SVM classifier should stay constant for the final production system.

Because the overall performance in terms of precision and recall are crucial for the entire system, we implemented a performance tracking system that ran performance tests on a small set of gold data to keep track of the impact of any code changes.

7.5.2.1 Performance Recording
The overall performance of the system is evaluated by using a set of 275 hand-annotated documents that were split into 3 folds and used as a development set. Results for the development set and 3-fold cross-validation was computed every time a change of the code base was checked into the version control system. As soon as a change is checked in the performance tests are run and recorded in a mySQL database. In addition to the time stamp, the change list and the person who checked in the change is recorded.

7.5.3 Performance Reporting
The changes in the database are also easily accessible via a web page that displays the current performance but also the history of changes and the impact on the performance. The overall performance in F-score is displayed on a web page as a Gauge meter, as indicated in Figure 7.6.

The performance tracking website also displays the history of all changes and makes it easily accessible to researchers, developers and project managers. Figure 7.7 shows a list of changes and increases and decreases in performance indicated by colour changes. Moreover, the change list is linked directly to the change list description of the version control system and allows somebody to drill down directly to the respective code change, if desired (see Figure 7.8).

Figure 7.6 Gauge meter display for F-score performance.

ChangeList	Name	P4_Checkin_Time	Org_precision	Org_recall	Org_F_Score	Org_Res_Prec	Org_Res_recall	Org_Res_F	Org_Comb_Prec	Org_Comb_Recall	Org_Comb_F
77810	sudhanshu	Dec 30 2012 10:35AM	0.889	0.766	0.822	0.943	0.960	0.944	0.839	0.726	0.778
78816	merine	Jan 2 2013 9:23AM	0.889	0.768 ↓	0.822	0.943	0.947 ↓	0.944	0.839	0.726	0.778
79820	sudhanshu	Jan 12 2013 5:47AM	0.889	0.764 ↓	0.821 ↓	0.944 ↑	0.947	0.945 ↓	0.839	0.725 ↓	0.777 ↓
80820	merine	Feb 1 2013 11:02AM	0.889	0.764	0.821	0.944	0.947	0.945	0.839	0.725	0.777
80825	frank	Feb 6 2013 8:38AM	0.889	0.764	0.821	0.944	0.947	0.945	0.839	0.725	0.777

Figure 7.7 History of code changes and their impact of overall performance.

Figure 7.8 Link to the change list details in the version control system.

Tracking the performance of the entire system proved to be very helpful for catching unintended decreases of the overall performance early, and detecting the change was easily done from this web page. At the same time, the performance tracker did not affect a researcher the same way a unit test would prevent a successful build on a Hudson server. The drop in performance was, however, recorded and one could go back and reproduce the same performance from the respective change list. Running experiments or experimenting with different feature extractors is made much easier compared to a rigid unit test harness.

7.6 CONCLUSIONS

We presented a text mining system called Newton that automatically tags companies in text and resolves them automatically against an entity store of 32,000 companies.

- We designed a text mining framework utilising UIMA and the pipeline presented in this paper is the Newton system for tagging and resolving companies. The Newton system was embedded in a bigger text mining framework that allows reusability of commonly used components (e.g., tokeniser) and easy deployment of new pipelines by combining already existing components with newly developed ones.
- We proposed a method for creating precise company names that enabled us to extract large amounts of silver data and increased precision of the overall tagging pipeline.

- We utilised a large data set (i.e., the Reuters News Archive) to quickly generate large amounts of training data.
- The authority-based approach gave us the flexibility to update the set of companies that need to be resolved without any retraining of the classifier.
- The developed company tagging and resolution system has a state-of-the-art performance level of 84 precision and 72 recall for the entire pipeline (tagging and resolution combined).
- We designed safeguards against detrimental changes in the code base by developing consistency tests and instantiating performance tracking.
- We developed a programming environment that allowed 6 researchers and developers to safely work on the same code base at the same time.

Current work focuses on how well the Newton system can be applied to different news sources other than the Reuters News Archive or even other text types (e.g., social media).

ACKNOWLEDGEMENTS

This research is made possible with the support of Thomson Reuters Global Resources. Thanks are also to Khalid Al-Kofahi for encouragement, Giles Mayley and Andrew Shaw for providing us with the company authority and further assistance with building the overall pipeline and the anonymous reviewers for critical feedback.

REFERENCES

Benjelloun, O., Garcia-Molina, H., Menestrina, D., Su, Q., Whang, S.E., Widom, J., 2009. Swoosh: a generic approach to entity resolution. VLDB J. 18 (1), 255–276.

Canisius, S., Sporleder, C., 2007. Bootstrapping information extraction from field books. In: Proceedings of the Joint Conference on Empirical Methods in Natural Language Processing and Computational Natural Language Learning, pp. 827–836.

Carpenter, B., 2007. LingPipe for 99.99% recall of gene mentions. In: Proceedings of BioCreAtIvE, pp. 307–309.

Chang, C.C., Lin, C.J., 2011. LIBSVM: a library for support vector machines. ACM Trans. Intell. Syst. Tech. 2, 27:1–27:27. Software available at http://www.csie.ntu.edu.tw/cjlin/libsvm.

Clarke, J., Srikumar, V., Sammons, M., Roth, D., 2012. An NLP curator (or: how i learned to stop worrying and love NLP pipelines). In: Proceedings of the International Conference on Language Resources and Evaluation, pp. 3276–3283.

Cucerzan, S., 2007. Large-scale named entity disambiguation based on Wikipedia data. In: Proceedings of the Joint Conference on Empirical Methods in Natural Language Processing and Computational Natural Language Learning, pp. 708–716.

Curran, J.R., Clark, S., 2003. Language independent NER using a maximum entropy tagger. In: Proceedings of the Conference on Natural Language Learning, pp. 164–167.

Dozier, C., Haschart, R., 2000. Automatic extraction and linking of person names in legal text. In: Proceedings of the International Conference on Computer-Assisted Information Retrieval, pp. 1305–1321.

Fan, R.E., Chang, K.W., Hsieh, C.J., Wang, X.R., Lin, C.J., 2008. LIBLINEAR: a library for large linear classification. J. Mach. Learn. Res. 9, 1871–1874.

Fellbaum, C., 2005. Wordnet and wordnets. In: Brown, K. (Ed.), Encyclopedia of Language and Linguistics. Elsevier, Oxford, pp. 665–670, http://wordnet.princeton.edu/.

Ferrucci, D., Lally, A., 2004. UIMA: An architectural approach to unstructured information processing in the corporate research environment. Natural Lang. Eng. 10 (3-4), 327–348.

Ferrucci, D.A., 2012. Introduction to "This is Watson. IBM J. Res. Dev. 56 (3), 1.

Finkel, J.R., Grenager, T., Manning, C., 2005. Incorporating non-local information into information extraction systems by Gibbs sampling. In: Proceedings of the Annual Meeting of the Association for Computational Linguistics, pp. 363–370.

Hachey, B., Radford, W., Nothman, J., Honnibal, M., Curran, J.R., 2013. Evaluating entity linking with Wikipedia. Artif. Intell. 194, 130–150.

Hakenberg, J., Royer, L., Plake, C., Strobelt, H., Schroeder, M., 2007. Me and my friends: gene mention normalization with background knowledge. In: Proceedings of BioCreAtIvE, pp. 141–144.

Hirschman, L., Colosimo, M., Morgan, A., Yeh, A., 2005. Overview of BioCreAtIvE task 1B: normalized gene lists. BMC BioInformatics 6 (Suppl. 1), S11.

Ji, H., Grishman, R., Dang, H.T., 2011. An overview of the TAC2011 knowledge base population track. In: Proceedings of the Text Analysis Conference.

Kulkarni, S., Singh, A., Ramakrishnan, G., Chakrabarti, S., 2009. Collective annotation of Wikipedia entities in web text. In: Proceedings of the International Conference on Knowledge Discovery and Data Mining, pp. 457–466.

Liao, W., Veeramachaneni, S., 2009. A simple semi-supervised algorithm for named entity recognition. In: Proceedings of the NAACL HLT 2009 Workshop on Semi-supervised Learning for Natural Language Processing. Association for Computational Linguistics, Boulder, CO, pp. 58–65, http://www.aclweb.org/anthology/W09-2208.

Lin, D., Wu, X., 2009. Phrase clustering for discriminative learning. In: Proceedings of the Annual Meeting of the ACL and IJCNLP, pp. 1030–1038.

Lu, Z., Kao, H.Y., Wei, C.H., Huang, M., Liu, J., Kuo, C.J., et al., 2011. The gene normalization task in BioCreative III. BMC Bioinformatics 12 (Suppl 8), S2.

McCallum, A., Schultz, K., Singh, S., 2009. FACTORIE: probabilistic programming via imperatively defined factor graphs. In: Advances on Neural Information Processing Systems. pp. 1249–1257.

McCallum, A.K., 2002. Mallet: A machine learning for language toolkit. http://www.cs.umass.edu/mccallum/mallet.

Milne, D., Witten, I.H., 2008. Learning to link with Wikipedia. In: Proceedings of the Conference on Information and Knowledge Management, pp. 509–518.

Morgan, A.A., Lu, Z., Wang, X., Cohen, A.M., Fluck, J., Ruch, P., et al., 2008. Overview of BioCreative II gene normalization. Genome Biol. 9 (Suppl. 2), S3.

Ogren, P.V., Wetzler, P.G., Bethard, S.J., 2009. ClearTK: a framework for statistical natural language processing. In: Unstructured Information Management Architecture Workshop at the Conference of the German Society for Computational Linguistics and Language Technology.

Ratinov, L., Roth, D., 2009. Design challenges and misconceptions in named entity recognition. In: Proceedings of the Conference on Computational Natural Language Learning, pp. 147–155.

Sundheim, B.M., Chinchor, N.A., 1993. Survey of the Message Understanding Conferences. In: Proceedings of the workshop on Human Language Technology, HLT '93. Association for Computational Linguistics, Stroudsburg, PA, USA, pp. 56–60, http://dx.doi.org/10.3115/1075671.1075684.

Tjong Kim Sang, E.F., De Meulder, F., 2003. Introduction to the conll-2003 shared task: Language-independent named entity recognition. In: Daelemans, W., Osborne, M. (Eds.), Proceedings of CoNLL-2003. Edmonton, Canada, pp. 142–147.

Turian, J., Ratinov, L.A., Bengio, Y., 2010. Word representations: a simple and general method for semi-supervised learning. In: Proceedings of the Annual Meeting of the Association for Computational Linguistics, pp. 384–394.

Vapnik, V.N., 1999. The Nature of Statistical Learning Theory, second Springer, New York.

Wu, F., Hoffmann, R., Weld, D.S., 2008. Information extraction from Wikipedia: moving down the long tail. In: Proceedings of the International Conference on Knowledge Discovery and Data Mining, pp. 731–739.

Wu, T.f., Lin, C.J., Weng, R.C., 2003. Probability estimates for multi-class classification by pairwise coupling. J. Mach. Learn. Res. 5, 975–1005.

Yao, L., Riedel, S., McCallum, A., 2010. Collective cross-document relation extraction without labelled data. In: Proceedings of the Conference on Empirical Methods in Natural Language Processing, pp. 1013–1023.

CHAPTER 8

Automatic Language Identification

M. Zampieri*,†
*Saarland University, Saarbrücken, Germany
†German Research Center for Artificial Intelligence (DFKI), Saarbrücken, Germany

8.1 INTRODUCTION

This chapter presents the task of automatic language identification or simply *language identification* and its relevance for text processing applications. Language identification is the task of automatically identifying the language contained in a given document.

There are a number of situations in which the source language of a document is unknown and computational methods can be applied to determine its source language. State-of-the-art methods for this task apply n-gram based language models at the character or word level to distinguish a set of languages automatically. The results obtained by these methods are usually well over 95% accuracy (Lui and Baldwin, 2012).

Consider the following three lists of characters combinations:
1. ing, the, to, off, wha, thr, and
2. der, ung, sch, aus, ät, ein, ich
3. oja, ón, año, lle, aza, la, un

Any native or competent speaker of English would have no doubt that the first list has more letter combinations that are used in English than the other two. Moreover, a competent speaker of English would easily recognise well-formed words such as *and*, *off*, *to* and *the*. Looking a bit more closely, a speaker might even recall words that are formed using these character sequences such as *what*, *going*, *three*, *there* or *tomorrow*.

It is fairly easy to recognise patterns in lists two and three, even if a person doesn't speak a foreign language but had any contact with foreign language texts. Character combinations such as *ung* and *sch* often belong to Germanic languages, most notably high German, whereas *año*, *ión* contain graphical signs such as *ñ* and *ó* that are not used in English or German, but are used in Spanish.

Working with Text
http://dx.doi.org/10.1016/B978-1-84334-749-1.00008-1

This simple example shows the basic idea behind state-of-the-art language identification methods. One doesn't have to be proficient in English, German or Spanish to distinguish character sequences of these three languages and the same is expected from computational methods. Language identification methods are trained to identify languages automatically without explicit linguistic knowledge.

As described in Palmer (2010), it is very common for language identification methods to perform almost perfectly when distinguishing languages that are typologically not closely related (e.g., Turkish and Spanish or Finnish and French) as well as when recognising languages with unique character sets as is the case with Hebrew. This explains the success obtained by most state-of-the-art general purpose language identification methods that will be presented in this chapter.

There are basically two main difficulties faced by state-of-the-art systems. First of these is the identification of closely related languages. Closely related languages share similar character sequences and lexical units such as the case of Croatian and Serbian and to a lesser extent Portuguese and Spanish or Danish and Swedish. Secondly, systems have difficulty when confronted with small pieces of texts, particularly those available on the Internet, because they often contain nonstandard spelling. Methods designed in recent years to tackle these two aspects of language identification will be presented in this chapter.

The chapter will also discuss related applications such as the task of identification of language varieties (e.g., distinguishing British English from American English texts or Brazilian Portuguese from European Portuguese) and the identification of the native language of an author based on his/her production of second language, most notably English.

8.1.1 Language Identification: A Classification Task

Language identification is essentially a document classification task that consists of assigning documents to classes or categories that are represented by a finite set of labels. In our examples, documents are texts whose source language is unknown.

The type of classification used for language identification is called single-label classification. This kind of classification allows only one label to be attributed to each instance. The language of a text can be either English or German or Portuguese or Chinese, but not two of them at the same time.[1]

---

[1] Please note that there are some specific situations in which multilabel classification could be used, such as multilingual documents.

The term single-label classification is used in contrast to multilabel classification, which allows more than one label to be attributed to the same instance.

Formally, single-label classification can be represented by the following function:

$$f_{\text{class}} : \chi \rightarrow \lambda \tag{8.1}$$

In Equation (8.1), χ is the sample space and λ is a set of class labels. The classification function then maps the relation between a label $y \in \lambda$ to all instances of a given data set. In language identification, the labels $y \in \lambda$ are a set of languages that the method tries to attribute to each text.

Conceptually, language identification is no different from other text classification tasks with which the reader might be familiar (e.g., text categorisation). The kind of features and algorithms used might differ, but the basic idea behind the task is the same.

8.2 HISTORICAL OVERVIEW

Language identification is a well-known task in natural language processing (NLP) and it is part of a number of NLP applications such as machine translation or information retrieval. This section will briefly present several approaches to language identification published over the years.

The aforementioned study published by Ingle (1980) is the first well-known attempt to solve the language identification problem. In this early approach, Ingle applied Zipf's law distribution to order the frequency of short words in a text and used this information as the main aspect of language identification. The studies published by Beesley (1988) and later by Dunning (1994) were among the first to use character n-grams for language identification. Character n-grams are the basis of several state-of-the-art methods in language identification. Dunning (1994) reports over 99% accuracy in distinguishing English and Spanish texts. In this approach, the likelihood of character n-grams is calculated using Markov models and Bayesian decision rules are applied to minimise errors.

After Dunning, several studies using n-gram language models were published, among them is the work of Cavnar and Trenkle (1994). This study employs n-gram methods that make use of the list of the most frequent character n-grams in a corpus. The tool is available online and is called *TextCat*.[2]

[2] http://odur.let.rug.nl/vannoord/TextCat/.

TextCat can be customised to user's needs as it allows users to train the system with one's own data.

Grefenstette (1995) compares two methods of language identification: a trigram approach inspired by the work of Beesley (1988) and Cavnar and Trenkle (1994) and the frequent word approach proposed by Ingle (1980). Grafenstette points out the simplicity of both methods and the advantage of character-based approaches when dealing with short texts (less than 15 words). According to this study, shorter sentences are often titles and section headings, which might not contain any of the short words used for classification in Ingle's approach.

A couple of other comparative studies have been published and they aim to investigate the performance of statistical methods and features in language identification. Vojtek and Belikova (2007) compares two methods based on Markov processes including the aforementioned method proposed by Dunning (1994). Padró and Padró (2004) compared the performance of three methods: Markov models, trigram frequency vectors and n-gram-based text categorisation (Cavnar and Trenkle, 1994) and finally, Groethe et al. (2008) compare methods based on three features: short words, frequent words and character n-grams.

The Internet is an interesting application for language identification and this will be discussed in more detail in Section 8.4.1. Documents available on the Internet are often unidentified regarding source language. Moreover, the same document may contain more than one language, making it difficult for computer programs to process them. In the last few years, a number of language identification methods were proposed for this kind of data, including Martins and Silva (2005), Rehurek and Kolkus (2009), Tromp and Pechnizkiy (2012) and Vogel and Tresner-Kirsch (2012). The two last methods focus on short and often noisy Internet texts such as *tweets* using the LIGA algorithm.

Martins and Silva (2005) proposed a method to identify a set of 12 languages and their results varied by language, ranging from 99% accuracy for English to 80% for Italian. Their study provides an example of one of the two aforementioned bottlenecks of language identification: the identification of closely related languages. The performance obtained when identifying Italian is particularly representative of this difficulty: among 500 texts classified, 20 were tagged as Portuguese and 42 as Spanish. Given that Italian, Portuguese and Spanish are all Romance languages, it is evident why algorithms have difficulty classifying Italian documents.

Lui and Baldwin (2012) developed a language identification tool called *langid.py*. The system contains language models for 97 languages, using various data sources such as the EMEA biomedical corpus, the EuroPARL Corpus and Wikipedia. The study reports 91.3% accuracy for a set of 67 languages using Wikipedia data. The tool is off-the-shelf and can be trained to identify new languages. Another recent study is the one by Takçi and Güngör (2012), who propose a centroid-based classification approach for language identification. The authors report results of 97.5% accuracy.

Brown's work is among the most recent studies in language identification (Brown, 2013, 2014). His work focuses on building robust methods to identify a wide range of languages. In his most recent publication Brown reports results of a system trained to identify over 1300 languages (Brown, 2014).

8.2.1 Distinguishing between Similar Languages

As previously mentioned, distinguishing similar languages is one of the bottlenecks of language identification and there is still a lack of studies in this area. Only recently has this aspect of language identification received more attention, with a few studies published about it and a shared task organised for this purpose.

Ljubešić et al. (2007) proposed a computational model for the identification of Croatian texts in comparison to other South Slavic languages, namely: Slovene and Serbian. The study reports 99% recall and precision in three processing stages. One of these processing stages includes a list of forbidden words that appear only in Croatian texts, making the algorithm perform better. Tiedemann and Ljubešić (2012) improves this method and applies it to Bosnian, Serbian and Croatian texts. The study reports significantly higher performance than the accuracy of general purpose methods, such as *TextCat* and *langid.py*.

Ranaivo-Malançon (2006) presents a semisupervised character-based model to distinguish between Indonesian and Malay, two closely related languages from the Austronesian family. The study uses the frequency and rank of character trigrams derived from the most frequent words in each language, lists of exclusive words and the format of numbers (Malay uses decimal point whereas Indonesian uses comma). The authors compare the performance obtained by their approach with the one obtained by the aforementioned *TextCat* tool.

Recently, within the scope of the VarDial workshop held at the 2014 edition of COLING, the discriminating between similar languages (DSL) (Zampieri et al., 2014) shared task was organised. In this shared task, participants were requested to train systems to discriminate between 13 languages in 6 language groups, each of them including two or more similar languages and language varieties. Participants received a data set comprising sentences extracted from journalistic texts (Tan et al., 2014).

The top five teams obtained above 90% accuracy and the best scores were obtained by Goutte et al. (2014) using a two-step approach to predict first the language group then the language of each instance. Two systems used information gain (IG) to select the best features for classification, namely King et al. (2014) and Lui et al. (2014), which made use of the aforementioned *langid.py* software. The other two top five results were obtained by Porta and Sancho (2014) and Purver (2014) using a linear SVM classifier with words and characters as features.

The methods applied to the distinction between similar languages have a lot in common with those applied to distinguish varieties and dialects. This application of language identification will be discussed in Section 8.4.2.

8.3 COMPUTATIONAL TECHNIQUES

This section discusses the techniques used in the methods presented in Section 8.2. It begins by presenting short word-based methods and subsequently describes n-gram calculation, which is the core component of state-of-the-art language identification methods. Finally, it presents some of the classification methods used for language identification.

8.3.1 Short Words

Introduced by Ingle (1980), short words can be good clues for language identification methods. These words are often grammatical words such as determiners, conjunctions and prepositions and they are very frequent in natural language corpora. The idea behind this approach is that short words are highly discriminative because the frequency of words in a corpus follows a Zipfian distribution (Zipf, 1949).

Zipf's law states that for every corpus, the frequency of any word is inversely proportional to its rank in a frequency list. According to this principle, the most frequent word occurs approximately twice as often as the second most frequent word, three times as often as the third most frequent word and so on. Zipf's law also suggests that short words are on average more frequent than long ones. A personal pronoun in its first person singular form, which is used very often in a language, would probably never be more than two or three characters long. Zipf states that the distribution of words in a language is due to the tendency to communicate efficiently with least effort: "Principle of Least Effort".

Table 8.1 Top five short words presented by Grefenstette (1995)

Dutch	English	French	German	Portuguese	Spanish
de	the	de	der	de	de
van	and	la	die	a	la
het	to	le	und	que	que
een	of	et	den	o	el
en	a	des	in	e	en

Grefenstette (1995) presents a short word list calculated based on the ECI corpus. Table 8.1 presents the top five words of this table for Dutch, English, French, German, Portuguese and Spanish.

Even though the likelihood of occurrence of these short words is very high, by looking at Table 8.1, one can see a shortcoming of this method. Short word-based approaches have difficulty in providing information to distinguish between similar languages. Portuguese and Spanish share two of the most frequent short words, namely *de* and *que* and the same is true for French and Spanish with *de* and *la*. All three of these languages have *de* as their most frequent word.

8.3.2 N-Gram Language Models

Most state-of-the-art methods in language identification, starting with Dunning (1994) rely on n-gram language models. These models are simple statistical language models calculated based on the cooccurrence of words or characters. The basic idea is to consider a text or corpus as the probability of different words or characters occurring alone or occurring in sequence.

In language identification, character models are often modelled as bigrams, trigrams and 4-grams, whereas unigrams are mostly used for words. For a more detailed explanation of n-gram language models, I recommend reading Manning and Schütze (1999), Chapter 6.

8.3.2.1 Unigrams

Unigram models are the simplest language models. They treat units (in our example, words) in isolation. Each word is assigned a probability and the model assumes independence between them. Take the following sentence as an example:

John went to the supermarket to buy a bottle of wine.

This is a well-formed English sentence that could be part of a natural language corpus. Our example contains 11 words.[3] The words *John* and *went* occur only once, and each has a probability of $\frac{1}{11}$ or 0.0909. The word *to* occurs twice and receives $\frac{2}{11}$ or 0.1818. This information is then used to calculate more interesting information; for example, the probability of a sentence or string of words occurring in a corpus.

The calculation of the probability of *John went to* occurring in our corpus is done simply by multiplying the individual probabilities: $0.0909 \times 0.0909 \times 0.1818 = 0.0015$. This calculation is simple and does not make any distinction in terms of word order. *John to went* would also receive 0.0015 probability, although it is not a well-formed combination. Formally a unigram language model calculated for three words can be represented by the following equation:

$$P_{\text{uni}}(w_1 w_2 w_3) = P(w_1)P(w_2)P(w_3) \qquad (8.2)$$

The probability of the words w_1, w_2 and w_3 occurring in a corpus is the product of their individual probabilities. An example of the usage of unigrams in language identification is the work of Souter et al. (1994). In their approach, texts were analysed word-by-word with a likelihood calculated for each. At the end of the text, the program returns the most likely language according to the word unigram probabilities. There are, however, more sophisticated ways of calculating language models that take context into account, as will be presented next.

8.3.2.2 Bigrams and Higher-Order N-Grams

Every natural language has a number of word ordering restrictions. Returning to our example, *John went to* is an acceptable combination in English, whereas *John to went* is not. The same is true for character combinations: *th* is a very frequent character combination in English, whereas *ht* is not.

Language models may take ordering restrictions into consideration, and one of the ways of doing so is by using bigrams and higher-order n-grams (trigrams, 4-grams, etc.). Bigrams are first-order language models that aim to capture some of the ordering restrictions that occur in natural language. They consider the probability of a word occurring as a function of its immediate context, as shown next:

$$P(w_1 w_2) = P(w_1)P(w_2|w_1) \qquad (8.3)$$

---

[3] In this example, we do not take punctuation into account.

In Equation (8.3), w_2 represents the antecedent of a given w_1 word. The assumption that only the local context affects the next word is a *Markov* assumption. Markov models are used in several language identification methods such as Dunning (1994).

Understanding the calculation of bigrams allows us to understand the logic behind higher-order language models that take a bigger set of context into account. Before we proceed to higher-order models let us look at an example for character n-grams. Our example adapted from Cavnar and Trenkle (1994) takes the word *park* and models it into bigrams, trigrams and 4-grams. The symbol * represents blanks.

- bigrams: *p, pa, ar, rk, k*
- trigrams: **p, *pa, par, ark, rk*, k**
- 4-grams: ***p, **pa *par, park, ark*, rk**, k***

In this example one can see that the higher the order of the n-gram model, the more lexical units the model will consider. The word *park* is considered as a whole in a 4-gram model. In this language model, we will therefore not only be considering the character sequences, but also complete words.

Most language identification methods use character trigrams, nevertheless bigrams and 4-grams were also substantially explored. Character and word trigrams can be calculated using the following formula:

$$P(w_1w_2w_3) = P(w_1)P(w_2|w_1)P(w_3|w_2w_1) \qquad (8.4)$$

Given the n-gram calculations discussed so far, what happens if a word exists in the language and it does not appear in a given corpus? Should it be part of the language model? No matter how big a corpus is, some words will be rare and will simply not occur in the corpus. However, this does not mean they will not occur in other samples. The same is true for character sequences, where some are more frequent than others. Take the word *rhythm* as an example. Is the combination of *rhyt* a frequent character combination in English? It might not be as frequent as other combinations, but it is certainly valid.

As Manning and Schütze (1999) stated: "regardless of how the probability is computed, there is still the need to assign a non-zero probability estimate to words or n-grams that are not present in our training corpus". This kind of strategy is called smoothing and there are a number of techniques that are used in language identification. A very simple one used in Dunning (1994) and Zampieri and Gebre (2012) is the Laplace distribution, also referred to as add one smoothing:

$$P_{\text{lap}}(w_1 \ldots w_n) = \frac{C(w_1 \ldots w_n) + 1}{N + B} \qquad (8.5)$$

In Equation (8.5), C is the count of the frequency of w_1 to w_n in the training data, N is the total number of n-grams and B is the unique number of n-grams. The biggest criticism regarding the simplicity of the Laplace smoothing is that it leads to overestimation of the probabilities of unseen n-grams.

There are other smoothing techniques worth mentioning that are used not only for language identification but also in other NLP tasks.[4] One example of a technique is Good–Turing discounting, published by Good (1953), which credits Alan Turing for the original idea. The basic intuition of this method is to use the count of items that appear once in a data set to estimate the count of unseen items. Other smoothing techniques include backoff models, such as the one proposed by Katz (1987), widely used in speech processing, and absolute discount, by Ney et al. (1994).

The language models presented so far are an important part of state-of-the-art n-gram-based language identification methods. These n-gram models are used as input for classification methods. They serve as a source of information to calculate the probability of a document belonging to a given class (language), as previously described in Section 8.1.1.

8.3.3 Classification Methods

For the document classification stage, different approaches have been proposed. Algorithms that rely on random sampling to obtain numerical results, known as Monte Carlo sampling, were used by Poutsma (2001). The aforementioned Markov chains were proposed by Dunning (1994) in combination with Bayesian decision rules. Xafopoulos et al. (2004) also used Markov-based methods, applying HMM to calculate the probability of documents belonging to a given class.

Cavnar and Trenkle (1994) proposed an out-of-place metric applied to ordered lists of n-grams to distinguish languages. The same basic idea was later explored by other studies such as Grefenstette (1995) and the comparative study proposed by Groethe et al. (2008). Due to its relevance, this model will be discussed in more detail in Section 8.3.3.1.

Machine learning techniques were also used in language identification. Combrinck and Botha (1994) proposed the use of machine learning as an alternative to Markov-based approaches. Takçi and Güngör (2012) applies a centroid-based classification approach, widely used in text classification.

---

[4] Chapter 4 of Jurafsky and Martin (2009) provides a very good introduction to several smoothing techniques.

Lui and Baldwin (2011) proposes the use of a multinomial naive Bayes classifier with very good results.

Most language identification studies involve supervised learning strategies. Nevertheless, there were a couple of attempts to perform the task by using unsupervised methods such as Amine et al. (2010). In this study, the authors propose a hybrid method for language identification that includes k-means clustering.

8.3.3.1 Out-of-Place Metric

The classification method proposed by Cavnar and Trenkle (1994) is conceptually a ranking method. The core of this classification method relies on the out-of-place metric. This metric establishes n-gram profiles and calculates a simple rank-order statistics that determines how far out of place an n-gram in one profile is from its place in the category. The idea can be best understood by looking at Figure 8.1.

Based on the authors' example and description (Cavnar and Trenkle, 1994), the n-gram "ING" is at rank 2 in the document, but at rank 5 in the category, therefore 3 ranks out of place. If an n-gram (e.g., "ED") is not in the category profile, it takes a maximum out-of-place value (arbitrarily defined). The sum of all of the out-of-place values for all n-grams is the distance measure for the document from the category. The algorithm then applies what they called a "find minimum distance" function. This function takes the distance measures from all of the category profiles to the document profile, and picks the smallest one.

8.3.3.2 Information Gain: Estimating the Best Features

The aforementioned *langid.py* (Lui and Baldwin, 2012; Lui and Baldwin, 2011) is a state-of-the-art off-the-shelf general purpose language

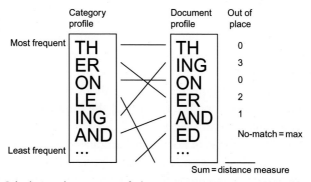

Figure 8.1 Calculating the two out-of-place measure (Cavnar and Trenkle, 1994).

identification tool. The method achieved results of up to 94.7% accuracy, thus outperforming similar tools such as *TextCat* (Cavnar and Trenkle, 1994).

The approach uses a multinomial naive Bayes classifier combined with IG for feature selection. IG minimises the impact of the topic influence in language identification and it is the main innovative aspect of *langid.py*.

According to Lui and Baldwin (2011), their approach considers the IG of particular n-gram features in three dimensions: (1) the set of all languages; (2) within a given language; and (3) within the domain the data was obtained from. The method aims to use this information to identify features that have high IG with respect to language but low IG with respect to domain. The method was tested using a data set containing 97 languages and 5 different domains. It obtained performance and speed superior to other off-the-shelf tools such as *GoogleAPI* and *TextCat*.

8.4 APPLICATIONS AND RELATED TASKS

After providing an overview of the most important approaches to automatic language identification, this section presents a couple of applications and related tasks.

Methods designed to work on short texts such as those available on the Internet are discussed. Another application explored in this section is language identification methods applied to distinguish language varieties (e.g., American and British English or Brazilian and European Portuguese) and dialects. Finally, I discuss a relevant and more complex task similar to language identification, called native language identification (NLI).

8.4.1 Internet Data and Short Texts

As previously mentioned, there are two bottlenecks in state-of-the-art language identification. One of them is the identification of closely related languages and the other is the performance of language identification of short pieces of text. Short texts might not contain the necessary amount of information that would allow general purpose methods to perform well. These kinds of texts are frequent on the Internet in the form of short query texts and on social media such as *Twitter*.

Identifying the language of documents originated from the Internet is a difficult task. Firstly, because a number of computer-mediated communication contexts make use of nonstandard spelling that identification methods need to be trained to recognise. Secondly, because of their multilingual nature, texts on the Internet often contain code-switching, resulting in multilingual documents. Given these challenges, in the last few years, a number of language identification methods were developed for Internet data. These methods include the aforementioned study by Martins and Silva (2005), which aimed to distinguish a set of 12 languages using Internet data.

Another study, published by Rehurek and Kolkus (2009), investigates the limitations of Markov-based approaches when applied to real-world web pages. The authors point out the difficulty that these methods face when they are used to identify very short texts and multilingual texts. They propose an approach that constructs language models based on word relevance. To classify multilingual documents, the method segments multilingual texts automatically into blocks of individual languages.

The Ceylan and Kim (2009) study aims to identify languages in short query texts used in search engines. Authors use logs from *Yahoo!* to train machine learning algorithms. They train two decision tree classifiers: one that only uses linguistic features and another that includes nonlinguistic features. More recently, Tromp and Pechnizkiy (2012) developed the LIGA algorithm. This method was developed to identify the language of short texts and it was evaluated on texts extracted from *Twitter*. The LIGA algorithm was later improved by Vogel and Tresner-Kirsch (2012).

A recent shared task on language identification on *Twitter* messages was held at the 2014 edition of the Conference of the Spanish Society for NLP (SEPLN) (Zubiaga et al., 2014). In the data provided by the organisers, *tweets* were written in Spanish, Portuguese, Catalan, English, Galician and Basque (ordered by the number of *tweets*). The top scoring system obtained a 75.2% F1 score (Hurtado et al., 2014).

8.4.2 Discriminating and Language Varieties

Most language identification methods developed so far do not take language variation into account. For computational applications it is in most cases enough to identify whether a text is written in English, German or Spanish regardless of language variety or dialectal information.

It is, however, understood that language variation influences perception and allows speakers to identify texts or speech production (accent) that belong to a certain variety or dialect. Some languages have more than one national written standard and these are called pluricentric languages.[5] This is the case of English, which is the official language of several countries and therefore has a number of language varieties, each of them with unique characteristics.

For example, British and American English are two varieties of the same language that are distinct from one another. Their differences include: lexical choices (e.g., *rubbish* (UK) and *garbage* (US) or *trousers* (UK) and *pants* (US)), moderate differences in orthography (e.g., *neighbour* (UK) and *neighbor* (US)) and substantial differences in phonology. If the purpose of language identification methods is to distinguish different linguistic systems, it would also be possible to distinguish subtle differences automatically. A number of text processing applications might benefit from the identification of the correct variety of the text, including text mining.

The methods applied to varieties and dialects are similar to those discussed in Section 8.2.1 for similar languages. One of the methods proposed to identify language varieties is by Huang and Lee (2008). This study presented a bag-of-words approach to distinguish Chinese texts from the mainland and Taiwan with results of up to 92% accuracy. Another study is the one presented by Zampieri and Gebre (2012) for Portuguese. In this study, the authors proposed a log-likelihood estimation method along with Laplace smoothing to identify two varieties of Portuguese (Brazilian and European). Their approach was trained and tested in a binary setting using journalistic texts, with accuracy results above 99.5% for character n-grams. The algorithm was later adapted to classify Spanish texts using not only the classical word and character n-grams but also part-of-speech (POS) distribution Zampieri et al. (2013).

The DEFT2010 (Grouin et al., 2010) shared task held in Montreal provided French journalistic data for participants to train their system to classify texts not only with respect to their geographical location but also according to the decade in which they were published. Among the participants, Mokhov (2010) trained the MARF pattern recognition software for the task. Along similar lines, Trieschnigg et al. (2012) describes a classification experiment for Dutch dialects from the Dutch Folktale Database, which also

---

[5] Note that here I will not discuss the fine line between languages in their own right, language varieties and dialects. It would be beyond the scope of this chapter and it is a long-standing debate in linguistics. Nevertheless, I recommend Clyne (1992) as a reference work on pluricentric languages and Chambers and Trudgill (1998) for a concise yet complete introduction to dialectology.

contains historical texts. In this study researchers report micro average f-measure results of 79.9% with the best f-measure result reaching 98.7% for one of the classes.

Lui and Cook (2013) investigate computational methods to discriminate between texts from three English national varieties (Canadian, Australian and British) across different domains and text types. According to the authors, the results obtained suggest that each variety contains characteristics that are consistent across multiple domains, which enables algorithms to distinguish them regardless of the data source.

More recently, attention has been given to the discrimination between Arabic dialects. This is reflected in a number of studies published in the last few years (Elfardy and Diab, 2014; Zaidan and Callison-Burch, 2014; Tillmann et al., 2014; Sadat et al., 2014).

8.4.3 Native Language Identification

Another related task to language identification is NLI. NLI is the task of automatically identifying the native language of a writer based on the writer's foreign language production. The task is often regarded as part of the broader task of authorship profiling. Authorship profiling methods try to assert attributes of the author such as age, gender and native language.

NLI methods are particularly relevant for languages with a significant number of foreign speakers, most notably, English. According to *Ethnologue* data (Lewis et al., 2013), it is estimated that the number of nonnative English speakers outnumbers native speakers by two to one. The nonnative speakers' production is present on the Internet where English is used as lingua franca.

The task is by no means trivial and it is based on the assumption that the mother tongue influences second language acquisition and production (Lado, 1957). NLI might be a useful component in text mining applications, particularly those applied to Internet data. NLI methods can be used firstly to identify native from nonnative texts and secondly to assert the native language or language family (e.g., Slavic, Germanic, Romance) of an individual. A number of attempts at identifying native language have been made. Tomokiyo and Jones (2001) uses a naive Bayes classifier and their experiments used transcribed data from three native languages: Chinese, Japanese and English. The algorithm reached 96% accuracy when distinguishing native from nonnative texts and 100% when distinguishing English native speakers from Chinese native speakers.

Koppel et al. (2005) used a machine learning approach to identify the native languages of nonnative English speakers with five different mother tongues (Bulgarian, Czech, French, Russian and Spanish). Authors used data from the International Corpus of Learner English (Granger et al., 2009) and the features considered were function words, character n-grams, and POS bigrams. Tsur and Rappoport (2007) investigated the influence of the phonology of a writer's mother tongue through native language syllables modelled by character bigrams.

Kochmar (2011) used support vector machines (SVM) for NLI. The author identified error types that are typical for speakers of different native languages, and compiled a set of features based on these error types to improve the classification's performance.

Recently, the NLI shared task[6] (Tetreault et al., 2013) featured 29 systems trying to identify a set of 11 native languages in students essays from the TOEFL11 collection (Blanchard et al., 2013). Among the participants, Gebre et al. (2013) used TF-IDF weighting for NLI with results reaching 81.4% accuracy and the overall best result was 83.6% accuracy obtained by Jarvis et al. (2013).

The most recent work on NLI is, to my knowledge, that of Ionescu et al. (2014). In this paper researchers approach the task using character n-grams as features and report results 1.7% higher than the top scoring system of the 2013 NLI shared task.

8.5 CONCLUSION

This chapter discussed the task of automatic language identification focusing on the use of n-gram language models.

The chapter presented solely methods designed to work on written data. Although the identification of spoken language uses similar methods to those applied to written language, I believe that spoken language would not be within the scope of a handbook in text mining. Instead, I presented relevant related tasks to language identification that could be adapted to real text mining applications, including identification of language varieties and dialects and native language identification.

Researchers who wish to investigate and implement new or existing methods in language identification can use this chapter as a starting point and look in more detail to the references presented here. The textbooks by Jurafsky and Martin (2009) and Manning and Schütze (1999) provide a solid background on n-gram and statistical models applied to text

---

[6] https://sites.google.com/site/nlisharedtask2013/.

processing. The technical report published by Dunning (1994) may also be recommended as a concise introduction to language identification. A couple of tools such as *TextCat* (Cavnar and Trenkle, 1994), *langid.py* (Lui and Baldwin, 2012) or *VarClass* (Zampieri and Gebre, 2014) are available online and may be integrated into text processing applications.

ACKNOWLEDGEMENTS

The author would like to thank Binyam Gebrekidan Gebre and Nikola Ljubešić for commenting on a draft version of this chapter and the editors of this handbook for their valuable help throughout the whole editorial process.

REFERENCES

Amine, A., Elberrichi, Z., Simonet, M., 2010. Automatic language identification: an alternative unsupervised approach using a new hybrid algorithm. Int. J. Comput. Sci. Appl. 7, 94–107.

Beesley, K., 1988. Language identifier: a computer program for automatic natural-language identification of on-line text. In: Proceedings of the Annual Conference of the American Translators Association, Pages 57, 54.

Blanchard, D., Tetreault, J., Higgins, D., Cahill, A., Chodorow, M., 2013. TOEFL11: a corpus of non-native English. Technical report, Educational Testing Service.

Brown, R., 2013. Selecting and weighting n-grams to identify 1100 languages. In: Proceedings of the 16th International Conference on Text Speech and Dialogue (TSD2013), Lecture Notes in Artificial Intelligence (LNAI 8082). Springer, Pilsen, Czech Republic, pp. 519–526.

Brown, R.D., 2014. Non-linear mapping for improved identification of 1300 + languages. In: Proceedings of EMNLP.

Cavnar, W., Trenkle, J., 1994. N-gram-based text catogorization. In: 3rd Symposium on Document Analysis and Information Retrieval (SDAIR-94).

Ceylan, H., Kim, Y., 2009. Language identification of search engine queries. In: Proceedings of the Annual Meeting of the ACL, pp. 1066–1074.

Chambers, J., Trudgill, P., 1998. Dialectology, second ed. Cambridge University Press, Cambridge, UK.

Clyne, M., 1992. Pluricentric Languages: Different Norms in Different Nations. CRC Press.

Combrinck, H., Botha, E., 1994. Text-based automatic language identification. In: Proceedings of the 6th Annual South African Workshop on Pattern Recognition.

Dunning, T., 1994. Statistical identification of language. Technical report, Computing Research Lab – New Mexico State University.

Elfardy, H., Diab, M.T., 2014. Sentence level dialect identification in Arabic. In: Proceedings of ACL.

Gebre, B.G., Zampieri, M., Wittenburg, P., Heskens, T., 2013. Improving native language identification with TF-IDF weighting. In: Proceedings of the 8th NAACL Workshop on Innovative Use of NLP for Building Educational Applications (BEA8), Atlanta, USA.

Good, J., 1953. The population frequencies of species and the estimation of population parameters. Biometrika 40, 237–264.

Goutte, C., Léger, S., Carpuat, M., 2014. The NRC system for discriminating similar languages. In: Proceedings of the 1st Workshop on Applying NLP Tools to Similar Languages, Varieties and Dialects (VarDial), Dublin, Ireland.

Granger, S., Dagneaux, E., Meunier, F., 2009. International Corpus of Learner English (Version 2). Presses Universitaires de Louvain, Louvain-la-Neuve, Belgium.

Grefenstette, G., 1995. Comparing two language identification schemes. In: Proceedings of JADT 1995, 3rd International Conference on Statistical Analysis of Textual Data, Rome.

Groethe, L., De Luca, E., Nürnberger, A., 2008. A comparative study on language identification methods. In: Proceedings of LREC.

Grouin, C., Forest, D., Da Sylva, L., Paroubek, P., Zweigenbaum, P., 2010. Présentation et résultats du défi fouille de texte DEFT2010 où et quand un article de presse a-t-il été écrit? In: Actes du sixième DÉfi Fouille de Textes.

Huang, C., Lee, L., 2008. Contrastive approach towards text source classification based on top-bag-of-word similarity. In: Proceedings of PACLIC 2008, pp. 404–410.

Hurtado, L.-F., Pla, F., Giménez, M., Sanchis, E., 2014. Elirf-upv en tweetlid: Identificatión del idioma en twitter. In: Proceedings of the Tweet Language Identification Workshop (TweetLID), Girona, Spain.

Ingle, N., 1980. A Language Identification Table. Technical Translation International.

Ionescu, R.T., Popescu, M., Cahill, A., 2014. Can characters reveal your native language? a language-independent approach to native language identification. In: Proceedings of EMNLP, Doha, Qatar.

Jarvis, S., Bestgen, Y., Pepper, S., 2013. Maximizing classification accuracy in native language identification. In: Proceedings of the 8th NAACL Workshop on Innovative Use of NLP for Building Educational Applications (BEA8), Atlanta, GA, USA.

Jurafsky, D., Martin, J., 2009. Speech and Language Processing, second ed. Prentice Hall, New Jersey, NJ, USA.

Katz, S., 1987. Estimation of probabilities from sparse data for the language model component of a speech recognizer. IEEE Trans. Acoust. Speech Signal Process. 35, 400–401.

King, B., Radev, D., Abney, S., 2014. Experiments in sentence language identification with groups of similar languages. In: Proceedings of the 1st Workshop on Applying NLP Tools to Similar Languages, Varieties and Dialects (VarDial), Dublin, Ireland.

Kochmar, E., 2011. Identification of a writer's native language by error analysis. Master's Thesis, University of Cambridge, Cambridge, United Kingdom.

Koppel, M., Schler, J., Zigon, K, 2005. Automatically determining an anonymous author's native language. In: Lecture Notes in Computer Science, vol. 3495. pp. 209–217.

Lado, R., 1957. Applied Linguistics for Language Teachers. University of Michigan Press, Ann Arbor, MI, USA.

Lewis, P., Simons, G., Fennig, C., 2013. Ethnologue: Languages of the World, 17th ed. SIL International, Dallas, TX, USA.

Ljubešić, N., Mikelic, N., Boras, D., 2007. Language identification: how to distinguish similar languages? In: Proceedings of the 29th International Conference on Information Technology Interfaces.

Lui, M., Baldwin, T., 2011. Cross-domain feature selection for language identification. In: Proceedings of 5th International Joint Conference on Natural Language Processing. Asian Federation of Natural Language Processing, Chiang Mai, Thailand, pp. 553–561.

Lui, M., Baldwin, T., 2012. langid.py: an off-the-shelf language identification tool. In: Proceedings of the 50th Meeting of the ACL.

Lui, M., Cook, P., 2013. Classifying English documents by national dialect. In: Proceedings of Australasian Language Technology Workshop, pp. 5–15.

Lui, M., Letcher, N., Adams, O., Duong, L., Cook, P., Baldwin, T., 2014. Exploring methods and resources for discriminating similar languages. In: Proceedings of the 1st Workshop on Applying NLP Tools to Similar Languages, Varieties and Dialects (VarDial), Dublin, Ireland.

Manning, C., Schütze, H., 1999. Foundations of statistical natural language processing. MIT Press, Cambridge, MA, USA.

Martins, B., Silva, M., 2005. Language identification in web pages. In: Proceedings of the 20th ACM Symposium on Applied Computing (SAC), Document Engineering Track. EUA, Santa Fe, NM, USA, pp. 763–768.

Mokhov, S., 2010. A marf approach to deft2010. In: Proceedings of TALN2010, Montreal, Canada.

Ney, H., Essen, U., Kneser, R., 1994. On structuring probabilistic dependence in stochastic language modelling. Comput. Speech Lang. 8, 1–38.

Padró, M., Padró, L., 2004. Comparing methods for language identification. Procesamiento del Lenguaje Natural 33, 155–162.

Palmer, D., 2010. Text processing, In: Indurkhya, N., Damerau, F. (Eds.), Handbook of Natural Language Processing. second ed. CRC Press, Boca Raton, FL, USA, pp. 9–30.

Porta, J., Sancho, J.-L., 2014. Using maximum entropy models to discriminate between similar languages and varieties. In: Proceedings of the 1st Workshop on Applying NLP Tools to Similar Languages, Varieties and Dialects (VarDial), Dublin, Ireland.

Poutsma, A., 2001. Applying Monte Carlo techniques to language identification. In: Proceedings of Computational Linguistics in the Netherlands.

Purver, M., 2014. A simple baseline for discriminating similar language. In: Proceedings of the 1st Workshop on Applying NLP Tools to Similar Languages, Varieties and Dialects (VarDial), Dublin, Ireland.

Ranaivo-Malançon, B., 2006. Automatic identification of close languages – case study: Malay and Indonesian. ECTI Transactions on Computer and Information Technology 2, 126–134.

Rehurek, R., Kolkus, M., 2009. Language identification on the web: extending the dictionary method. In: Proceedings of CICLing. Lecture Notes in Computer Science. Springer, Berlin, Heidelberg, Germany, pp. 357–368.

Sadat, F., Kazemi, F., Farzindar, A., 2014. Automatic identification of Arabic language varieties and dialects in social media. In: Proceedings of SocialNLP 2014.

Souter, C., Churcher, G., Hayes, J., Hughes, J., Johnson, S., 1994. Natural language identification using corpus-based models. Hermes J. Linguistics 13, 183–203.

Takçi, H., Güngör, T., 2012. A high performance centroid-based classification approach for language identification. Pattern Recogn. Lett. 3, 2077–2084.

Tan, L., Zampieri, M., Ljubešić, N., Tiedemann, J., 2014. Merging comparable data sources for the discrimination of similar languages: the DSL corpus collection. In: Proceedings of the Workshop on Building and Using Comparable Corpora (BUCC), Reykjavik, Iceland.

Tetreault, J., Blanchard, D., Cahill, A., 2013. A report on the first native language identification shared task. In: Proceedings of the Eighth Workshop on Innovative Use of NLP for Building Educational Applications. Association for Computational Linguistics, Atlanta, GA, USA.

Tiedemann, J., Ljubešić, N., 2012. Efficient discrimination between closely related languages. In: Proceedings of COLING 2012, Mumbai, India, pp. 2619–2634.

Tillmann, C., Mansour, S., Al-Onaizan, Y., 2014. Improved sentence-level Arabic dialect classification. In: Proceedings of the First Workshop on Applying NLP Tools to Similar Languages, Varieties and Dialects. Association for Computational Linguistics and Dublin City University, Dublin, Ireland, pp. 110–119.

Tomokiyo, L., Jones, R., 2001. You're not from 'round here, are you'?: naive Bayes detection of non-native utterance text. In: Proceedings of the Second Meeting of the North American Chapter of the Association for Computational Linguistics on Language Technologies (NAACL '01).

Trieschnigg, D., Hiemstra, D., Theune, M., de Jong, F., Meder, T., 2012. An exploration of language identification techniques for the Dutch folktale database. In: Proceedings of LREC2012.

Tromp, E., Pechnizkiy, M., 2012. Graph-based N-gram language identification on short texts. In: Proceedings of the Twentieth Belgian Dutch Conference on Machine Learning (Benelearn 2011), pp. 27–34.

Tsur, O., Rappoport, A., 2007. Using classifier features for studying the effect of native language on the choice of written second language words. In: Proceedings of the Workshop on Cognitive Aspects of Computational Language Acquisition, pp. 9–16.

Vogel, J., Tresner-Kirsch, D., 2012. Robust language identification in short, noisy texts: improvements to LIGA. In: Third International Workshop on Mining Ubiquitous and Social Environments (MUSE 2012).

Vojtek, P., Belikova, M., 2007. Comparing language identification methods based on Markov processes. In: Slovko, International Seminar on Computer Treatment of Slavic and East European Languages.

Xafopoulos, A., Kotropoulos, C., Almpanidis, G., Pitas, I., 2004. Language identification in web documents using discrete HMMs. Pattern Recogn. 37, 583–594.

Zaidan, O.F., Callison-Burch, C., 2014. Arabic dialect identification. Comput. Linguist. 40, 171–202.

Zampieri, M., Gebre, B.G., 2012. Automatic identification of language varieties: the case of Portuguese. In: Proceedings of KONVENS2012, Vienna, Austria, pp. 233–237.

Zampieri, M., Gebre, B.G., 2014. Varclass: an open source language identification tool for language varieties. In: Language Resources and Evaluation (LREC).

Zampieri, M., Gebre, B.G., Diwersy, S., 2013. N-gram language models and POS distribution for the identification of Spanish varieties. In: Proceedings of TALN2013, Sable d'Olonne, France, pp. 580–587.

Zampieri, M., Tan, L., Ljubešić, N., Tiedemann, J., 2014. A report on the DSL shared task 2014. In: Proceedings of the First Workshop on Applying NLP Tools to Similar Languages, Varieties and Dialects. Association for Computational Linguistics and Dublin City University, Dublin, Ireland, pp. 58–67.

Zipf, G., 1949. Human Behavior and the Principle of Least Effort. Addison-Wesley, Cambridge, MA.

Zubiaga, A., San Vicente, I., Gamallo, P., Pichel, J.R., Alegria, I., Aranberri, N., Ezeiza, A., Fresno, V., 2014. Overview of TweetLID: Tweet language identification at SEPLN 2014. In: Proceedings of the Tweet Language Identification Workshop (TweetLID), Girona, Spain.

CHAPTER 9

User-Driven Text Mining of Historical Text

B. Alex, C. Grover, E. Klein, C. Llewellyn, R. Tobin
School of Informatics, University of Edinburgh, Edinburgh, UK

This chapter presents a summary of work on text mining (TM) of historical documents for the discovery of 19th century trade in the British Empire as part of the Digging into Data (http://www.diggingintodata.org) project TRADING CONSEQUENCES (http://tradingconsequences.blogs. edina.ac.uk). The project aimed to assist environmental historians in understanding the economic and environmental consequences of commodity trading during the 19th century. We applied TM to large quantities of historical text, converting unstructured textual information into structured data. The structured data was used to populate a relational database that is in turn the back end for querying and different types of online visualisations. We will discuss some of the challenges involved when processing digitised historical text which originally appeared in printed form.

Prior historical research into commodity flows has focused on a small number of widely traded natural resources such as coffee, timber or cinchona. Tully, for example, examined trade in gutta percha (Tully, 2009) and Cronon researched the history of beef, lumber and wheat (Cronon, 1992). By contrast, this project provides historians with data from large corpora of digitised documents, thereby enabling them to analyse a much broader range of commodities. A detailed appraisal of trade in these resources yields a significantly more complete picture of globalisation and its environmental consequences. The TRADING CONSEQUENCES system allows historians to explore global trends of commodity trading at different times and at different locations while still being able to investigate mentions of individual commodities in context.

We begin this chapter by discussing related work on TM for historical document collections (see Section 9.1). In Section 9.2, we provide an overview of the TRADING CONSEQUENCES system and partners. We describe all the collections that were processed as part of the project in Section 9.3. We then discuss the challenges involved in processing digitised

Working with Text
http://dx.doi.org/10.1016/B978-1-84334-749-1.00009-3

209

historical text and language, particularly the low quality of optical character recognition (OCR) and the difficulty of mining tables, and discuss ways to improve them in Section 9.4. We outline the different stages of our TM pipeline and its output in Section 9.5 and describe how we advanced our research in a user-driven way by means of rapid prototyping in Section 9.6.

9.1 RELATED WORK ON TEXT MINING HISTORICAL DOCUMENTS

Text mining historical documents to extract interesting information, that is, turning unstructured text into structured data, has only become possible with the digitisation of document archives and collections and has gained some traction in the last 10 years. For example, Smith and Crane (2001) and Nissim et al. (2004) worked on extracting geographical names from historical digital collections and geogrounding, that is, disambiguating extracted location mentions and determining their latitudes and longitudes. With the recent increase in digitisation efforts, this field is beginning to establish itself in the context of digital humanities. For example, the GeoDigRef and Embedding GeoCrossWalk projects (Grover et al., 2008, 2010) were both concerned with georeferencing digitised historical collections: for GeoDigRef the collections were the Online Historical Population Reports for Britain and Ireland from 1801 to 1937 (Histpop) and the Journals of the House of Lords (1688 to 1854) from the BOPCRIS 18th Century Parliamentary Publications; for Embedding GeoCrossWalk the collection was the Stormont Papers, parliamentary debates from the start of the Northern Irish Parliament in 1921 to the end of Home Rule in 1972. The two projects used the Edinburgh Geoparser[1] (Tobin et al., 2010) to enrich their existing metadata collections with georeference information extracted as a result of TM. Another method that is often used to analyse pieces of text is topic modelling (for a review article on this technique see Blei (2012)). In the context of historical text analysis, Underwood, for example, has applied topic modelling and topic similarity to 19th century literary text to examine how topics are distributed among genre.[2]

So far, the most frequent use of TM has been to facilitate information retrieval (IR) beyond keyword search. Launched in 2011, Connected Histories[3] provides integrated access to a wide range of distributed digital resources relating to early modern and 19th century British history. The

[1] http://www.ltg.ed.ac.uk/clusters/Edinburgh_Geoparser.
[2] http://tedunderwood.com/.
[3] http://www.connectedhistories.org.

resources were processed to extract person, location and date mentions within each of the documents and this information is used for indexing the collections. The Connected Histories search engine interface allows users to search for person or location names in combination with a date range and therefore goes beyond the standard key word search that is typical for online search engines. The search results are then listed in the form of document titles and summaries with search terms highlighted. A similar service is provided by Manuscripts Online[4] with additional options to search within references, search for spelling variants and search in French and Latin besides English. In both projects, ANNIE,[5] an open-source information extraction system, was used as the basis for the named entity recognition.

In the last few years, there has been a strong focus on text mining large data sets for digital humanities research. For example, the Digging Into Data (DID) program, which was launched in 2009, aims to understand how big data changes humanities and social sciences research. Scholars in these fields make use of large data sets of various types, including historical collections of textual documents. The DID Challenge aims to discover how state-of-the-art computational techniques, including TM, can be applied to such sources to facilitate existing research methods and answer experts' hypotheses or provide new angles on their research. DID funded a series of projects including ChartEx[6] which applied natural language processing (NLP) to medieval charters from the 12th to the 16th century to identify person and place names and relational information. TRADING CONSEQUENCES, also funded by DID, combined TM with advanced visualisation methods. Visualising the extracted textual information from millions of digitised images using maps, timelines or in combination with other data sets, for example, climate data or railroads information, can become a powerful tool to researchers in the humanities and social sciences.

With respect to processing digitised historical documents specifically, there has been some work on determining the effect of OCR accuracy on text processing, be it IR or TM. Direct access to historical documents is hindered through language change and historical words have to be associated with their modern variants to improve recall. Hauser et al. (2007), for example, designed special fuzzy matching strategies to relate modern language keywords with old variants in German documents from the Early New High German period. Gotscharek et al. (2011) argue that such matching procedures need to be used

---

[4] http://www.manuscriptsonline.org.
[5] http://gate.ac.uk/sale/tao/splitch6.html#chap:annie.
[6] http://www.chartex.org.

in combination with specially constructed historical lexica to improve recall in IR. The latter work was carried out as part of IMPACT,[7] a large EU project aiming to enhance the capabilities of OCR engines and thereby improve the accessibility of digitised text for mass digitisation effort. OCR errors have been shown to have a negative effect on NLP in general. Lopresti (2005, 2008a, b), for example, examines the effect that varying degrees of OCR accuracy have on sentence boundary detection, tokenisation and part-of-speech tagging, all steps that are typically carried out as early stages of TM. Kolak and Resnik (2005) carried out an extrinsic evaluation of OCR postprocessing for machine translation from Spanish into English and show that translation quality increases after postcorrecting the OCRed text. Furthermore, the NLP work carried out in the Connected Histories project showed that performance for named entity recognition is higher for rekeyed collections than for raw OCRed text.[8] To what extent the correction of OCR can affect the quality of TM and whether it is necessary when processing Big Data are questions that still require further research.

9.2 THE TRADING CONSEQUENCES SYSTEM

TRADING CONSEQUENCES is a collaborative project between environmental historians at York University[9] and the University of Saskatchewan,[10] computational linguists at the Edinburgh Language Technology Group[11] at the School of Informatics, database engineers at EDINA[12] and computer visualisation experts at the St. Andrews Computer Human Interaction research group.[13] The project aims to assist environmental historians in understanding the economic and environmental consequences of commodity trading during the 19th century. We applied TM to large quantities of historical text, converting unstructured textual information into structured data used to populate a relational database. Prior historical research into commodity trading has focused on a small number of widely traded natural resources. By contrast, this project provides historians with data from large corpora of digitised documents, thereby enabling them to analyse a broader range of commodities. Equally, they will be able to drill down to individual

---

[7] http://www.impact-project.eu/home/.
[8] http://www.connectedhistories.org/about.aspx#evaluation.
[9] http://www.yorku.ca.
[10] http://www.usask.ca/.
[11] http://www.ltg.ed.ac.uk/.
[12] http://edina.ac.uk/.
[13] http://sachi.cs.st-andrews.ac.uk.

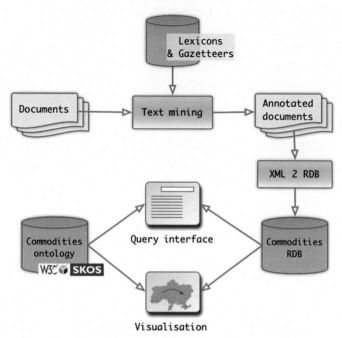

Figure 9.1 Architecture of the TRADING CONSEQUENCES prototype.

documents and see which documents are most relevant for a given commodity and study the mentions of commodities in context.

Within TRADING CONSEQUENCES, our intention was to develop a series of prototypes of the overall system. Initially, they had limited functionality, but they became increasingly powerful. After delivering the first prototype of the TRADING CONSEQUENCES system, we improved the technology based on user feedback and repeated this process iteratively. Figure 9.1 shows an overview of the final system architecture. The system takes in documents from a number of different collections. The main processing of the TM component involves various types of shallow linguistic analysis of the text, lexicon and gazetteer lookup, named entity recognition and grounding, and relation extraction (see Section 9.5). We determine which commodities were traded when and in relation to which georeferenced locations (Alex et al., 2015). We also determine whether locations are mentioned as points of origin, transit or destination and whether vocabulary relating to diseases and disasters appears in the text. All mined information is added back into the XML documents as different layers of annotation.

The entire annotated XML corpus is parsed to create a relational database (RDB). This stores not just metadata about the individual document, but also detailed information that results from the TM, such as named entities, relations, and how these are expressed in the relevant document. Visualisations and a query interface access the database so that users can either search the mined information directly through textual queries or browse the data in a more exploratory manner. All information mined from the collections is linked back to the original documents of the data providers.

9.3 DATA COLLECTIONS

We analyse textual data from major British and Canadian data sets, most importantly the House of Commons Parliamentary Papers (HCPP)[14] from ProQuest,[15] the Early Canadiana Online data archive (ECO)[16] and a subpart of the Foreign and Commonwealth Office Collection (FCOC) from JSTOR.[17] We also analyse Adam Matthew's Confidential Print collections for Africa, Latin America, the Middle East and North America (CPRINT),[18] the Directors' Correspondence Collection from the Archives at Kew Gardens available at JSTOR Plant Science (LETTERS)[19] and a number of books relevant to trading in the 19th century. Together these sources amount to millions of pages of text. Table 9.1 provides an overview of the number of documents and images per collection or subcollection available to TRADING CONSEQUENCES.[20] The data sets include a wide range of official records from the British and Canadian governments, making them ideal for historical TM. The frequency distribution of the year of publication of all documents process in TRADING CONSEQUENCES

Table 9.1 Overview of the number of documents and scanned images per collection

Collection	No. of docs	No. of scanned images
HCPP	118,526	6,448,739
ECO	83,016	3,938,758
LETTERS	24,765	n/a
CPRINT	1,315	140,010
FCOC	1,000	41,611

With the exception of CPRINT, one scanned image usually corresponds to one document page. In the case of CPRINT, one image mostly corresponds to 2 document pages. The LETTERS are manually written, electronic summaries of the actual letters and therefore did not require OCR.

[14] http://parlipapers.chadwyck.co.uk/home.do.
[15] http://www.proquest.co.uk.
[16] http://eco.canadiana.ca.
[17] http://www.jstor.org/.
[18] http://www.amdigital.co.uk.
[19] http://plants.jstor.org/.
[20] We do not provide statistics for the books as they do not belong to one specific collection.

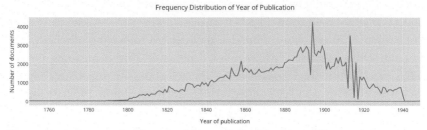

Frequency Distribution of Year of Publication

Figure 9.2 Frequency distribution of the year of publication of all mined documents.

is presented in Figure 9.2. It shows that the bulk of the corpus was written in the second half of the 19th and beginning of the 20th century. We describe each collection in more detail below.

HCPP: We analysed a subpart of the House of Commons Parliamentary Papers, namely all of the 19th century sessional papers from (1801–1900) to part of the 20th century papers (1901–1940). This collection includes bills, House of Commons papers, command papers, reports and accounts of the British government. They amount to 118,526 documents and almost 6.5 million scanned images where an image usually corresponds to one document page.

ECO: Early Canadiana Online contains books, magazines and government publications relevant to Canada's history ranging from 1600 to the 1940s. This collection comprises 83,016 documents amounting to a total of almost 4 million images written mostly in English and French but also in 10 First Nation languages and other European languages as well as Latin. We only processed the proportion of documents identified as written in English (55,277).

LETTERS: The directors' Correspondence Collection from the Archives at Kew Gardens contains handwritten, scientific letters and memorandum received by Kew's Directors and senior staff from the 1840s to 1928, as well as correspondence received by Sir William Jackson Hooker prior to 1841. It provides first hand accounts and observations on botany, ethnobotany, history, natural history, science and politics around the world. In TRADING CON-SEQUENCES, we worked with the letters specifically relevant to Africa, Asia and Latin America. We did not process the letters themselves but the metadata attached to each document, and particularly a written summary of the content of each piece of correspondence. This collection continuously increased over the course of the project as staff in the digitisation team at Kew Gardens made it available to our project. In total, we processed summaries for 24,765 documents. This is the only electronic data set processed in TRADING CON-SEQUENCES that did not require OCR.

CPRINT: The Confidential Print series (split further into Africa, Latin America, the Middle East and North America) contains official British documents generated by the Foreign and Colonial Offices between c. 1820 and 1970 all sourced from The National Archives, Kew. All items marked "Confidential Print" were printed and circulated to leading officials in the Foreign Office, to the Cabinet, and to heads of British missions abroad. They range from single-page letters and telegrams to dispatches, reports and treaties. This data set contains 1,315 documents and 140,010 images where an image corresponds to 2 pages in a document in the majority of cases.

FCOC: JSTOR's Foreign and Commonwealth Office Collection contains material sent to London by British ambassadors and related to South America, the Near East and to various European political "questions" of the 19th century. The collection also contains pamphlets sent back from Britain's colonies, including early material from Australasia. It contains mostly 19th century documents written in English and French but also in other European languages. Some of the material ranges as far back as the 1540s. In TRADING CONSEQUENCES, we had access to 1,000 documents, approximately 25% of the entire collection, which amount to 41,611 scanned images. We applied TM to the proportion of documents identified as written in English (734).

9.4 CHALLENGES OF PROCESSING DIGITISED HISTORICAL TEXT

There are significant challenges in the initial step of transforming these document collections into a format that is suitable for subsequent TM. Here we do not refer to document formats, as converting a document from one format into another is a straight forward task. We rather mean challenges related to the text quality of OCRed output. Documents not only contain running text but may contain text interspersed with tables and figures or pages scanned at an angle or upside down. They may contain headers or even hand written notes in book margins all of which might interrupt the flow of the text. Additionally, an issue for any kind of textual data is that documents may be written in different languages or may contain tables. In summary, we are dealing with very noisy text as input into our TM tools.

9.4.1 Optical Character Recognition Errors

Poor OCR quality, together with artefacts introduced by the scanning process and 19th century language, are major factors influencing the performance of the TM component. For most of the collections, the OCR was carried out several years ago, and is far inferior to what can be achieved nowadays with contemporary scanning hardware and OCR technology. The problems of OCR are aggravated for our corpus by the use of old fonts, poor print and paper quality, and 19th century language. The only collection where the output is relatively clean is the CPRINT series, which was digitised relatively recently using the ABBYY OCR engine, the recognised market leader.[21] This collection also contains many documents published in the 20th century, which means that their original fonts are likely to be more consistent and their print more modern and of higher quality than that of the other OCRed data sets.

In a small study, we investigated the effects of OCR on text quality of a random sample of 25 text records from the ECO collection. We found an error rate of 0.224 in the OCRed text compared to a manually corrected version (Alex et al., 2012). We also found that by applying just two systematic postcorrection steps, namely end–of–line soft hyphen deletion and $f{\rightarrow}s$ character conversion, the word error rate could be reduced by over 12%. While both correction steps proved highly effective, a large number of OCR errors remain in the text. We also carried out a thorough analysis of the effect of OCR errors on named entity recognition and investigated whether it it is worth postcorrecting the OCR when processing big text collections where the sheer size of the data might make noise irrelevant when identifying global trends. The results of these studies show that OCR errors are more severe for proper nouns than for common nouns but that in both cases recall is affected considerably. When looking at commodity distributions within very large data sets, individual OCR errors, depending on their type, can either become irrelevant in the sheer size of the data or can have a very detrimental effect (Alex and Burns, 2014).

In some cases, the historic text can be so garbled that automatic correction is unlikely to improve TM performance even in the slightest. The following four lines of text represent an example of an incomprehensible text extract, the electronic text corresponding to the first four lines of text in the scanned image shown in Figure 9.3. The reason is that the document page was scanned upside down or at least OCRed the wrong way up.[22]

[21] http://www.abbyy.com/.
[22] The original image is available at: http://www.jstor.org/stable/60238580?seq=2.

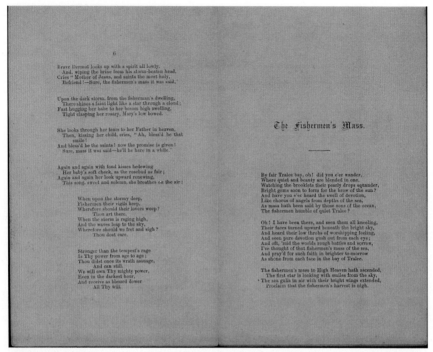

Figure 9.3 Upside down scanned image in the FCOC collection from 1862 (Rupertino, 1862).

```
1  qBiu si }S3A:req s,uauuaqsu aq} }Bq} uirepo.ifT
2  'papua}X3 sSuiav }qSuq Jiaq} qiiM jib ui snnS bbs aqx
3  'a"3(s aq} tnojj ssfitns q}TM Sni5[ooi si jb}s }S.ii; aqx
4  'papnaoSB q}Bq naABSjj qS;H°1 ssbui s.uauuaqsu aqx
```

Extract from document 10.2307/60238580 in FCOC (Rupertino, 1862)

One way of dealing with such completely garbled text would be to reject those documents from processing whose text accuracy falls below a certain threshold. We have developed a system for automatic scoring of text quality and tested its accuracy by correlating its performance with manual text quality rating (Alex and Burns, 2014). The results show that it is worth processing only documents with a threshold above which they are considered of mediocre or good quality to a human reader. When setting an exact threshold the percentage of document discarded as a result must be considered as this step can significantly decrease the amount of data available for processing.

In fact, our TM component also rejects the file shown in Figure 9.3 at the language identification stage. As the FCOC collection contains documents in different languages but without language meta information, we employ a language identification step that rejects any documents written in languages other than English. We use TEXTCAT[23] for the language identification, which determines the distance of a text string to a series of character n–gram models, a technique proposed in Cavnar and Trenkle (1994) that was shown to perform extremely well on longer passages of text. We first determine the language for each paragraph in the document and then infer the language of the document by taking the most frequent language assigned. Of the 1000 FCOC documents, 734 are classified as English. For the above example, TextCat is unable to assign a language as the text is too distant from any of its pretrained language models.

9.4.2 Text Mining Tables

Information presented in tables is another challenge when mining relational data from text. While this is not an issue specific to historical documents alone, it is very prevalent in TRADING CONSEQUENCES as the HCPP data, the biggest collection we are processing, contains at least one table more than 3 million scanned images; that is, almost every second page contains a table. They often list very useful information on shipments of goods, including specific types of commodities, quantities, dates relevant to the shipment and ports of origin or destination. A typical table in the HCPP collection is shown in Figure 9.4. It contains an entry dated *Feb. 17th 1834* for the ship *Elphinstone*, whose master was *J. Short*, to transport *20 bundles of goatskins* from *Madras & Cape* to *London*. It also states that this report was amended on *March 3rd 1834* when it was noted that *18 should have been sheepskins*.

This type of data contains very explicit commodity-location relations where both the commodity mentions and the origin or destination locations of a shipment are very obvious for human readers to parse and understand. A computer would need to know how to relate information in rows and columns, and be able to interpret ditto marks where a typographical symbol (- " -, " or –) is used to indicate that the word(s) or figure(s) above it are to be repeated. Another difficulty is the fact that the structure of tables will not always be the same. The digitised OCRed HCPP data contains w elements around words with p attributes capturing the x , y coordinates of each word in the image of the page, which means that the TM results can be mapped back onto the image if desired:

---

[23] TextCat version 1.10, pre-trained for 74 languages: http://odur.let.rug.nl/~vannoord/TextCat/.

RETURN OF THE NUMBER OF SHIPS' REPORTS THAT REQUIRED

Date of Report.	SHIP.	MASTER.	From whence.	Total Quantity and Description of Goods reported, in respect of which the Error arose.		NATURE OF ERROR.	Date at which the amended Report was completed.
				Description.	Quantity.		
1834:	LONDON—*continued.*						1834:
Feb. 14	Cadiz Packet	W. Williamson	Cadiz	Saffron / Silk	16 bales / 7 "	15 should be Wild Saffron / should be Waste Silk	16 Feb.
–	Emma	W. Cobb	Singapore	Rice	182 bags	100 bags, excess	16 June
–	Shepherd	G. N. Livesay	Mauritius	–	–	1 Pig, omitted	19 Feb.
27	Collingwood	W. Swain	Charente	–	–	6 boxes, Pies, omitted	19 April
–	Elphinstone	J. Short	Madras & Cape	Goatskins	20 bundles	– 16 should be Sheepskins / sundry Stores, omitted / Live Stock, omitted	3 March / 20 Feb.
–	Guten Freunde	A. Gunther	Rostock	Bags	120	72 to remain on board	27 –
18	Peter Procter	J. Terry	Mauritius and Cape	–	–	one half aum, Wine, omitted	28 –
–	Ferdinand	H. Hoff	Dantzic	Spirits (stores)	6 gallons	16 gallons, excess	3 March
–	London Packet	C. W. Kegut	Dantzic	Flour	1,403 barrels	1 barrel, excess	5 –
25	George Canning	J. Nichols	Para	Cocoa	64 bags	1 bag, excess	6 –
–	Nameless	L. Lefeuvre	Valentia	Onions / Raisins	3 quintals / 15 boxes	– the words "for exportation in same ship" omitted	1 –
–	Vibilia	E. Watts	St. John's	Timber / Staves / Deals	85 pieces / 6,600 pieces / 7,564 pieces	4 pieces, deficient / 76 pieces, deficient / 136 pieces, excess	15 –
–	Violante	S. Taglioferro	Odessa	Wool	34 bales	50 bales, excess	5 –
–	Ontario	W. S. Sebor	New York	Turpentine	2,000 barrels	12 barrels, excess	12 –
27	Glory	J. Latta	Marseilles	Verdigris	1 cask	should bu 1 cake	11 –
–	Hebe	W. Currie	Singapore	–	–	1 case, Presents, omi t	4 June / 8 July
–	Margaret & Ann	C. L. Back	– Cape und St. Helena	Coffee	141 bags	1 coir hawser, omitted	1 March

Figure 9.4 Typical table in the HCPP collection (hcp, 1836).

```
1   <w p="194,653,275,684">Feb.</w>
2   <w p="289,659,328,683">14</w>
3   <w p="212,822,252,836">-</w>
4   <w p="287,809,327,836">17</w>
5   <w p="214,1013,254,1027">-</w>
6   ...
7   <w p="372,844,557,871">Elphinitone</w>
8   ...
9   <w p="678,841,719,872">J.</w>
10  <w p="719,840,802,871">Short</w>
11  ...
12  <w p="951,839,1200,867">Madras&Cape</w>
13  <w p="1220,836,1368,866">Goatskins</w>
14  ...
15  <w p="1488,839,1537,866">20</w>
16  <w p="1537,836,1668,866">bundles</w>
17  ...
18  <w p="1797,837,1847,866">18</w>
19  <w p="1847,843,1959,866">should</w>
20  <w p="1959,836,2006,866">be</w>
21  <w p="2006,836,2191,866">Sheepskins</w>
22  ...
23  <w p="2329,842,2355,874">3</w>
24  <w p="2355,842,2436,878">March,</w>
```

Extract from document 1836-016588 in HCPP (hcp, 1836)

Given page coordinates, it is possible to identify text that appears on a line or table row. For example, the characters of the strings *Elphinitone*[24], *J. Short, Madras&Cape, Goatskins, 20 bundles, 18 should be Sheepskins* and *3 March,* all appear at a height ranging between 836 to 844 and 866 to 878. None of the other words or symbols in that image appear at that height. However, the related date *Feb. 17* appears higher up in the image and is simply repeated using ditto marks that were not picked up by the OCR engine. Aside from OCR errors, this example illustrates that TM tools that are typically developed for running text will struggle to process such information correctly as there is no context information around each table cell entry and the positioning of strings on a page is crucial to understand the different pieces of knowledge and how they are related to one another.

9.5 TEXT MINING COMPONENT

The TM component (see Figure 9.5) takes documents from a number of different collections in different formats as input, and is the first processing step in the TRADING CONSEQUENCES system. It consists of an initial preprocessing stage that converts each document to a consistent XML format. Depending on the corpus, a language identification step may be performed to ensure that the current document is in English. The OCRed

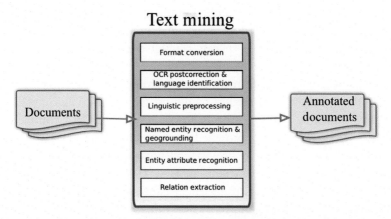

Figure 9.5 Processing steps in the TRADING CONSEQUENCES TM component.

---

[24] This is an error in the OCR, it should say *Elphinstone.*

text is then automatically improved by correcting and normalising a number of issues.

The project's underlying TM tools are built on the LT–XML2[25] and LT–TTT2[26] tools. While they are robust and achieve state-of-the-art results for modern digital newspaper text, their output for historical text will necessarily involve errors. Apart from OCR imperfections, the data is not continuous running text but passages interspersed with page breaks, page numbers, headers and occasionally handwritten notations in page margins. For our TM tools to extract the maximum amount of information, we are carrying out a limited amount of automatic correction of the text as a preliminary processing step.

We perform two automatic OCR postprocessing steps, the first being the deletion of end-of-line soft hyphens splitting word tokens and the second being the correction of the "long *s*"-to-*f* confusion. The first issue is not specific to historical documents but can affect any running text where a word is longer than the remaining space on the line and therefore split in two using a hyphen. The second issue is very relevant to processing historical text as this character was used in ligatures in various languages, specifically text written prior to the late 18th and early 19th century when the "long *s*" fell out of use. For more detailed information on how each of these steps functions and how well they perform in an intrinsic evaluation see Alex et al. (2012).

The main processing of the TM component involves various types of shallow linguistic analysis of the text, lexicon and gazetteer lookup, named entity recognition and geogrounding, and relation extraction. After performing the necessary preprocessing including tokenisation, sentence boundary detection, part-of-speech tagging and lemmatisation, various types of named entities (including commodity, location, organisation and person names), temporal information, amounts and units are extracted. With respect to identifying commodity mentions, we rely heavily on gazetteer matching and bootstrapping from a list of several hundred commodities and their alternative names provided to us by the historians Jim Clifford and Prof. Colin Coates, our project collaborators at York University in Toronto. They manually extracted a list of 400 raw materials or lightly processed commodities from customs ledgers stored at the National Archives (collection CUST 5), ranging from live animals to natural resources and related staples imported into Great Britain during the 19th century. We then

[25] http://www.ltg.ed.ac.uk/software/ltxml2.
[26] http://www.ltg.ed.ac.uk/software/lt-ttt2.

used this data as a seed set to create a much larger commodity lexicon automatically (Klein et al., 2014).

For extracting the other types of entities, we use an existing rule-based named entity recognition system that has been developed inhouse over a number of years and adapted to different types of text. It was last used in the SYNC3 project (Sarris et al., 2011) and includes the Edinburgh Geoparser (Tobin et al., 2010), which extracts location names and grounds them to the GeoNames gazetteer.[27] It has also been applied in the GeoDigRef and Embedding GeoCrossWalk projects to identify named entities in 18th century parliamentary papers and enable more sophisticated indexing and search (see Grover et al. (2008, 2010)). We also determine date attributes for commodity entities and direction attributes (destination, origin or transit) for location entities, if available. In the case of the former, we choose date entities in close textual proximity to a commodity mention as the attribute value. If none are available, we assign the year of the document's publication date as the date attribute value. The direction attributes are assigned on the basis of prepositions that signal direction occurring in front of locations (e.g., *to/ from/in*, etc.). We also identify vocabulary referring to animal diseases and natural disasters in the text by means of two small manually compiled gazetteers. They contain entries like *scabies*, *Rinderpest* and *ticks* as well as *drought*, *flood* and *tsunami*, respectively.

Once the various entity mentions are recognised, a relation extraction step is performed where we determine which commodities are related to which locations. We applied the simple rule that a relation holds between a commodity and a location (with a population size greater than zero) occurring in the same sentence. We decided against using syntactic parsing to identify such relations as we expected the OCRed text to be too noisy, resulting in too many failed parses. We also prepared a human annotated gold standard annotated with commodity and location entity mentions and commodity-location relations to monitor the performance of the TM component (some information on this intrinsic evaluation can be found in Klein et al. (2014)).

In summary, we determine which commodities were traded when and in relation to which locations. We also determine whether locations are mentioned as points of origin, transit or destination, reflecting trade movements to and from certain locations and whether vocabulary relating to diseases and disasters appears in the text. All these pieces of information are added back into

---

[27] http://www.geonames.org.

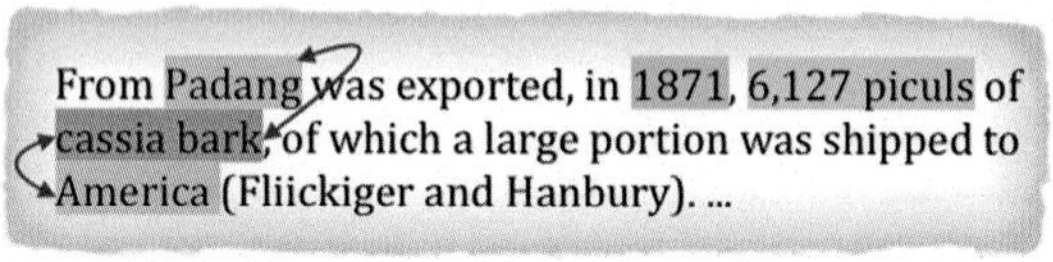
From Padang was exported, in 1871, 6,127 piculs of cassia bark, of which a large portion was shipped to America (Fliickiger and Hanbury). ...

Figure 9.6 Excerpt from "Spices" (Ridley, 1912), extracted entities highlighted in colour and relations visualised using arrows.

the XML document as different layers of annotation. This allows us to visualise documents for the purpose of error analysis. Figure 9.6 shows some of the entities that we extract from the text; for example, the locations *Padang* and *America*, the year *1871*, the commodity *cassia bark* and the quantity and unit *6,127 piculs*. The TM component further extracts that *Padang* is an origin location and *America* is a destination location and geogrounds both locations to latitudes and longitudes, information not visible in this figure. The commodity-location relations *cassia bark – Padang* and *cassia bark – America*, visualised by the red arrows in Figure 9.6, are also identified.

The extracted information is entered into the TRADING CONSEQUENCES database along with text snippets of its surrounding context. Figure 9.7 shows the database entries for the extracted commodity entity *cassia bark*, its relation to the grounded location entity *Pandang*, its date attribute expressed by the date entity *1871*, and the quantity entity *6,127 piculs*. All of this information is linked back to the database entry for the document via identifiers. Commodity mentions are also linked to a commodity ontology that we developed as part of TRADING CONSEQUENCES via their preferred labels (skos:prefLabel).[28] Some additional document meta information, including document identifier, URL, language (if available) and name of the collection is also stored in the database. Essentially we use TM to transform unstructured text into structured data that can be queried and visualised in many different ways.

9.6 USER-DRIVEN TEXT MINING

When the database is populated with information mined from all the collections, users are able to query it, for example, for *all commodities mentioned in a given year, all commodities mentioned in relation to London, UK* or even *all mentions of cassia bark in relation to all locations over a given time span*. This type of

[28] http://www.w3.org/2004/02/skos/.

Figure 9.7 Database example.

information can then be offered to the user in different ways using the search interface combined with dynamic visualisation of the structured data, both of which were developed as part of the project.[29] All mined information is linked back to the original documents, thereby enabling not only distant but also close reading. TRADING CONSEQUENCES users are able to get a global view of trade of different commodities over time but can also investigate how specific commodities were relevant to a particular location, year or to other commodities. This means that historians are able to find out information about overall trends of trade in the past while at the same time being able to research very specific mentions of a commodity in a given piece of text.

---

[29] The different user interfaces to the TRADING CONSEQUENCES database can be accessed here: http://tradingconsequences.blogs.edina.ac.uk/access-the-data/.

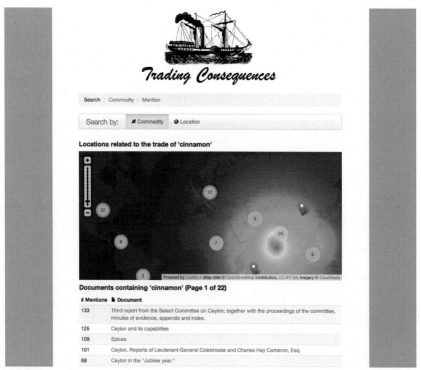

Figure 9.8 Screenshot of the initial TRADING CONSEQUENCES database query interface.

When the first TRADING CONSEQUENCES prototype was made available, historians were able to query for commodities and locations separately in a search interface developed at Edina (see a screenshot in Figure 9.8).[30] The output shows a list of variants of commodity types relevant to the initial search as well as their frequencies in relation to particular locations both within all of the collections and per document. This information was visualised on a map and also linked back to the source documents. The historians were able to test our system early on and get a good overview of what can be extracted by the TM tools and where the difficulties lie. Whenever they spotted something unusual in the visualisation of the mined commodity data, they looked more closely at whether that information was true or whether an error could have occurred in any of the TM steps, or downstream processing (database or visualisation). In the case of the latter,

---

[30] This interface has since been updated and is publicly accessible at http://tcqdev.edina.ac. uk/search/.

they then flagged an issue to the relevant team, which was then further investigated and fixed if necessary.

The continuous user feedback (positive or negative) proved extremely useful as it helped to steer the TM research and development directly toward better performance in each subsequent processing round. We continued this rapid prototyping throughout the entire project and also ran a user work-shop at the Canadian History and Environment Summer School 2013 (Hinrichs et al., 2015). The historians essentially carried out extrinsic manual evaluation of the TM component by means of data analysis.

Following this process, the historians alerted us to named entity recog-nition errors, in particular missed commodities and location names, entity boundary errors and entities with the wrong type, as well as errors in the georeferencing. For example, the output of the first prototype contained an unusually high frequency of the location entity *Markham* geogrounded to a suburb north of Toronto. The historians recognised that this entity actu-ally referred to *Clements Robert Markham*, a British official who smuggled cinchona seeds out of Peru (see Figure 9.9).[31] Subsequently, we adapted our code that distinguishes people from places to correct this error. Via this continuous feedback mechanism, we had improved the system output sig-nificantly by the time development stopped. It also helped the historians to become familiar with the strengths and weaknesses of the final technology.

Figure 9.9 Clements Robert Markham.

---

[31] http://en.wikipedia.org/wiki/Clements_Markham.

If they know when to trust its correctness and when to treat it more care-fully, then the TRADING CONSEQUENCES system, and for that matter TM software in general, can become a very powerful tool in assisting research in social science and the humanities.

9.7 CONCLUSION

In this chapter, we have reviewed related work on historical text mining and have discussed studies testing the effect of OCR quality on NLP in general. We introduced the TRADING CONSEQUENCES project with an over-view of the entire system architecture and provided a more concrete descrip-tion of the TM component itself. We have also described all the data collections processed as part of TRADING CONSEQUENCES, digitised versions of over 10.5 million scanned images. We have outlined some of the challenges of processing such digitised historical collections and have dis-cussed possible solutions. Two of the biggest challenges encountered were the bad quality of the OCRed text and the difficulty in mining information from tables. We have made some progress in tackling the former issue and will focus our attention on the latter in future work.

We have also described our user-driven approach to taking our TM research forward and to developing the TRADING CONSEQUENCES system as a whole. We have seen some clear benefits in taking such a user-centric approach to research and development from very early on in the project. We believe that better TM results can be achieved when com-bining user-based feedback with performance optimisations based on the more formal, intrinsic evaluation that is typically carried out in the area of natural language processing.

ACKNOWLEDGEMENTS

We would like to thank our TRADING CONSEQUENCES project partners at York Uni-versity and University of Saskatchewan, University of St. Andrews and EDINA for their feedback and support (Digging Into Data: CIINN01).

REFERENCES

Ships' Reports, 1836. Return to an order of the Honourable the House of Commons, dated 31 May 1836;-for, a return of the number of ships' reports that required amendment dur-ing the two years ending 5th January 1836; the date of each ship's arrival; and the date at which the amended report was completed; stating the nature of the error in each case.

In: House of Commons Parliamentary Papers, URL http://gateway.proquest.com/openurl?url_ver=Z39.88-2004&res_dat=xri:hcpp&rft_dat=xri:hcpp:fulltext:1836-016588.

Alex, B., Burns, J., 2014. Estimating and rating the quality of optically character recognised text. In: Proceedings of the First International Conference on Digital Access to Textual Cultural Heritage, DATeCH 2014. ACM, pp. 97–102.

Alex, B., Byrne, K., Grover, C., Tobin, R., 2015. Adapting the Edinburgh geoparser for historical georeferencing. Int. J. Humanit. Arts Comput. 9 (1), 15–35.

Alex, B., Grover, C., Klein, E., Tobin, R., 2012. Digitised historical text: Does it have to be mediOCRe? In: Proceedings of the LThist 2012 workshop at KONVENS 2012, pp. 401–409.

Blei, D.M., 2012. Probabilistic topic models. Commun. ACM 55 (4), 77–84.

Cavnar, W.B., Trenkle, J.M., 1994. N-gram-based text categorization. In: In Proceedings of Third Annual Symposium on Document Analysis and Information Retrieval. Las Vegas, US, pp. 161–175.

Cronon, W., 1992. Nature's Metropolis: Chicago and the Great West. W.W. Norton & Company, New York.

Gotscharek, A., Reffle, U., Ringlstetter, C., Schulz, K.U., Neumann, A., 2011. Towards information retrieval on historical document collections: the role of matching procedures and special lexica. IJDAR 14 (2), 159–171.

Grover, C., Givon, S., Tobin, R., Ball, J., 2008. Named entity recognition for digitised historical texts. In: Proceedings of the Sixth International Conference on Language Resources and Evaluation (LREC'08). Marrakech, Morocco, pp. 1343–1346.

Grover, C., Tobin, R., Byrne, K., Woollard, M., Reid, J., Dunn, S., et al., 2010. Use of the Edinburgh Geoparser for georeferencing digitised historical collections. Phil. Trans. Roy. Soc. A 368 (1925), 3875–3889.

Hauser, A., Heller, M., Leiss, E., Schulz, K.U., Wanzeck, C., 2007. Information access to historical documents from the Early New High German period. In: Burnard, L., Dobreva, M., Fuhr, N., Lüdeling, A. (Eds.), Digital Historical Corpora- Architecture, Annotation, and Retrieval. Dagstuhl, Germany.

Hinrichs, U., Alex, B., Clifford, J., Quigley, A., 2015. Trading Consequences: A Case Study of Combining Text Mining and Visualisation to Facilitate Document Exploration. In: Digital Scholarship in the Humanities (DSH); DH2014 Special Issue.

Klein, E., Alex, B., Clifford, J., 2014. Bootstrapping a historical commodities lexicon with SKOS and DBpedia. In: Proceedings of the 8th Workshop on Language Technology for Cultural Heritage, Social Sciences, and Humanities (LaTeCH). Association for Computational Linguistics, Gothenburg, Sweden, pp. 13–21.

Kolak, O., Resnik, P., 2005. OCR post-processing for low density languages. In: Proceedings of the conference on Human Language Technology and Empirical Methods in Natural Language Processing, pp. 867–874.

Lopresti, D., 2005. Performance evaluation for text processing of noisy inputs. In: Proceedings of the Symposium on Applied Computing, pp. 759–763.

Lopresti, D., 2008a. Measuring the impact of character recognition errors on downstream text analysis. In: Yanikoglu, B.A., Berkner, K. (Eds.), In: Document Recognition and Retrieval, vol. 6815. SPIE.

Lopresti, D., 2008b. Optical character recognition errors and their effects on natural language processing. In: Proceedings of the second workshop on Analytics for Noisy Unstructured Text Data, pp. 9–16.

Nissim, M., Matheson, C., Reid, J., 2004. Recognising geographical entities in Scottish historical documents. In: Proceedings of the Workshop on Geographic Information Retrieval held at the 27th Annual International ACM SIGIR Conference.

Ridley, H.N., 1912. Spices. Macmillan and Co., Ltd., London.

Rupertino, 1862. The fishermen's mass: a poem. In: Foreign and Commonwealth Office Collection,http://www.jstor.org/stable/60238580.

Sarris, N., Potamianos, G., Renders, J.M., Grover, C., Karstens, E., Kallipolitis, L., et al., 2011. A system for synergistically structuring news content from traditional media and the blogosphere. In: eChallenges 2011.

Smith, D.A., Crane, G., 2001. Disambiguating geographic names in a historical digital library. In: Proceedings of ECDL. Springer-Verlag, New York, pp. 127–136.

Tobin, R., Grover, C., Byrne, K., Reid, J., Walsh, J., 2010. Evaluation of georeferencing. In: Proceedings of the 6th Workshop on Geographic Information Retrieval, GIR '10. ACM, New York, NY, USA, pp. 7:1–7:8, http://doi.acm.org/10.1145/1722080. 1722089.

Tully, J., 2009. A victorian ecological disaster: Imperialism, the telegraph and gutta-percha. J. World Hist. 20 (4), 559–579.

CHAPTER 10

Automatic Text Indexing with SKOS Vocabularies in HIVE

G. Bueno-de-la-Fuente*, D. Rodríguez Mateos*, J. Greenberg‡
*University Carlos III of Madrid, Madrid, Spain
‡Drexel University, Philadelphia, PA, USA

10.1 INTRODUCTION

The exponential growth of digital information is staggering when one considers output generated across the global web and from personal and social information devices (e.g. cell phones, tablets, etc.). The growth is extended via traditionally closed systems such as the bibliographical databases and abstracting and indexing services systems that are increasingly accessible via the web. These types of information systems generally include structured information that may follow a specific standard; and they may use a controlled vocabulary.

Controlled vocabularies are important tools; they help information professionals to ensure consistency in document analysis and representation and aid the end users in selecting appropriate search terms (Svenious, 1986, 2003; Rowley, 1994). Despite the demonstrated benefits of controlled vocabularies, their use is limited, due to cost, interoperability and usability challenges (Greenberg et al., 2011). These challenges are more pressing when information professionals are working with multidisciplinary and transdisciplinary resources and have an interest in using several vocabularies to adequately cover a topic. Perhaps the most obvious, simple solution in this case is for the information professional to have access to a set of desired vocabularies at the time of indexing, and to select appropriate terms. The appeal of this approach quickly diminishes, given that searching multiple vocabularies is both time-consuming and expensive. Even if the vocabularies of interest are accessible online, searching several vocabularies to index a single document becomes very costly.

One way to address this challenge is via applying automatic indexing processes across multiple controlled vocabularies in a single setting. This is how the HIVE technology operates. HIVE technology uses automatic indexing, machine learning and mapping to controlled vocabularies that provide a knowledge base. HIVE also leverages the Simple Knowledge Organization System (SKOS) (Miles and Bechhofer, 2009), a World Wide Web Consortium (W3C) encoding standard.

This chapter reports on the HIVE approach. The chapter begins by briefly reviewing automatic indexing. Next, the KEA, KEA++ and MAUI automatic indexing algorithms are discussed; followed by an introduction to the HIVE technology and HIVE-ES (España) initiative. Following this, the chapter reports on research experiences and their results on automatic indexing using SKOS vocabularies in a HIVE instance. The conclusion summarises the work presented, reflects on the main achievements and shortcomings faced, and identifies several next steps.

10.2 AUTOMATIC INDEXING WITH MACHINE LEARNING

There are a number of ways information systems use automatic indexing for document representation. Systems may simply automatically extract a collection of terms or generate a vector for document representation. The representation serves as the chief document that is searched during an information retrieval activity. That is, a search will be directed to this representation, not the document's full text. Another approach that can be combined is placing terms that represent the document in an inverted file. Automatic indexing techniques are based on statistical algorithms that analyse document properties and identify key terms or key phrases by frequency of occurrence and length. Among basic approaches are term/documentation ratios (tf^*idf), co-occurrence and key phrase extraction:

- The most popular algorithm is tf^*idf, that stands for Term Frequency per Inverse Document Frequency. This method allows one to measure how important a term is. It counts the number of times a term appears in a particular document (tf) and compares it to the time it occurs in a full collection of documents (Salton and Buckley, 1988).
- Another common approach is *co-occurrence*, which is when terms that frequently occur together are indicators of a domain (van Rijsbergen, 1977). For example, if the word "labour" appears with "human resources" and "employment", we know that the domain is related to "work" or "vocation", whereas if the word "labour" co-occurs with "pregnancy", the domain is more likely woman's health and may be about "child birth".

- *Keyphrase extraction* is another common method that includes knowledge of semantic and syntactic relationships. The approach extends beyond co-occurrence to include "phrases"; that is, terms that generally appear next to each other in a syntactic order. This approach is powerful, because concepts often require a number of terms. However, key phrase extraction is challenging at times and can generate phrases that are not grammatically correct (Medelyan, 2009:51).

Less common in basic IR, but having great appeal in the metadata community are algorithms that not only generate representations, but also integrate ontologies or controlled vocabularies into the process. For example, the vector or automatic key phrases extracted during the initial indexing operations is mapped to a controlled vocabulary or set of terminologies to aid in selecting the best candidate terms for representation (Anderson and Pérez-Carballo, 2001a,b). This approach replicates the work of an information professional and can be cost-effective because it is very time-consuming and costly to work with controlled vocabularies, although the benefits of such systems are well-known and desired.

Algorithms and automated workflows that integrate controlled vocabularies are far from perfect, because they do not disambiguate like a human. This is because natural language is extremely rich and it can be very difficult for these algorithms to achieve high degrees of representativeness. One way to improve an automatic indexing algorithm's performance is the application of machine learning strategies to train the system from a previous set of documents indexed by human professional indexers.

These learning activities require a set of training documents that have been previously indexed by a human, specifically a knowledgeable information professional representing the "gold standard" because such person knows not only how to disambiguate meanings, but also being a domain specialist on some level in a discipline, have knowledge of indexing principles, such as specificity. The integration of a machine learning algorithm can provide positive and negative examples and build rules that can predict the indexing of new documents (Medelyan and Witten, 2008).

HIVE technology uses indexing algorithms that include machine learning, specifically the key phrase extraction algorithm (KEA) and MAUI (Medelyan et al., 2009). These algorithms, which are explained in the next section, combine the processes of extraction and assignment: key phrases are extracted from the document and used to select terms from a controlled vocabulary. These key phrases help make sense of the underlying semantics relationships. This combined approach has been shown to improve indexing consistency as well as achieve a higher degree of efficiency (White et al., 2012). There are a variety of algorithms available for automatic indexing, and some perform fairly well for pulling out key concepts, but many fall short of matching concepts to a controlled vocabulary. HIVE technology addresses this shortcoming by leveraging the automatically extracting key phrases from textual documents and mapping the results to one or more controlled vocabularies. Finally, HIVE enables intervention of humans to ensure quality.

10.3 ALGORITHMS FOR TEXT DATA MINING: KEA, KEA++ AND MAUI

The HIVE technology uses automatic indexing that emulates professional indexers, while also leveraging automatic indexing capabilities. The initial HIVE system used KEA (Witten et al., 1999). KEA was originally designed as an automatic keyword extraction and indexing system. Nevertheless, KEA was extended to some available versions that combine this automatic approach with preliminary training based on a manual text treatment, based on the use of a set of documents. Each document includes full text, plus an extra file containing keywords assigned by professional indexers. This new KEA was called KEA++.

The HIVE technology includes two phases. First, the training phase, when KEA starts using another text mining algorithm called WEKA that filters the stopwords and applies a stemming process and extracts a number of expressions called n-grams (Hall et al., 2009). This means that, given an n number, WEKA extracts chains of groups with a number of chains lower or equal to n (i.e. if n equal to 3, WEKA allows chains with 1, 2 or 3 chains of letters, or pseudowords). KEA includes its own stemming tools that work into English, French and Spanish.

Any n-gram contains parts of words literally similar to the beginnings of others included on a thesaurus. The system selects a series of keywords from the available thesauri and executes a calculation via the following processes:

1. A combination of $tf * df$, that stands for Term Frequency per Inverse Distance Frequency. As described above, this calculates the number of times that a term is included in a document and the number of times the same term is included in the total amount of documents analysed (Salton and Buckley, 1988; Medelyan, 2009:91).

2. First occurrence: percentage of the document when the candidate term appears at the first place. If the expression is near the beginning of the

document, its weight for this reason increases, because it is supposed that this term could appear on the title, the abstract or the table of contents.

3. Length of a phrase: A two-word expression is preferred to a single word, because some studies (Medelyan and Witten, 2008) have shown that professional indexers prefer expressions to individual words.

4. Node degree: Given an equivalence that matches a candidate term to a similar term in a thesaurus, this feature measures the total amount of other thesaurus terms that have any relationship to the thesaurus term matching.

This last feature is one of the two main differences between KEA and KEA++ (that uses node degree), although it is possible to deactivate it.

The other difference between both algorithms is previous training. KEA++ uses a list of documents and keywords previously matched by professional indexers, so that KEA++ can create a model of equivalent rules among texts and keywords already matched by professional indexers.

10.4 ALGORITHM TRAINING AND WORKFLOW

The ideal training process is based on a SKOS formatted thesaurus. It starts with a set of 50 documents, converted to a plain text format. Each document has been indexed by a human indexer to extract manual keywords, taken from the previous thesaurus (there is a plain text keywords file for any document). Figure 10.1 provides an example, with keywords assigned by a metadata professional. This represents a gold standard.

In a parallel process, the same text documents are automatically indexed through WEKA. Results from these two processes are compared: WEKA features and values achieved only from keywords matching with manual keywords are computed in a new model. This final model is then used to calculate the likelihood of further expressions in a document in the future. In other words, the *learning* relationship between the document and officially assigned keywords, representing a gold standard, aids the automatic selection of appropriate keywords for a next automatic indexing sequence (Figure 10.2).

The size of the initial document set is based on previous studies that have proved that a higher number of documents in a training set do not improve the results (Medelyan, 2009).

A second algorithm used to index terms is Maui (Medelyan, 2009). Maui boosts KEA with some additional features:

- Position of the last occurrence: KEA++ only considers a word position near the top of the document. Maui also considers if a word is at the end

Every text document...

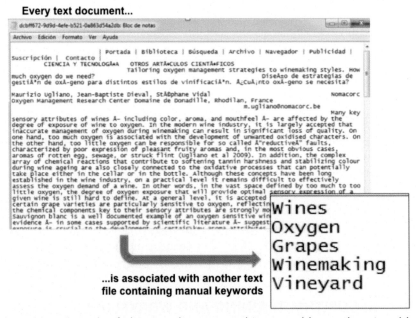

Figure 10.1 Example of plain text document and its manual keywords assigned by metadata expert.

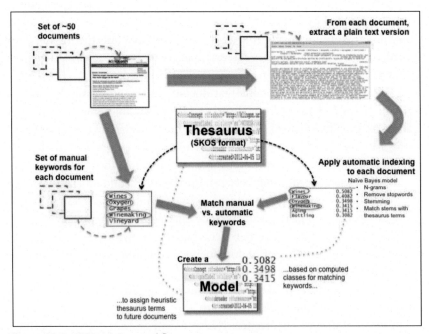

Figure 10.2 HIVE training workflow.

of a document, because the word also could be at the results or final conclusion sections.

- Spread: Distance between the first occurrence and the last occurrence of a word in a document, normalised by the document's length in words.
- Domain key phraseness: If the candidate keyword never appears in a manually assigned topic on a training, the value is 0. And this value is higher, on the contrary.
- Semantic relatedness: In addition to the node degree used by KEA, Maui adds a comparison between candidates appearing in the text and terms included in the thesaurus, even if the matching algorithm has not recognised these text terms. Moreover, according to Medelyan (2009: 99), keywords have higher co-occurrence to related terms included in the thesaurus.
- Wikipedia key phraseness: This feature and others related to Wikipedia are possible because of the Wikipedia Miner (Milne, 2009) a Maui module that makes some calculations based on Wikimedia terms. This feature is related to the number of Wikipedia links anchors that point out to a term. If a candidate term is related to this term, its weight increases as well.
- Wikipedia frequency and Wikipedia inverse frequency: are a measure of $tf * idf$ but only on Wikipedia pages.
- Generality: The more general the candidate terms are, the poorer the performance obtained on keywords extraction.
- Use of a higher number of WEKA classes: KEA only uses some of the WEKA classes, whereas MAUI plugs in the complete class library. KEA uses naive Bayes whereas Maui uses another classifier called "bagged decision trees".

For each term candidate, Maui computes a value related to each feature. After that, all these values are multiplied among them to obtain a likelihood total value. The terms with higher final values are considered to be keywords.

10.5 THE HIVE SYSTEM

The Helping Interdisciplinary Vocabulary Engineering (HIVE) (Greenberg et al., 2011) initiative was launched with support from the U.S. Institute of Museum and Library Studies (IMLS), and has subsequently been supported by the National Science Foundation in connection with the DataNet initiatives. The HIVE technology demonstrates an approach for addressing cost, interoperability and usability challenges associated with traditional vocabulary frameworks. The HIVE-ES (España) (Méndez and Greenberg, 2012) initiative has extended this work to Spanish language vocabularies.

These HIVE projects align with the endeavours of the linked open data (LOD), and more specifically the linked open vocabularies (LOV) movement, facilitating open, accessible, and, on some level, interoperable vocabularies. HIVE is initiated by converting several vocabularies to SKOS (NBII Thesaurus, TGN, ITIS and MeSH) and creating a framework in which they are interoperable with existing SKOSed vocabularies (e.g. AGROVOC and LCSH). HIVE-ES was launched by SKOSifying the EMBNE (the Spanish LCSH) and integrating this with the LEM SKOSed vocabulary and the newly generated Wine Thesaurus.

The HIVE software has three different modules: (1) HIVE Core, (2) HIVE Web and (3) HIVE REST. HIVE Core implements the main features of the system, like automatic metadata extraction and topic detection, using KEA++/Maui. Concept retrieval is supported via Lucene, and RDF storage and management uses SESAME/Elmo. HIVE Web includes a web user interface based on the GoogleWeb Toolkit, offering human users a comfortable interface to browse and search through vocabularies. Additionally, HIVE REST provides a machine-oriented interface based on Web Services to ease integration with third-party software. HIVE installation procedures are documented via the project wiki and the source code is all open-source.

HIVE offers two indexing options: KEA++ or MAUI. Each one might be also trained, based on your own previous document corpus. You can also use any of these algorithms without training, although this option increases the risk of noisy results.

HIVE Core is based on Java and requires an installation of Tomcat. Its main purpose is to help libraries and archive institutions to increase spread and appropriateness indexing, by using controlled vocabulary. HIVE allows people to choose some indexing options, but without requiring them to be professional indexers: they only need to choose accurate options, adding documents, indexing them and sharing these results with others. This would all be possible by means of HIVE Web.

Therefore, HIVE Core controls the addition of available vocabularies on the system plus the ingestion of the training set and the keywords assigned to each document included in this set.

HIVE Web is made up of two different web interfaces. The first one is called "concept browser", and includes a list of available thesauruses.

Any user could access this list. Every thesaurus is browsable, starting from a first-level A–Z list, unfolding at any term to extend subterms. Each term includes a file with data as concept label, term URI in the online thesaurus version out of HIVE, if available; alternative label, broader and narrower concepts, related contents and scope notes. If possible, each of these concepts is also browsable by means of a link. HIVE Web Concept Browser includes a search engine on any available thesaurus.

The second interface is called "indexing". This interface support the indexing of a single document, using one or more vocabularies. The document is uploaded from or referenced via a URL. The optional settings are the following:

- The indexing algorithm, between Kea++ (called "Kea") and Maui;
- The number of hops, concerning the level of thesaurus terms that will be checked, with 0 – zero – value related only to the broadest terms, 1 value equivalent to broader terms and narrower terms directly related to them, and so on;
- The maximum number of terms that will be extracted and related to the document file created at the end of the process, with options of 5, 10, 15 or 20;
- The minimum number of occurrences of a term in the document to be considered as a keyword candidate;
- An extra option to index only the differences, in the case of reindexing a document already available at the database.

Once a document is added to the HIVE system, and based on the aforementioned criteria, the document is indexed and a tag cloud with the added keywords is shown. Every document is indexed over all the vocabularies included in the list, and the final tag cloud shows all the keywords, distinguishing the different sets of keywords from every thesaurus by means of different font colours. Results are also available in SKOS/RDF, SKOS-N Triples, Dublin Core/RDF, MODS/XML and MARC/XML formats.

Concerning HIVE Core, all their tools are controlled via a terminal access. The chief use is the addition of a new thesaurus and the system training from this through a new set of documents and keywords.

Each new thesaurus requires a well-formed SKOS file, based on RDF format. Any encoding problems with a SKOS file prevents the "setting" process. The preliminary files "generated" must be fully cleared to restart the HIVE process.

Every thesaurus' set of training documents must be uploaded on a local repository. Each document must include another plain text (with key extension), with one line for every keyword. The system must also have a list of stopwords, and it is mandatory to choose one of the HIVE stemmers. HIVE includes a standard list of stemmers for both KEA and Maui, although experienced administrators can modify them or choose other stemmers, some of them also available via the HIVE standard installation. It is also required to create a short, fixed structured configuration file, on a plain text that points out to all the required file paths into the local server.

Every thesaurus training is run by Java commands, with some customizable options.

Last but not least, Sesame (http://openrdf.callimachus.net/) is used as a semantic web framework that allows the storage and query of a large amount of terms and association included in SKOS thesaurus files.

10.6 TEXT MINING FOR DOCUMENTS INDEXING USING SKOS VOCABULARIES IN HIVE

A first HIVE original website application is available at http://hive.cci.drexel.edu:8080/home.html. This installation hosts several different vocabularies, including the aforementioned AGROVOC, an agricultural thesaurus from the FAO; ITIS, the integrated taxonomic information system, focused on plants and animals; MeSH, a specific medical thesaurus from the NLM; NBII, a biological thesaurus; TGN, a geographical thesaurus; and the more general LCSH, the list of subject headings from the US Library of Congress.

In an effort to expand HIVE across the United States, and specifically over the Spanish-speaking world, a collaboration was established between one of the HIVE leading institutions, the Metadata Research Center (MRC) from the University of North Carolina at Chapel Hill, and Carlos III University of Madrid, Spain. An article about the HIVE system (Méndez and Greenberg, 2012) summarises this collaboration. Moreover, the MRC director carried out a research stay at UC3M, by the means of a Chair of Excellence.

The main agreement from this collaboration process was to set up a HIVE mirror in Spain, called HIVE-ES. Moreover, a further agreement with the National Library of Spain (in Spanish, BNE) was also settled. A HIVE-ES test server was set up by the Tecnodoc research group, Department of Library and Information Science, University Carlos III of Madrid (Spain).

HIVE-ES also disseminated information about HIVE technology and processes through a seminar held in June 2012. Documentation is available at http://tecnodoc.uc3m.es/hive-es/wiki.

The HIVE-ES group carried out two different studies using HIVE technology. The first one was focused on the collaboration with Spanish official institutions on public libraries, as BNE and the Spanish Ministry of Culture. BNE maintains EMBNE, the Spanish National Library Subject Headings, meanwhile the Ministry of Culture oversees the Spanish Public Libraries Subject Headings list. The main aim was the creation of their own SKOS versions of both products to test their future development as possible vocabularies available through HIVE-ES. As a second phase, the aim was also to test HIVE-ES as a tool to improve both BNE and Spanish national public libraries system.

Concerning LEM, it was not possible to test its use, given practical research contraints. The SKOS version of the vocabulary presented some technical problems related to its file format. HIVE-ES was able to offer a browsable and searchable version of LEM, although we did not have time to fully implement the indexing process. Previous training process also encountered some problems because of the LEM SKOS version structure.

About EMBNE, a primary version was offered directly from professional cataloguers from the BNE. Nevertheless, this EMBNE SKOS revealed several difficulties. First, its size made it difficult to detect some mistakes that appeared during the configuration and training process, related to some shortcomings found on the EMBNE thesaurus file. Second, only a small set of training documents were provided by BNE, so previous training was done with general documents (EMBNE is a general and universal cataloguing list). Third, EMBNE is a plain list vocabulary: although formally the EMBNE version used is SKOSed, it was not really a thesaurus but a subject headings list with one hierarchical level. This can decrease the weight of some Maui features during the training process.

This combination of factors could be the reason for having a formally browsable and searchable EMBNE version on the HIVE-ES server, ready technically to index documents, but whose results are not really useful at all.

A further series of tests were done with a more specific thesaurus about wine products, based on a thesaurus developed by professional wine indexers. This product is called "vino" (wine, in Spanish). Vino contains about 300 Spanish keywords concerning every wine product and facets from this product and its industry in Spain.

Vino was also trained with a set of 20 documents, extracted from different Spanish shop websites, mainly files about different wine brands, adding some Wikipedia Spanish entries focused on wine. The training process went right, and all documents and keywords for this were written in Spanish. All the documents had the same number of five keywords. A number of different tests were done, combining all the possibilities offered on HIVE Web, described in Section 10.4 of this chapter.

Best results were obtained with the Maui algorithm, with a number of hops equal to 0 and only a minimum number of occurrences equal to 1, with 5 as a maximum number of terms. 80% of the received keywords, as an average, could be considered as acceptable.

Despite the short number of training documents, we could suggest that a HIVE system is able to train and index on different languages than English (also in Spanish, at least). These results could be achieved with a relatively small effort by the means of a scoped domain specific thesaurus and a subject related training set of documents and keywords.

This test also shows that better results were obtained with a number of keywords lower or equal to the number of keywords added to every document from the training set. Searching a higher number of keywords on HIVE web increases the risk of assigning incorrect keywords to future documents at the end of the indexing process.

10.7 CONCLUSIONS

Although a large set of measures could be applied to improve HIVE-ES performance, some accurate conclusions are achieved.

First, HIVE-ES works properly as the HIVE original system, and that means Maui configuration, also in Spanish, with very little development. These results point to future HIVE-ES adjustments, concerning tests with different stemmers, the creation of more extensive training sets and, specifically, a search of collaboration through thesaurus obtained from different Spanish-speaking world institutions.

Second, Maui has proved its better performance over the KEA++ version available from HIVE, although future tests must be done to compare Maui with KEA 5.0, both still available from the University of Waikato website in New Zealand. Further Maui improvements are supposed to have been added to KEA 5.0, but the same university that holds the rights to both indexing systems offers both of them.

There are still a number of questions about the stemmers used. We do not have full evidence about using all different stemmers available, as for applying some specific stemmers for Spanish language documents.

On the contrary, tests with consolidated Spanish cataloguing systems have failed. A main reason could be the use of cataloguing systems instead of classification systems. An additional factor concerns the very general purpose of both heading lists. So, these tools will be more useful if documents involved on HIVE-ES use were focused on a specific topic. Using such a general and plain vocabulary was not the best strategy.

A possible future approach could be to focus on extracting narrower topic subsets from these description tools, and extending their information skills more on classification than cataloguing. This proposal must be discussed, considering previous experiences from the digital libraries' world.

HIVE-ES and the HIVE system have proved to be useful tools to manage a thesaurus, making an easier and faster indexing process, but more research on their capabilities has to be done. A combination with a specific retrieval tool would increase its visibility for indexers, and so would a tool designed for linking terms from different vocabularies hosted on the same HIVE server.

Nevertheless, the major requirement for future HIVE success does not depends on the system itself. A larger list of SKOS-based thematic thesaurus must be able to extend its use.

Gema Bueno de la Fuente holds a Ph.D. in Library and Information Science (2010). Assistant professor at the Library and Information Science Department, University Carlos III of Madrid, she teaches since 2005 in many Undergraduate and Master programmes, for example, the Master on Digital Libraries and Information Services. She has participated in many research projects as a member of the Tecnodoc group, and has published in national and international journals mainly in the area of Library and Information Science. She has made several research stays as a visiting scholar in the University of Minho (Portugal), the School of Information and Library Science of UNC-Chapel Hill (USA) and CAPLE/CETIS (UK). Her teaching and research focuses on open access to science and education, digital libraries, digital preservation, vocabularies, semantic web standards and linked data.

David Rodríguez Mateos holds a Ph.D. in Library and Information Science (2004). Currently, he is an assistant professor at Journalism and Audiovisual Communication Department (and a former member of the LIS department), University Carlos III of Madrid, where he has taught several topics related to information technology since 2000, in undergraduate and Master programmes. He belongs to Tecnodoc research group, and has been a member or PI in more than 20 research projects since 2000. He has made several research stays as a visiting scholar in Loughborough University (UK) and Syracuse University (USA). His teaching and research focuses on digital media, markup languages, text processing and content management systems applied to media, journalism, law, education and science.

Jane Greenberg is the A. B. Kroeger professor and director of the Metadata Research Center at the College of Computing & Informatics, Drexel University, Philadelphia, PA. She is also a 2014 Data Science Fellow at the National Consortium for Data Science at the Renaissance Computing Initiative (RENCI) in Chapel Hill, NC, and a senior scientist at the National Evolutionary Synthesis Center (NESCent) in Durham, North Carolina. Her research and teaching focus in the area of metadata, knowledge organisation and ontology/semantics, with an emphasis on data science problems and solutions. She is the PI for the HIVE (Helping Interdisciplinary Vocabulary Engineering) project and the MetaDataCAPT'L initiative, a coPI for Dryad repository.

ACKNOWLEDGEMENTS

Special thanks to Eva Méndez for making this possible. Thanks to all the team members from Metadata Research Center, Tecnodoc research group and Biblioteca Nacional de España for their support and hard work.

REFERENCES

Anderson, J.D., Perez-Carballo, J., 2001a. The nature of indexing: how humans and machines analyse messages and text for retrieval. Part I: research, and the nature of human indexing. Inf. Process. Manag. 37, 231–254.

Anderson, J.D., Perez-Carballo, J., 2001b. The nature of indexing: how humans and machines analyse messages and text for retrieval. Part II: machine indexing, and the allocation of human versus machine effort. Inf. Process. Manag. 37, 255–277.

Greenberg, J., Losee, R., Pérez Agüera, J.R., Scherle, R., White, H., Willis, C., 2011. HIVE: helping interdisciplinary vocabulary engineering. Bull. Am. Soc. Inf. Sci. Technol. 37 (4) Available at: http://www.asis.org/Bulletin/Apr-11/AprMay11_Greenberg_etAl.html.

Hall, M., Frank, E., Holmes, G., Pfahringer, B., Reutemann, P., Witten, I.H., 2009. The WEKA data mining software: an update. SIGKDD Explor. 11 (1), 10–18.

Medelyan, O., 2009. Human-competitive automatic topic indexing. PhD Thesis, University of Waikato, New Zealand. Available at: http://www.medelyan.com/files/phd2009.pdf.

Medelyan, O., Witten, I.H., 2008. Domain independent automatic keyphrase indexing with small training sets. J. Am. Soc. Inf. Sci. Technol. 59 (7), 1026–1040.

Medelyan, O., Frank, E., Witten, I.H., 2009. Human-competitive tagging using automatic keyphrase extraction. In: Proceedings of the 2009 Conference on Empirical Methods in Natural Language Processing: Volume 3. Association for Computational Linguistics. Available at http://www.cs.waikato.ac.nz/ml/publications/2009/maui_emnlp2009_1dataset.pdf.

Méndez, E., Greenberg, J., 2012. Linked data for open vocabularies and HIVE's global framework – datos enlazados para vocabularios abiertos: marco global de HIVE. El Profesional de la Información 21 (3), 236–244.

Miles, A., Bechhofer, S., 2009. SKOS simple knowledge organization system reference. W3C Recommendation 18 August 2009. Available at: http://www.w3.org/TR/2009/REC-skos-reference-20090818/.

Milne, D., 2009. An open-source toolkit for mining Wikipedia. In: Proc. New Zealand Computer Science Research Student Conf., NZCSRSC'09, Auckland, New Zealand. Available at: http://cs.smith.edu/classwiki/images/c/c8/Open_source_mining_wikipedia.pdf.

Rowley, J., 1994. The controlled versus natural indexing languages debate revisited: a perspective on information retrieval practice and research. J. Inf. Sci. 20 (2), 108–119.

Salton, G., Buckley, C., 1988. Term-weighting approaches in automatic text retrieval. Inf. Process. Manag. 24 (5), 513–523. 0.1016/0306-4573(88)90021-0.

Svenious, E., 1986. Unanswered questions in the design of controlled vocabularies. J. Am. Soc. Inf. Sci. 37, 331–340. http://dx.doi.org/10.1002/(SICI)1097-4571(198609)37:5<331::AID-ASI8>3.0.CO;2-5.

Svenious, E., 2003. Design of controlled vocabularies. In: Drake, M. (Ed.), second ed. In: Encyclopedia of Library and Information Sciences, vol. II. CRC, Boca Raton, ISBN 978-0824720780, p. 800.

van Rijsbergen, C.J., 1977. A theoretical basis for the use of co-occurrence data in information retrieval. J. Doc. 33 (2), 106–119.

White, H., Willis, C., Greenberg, J., 2012. The HIVE impact: contributing to consistency via automatic indexing. In: iConference 2012, February 7–10 2012, Toronto, Ontario, Canada. ACM ISBN: 978-1-4503-0782-6/12/02.

Witten, I.H., Paynter, G.W., Frank, E., Gutwin, C., Nevill-Manning, C.G., 1999. KEA: practical automatic keyphrase extraction. In: Proc. DL '99, pp. 254–256. Available at: http://www.nzdl.org/Kea/Nevill-et-al-1999-DL99-poster.pdf.

CHAPTER 11

The PIMMS Project and Natural Language Processing for Climate Science

Extending the ChemicalTagger Natural Language Processing Tool with Climate Science Controlled Vocabularies

C.L. Pascoe*,†, H. Barjat‡, B.N. Lawrence*,†,§, G.J.L. Tourte¶, P. Murray-Rust**, L. Hawizy**

*National Centre for Atmospheric Science, Natural Environment Research Council, UK
†Centre for Environmental Data Archival, STFC Rutherford Appleton Laboratory, UK
‡Barjat Consulting, Langley, Macclesfield, UK
§Department of Meteorology, University of Reading, UK
¶School of Geographical Sciences, University of Bristol, UK
**University of Cambridge, Cambridge, UK

11.1 INTRODUCTION

The PIMMS (Portable Infrastructure for the Metafor Metadata System) project aims to provide institutions with tools to capture information about the workflow of running climate simulations from the initial design of experiments to the final implementation. PIMMS uses the METAFOR methodology for simulation documentation, which consists of a common information model (CIM) and a set of controlled vocabularies (CV) and software tools (see Lawrence et al., 2012; Guilyardi et al., 2011; Callaghan et al., 2011). PIMMS software tools provide for the creation and consumption of CIM content via a web infrastructure and portal (Figure 11.1).

The main PIMMS effort involves refactoring the "CMIP5 questionnaire" metadata management tool[1] (Lawrence et al., 2012; Guilyardi et al., 2011) used for collecting climate model metadata for the CMIP5 model intercomparison project (Taylor et al., 2011), so that it can be more easily ported into stand-alone installations within the university environment,

---

[1] http://q.cmip5.ceda.ac.uk/.

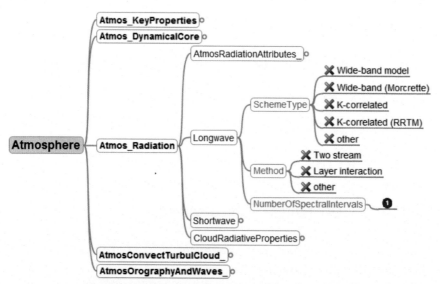

Figure 11.1 The PIMMS framework captures metadata about the life cycle of a climate simulation. Here we see a UML view of the CIM elements that are populated by PIMMS; they explain why and how the simulated data was created. It is important to know this if you want to use another researcher's data.

and customised to address the specific requirements of individual research groups. With this technology, initial model descriptions may take time to complete but once they have been created the PIMMS infrastructure can be used to document subsequent variations by describing only those elements that are changed. An established PIMMS infrastructure will fit seamlessly into the research metadata workflow and significantly reduce subsequent documentation effort.

The key to the customisation of PIMMS is in the modularity of its tools and the clear separation of structure (CIM) from content (CV). The PIMMS project is extending the CMIP5 controlled vocabulary for domain specific documentation and demonstrating how the CIM can be used, amongst other applications, to document an integrated assessment model. These extensions to controlled vocabularies are an integral part of making the PIMMS system applicable outside of CMIP5.

The controlled vocabularies can both be exploited by, and informed by, text mining tools. To that end, PIMMS has been exploring how these controlled vocabularies can be used in an adapted version of the University of Cambridge ChemicalTagger tool.

The ChemicalTagger parser was developed, by researchers at the University of Cambridge, as a medium-depth, phrase-based semantic natural language processing (NLP) tool for the language of chemical experiments. An overview of ChemicalTagger is given by Hawizy et al. (2011). Tagging is based on a modular architecture and uses a combination of OSCAR (for identifying chemical entities), chemistry domain-specific regular expressions (regexes) and English taggers to identify parts of speech. In the work by Hawizy et al. (2011), using a metric that allows for overlapping annotations, the authors achieved machine-annotator agreements of 88.9% for phrase recognition and 91.9% for phrase-type identification (*Action* names).

ChemicalTagger has primarily been deployed to text mine research publications for content of interest in chemistry, but a modified version was developed in the ACPGeo project, to additionally search for wider information of interest to atmospheric scientists. In particular, the domain-specific regex was extended to cover temporal and geographical descriptions, as well as vocabulary more specific to the subject area.

In the context of PIMMS, this work has been extended, initially with the aim of exploiting the CIM vocabularies and content to find publications of relevance to specific models and the domains they simulate, and then to use ACPGeo to present such abstracts in an interactive way that categorises the content. However, as the project matured, the ACPGeo work has followed three separate threads to:

(1) Investigate the PIMMS vocabulary and language structures that are "new" to the existing CV compiled during METAFOR (i.e. palaeoclimate language).

(2) Adapt the ACPGeo version of ChemicalTagger to include terms of importance to climate modelling (e.g. model resolution).

(3) Develop tools for extraction of the tagged information into the CIM format.

In completing this work, additional improvements to the tagging of existing language structures have been made through iteration over a wider range of sample material, for example, the phrases used to highlight model names or acronyms have been improved and incidental work has been carried out to distinguish caption phrases (i.e. Figure/Table), as often important model metadata is held in tabular forms.

In the remainder of this chapter we briefly describe the questionnaire process, the controlled vocabularies and the CIM in more detail, before concentrating on the details of the modifications to the ChemicalTaggers system, and presenting the results of its use in analysing climate publications.

11.2 METHODOLOGY

11.2.1 Controlled Vocabularies and Common Information Model

Controlled vocabularies are currently built by an interactive process of consultation with domain experts and stakeholders. Mind maps are used to capture the information that eventually forms part of an information pipeline, which results in assimilation into the PIMMS questionnaire. An example excerpt of a mind map, showing a portion of the controlled vocabulary for atmospheric radiation code, is shown in Figure 11.2. The community finds use of mind maps intuitive and free software is readily available. Once the vocabulary has been agreed upon, the mind maps are parsed and converted to an XML format suitable for the pipeline. Code for parsing mind maps has been written in Python and is available from the PIMMS website.

The PIMMS methodology assumes an initial effort to document standard model configurations. Once these descriptions have been created, users need only describe the specific way in which their model configuration is different from the standard. Thus, the documentation burden on the user is specific to the experiment they are performing and fits easily into the workflow of their science. A schematic illustration of the questionnaire metadata pipeline is shown in Figure 11.3.

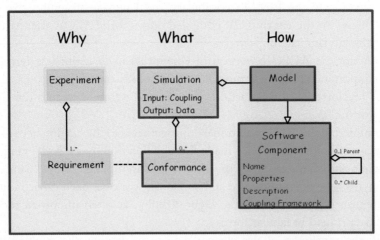

Figure 11.2 An example excerpt of a mind map, focusing on controlled vocabulary for atmospheric radiation code. The community finds use of mind maps intuitive and free software is readily available (http://freemind.sourceforge.net/wiki/index.php/Main_Page).

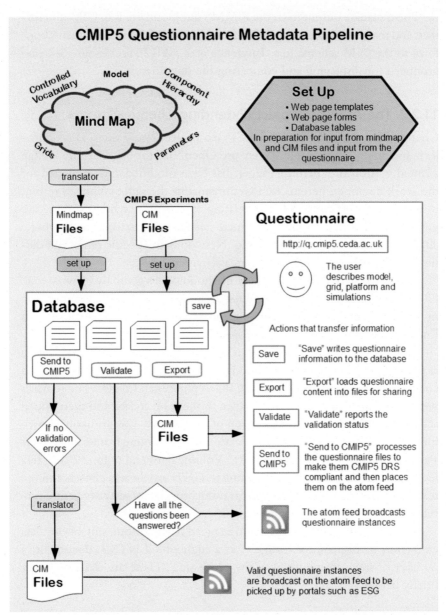

Figure 11.3 The CMIP5 Questionnaire Metadata Pipeline, which is being refactored by PIMMS so that it can be more easily portable into stand-alone installations within the university environment and customised to address the specific requirements of individual research groups.

The metadata output from the PIMMS questionnaire is in CIM xml format, and made available using Atom feeds. The CIM XML documents conform to the CIM schema (e.g. Lawrence et al., 2012), and tooling is being produced for displaying and comparing the documents.

11.2.2 The ACPGeo Project (Extending ChemicalTagger)

ChemicalTagger, and its related ACPGeo project, are written as Java projects and are freely available.[2] They use OpenNLP for NLP.[3] ACPGeo, an adapted version of ChemicalTagger, has been modified and employed for the work described herein. ACPGeo maintains the same architecture but, in place of the grammar phrases relating to chemical synthesis, there are phrases more suited to environmental science, in particular atmospheric chemistry: field work and modelling. New domain-specific regex and dictionaries have been added for the areas covered.

An overview of ChemicalTagger methodology is given by Hawizy et al. (2011). Tagging is based on a modular architecture and uses a combination of OSCAR, chemistry domain-specific regex (regular expressions) and English taggers to identify parts of speech.

Sample texts from the European Geophysical Union's journals *Climates of the Past*[4] and *Geophysical Model Development (GMD)*[5] have been used as a corpus to iteratively develop the ACPGeo phrases and regex. The journals were chosen because of their relevance to the subject area and their "open access" availability. The XML version of the abstracts was primarily chosen for study with the work detailed in Section 11.3.1 coming from *Climate of the Past* abstracts from Volume 1 (2005) to Volume 8 (to end of June 2012). In a few cases, see Section 11.3.2, a complete *GMD* article was chosen and the text was extracted from the pdf format using proprietary software before carrying out the processing described below.

To parse a text and convert it into a tagged XML output, suitable for data extraction or display, for example, as a highlighted HTML document, a number of steps are required in the processing. These are described very briefly below.

---

[2] https://bitbucket.org/wwmm/chemicaltagger and https://bitbucket.org/wwmm/acpgeo.
[3] http://opennlp.apache.org.
[4] http://www.climate-of-the-past.net/home.html.
[5] http://www.geoscientific-model-development.net.

Text normalisation is a preprocessing step that transforms the text into a format that is consistent for tagging. This involves removing nonprinting unicode characters from text and normalising the spacing between the words. The exact requirements of the preprocessing are dependent upon the source text. For example, the ACPGeo project was set up to read abstracts from journals that were presented in XHTML and, thus, removal of formatting tags (e.g.) was carried out prior to further processing.

Multiword regular expression preprocessing has been added during this project, to reduce the NLP burden, and it is carried out for two very set phrases: citation phrases (e.g. "Held and George, 2000"), and a subset of the acronym phrases (i.e. those of the type "This Is An Acronym (TIAA)") whereby a simple multiword regular expression may be more reliable than NLP. In the reference phrase shown as an example, "Held" may be interpreted as a verb rather than a proper noun and, thus, may have been missed with the NLP approach. Likewise, the surnames "Black" or "England" could be incorrectly tagged as an adjective and location, respectively. Whilst it would be possible to extract these phrases using other methods (see, e.g. Yeates (1999) and Kaplan et al. (2009)), the inclusion of these multiword regex keeps the processing simple.

Tokenisation is the process of splitting a phrase into a sequence of meaningful elements called tokens. A token can be made up of one or more words and it is not necessarily alphanumeric (e.g. commas, exclamation marks, full stops, etc.). Many different splitting patterns are conceivable in NLP. Hence, many different tokenisers exist, with the most common one being the white space tokeniser. The tokenisers used in ChemicalTagger and the ACPGeo project are slightly different with both being based on a white space tokeniser. The exact choice of whether to break on periods (full stops), brackets, hyphens and colons, for example, depends upon the surrounding text and whether it matches regular expressions such as might fit a chemical name, a time description, an acronym, a numeric quantity, an abbreviation and so forth.

Tagging is the process of assigning grammatical roles to the tokens. ChemicalTagger uses a three-step cascading tagger. The first step involves running a chemical entity recogniser (OSCAR) on the tokens. Chemical-Tagger then falls back on a customised regex tagger, which has been further modified for the ACPGeo project, and finally a parts of speech tagger for the tokens that have not been identified. In addition to the customised regex tagger the ACPGeo project also contains a number of dictionaries, which may be relevant depending on context. The taggers will be discussed further below.

OSCAR tagging: Open source chemistry analysis routines (OSCAR) is used for the recognition of chemical entities in text. OSCAR is an open source extensible system for the automated annotation of chemistry in scientific articles (Corbett and Murray-Rust, 2006; Jessop et al., 2011). It can be used to identify chemical names and ontology terms. In addition, where possible, any chemical names detected will be annotated with structures derived either by lookup, or name-to-structure parsing using "OPSIN" (Lowe et al., 2011), or with identifiers from the ChEBI ("Chemical Entities of Biological Interest") ontology (Degtyarenko et al., 2008).

The Regex tagger is used to mark up *subject-related* terms that are not recognised by OSCAR. The regex tagger uses regular expressions that are stored in a *rules* file together with the customised tags. The regex tagger rules can be altered depending upon the requirements of the subject area. In ChemicalTagger the rules include, for example, nouns and verbs relevant to chemical synthesis. In ACPGeo the regex tagger includes units, common acronyms or likely acronyms, location specific words (e.g. regex to match coordinates or words such as "Island", "lake" etc.), number patterns likely to be dates or times and so on, and words that are likely to have a specific meaning in the context; for example, "interval", "period", "present" might all relate to timescales. Careful choice of these words and regex has to be made to avoid too many false positives. In addition to the regex rules file, the ACPGeo project uses *dictionaries* relevant to the subject area. These may be specific to a certain topic area. Those currently in use are a dictionary of well-known field sites commonly used for atmospheric research, for example, Global Atmospheric Watch (GAWSIS)[6] stations and EMEP European Monitoring and Evaluation Program (monitoring and evaluation of long-range transmission of air pollution) stations[7] a general dictionary of atmospheric science terms and, as part of this work, a palaeotimes dictionary, has been complied, primarily using Wikipedia[8] as a source.

---

[6] http://gaw.empa.ch/gawsis/StationList.asp.
[7] http://www.nilu.no/projects/ccc/network/index.html.
[8] http://en.wikipedia.org/wiki/Geologic_time_scale.

English parts of speech tagger involves marking up the general English language tokens. English parts of speech (POS) taggers are widely available and for the purposes of this work, the Penn Treebank[9] is used. A treebank is a parsed text corpus (i.e. annotated with syntactic structure) that is used in corpus linguistics. The Penn Treebank is commonly used for English parts of speech tagging and is made up of 4.5 million American English words. Typical tags include:

- **NN** singular or mass noun
- **NNS** plural noun
- **VB** verb, base form
- **VBD** verb, past tense
- **CD** cardinal number (one, two, 2, etc.)
- **CC** Conjunctions (and, or, plus, etc.)

This treebank is used within a parts of speech tagger, provided by OpenNLP. OpenNLP is a suite of open-source Java projects, data sets and tutorials supporting research and development in NLP.

11.2.3 Phrase Parsing

Parsers build on tagged tokens to assign syntactical structure to text. The goal of phrase parsing in ChemicalTagger is to build the chemical equivalent of a Chomsky tree structure of a sentence (Chomsky, 1957).

In human discourse, sentences are parsed in multiple valid ways. However, the formulaic structure of many scientific publications leads to fewer probable parses for a given sentence. Therefore, a formal approach was decided on for phrase parsing, so ChemicalTagger uses ANTLR, Parr, 2007. ANTLR (ANother Tool for Language Recognition) is a parser generator that uses LL(*) parsing to automate the construction of language recognisers. It was designed to generate grammars for formal programming languages, but it is applicable to any domain where an underlying implicit grammar exists. LL(*) parsers are recursive descent parsers; they analyse input sequences by working their way down from the topmost nonterminal symbol until they reach a terminal node. In natural language these terminal nodes are the tokens.

To demonstrate how ANTLR is used, a simplified version of ACPGeo's grammar is described below. For clarity, uppercase symbols represent terminals (symbols that cannot be broken down into smaller constituents) while

---

[9] http://www.cis.upenn.edu/%7Etreebank/.

lowercase words represent nonterminals (symbols that can be broken down into smaller constituents).

The top rule in our grammar is a *sentence* and it can be made up of a *transitionphrase* (e.g. "However",) *verbphrase(s), prepphrase(s), nounphrase(s), referencephrase(s)* (i.e. a reference to a publication). A small number of tokens are allowed to be part of a *sentence*, even where they do not fit into one of the phrases above (e.g. punctuation and conjunctions, etc.). Where the word structure does not meet the *sentence* criteria an "unmatched" phrase is reported.

A *verbphrase* could consist of an *adverb, verb(s) and may be* followed by a *prepphrase,* which may in turn contain another *prepphrase* and, hence, *nounphrase*.

A *prepphrase* contains at least one preposition and a *nounphrase* (or *referencephrase,* i.e. a citation) but it may also contain additional adverbs, adjectives and determiners. There are *prepphrases* specific to location and time. These can be useful for looking for possible locations where there is no dictionary location stored (e.g. "in Newplace"). However, this has to be balanced by false positives such as "in Newmodel". Once recursion down the *prepphrase* tree is completed, *nounphrase* is next.

A *nounphrase* can be made up of a *determiner, adjective(s)* and *noun(s)*. A *noun* can include numbers, molecules and various proper nouns/nouns from relevant dictionaries. There are phrases within *nounphrase* relating to the sentence structure such as *parentheticalphrase* and *acronymphrase*. There are also phrases within noun phrases based more on content than grammar; for example, *time, campaign, model, location, quantity, mathexpression* and *mathequation*. More phrases can be added to look at particular areas of a subject, for example, *resolution* phrases have been added in this work, or areas relating to the structure of a paper; for example, a *captionphrase* has also been recently added.

The subject area phrases relate key words to other likely words or phrases. For example, the *campaign* phrase will link words such as "campaign", "experiment", "project", "study" and "programme" with likely phrases/words (e.g. acronym phrases, proper nouns, times, etc.). Figure 11.4 shows a how the *campaign* phrase can be constructed; for example, an acronym phrase (acronymphrase) or unspecified proper nouns (nnp, nnps) or other nouns specified within ACPGeo's regex file (nndomain, nnplocationType, nnpacronym), followed by any number of time phrases (time), alpha-numerics (cd, nnidentifierAll), other nouns (nn, nnp, nndomain, nnplocationType, moleculeNoun) or adjectives and

```
campaign
   :   (   campaignContent1 | campaignContent2
       )
   -> ^( CAMPAIGN campaignContent1? campaignContent2?)
   ;

campaignContent1
   :   (   acronymphrase | nnp | nndomain | nnplocationType | nnps | nnpacronym
       )
       (   time | cd | nnidentifierAll | nn | nnp | nndomain | nnplocationType | adj | moleculeNoun
       )* nncampaign
   ;

campaignContent2
   :   acronymphrase
       (   time | cd | nnp | nndomain | adj | moleculeNoun | nnplocationType
       )* nnstudy
   ;
```

Figure 11.4 An extract from the ANTLR grammar file showing the structure of the campaign phrase. Campaign phrases can contain acronym and time phrases, alphanumerics (cd, nnidentifierAll), adjectives (adj), undefined proper nouns (nnp), a number of other proper nouns (starting nnp), undefined nouns (nn) and other nouns (starting nn).

finally a campaign keyword (nncampaign) matching the regex `^((EU-)?(p|P)re)?((C|c)ampaign|(EU-)?(p|P)roject|(EU-)?(p|P)rogram(me)?)(s)?$`.[10] The second possible description must contain an *acronymphrase*, without which the key word "`[S|s]tudy`" (nnstudy) would not strongly indicate a campaign phrase, but might be used as a verb or something else.

Further work could be carried out to add more phrases. However, problems arise when the text could be assigned to one or more phrases. Hence, there is a need to prioritise phrases, such that the maximum information is retrieved for the effort employed. This is an iterative process, whereby texts are parsed and the resultant phrases observed manually. Machine learning could enhance this process given adequate resources.

11.3 RESULTS

11.3.1 Overview of ACPGeo Phrases

Table 11.1 shows selected phrases that are output from the ACPGeo tagging of relevant publications and typical example phrase content. The different phrases have different importance depending on the exact usage of ACPGeo. For example, in field work, the campaign phrase would be found more often than in climate modelling papers. However, it is still useful to know whether or not a published piece of work is part of a larger project. Running

---

[10] This would match words such as EU-Project or pre-campaign *etc.*

Table 11.1 Example phrases together with their output tags and a brief comment

Tag	Example(s)	Comment
$<$CAMPAIGN$>$	(i) Palaeoclimate modelling Intercomparison Project (PMIP), (ii) PANASH (Paleoclimates of the Northern and Southern Hemisphere) programme	In these examples $<$CAMPAIGN$>$ refers to modelling projects rather than field campaigns
$<$MODEL$>$	(i) REVEALS model, (ii) ECBILT-CLIO intermediate complexity climate model	$<$MODEL$>$ will also identify generic acronyms such as GCM as a model
$<$acronymPhrase$>$	(i) Modern analogues technique (MAT), (ii) REVEALS (Regional Estimates of VEgetation Abundance from Large Sites)	See note on multiword regular expression preprocessing above
$<$QUANTITY$>$	(i) 10 ppm, (ii) 0.53 mm/day	The units dictionary could be more extensive
$<$MOLECULE$>$	(i) CO_2, (ii) calcium carbonate	There are some false positives (e.g. where acronyms may look similar to a chemical formula)
$<$timePhrase$>$	(i) during the meteorological autumn of 2006	Ranges from time of day to PALAEOTIME time ranges
$<$PALAEOTIME$>$	(i) Holocene, (ii) 8 ky BP	A subset of timePhrase
$<$CITATION$>$	(i) Otto et al. (2009b), (ii) Giraudeau et al. (2000)	Important to distinguish year pattern from dates relevant to the study
$<$locationPhrase$>$	(i) around Lake Kotokel, (ii) over Tibetan Plateau	False positives (e.g. "from Sphagnum")
$<$LOCATION$>$	(i) 52°47′N, 108°07′E, 458 m a.s.l, (ii) London	Degrees sign not always accessible from sources (e.g. when pdf→text used)
$<$resolution$>$	(i) Horizontal resolution of approximately 2.8° × 2.8°	Degrees sign not always accessible from sources (e.g. when pdf→text used)
$<$horizontalGrid$>$	(i) 256 equally spaced grid points	T42′ will be identified as $<$NN-IDENTIFIER$>$
$<$verticalResolution$>$	(ii) 20 vertical σ levels	Further information generally required from the text
$<$MATHEXPRESSION$>$	$(1° × 1°)$	This information may make part of another phrase
$<$MATHEQUATION$>$	$R^2 = 0.4$	Despite tag name, also includes inequalities

the ACPGeo code on example abstracts from *Climates of the Past* gives phrases such as "PANASH (Paleoclimates of the Northern and Southern Hemisphere) programme". Many of the phrases may contribute to others; for example, a *timephrase* may have *year, month* or *palaeotime* phrases.

11.3.1.1 Palaeotime Phrases

Given that one of our journals was *Climate of the Past*, it became necessary to construct a new specific phrase for *palaeotime*. The phrase is based on a palaeo-time dictionary containing a glossary of *timeperiod* words (e.g. "Holocene"), together with other common time references and development of related grammar rules.

In addition, time units were extended to include units such as "mya" (million years ago), b.y. (billion years) and words such as "decade" and "mil-lenia", and so forth. The language processing of time units is complicated by the lack of adoption of a standard representation of "year" (i.e. y, yr, ya, a, cal). Qualifiers to the time units were separately tagged and include acro-nyms and words such as "AD", "BC" and "ago". For the most part, these additional units and qualifiers have not caused a problem with existing inputs to the tagging process. However, there is some overlap with existing acro-nyms; for example, BC could also be used to represent "Black Carbon".

Other nouns relating to time are also given a separate tag. These include words such as "era", "epoch", "eon" and so on, and more general words such as "Time", "interval" and so forth. Time period adjectives have also been specified; for example, "stadial" is considered an adjective but "Stadial" is considered as a proper noun and is contained within the palaeotime dic-tionary. In reality, words such as "stadial" and "glacial" may be used as proper nouns, nouns or adjectives.

From the 382 abstracts processed, 1289 *palaeotime* structures were found. These ranged from single words (e.g. "Holocene") to more complex phrases (e.g. "seventeenth and eighteenth centuries" (Hamza et al., 2007) or "Roman Classical Period" (Taricco et al., 2009)). These *palaeotime* structures are included as a subset of *time* structures, of which 2135 were found. As a consequence, *time* structures range from single words such as "afternoon", to times such as "12:00" and to phrases such as "Last Glacial Maximum to the Late Holocene" (Albani et al., 2012). *Time* structures may or may not be included within *timephrase*, which is a special case of the *prepphrase*; that is, phrases beginning with a selected preposition and containing a *time* phrase. A total of 768 *timephrase*s were found. These range from simple phrases such as "in summer" (Hofer et al., 2012) to numeric quantities such as "from 9 to

6 ky BP" (Jin et al., 2009) or more descriptive phrases such as "during the relatively warm Jurassic and Cretaceous Periods" (Jenkyns et al., 2012) and "in the Middle Miocene around 13.9 million years ago" (Langebroek et al., 2009). The latter example is shown in Figure 11.5, to give an idea of the structure of the tags (tokens).

11.3.1.2 Palaeotime Phrase Omissions and False Positives

Very few (6) unambiguous false positives were found; for example, "confidence intervals" (Christiansen and Ljungqvist, 2012). Other phrases could be correctly identified as *palaeotime* references but they might not be particularly useful, as they do not clearly identify a single period in time; for example, "glacial period" (Peavoy and Franzke, 2010).

There are a number of known omissions; for example, it is not possible to recognise the phrase "Greenland Interstadial" as *palaeotime*, as with this method the *location* phrase has higher priority than the time phrase. In this example, the result would be a *location* phrase preceding the *palaeotime* phrase, which, itself, would only contain "Interstadial". Hence, postprocessing is required to correct for *palaeotime* phrases that include a location. Phrases such as the "pre-Vostok period" might relate to a well-defined time period. However, as the NLP tagging of "pre-Vostok" is as an adjective and not a proper noun, this phrase is not matched and further work would be required to determine the importance of similar phrases.

```
- <TimePhrase>
    <IN-IN>in</IN-IN>
    <DT-THE>the</DT-THE>
  - <TIME>
      <JJ-TIMEPERIOD>Middle</JJ-TIMEPERIOD>
    - <PALAEOTIME>
        <NNP-TIMEPERIOD>Miocene</NNP-TIMEPERIOD>
      </PALAEOTIME>
    </TIME>
    <IN-TIMLOC>around</IN-TIMLOC>
  - <TIME>
    - <PALAEOTIME>
        <CD>13.9</CD>
        <CD>million</CD>
        <NN-TIMEUNIT>years</NN-TIMEUNIT>
        <NN-PALAEOTIMEQUALIFIER>ago</NN-PALAEOTIMEQUALIFIER>
      </PALAEOTIME>
    </TIME>
  </TimePhrase>
```

Figure 11.5 An example of a time phrase that includes palaeotime phrases, from Langebroek et al. (2009).

Also omitted from the *palaeotime* structures are phrases such as "during the last four glacial cycles" (Köhler and Fischer, 2006), "between the current interglacial period and ..." (Masson-Delmotte et al., 2006) and "roughly a millennium ago" (Goosse et al., 2006). These can all be directly linked to a period in time. For the first two examples, it would be possible to look for phrases with multiple occurrences of time period adjectives (e.g. "last" and "glacial") or where time period adjectives are combined with time-related nouns particularly within a *prepphrase*. However, the majority of phrases retrieved in this way would not relate to a specific time and, in most cases, the time will be better defined elsewhere within the text. Out of the 340 abstracts there were 87 phrases with a key word that matched a time unit such as "millenium" and did not correspond to *palaeotime* or *time* structures. These can always be accessed by a slightly more complex extraction from the XML (e.g. using the *nounphrase* or *prepphrase* that encloses the time unit tag) but again, in most cases a clearer description of the time period is given elsewhere within the text.

11.3.2 Extraction of Tagged Metadata in a Format Suitable for Comparison with the CIM

The objective of this work was both to inform the ACPGeo tagger with vocabularies from PIMMS and previous projects, and be able to take the ouput of the ACPGeo tagger, and compare them with the formal descriptions obtained using questionnaires.

The ACPGeo tagger converts text documents into semantically tagged XML documents. Further processing of these XML documents is required to extract relevant phrases, quantities or key words.

For the purposes of this project it was necessary to compare identified phrases with the type of data stored within a CIM document. Text parsing and tagging of phrases or words such as time, location, mathematical expressions and chemical compounds, and so on, can be carried out with reasonable annotator-machine agreement as described in Section 11.3.1 above. However, extraction of information, to use within a given structure, is harder than the initial parsing, as the context is important.

A number of programming languages might have been chosen to extract information from the XML output of the ACPGeo language tagger. It was decided to use XSLT, which was developed for XML transformations, and might be reasonably easily adapted by others within the project. Essentially the controlled vocabularies from PIMMS were used as a "key word search" to relevant phrases or sentences within the tagged ACPGeo output.

In some cases the transformation of a phrase to CIM XML might be quite simple. In other cases the transformation may be more complex and possibly less reliable; for example, where all the required information is not present within one *phrase* or complete *sentence*. ACPGeo takes no account of text format and, hence, if the "search" for related data is extended outside of a single sentence then there is no information on whether neighbouring *sentences* are within the same paragraph, and so on. However, it may be possible to determine whether or not the sentences come under the same heading (although this has not been investigated within this work).

Within the time constraints of the project, it was only practical to look at one of the available controlled vocabularies, and so the atmosphere realm controlled vocabulary was used as the focus for the language used within the regular expression tagger.

One example of this process is presented here. Data was extracted from Chan et al., 2011 (from the journal *Geoscientific Model Development*) and placed in a CIM XML format. The result is shown here (Figure 11.6a–e) using the original generation of tools available to PIMMS (a new generation of tools is now available, but it was not possible to reprocess these figures for this chapter). We can see that in Figure 11.6a the CIM model is shortName, longName, description and type. The shortName (MIROC4m) was tagged as NNP-ACRONYM (but could equally be just NNP) and was associated with a *model* phrase from the ACPGeo output. As it is the first model mentioned in the paper it is assumed to be the model that is the subject of the paper. The longName is given as the model phrase in which the shortName first appears, failing this the first sentence was chosen. The description is arbitrarily the first sentence mentioning the model and a single subsequent sentence.

Figure 11.6b shows one atmospheric property (timing of the orbital parameter, part of the description of the top of atmosphere insolation). Other parameters such as volcano implementation and orography have not been matched, so there is no possibility with the CIM XML viewer to show these. However, details of the orbital parameters were found and these are displayed.

Similarly, in Figure 11.6c, we see that not all details of the atmospheric advection scheme used for the tracers has been obtained (e.g. the SchemeName is missing), but the grid name has been used to populate two of its properties. The tracers themselves are not easily identified from the paper.

The "AtmosRadiation" component properties are found with varying reliability. For example, more work needs to be done to isolate the correct time step. Unsurprisingly, the ACPGeo project is good at picking out the "GHG-Types" and "AerosolTypes" component properties and extraction of these is quite straightforward (see Figure 11.6d).

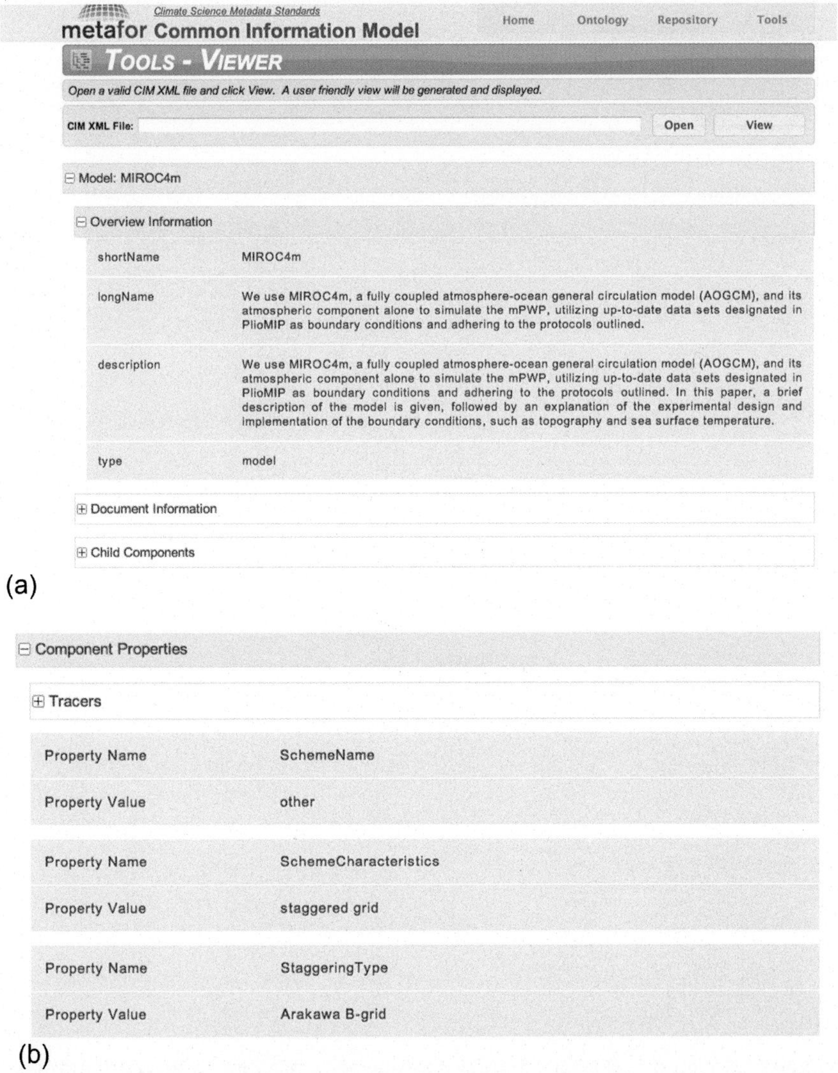

(a)

(b)

Figure 11.6 (a) Output from an example publication (Chan et al., 2011) to show how the high-level model elements are shown. (b) One example of a model property extracted from the text (Chan et al., 2011).

continued

Component Properties

⊞ Tracers

Property Name	SchemeName
Property Value	other

Property Name	SchemeCharacteristics
Property Value	staggered grid

Property Name	StaggeringType
Property Value	Arakawa B-grid

(c)

Property Name	AerosolTypes
Property Value	soil dust, black carbon, organic carbon, sulfate, seasalt

Property Name	GHG-Types
Property Value	CO2, CH4, N2O, O3

(d)

⊟ Longwave

Property Name	SchemeType
Property Value	k-distribution

Property Name	NumberOfSpectralIntervals
Property Value	None

⊟ Shortwave

Property Name	SchemeType
Property Value	two-stream

Property Name	NumberOfSpectralIntervals
Property Value	None

(e)

Figure 11.6, cont'd (c) Extract to show how the regex matching to keyword "Arakawa-B" is used to complete both property value "staggered grid" and property value "Arakawa B-grid" from Chan et al. (2011). (d) Extract to show how *molecule and aerosol*, found in the initial tagging, can be used within the Amos Key Properties' component property of the CIM XML, from Chan et al. (2011). (e) Extract to show how that whilst the "SchemeTypes" are correctly found the default answer of "None" is given to the "NumberofSpectralIntervals". This property value is not correct but there is no option of "NotFound" (Chan et al., 2011).

Information on longwave and shortwave scheme types is available but the number of spectral intervals was not found (see Figure 11.6e). The CIM display software does not allow for a value of "not found", as only valid CIM documents can be displayed. Hence, the number of spectral intervals is erroneously given as the default answer of "none". This is one example of simple feedback into the CIM vocabulary process: while "not found" might be specific to ACPGeo, a value of "not recorded yet" might be of more use. (One would not like to use a phrase like "not known", because obviously the information *is* known, but in this case not known by the software, and in a human-generated case, not known by the person filling out the form. In both cases, the information could be added in a subsequent step.)

11.4 OVERALL CONCLUSIONS AND SUGGESTIONS FOR FURTHER WORK

The work presented here has concentrated on the application of a modified version of the University of Cambridge ChemicalTagger to some climate science exemplars.

11.4.1 ACPGeo Phrases

Initial studies would indicate that ACPGeo can be used to highlight a number of phrases relevant to climate science. In particular, significant work has been carried out to identify palaeotime phrases (i.e. time phrases of relevance to the study of past climates). Some postprocessing of data is required to standardise the quantity phrase "2000 years" with the palaotime phrase "2 ky", and so forth. Likewise, phrases that don't meet the initial processing requirements (e.g. "Greenland Interstadial") must be identified in a postprocessing step. Further work to extend the palaeotime dictionary could be carried out, with iterations through more input texts, but it would seem that the dictionary entries do account for most common descriptions of past times.

Whilst a comparison of automated phrase retrieval compared with human annotation has been published for ChemicalTagger (Hawizy et al., 2011), such an analysis is not available for the new ACPGeo phrases. Meanwhile, we can be confident that this technique can highlight useful information, but further iterations over the phrases and inputs to the regular expression rules may be needed to give a better machine-annotator agreement.

11.4.2 XML Conversion to Compare with CV and CIM from PIMMS

The conversion from tagged information to structured CIM information has included a number of heuristics that could be improved. For example, the current conversion software includes some arbitrary choices about how far to look for related information. The software could be improved to further cheque for context and possibly add flags to indicate some form of reliability; for example, the reliability of extracting related information may get lower the further the extracted information is from the initial key word/phrase. The arbitrary choice to look for additional (related) information within five *sentences* of a phrase has been made in many areas. This has no scientific basis and should be investigated. Also, cheques on whether or not adjacent *sentences* are under the same heading are not made. There is sufficient information within the grammar file to try to extract heading information at present (e.g. usually an alpha numeric identifier followed by one or more proper nouns). It is envisaged that cheques on headings could be made in subsequent work.

Context needs to be improved to cheque for negatives (i.e. "We did not use the method of Blogs et al.") would correctly indicate a negative in the ACPGeo output but this is ignored in the current conversion. Context should also take account of intervening phrases. This is carried out within some parts of the conversion; for example, the software will only process information about a model component between the first mention of that model component and the first mention of a subsequent model component but this is not universally applied, nor tested for reliability.

11.4.3 CIM XML: Applicability

This work has shown limitations of the CIM schema itself: Some parts of the CIM are overly restrictive in terms of *allowed* content (e.g. the CIM schema does not allow comments within all elements); and some are overly restrictive in terms of *required* content. An example of the required information that is never likely to be found within a publication is the "responsible party" element of the CIM documents: all that is known is the responsible party for the paper itself, any others can only be hinted at through references within the paper.

Certainly, allowing extra information would be sensible: again, for example, allowing comments freely within the XML would aid comparison of what might be found (i.e. where there is some uncertainty) with what is expected. In this regard, the CIM schema needs to better respect foundation tenets of XML information processing: allow foreign markup, but potentially ignore it when processing (although viewers should attempt to display it).

Conversion of the ACPGeo tagged output XML into the CIM XML was carried out for expediency, as it would aid comparison of data extraction from papers with CIM documents. To make better use of the tagged output in this environment would require either modifications to the CIM itself or to the CIM ecosystem of tools.

11.4.4 Overall Conclusion

Whilst phrase parsing and tagging can be carried out with reasonable accuracy, provided there is sufficient iteration over likely text samples, there remains much work to be done to thoroughly study the context of phrases to automatically extract data for use in standardised data formats, such as the CIM. These initial studies would indicate that automated text processing can get much of the way toward highlighting likely phrases, but reliable data extraction would require considerably more work to be carried out on gauging the context of the phrases. It is likely that better use of the available controlled vocabularies can help inform the tagging process.

The success of ACPGeo has raised the question of how to interpret harvested CIM documents versus those created ab initio in a questionnaire environment. The CIM was designed to be populated by climate modellers, and was very technology focused in terms of the model description. However, CIM documents created by harvesting information from papers naturally concentrate on facets of the modelling process of direct interest to specific science goals. Inevitably that implies the likelihood that important information will be included in papers that is not covered by the controlled vocabularies, and much that is will not be included. Neither route to model documentation is likely to be complete, and so they are complementary. We are also aware of other projects concentrating on getting codes to be self-documenting. This means that projects aimed at delivering model documentation will need to support both different protocols for creating CIM documents, and comparison will need to be aware of the route to creation.

Clearly the more the process of model and workflow documentation that can be automated the better. Metadata collection is generally an onerous task. If some information can be captured from the narratives that appear in journal articles, and some from the codes themselves, then the more complete information required can be acquired incrementally in "questionnaires", rather than using them for the entire information acquisition. In any case, techniques of text mining are likely to be the only way retrospective model documentation will be accomplished in any significant manner.

ACKNOWLEDGEMENTS

We would like to thank JISC for funding of this work, under the JISC MRD (managing research data) project; Daniel Lowe for his invaluable help and advice on chemical tagging; Gerry Devine, for his help on the CIM structure and display software; and Greg Tourte for providing data on palaeoclimate language.

REFERENCES

Albani, S., Delmonte, B., Maggi, V., Baroni, C., Petit, J.-R., Stenni, B., Mazzola, C., Frezzotti, M., 2012. Interpreting last glacial to Holocene dust changes at Talos Dome (East Antarctica): implications for atmospheric variations from regional to hemispheric scales. Clim. Past 8, 741–750. http://dx.doi.org/10.5194/cp-8-741-2012.

Callaghan, S., Budich, R., Devine, G., Guilyardi, E., Lawrence, B., Valcke, S., 2011. Metafor: managing metadata for climate models. Zero-In Magazine. (Issue 3). Successful case studies of eScience/eResearch projects in Europe and globally.

Chan, W.-L., Abe-Ouchi, A., Ohgaito, R., 2011. Simulating the mid-Pliocene climate with the MIROC general circulation model: experimental design and initial results. Geosci. Model Dev. 4, 1035–1049. http://dx.doi.org/10.5194/gmd-4-1035-2011.

Chomsky, N., 1957. Syntactic Structures. Mouton, The Hague.

Christiansen, B., Ljungqvist, F.C., 2012. The extra-tropical Northern Hemisphere temperature in the last two millennia: reconstructions of low-frequency variability. Clim. Past 8, 765–786. http://dx.doi.org/10.5194/cp-8-765-2012.

Corbett, P., Murray-Rust, P., 2006. High-throughput identification of chemistry in life science texts. In: Berthold, M.R., Glen, R., Fischer, I. (Eds.), Computational Life Sciences II. Springer, Berlin/Heidelberg, pp. 107–118.

Degtyarenko, K., de Matos, P., Ennis, M., Hastings, J., Zbinden, M., McNaught, A., Alcántara, R., Darsow, M., Guedj, M., Ashburner, M., 2008. ChEBI: a database and ontology for chemical entities of biological interest. Nucleic Acids Res. 36, D344–D350.

Goosse, H., Arzel, O., Luterbacher, J., Mann, M.E., Renssen, H., Riedwyl, N., Timmermann, A., Xoplaki, E., Wanner, H., 2006. The origin of the European "Medieval Warm Period" Clim. Past 2, 99–113. http://dx.doi.org/10.5194/cp-2-99-2006.

Guilyardi, E., Balaji, V., Callaghan, S., DeLuca, C., Devine, G., Denvil, S., Ford, R., Pascoe, C., Lautenschlager, M., Lawrence, B., Steenman-Clark, L., Valcke, S., 2011. The CMIP5 model and simulation documentation: a new standard for climate modelling metadata. CLIVAR Exch. 16 (2), 42–46. Special Issue No. 56.

Hamza, V.M., Cavalcanti, A.S.B., Benyosef, L.C.C., 2007. Surface thermal perturbations of the recent past at low latitudes – inferences based on borehole temperature data from Eastern Brazil. Clim. Past 3, 513–526. http://dx.doi.org/10.5194/cp-3-513-2007.

Hawizy, L., Jessop, D.M., Adams, N., Murray-Rust, P., 2011. ChemicalTagger: a tool for semantic text-mining in chemistry. J. Cheminformatics 3, 17. http://dx.doi.org/10.1186/1758-2946-3-17.

Hofer, D., Raible, C.C., Dehnert, A., Kuhlemann, J., 2012. The impact of different glacial boundary conditions on atmospheric dynamics and precipitation in the North Atlantic region. Clim. Past 8, 935–949. http://dx.doi.org/10.5194/cp-8-935-2012.

Jenkyns, H.C., Schouten-Huibers, L., Schouten, S., Sinninghe Damsté, J.S., 2012. Warm Middle Jurassic–Early Cretaceous high-latitude sea-surface temperatures from the Southern Ocean. Clim. Past 8, 215–226. http://dx.doi.org/10.5194/cp-8-215-2012.

Jessop, D.M., Adams, S.E., Willighagen, E.L., Hawizy, L., Murray-Rust, P., 2011. OSCAR4: a flexible architecture for chemical text-mining. J. Cheminformatics 3, 41.

Jin, L., Peng, Y., Chen, F., Ganopolski, A., 2009. Modeling sensitivity study of the possible impact of snow and glaciers developing over Tibetan Plateau on Holocene African-Asian summer monsoon climate. Clim. Past 5, 457–469. http://dx.doi.org/10.5194/cp-5-457-2009.

Kaplan, D., Iida, R., Tokunaga, T., 2009. NLPIR4DL '09 Proceedings of the 2009 Workshop on Text and Citation Analysis for Scholarly Digital Libraries, pp. 88–95.

Köhler, P., Fischer, H., 2006. Simulating low frequency changes in atmospheric CO_2 during the last 740 000 years. Clim. Past 2, 57–78. http://dx.doi.org/10.5194/cp-2-57-2006.

Langebroek, P.M., Paul, A., Schulz, M., 2009. Antarctic ice-sheet response to atmospheric CO_2 and insolation in the Middle Miocene. Clim. Past 5, 633–646. http://dx.doi.org/10.5194/cp-5-633-2009.

Lawrence, B.N., Balaji, V., Bentley, P., Callaghan, S., DeLuca, C., Denvil, S., Devine, G., Elkington, M., Ford, R.W., Guilyardi, E., Lautenschlager, M., Morgan, M., Moine, M.-P., Murphy, S., Pascoe, C., Ramthun, H., Slavin, P., Steenman-Clark, L., Toussaint, F., Treshansky, A., Valcke, S., 2012. Describing Earth system simulations with the metafor CIM. Geosci. Model Dev. 5, 1493–1500. http://dx.doi.org/10.5194/gmd-5-1493-2012.

Lowe, D.M., Corbett, P.T., Murray-Rust, P., Glen, R.C., 2011. Chemical name to structure: OPSIN, an open source solution. J. Chem. Inf. Model. 51 (3), 739–753.

Masson-Delmotte, V., Dreyfus, G., Braconnot, P., Johnsen, S., Jouzel, J., Kageyama, M., Landais, A., Loutre, M.-F., Nouet, J., Parrenin, F., Raynaud, D., Stenni, B., Tuenter, E., 2006. Past temperature reconstructions from deep ice cores: relevance for future climate change. Clim. Past 2, 145–165. http://dx.doi.org/10.5194/cp-2-145-2006.

Parr, T., 2007. The Definitive ANTLR Reference: Building Domain-Specific Languages. The Pragmatic Bookshelf, Raleigh.

Peavoy, D., Franzke, C., 2010. Bayesian analysis of rapid climate change during the last glacial using Greenland $\delta^{18}O$ data. Clim. Past 6, 787–794. http://dx.doi.org/10.5194/cp-6-787-2010.

Taricco, C., Ghil, M., Alessio, S., Vivaldo, G., 2009. Two millennia of climate variability in the Central Mediterranean. Clim. Past 5, 171–181. http://dx.doi.org/10.5194/cp-5-171-2009.

Taylor, K.E., Stouffer, R.J., Meehl, G.A., 2011. An overview of CMIP5 and the experiment design. Bull. Am. Meteorol. Soc. 93, 485–498. http://dx.doi.org/10.1175/BAMS-D-11-00094.1.

Yeates, S., 1999. Automatic extraction of acronyms from text. In: New Zealand Computer Science Research Students' Conference, pp. 117–124.

CHAPTER 12

Building Better Mousetraps: A Linguist in NLP

E.L. Tonkin*,†
*Department of Digital Humanities, King's College London, London, UK
†Department of Electrical & Electronic Engineering, University of Bristol, Bristol, UK

These days, Christopher Phipps is a linguist. It wasn't always the case; he first joined the workforce during the early 1990s as an English teacher at a college in California. At the time, cultural critique was the name of the game: "Derrida and all that. I couldn't imagine teaching Hamlet for 30 years", he says, "so I quit. After 400 years of other peoples' analysis, there didn't seem many questions left to answer about Hamlet".

His teacher-training syllabus had included a linguistics class, which "contained a lot of language philosophy, such as [Leibniz's] Alphabet of human thought [a theoretical inventory of unambiguously represented elementary concepts]". The philosophy of language offered "interesting questions, to which there are still no answers. Compare with the progress of physics and chemistry. The mind remains a frontier of unknowns. In the 1750s–1850s, [those working in the] hard sciences felt the same way. In the hard sciences, a lot of questions have been solved". In linguistics, on the other hand, there are still more questions than answers.

"One sad fact that's often brought up", Phipps says, "is that of over seven thousand languages worldwide, fewer than a thousand have been studied at all. There's no information at all about most languages", at least beyond the most basic level. The social function of language complicates things further. Imagine 20 people from the same area stuck on a desert island. Would their dialects diverge? According to Phipps's graduate professor, the answer is "yes", because each subgroup (social clique) on the island needs to differentiate itself, and speech is a convenient means of achieving that end. Language, then, is a manifestation of human social behaviour.

What schools of linguistics are there? There are several, depending on what you want to study. "If you have an anthropological bent, you might want to go to the inner city and look at urban slang, or paddle up the Amazon. Then there are lab linguists working on psycholinguistics, such as phoneticians exploring the duration of vowels or reaction times", who are much in demand for specialised domains such as voice recognition. "Then there are pencil-and-paper linguists", such as syntaticians and semanticists. "For most natural language processing problems you're looking at syntax and semantics. The truth is, every linguist has to study at least a little of both".

Natural inclination is important. "Science people want to take things apart and see what [they] mean [...]", whilst engineers, on the whole, are more interested in constructing and improving ever-more-ingenious designs to fulfil familiar goals. "Computer scientists are people who are *good* at building mousetraps". Linguistics seems to exist across the prescriptive–descriptive attitudinal spectrum. At a few schools, it's possible to study linguistics from a bewildering variety of perspectives. Carnegie Mellon, for example, distribute their linguistics program across philosophy, modern languages, English, psychology and the Language Technologies Institute, which is part of the School of Computer Science.

Phipps applied for a PhD at the State University of New York (SUNY) at Buffalo, where he studied cognitive linguistics, "at the peak of the 1990s tech boom". The syllabus was in flux. Daniel Jurafsky and James H. Martin were in the process of writing their well-known textbook *Speech and Language Processing*. The class often used draft chapters.

A computer science professor at Buffalo, Rohini K. Srihari, was in the process of establishing a question answering (QA) startup. "They looked for fifteen to twenty linguistics grad students and funded them through the summers". Around six students worked at Cymfony each summer. "Fifteen dollars an hour – back then [it] was great money". QA is most often seen as an adjunct to the development either of systems able to reason over a typically large data set of information or a collection of natural language documents. A QA system is tasked with processing questions posed in natural language and generating the corresponding responses. "QA is spectacular tech, because it involves so many working parts of NLP".

The students developed corpora and wrote grammar rules, "doing everything from class, for pay". It wasn't quite a developer's job. The startup had developed an in-house, relatively linguist-friendly grammar writing tool, with a mechanism to compile the result in C. That meant that it offered an opportunity to learn about compilers, "first [about] using them. Then one smart guy got obsessed, so I wondered what I was missing ...".

I ask Phipps how true it is that linguists can't write code. "It's less true now than it was ten years ago", he says. "Different types of linguists have different approaches". Computational linguistics has a long history. Phipps mentions Zellig Harris of the University of Pennsylvania, whose 1940s work was data-led and focused on linguistics as applied mathematics. Despite the interdisciplinary approach of departments like Carnegie Mellon, the funding and departmental structures of linguistics in the United States mostly remain tied to anthropology and language. This can implant "bias about what linguists do and the kind of people who receive funding". Even so, the availability of computers mean that linguists are now better able to find and use corpora. So there are "more and more linguists, including grad students, who know how to code".

Tools have developed a new prominence in linguistics because of the rising interest in natural language processing. There's "finally enough data to start to make generalisations. Now, a million word corpora can be made by a grad student for a semester-long project [and] serious projects involve comparing two trillion-word web scale corpora. Nobody in history had access to such large-scale corpora". In the last 10 years, too, the explosion in social media has rapidly changed what can be studied.

The most important result of working with the QA startup in Buffalo was "a lightbulb moment: there are *jobs* out there [for linguists]. There were options. I could get a job at … Google. Not Facebook, which didn't exist yet, but whatever existed back then".

Fast-forward to 2004, once the bubble had burst. By now, Phipps was an advanced graduate student who'd "published a couple of things in small places". It had become clear how difficult it would be to get an academic job without publications. "Back in the 1970s–1980s, Buffalo was a good choice. By 2004, if you weren't doing a specific subject, there were no jobs. We saw maybe 15% of folks get jobs. Folks quit like mad. The attrition rate skyrocketed".

Sitting in the lab one day "bored out of my spine", Phipps found a consultancy job in DC advertised on the LinguistList job board. LinguistList invites advertisers to indicate the specialty required for the job. "They'd ticked every single box", he recalls. They weren't sure what they needed. "I sent a resume. It turned out to be a contract with the FBI". They needed translators to gather intelligence, and needed a better methodology for testing the translation skill of candidates. He wrote a proposal to improve the process; they liked it, and offered him a one-year contract.

The FBI recruiter's uncertainty about how and where to apply different branches of linguistics is based on misconceptions that are still a problem today. Even the term "linguist" engenders confusion. "To most government and military agencies, 'linguist' means 'translator'". To others, it means

"English teacher". The closest encounter with linguistics for most students in the United States is the surprisingly controversial inclusion of sentence diagramming in the standardised tests widely used for entry into higher education (SATs).[1] Grammar teachers in school, Phipps says, are generally "prescriptivists; people who tell us we don't speak proper English". The subject is not widely liked.

I'm reminded of Kitty Burns Florey, author of a 2007 book entitled *Sister Bernadette's Barking Dog: The Quirky History and Lost Art of Diagramming Sentences*, who wrote somewhat plaintively in a *New York Times* blog entry about the reactions that she received from readers of her book.[2] One message she received accused her "of succumbing to Stockholm syndrome because [she] wrote so benignly about the nun who brainwashed [her] into thinking diagramming [sentences] was fun".

If it is difficult to pin down the precise nature or contribution of linguistics, it's in part because the term "linguist" has too many meanings. Phipps suggests a few alternative terms for a language specialist, but none of them really seem to do justice to the metier. One term that was very popular in the 1990s, "knowledge engineer", strikes us both as carrying Orwellian overtones.

Before usability and human–computer interaction entered into the vocabulary of the marketplace, software engineers faced a similar problem. In the absence of today's acceptance of usability factors, it would be challenging to explain to a senior manager that the team should hire a cognitive psychologist to make a better solitaire application. Now there is broad acceptance that cognitive psychology has a role in software engineering; material drawn from psychology, such as Fitts's and Miller's Laws,[3] is widely (if unevenly) applied. It is surprising that software engineering appears to have made greater inroads into linguistics than linguistics into software engineering. Maybe it simply reflects the relative youth of the current set of NLP applications, or maybe the gulf between the humanities and the engineering worlds, so much wider than that which exists between engineering and the science of cognitive psychology, will take longer to cross.

Despite the challenge of nomenclature, Phipps found that linguistics was and remains in demand. Consequentially, he gave up the attempt at writing a

---

[1] SAT: The name originally referred to a 'Scholastic Aptitude Test'. SATs are standardised tests used to enter higher education in the USA.

[2] http://opinionator.blogs.nytimes.com/2012/06/18/taming-sentences/?_php=true&_type=blogs&_r=0.

[3] Fitts's law, originating with Paul Fitts in 1954, mathematically models the time taken to point to a given target of a certain size; Miller's law indicates that an individual can hold around seven "chunks" of data in working memory.

dissertation as "a silly idea; I wasn't going to become a professor" and took another job, this time "NLP for a defence contractor". There followed a string of other roles, many of which were linguistics-related. "Two years ago the federal government invested in a metaphor program. I was offered a job to work at Intelligence Advanced Research Projects Activity (IARPA http://www.iarpa.gov/index.php/research-programs/metaphor) as a local expert". But, Phipps reflects, "I get bored ...". [NOTE: I was a private contractor working for a private company named Strategic Analysis Inc https://www.sainc.com/ and they "placed" me at IARPA as a Scientific Engineering and Technical Assistant http://en.wikipedia.org/wiki/Systems_Engineering_and_Technical_Assistance. Note that some people say "scientific" others "systems", it's the same thing. In this capacity as a civilian employee, I supported government program managers as a linguist and NLP expert, but I did not work directly for the government. That's an important distinction.]

Then "a recruiter for Watson showed up a year ago". Watson is perhaps IBM's best-known achievement since the chess-playing computer Big Blue beat then-champion Gary Kasparov in 1996–1997. Instead of chess, Watson is geared to win games of general knowledge; specifically, it was originally designed to excel at the American quiz show, *Jeopardy*. Published reports on Watson's design show that the system's data sets include encyclopaedias, literary works, newswire articles and the full text of Wikipedia.[4] Although clearly far larger in scale than earlier systems, Watson's operation still involves QA, the topic of the original Buffalo startup. "It took a year for the job to come to pass. I can't talk about it too much, but I'm excited. Most [of my colleagues] come out of computer science".

Leaving Watson aside, I ask, at what point does a computer scientist need to call on a linguist? Computer scientists often have basic understanding of parsers, or parts of speech (POS) taggers, applications that attempt to guess at the grammatical function of words in a sentence ("noun", "verb", "adjective" and so on), Phipps explains, but there's "a deficit of tools for unfamiliar languages. Contrast the good [performance of tools] for English and German, versus how bad it is for Arabic and Farsi".

Problems arise when familiar tools are used in unfamiliar contexts. One example is the POS tagger; these are generally trained on manually annotated training data. "Can [a POS tagger for English] be tweaked for Turkish, or Lakota?" Phipps asks, somewhat rhetorically. Tools and assumptions fail

---

[4] http://www.aaai.org/Magazine/Watson/watson.php.

in a wide variety of languages. Some tools require "fundamental reimagining" when applied in different contexts. Internal structures can be quite different in more complex languages. A single token (space-delimited "word") can contain much more than one of "subject, object or verb" for example, so tokenisers tuned to work with English fail at the first hurdle. To resolve problems like that, you "have to work with linguists".

Sometimes it's also necessary to call on domain experts. This is particularly true in specific subject areas such as the medical domain, in which NLP tools are needed to interpret notes, descriptions, prescriptions and so on. In each of these cases, language use is specialised enough to damage the performance of plain vanilla kit-form solutions.

"Just building tools in a vacuum is proven to fail; off-the-shelf stuff to solve domain-specific problems failed in the 1990s". Tools usually don't fail entirely, but if their accuracy is impaired, it becomes more difficult to trust the system. Inaccuracy engenders mistrust. Worse: it invites derision.

"There's a danger in expecting audiences to tolerate error. It may lead to lowered expectations that hurt you". Phipps gives the example of autocorrect software on mobile phones which, he says, is "still a joke in peoples' minds. [Manufacturers] hurt themselves rolling it out too soon. People tolerated the errors, but it changed their perspective on it. Now, although it works well, we're biased against it". Promising too much "poisons the well".

We discuss the composition of ideal text mining teams, comparing two examples: I base the first on my current project, the Gascon Rolls, a collection of medieval French and Latin administrative documents spanning a hundred years. The second is a modern collection of papers drawn from climate science during the last decade or so.

Both projects would need to consider how to ingest data, whether it is via optical character recognition software or whether it is already available in digital format – "someone with an NLP bent to act as keymaster to the [backend] kingdom". Both would need "a solid [database] engineer on the backend". In both cases, "It's dangerous to go too far without questions about what should be asked [of the data]". Phipps recommends working with an experienced consultant to discuss scenarios and case studies of prior analyses. Like virtually any other project, text mining benefits from a clear set of requirements.

Domain experts are key to the historical example, as "you'll want people who know the historical trends. It may be a hard sell to get funding for full-timers". For this purpose, Phipps recommends working with graduate students. Given the age and variability of the text, it would be useful to work with linguists to ensure that the system provides adequate accuracy despite historical changes in the language. Time should be found for iterative testing – and "you'd need two or three solid straight-up Java gurus". Finally, the team would need a strong lead to draw it together.

The climate science project, on the other hand, can be tackled with off-the-peg tools. An imperfect solution could be "cobbled together using four or five resources in twenty minutes". The problem would become one of accuracy. "How do you know what went wrong – how do you back up and find the issues with your parser?"

I reflect that it's rare, in my experience, for projects in computer science to aspire to perfect accuracy. There's a trade-off between the convenience of off-the-shelf software, with its concomitant error, and a solution with higher specificity (and cost). Most projects can't afford high levels of precision. Pragmatically, three months of developer time is more than many projects can afford, especially in the humanities. Developing tools is particularly expensive (Phipps suggests that this type of activity may become restricted to a small number of elite schools). In some scenarios, Phipps suggests, projects can be designed to mitigate the effect of low precision; for example, a study of Twitter feeds in the months leading up to election time can use election results to validate the findings. "It's okay to be bad at language if you have enough data".

Then there is the qualitative aspect of validation; critical review of the assumptions and assertions made about study design and findings. Many applications of NLP fall foul of what Phipps calls the silver bullet fallacy of language. "People think words are a silver bullet into the brain".

He illustrates this by pointing to an unfounded belief that words directly indicate thought: for example, using "strong" words is taken to indicate that your personality shares this strength. Variants of this, I discover later, can be found in any number of business-focused articles and books: action verbs, strong or otherwise; power words; "elimination of weak words". In truth, "Language is inseparable from context. All words are biased. Language is inherently social". All of us choose words to fit our context.

"Code switching?" I suggest.

"Code switching. And subtler things". If a sufficiently large number of recruiters were to subscribe to a given belief, I suppose that applicants may tailor their writing accordingly. If this tells the recruiter anything, it is probably that the applicant has read the same book as she did.

Keeping this characteristic of language in mind helps when picking out biases in study methodologies, or identifying simplifying assumptions that often go unnoticed by researchers. Phipps gives the example of an article published in an online magazine, *Slate*, which discussed a dialect survey run by a gossip site that asked for opinions on "America's ugliest dialect". "That just shows deep[ly held] biases. Raw, hateful and ugly class and racial sentiment". We discuss another example previously reviewed in Phipps's blog, a book that uses Wikipedia as an "objective sample of human knowledge" to list history's most influential people. When you visualise Wikipedia, he notes, "you must understand that you're sampling young white men".

"Tools can pull a set of patterns out of a dataset. We can pull out patterns easily. The message that needs to be brought home [is this:] extracting the data isn't the point. It's the interpretation ...".

What should be done about that?

"Every text mining company should hire a sociologist".

Finally, I ask Phipps to give me a definition of text mining. "It's a branding term. Junk for marketers. There's no class called 'text mining'. It skyrocketed [as a result of] sentiment analysis, and was synonymous with sentiment analysis for some years. [Linguists] talk about QA, AI and NLP. In some cases, people dismiss text mining as 'just trivial data, like Twitter'. Sentiment analysis is a perfect example of overselling. It caught the public imagination ...". Phipps blames the Netflix million-dollar competition for the rapid growth of sentiment analysis. The size of the reward "lit a fire in engineering departments. Then companies formed around sentiment analysis".

Later, I run a web search, which tells me that various universities in the United Kingdom including Manchester, Westminster and Sheffield run degrees with a substantial focus on text mining. A Stanford MSc in computer science mentions text mining as a topic in the Information Management and Analytics track. Lewis University covers the topic as part of their Data Science M.S., CCSU as part of a Data Mining MSc. Georgia Tech run a Web Search and Text Mining module as an elective element of an M.S. in Analytics. Carnegie Mellon University offers a text mining module as part of the M.S. degree in Intelligent Information Systems offered by the School of Computer Science. There are others.

That said, the fact that there are indeed courses on text mining does not invalidate Phipps's charge: text mining is predominantly an engineering elective. Most of these are computer science courses. A rare exception is Stanford's Introduction to Critical Text Mining, an elective course intended for humanities students and run by the Department of English. If text mining is anything today, it is a piece of engineering jargon, as domain-specific an indicator of identity as any situated utterance ever was. Text mining, by and large, is exclusive of the humanities.

Some papers speak of "text miner" as an occupation, much as one might say "developer" or "linguist". Perhaps that is an encouraging sign, a first step in filling the descriptive gap that exists in this area. So far, though, it seems that the term is mostly used to refer to implementers. I wonder whether the number of well-funded text mining projects will ever be sufficiently large to make it necessary to develop terminology for "linguistically trained interdisciplinarians who help developers and researchers build better mousetraps". It is to be hoped that it will – such a move did human-computer interaction no harm at all – but in the end, only time will tell.

CHAPTER 13

Raúl Garreta, Co-founder of Tryolabs.com, Tells Emma Tonkin About the Journey from Software Engineering Graduate to Startup Entrepreneur

E.L. Tonkin*,†
*Department of Digital Humanities, King's College London, London, UK
†Department of Electrical & Electronic Engineering, University of Bristol, Bristol, UK

I set up my laptop in a borrowed home office. As the Skype call connects, I look out of the window at three New Forest ponies scratching their necks on a garden fence and wonder whether the rural English internet service will fail me at a critical moment. I apologise preemptively to Garreta, just in case. He laughs, soft-spoken and cheerful.

As the interview proceeds, I come to realise that for the staff of Tryolabs, putting folks at their ease from a distance of 7000 miles is all in a day's work. Their business is predicated on the ability to work fluidly with people from different industries anywhere in the world. Remote working skills are a necessary prerequisite.

Tryolabs is one of a number of start-ups working in the intersection between natural language processing, machine learning and software engineering. The organisation divides its work into two general areas. The first area involves agile consultancy and development services, which are designed to enable organisations to effectively bring specialist competences in-house. This has allowed Tryolabs staff to work as participants in in-house development teams. Interest in this service has come from very different areas: Garreta names Internet based start-ups, e-commerce and social media. The second area is the direct provision of services to end user developers, including the web-based platform MonkeyLearn, the service that first drew my attention.

Tryolabs describes what they do as text mining, so I ask for a definition. It's the use of "a combination of NLP and other techniques [including machine learning] to mine textual data, to extract and explore relevant data, and to build commercial applications". Mmm, I say, wondering about the

Working with Text
http://dx.doi.org/10.1016/B978-1-84334-749-1.00013-5

word "commercial". Garreta clarifies: "To do something *intelligent* with textual data".

I ask about the progression of events that drew Garreta into text mining entrepreneurship. He studied software engineering at the local university. He was generally interested in artificial intelligence, then "got into NLP and machine learning" and joined the NLP group at his computing science institute. But university wasn't the right setting to develop his ideas. "I thought about starting a masters or PhD", he explains, "but I didn't want to work in a lab, doing research in fields or on topics that are imposed by other researchers". It's about the freedom to choose one's own direction, as much as the subject area. "I thought that, working at a university, I'd be under someone else's control". No doubt many PhD students and post-docs would identify with that.

Garreta met his eventual business partner Ernesto Rodriguez as a co-worker at a local video game company, Powerful Robot Games, developing web-based games for clients including Cartoon Networks. It was an opportunity, Garreta explains, to use his AI knowledge and enjoy developing video games, a dream for many programmers. Parenthetically, the link isn't as tenuous as it sounds: the entrepreneur Elon Musk has taken to searching for talent at E3, the Electronic Entertainment Expo. Musk explained in an interview with FastCompany[1] that SpaceX "hire a lot of [their] best software engineers out of the gaming industry. In gaming there's a lot of smart engineering talent doing really complex things".

MonkeyLearn is not the first project on which Garreta and Rodriguez have collaborated. Their first company worked on an interface overlay for the Google search engine. It was "a small project, developed through the local university business incubator". Although the company ultimately dropped the idea, it helped the two to develop an understanding of the way start-ups work. In particular, the experience convinced the pair that the team needed skills that weren't yet represented. In the event, they sought a third partner who could bring the business focus that the startup required, and met Martin Alcala Rubi, a business professional looking for a technical partner. The result was Tryolabs.

Today, Tryolabs has about 21 employees. "We're all software engineers. Usually, employees have some university experience in NLP and machine learning. They join us because they want to work on that. Otherwise, if

[1] http://www.fastcompany.com/3031512/why-spacex-and-other-non-gaming-companies-are-scouting-talent-at-e3.

that's your field, you pretty much have to move to the USA". Looking more closely, within the research and development staff there are two general types of employee: "people who like NLP and machine learning – backend developers – and web application, frontend and user interface developers. Everybody has a full stack profile. We can all use databases and develop for the Internet".

It strikes me as interesting that there aren't any linguists on the team, so I say so. "Linguists don't know how to program or develop", he says. "We need software engineering and computer science…a good balance between algorithms and application development in a production-ready environment". It occurs to me later that most of the functionality that MonkeyLearn provides is based on relatively mature applications of NLP.

The team is headquartered in Uruguay, where the developers and researchers share offices on the shore. There's a business development officer in California, in easy reach of Silicon Valley, and another employee based in Paris who works with the project as a researcher and business developer. Both came in useful, for the "people [who] don't know where Uruguay is". The first step is the hardest. "Once you have a track record, it gets easier. After the first success stories, we got more referrals from clients". A big part of developing a company like Tryolabs is networking and, inevitably, Internet marketing.

"Why not move to Silicon Valley?" I wonder aloud.

There are problems with establishing start-ups in Silicon Valley. There's "tough competition for human resources", and though there's "a lot of money, resources are scarce. It's difficult for start-ups to take resources from bigger competitors". A small company would find it difficult to attract the specialised staff that they need. "It's very difficult to get people [with expertise in] NLP", he says. "Most of them work at Google or Facebook". So instead of moving to California, companies like Tryolabs can occupy a different niche, becoming one of the small outsourcing companies to which enterprises can look to develop specialised products. It means a heavy dependency on tools like Skype and Google Hangout, or whatever the customer prefers.

Machine learning, natural language processing and artificial intelligence are all interesting directions for Internet companies to take. Many companies have a lot of textual data and the ambition to use it, but perhaps surprisingly, there aren't many competing small companies in the text mining niche today. "Companies may prefer to hire an internal expert", Garreta suggests. "That's why we've identified two ways to embed our service within companies". The first is the MonkeyLearn offering: simple services that are designed to be easy for web developers to learn and use. The second is designed for larger projects: embedding Tryolabs developers in the team.

It's a challenge to get folks into working with text mining tools. The software tools are specialised, and it helps to have the right background. It takes a while to get into the subject, and developers who have a background in computer science and data structures will find it much easier. Even those with that background don't necessarily *"want* to dive into machine learning or NLP".

Even when developers are willing, the cost of failure is often too high for the parent enterprise to take the risk. "Sometimes prototypes may not work as expected. A priori, you can't tell, whereas with standard apps, it [the likelihood of a successful development process] is usually much clearer. So first-time machine learning and NLP projects are very risky". It helps, he says, if you have someone to blame, but ideally, minimising the risk in the first place helps more. Working with the simplest possible approach allows teams "to develop a solution in a lean and iterative way". He recommends "trying to give the customer, every time you have contact, some information about improvements that have been made, however, small. The sense that things are improving is important".

Even understanding the problem and the possible development paths can be challenging. Companies often approach text mining problems by analogy or through the examples of successful products – "[things that work] 'like Google does'". For example, many companies want to implement search or recommendation functions or improve their business analytics but simply don't know how. That means that a big part of the problem is a translation process, figuring out how to make use of low-level tools to fulfil a business aim. "It's difficult to get the pieces together to build a real product". That's where much of the motivation for MonkeyLearn comes from. "With MonkeyLearn, we want to allow users with standard backgrounds to create – without being an expert".

"It's designed to be fast: an easy-to-use tool for everyone".

Democratising natural language processing and machine learning? "Yes. It's a tough task. You're like a teacher, teaching machine learning and letting [ordinary] programmers see how it works, but without turning them off". To that end, the developers place a high value on instant gratification. The barriers to entry in NLP, like the complexity and specialised nature of the tools, are not attractive, and tools often require a lot of preparatory work.

Providing tools that use standard models for language detection or topic classification, or which provide user-friendly interfaces to configure and upload data, results in a trade-off between precision and stickiness. If it works today, the developer can improve it tomorrow. If it doesn't work today, what are the chances that the developer will keep trying?

User interface and user experience are further up the Tryolabs to-do list than one might expect. Documentation, demonstrations and introductory material are viewed as important. Sample code matters, too. Much of it is designed for "newbie" developers, the occasional developer or habitual developers with no text mining experience. But it's also important that the material and software provides the necessary functionality for experts seeking a rapid prototyping platform.

Server performance is an issue for MonkeyLearn, too. Text mining is generally resource-intensive. Tryolabs use distributed [elastic] infrastructure over Amazon's AWS, making it possible to extend computing power by adding servers. Different users require different plans and access to variable resources, with software-as-a-service at one extreme and local installations on company servers at the other.

How should such a service handle benchmarking, testing the performance of different tools or configurations? A lack of independent performance evaluation in text mining has long since been endemic to the sector, especially its commercial incarnations. Consequentially, many developers equate text mining with "snake oil", the too-good-to-be-true fake remedies peddled by charlatans and travelling salesmen.

Garreta is unfazed when I mention this. Whilst the functionality isn't all there yet, benchmarking is something they've thought about. Comparison with existing toolkits is useful, and they like to be able to show such data on the home page using a standard data set for comparison. I speculate that the most important thing for MonkeyLearn is ease of use, and that realistic benchmarking doesn't threaten that mission. Presumably, it just gives developers room to improve. Maybe that could enhance the "stickiness" of the site, relative to a textbook about machine learning. Incremental success is probably more fun than days of failure followed by eventual satisfaction.

Yes, he says, "the best technology available is often the simplest", although the accuracy does matter too. "A nice and easy toolkit, but also a toolkit that gives the best accuracy. And it's not just performance and accuracy that matter, but also a very fast response time, giving the customer a solution in a very short time". It's a lot to ask, but I guess it's a worthy ambition.

Still, text mining does sound too good to be true. What company would not want to eliminate the need for the crowdsourcing marketplace, or a reliance on human input, using a single impenetrably complicated script? Yes, please, you'd say, and many have followed just that thought process. A good number of them have eventually discovered that text mining is at least one of the following: fragile, annoyingly complex, a lot of work to train, resource-consuming to run, sufficiently abstruse that it resembles black magic, difficult, expensive, specialist and dull. The result has been overvaluation and disappointment, followed by a rapid descent into what Gartner calls the Trough of Disillusionment, into which we stumble on our way down from the Peak of Inflated Expectations, and where text mining (and, more recently, Big Data) are destined to spend more time than many other technologies.

Garreta agrees. "People who don't know these technologies assume that NLP can do anything. It's difficult to deal with high expectations. We try to teach the customer what to expect, what the difficulties are and how to manage them".

Despite the neatness of MonkeyLearn's drop-in black-box component/ service strategy, there's no one-size-fits-all solution. Assembling the different companies who view text mining as relevant results in an odd crowd indeed; we spend a few minutes discussing the contrasting requirements of two examples. E-commerce and real-estate marketing both have a real and increasing need for text mining, but "each vertical has to learn to use these tools for the value proposition of their businesses", says Garreta, briefly and disconcertingly shifting into hardcore business-speak. Other groups have very different expectations, too, such as "a legal group in New York that processes patents and legal documents", although "developers are pretty much the same in all of these different verticals of industry".

Tryolabs has now grown large enough to worry about raising its public profile, sponsoring conferences such as PyCon 2014 in Montreal. It's a long way from the university incubator where the team began, I think. Not so. Garreta "never [entirely] quit university. I also work as a lecturer in machine learning and natural language processing in university. I'm working on a Masters' degree, but [I'm] also teaching".

So, I speculate, the startup has been an educational experience despite the unconventional nature of the course? "Building this company taught me the technical stuff. It's taught me a lot more than I'd have learnt in academia. I've learned a lot about software engineering and the practical uses of natural language processing". Another benefit was the opportunity to gain experience of doing business with a complex technology. "I definitely wouldn't have learned that at university".

As the interview comes to a close, I wonder about everyday life in the long-distance Silicon Valley support industry. "What's the view from the office window?" I ask. Garreta laughs, surprised. Tryolabs are based in Montevideo, the capital and largest city of Uruguay, 7000 miles from my rural office. Their offices are on the coast, the Rambla, in front of the sea. "There is", he adds, "a very nice view".

He shares a link to the office Flickr account, which includes pictures both of their original incubator office and of their present office space. He's right. The view from the office window is idyllic, palm trees against sparkling sea. Exchanging ivory towers against palm trees may not be at the top of a conventional academic career development plan, but it strikes me as a very rational decision.

APPENDIX A

Resources for Text Mining

A.1 INTRODUCTION

Text and data mining are, as has been shown throughout this book, wide-ranging areas of practice. There is, therefore, no single short list of software or data resources. It is not possible to provide a comprehensive overview of all libraries and tools available for text and data mining, because this is an extensive area that would require a book of its own.

Miner et al. (2012) identify seven types of text mining, including:

1. Search and information retrieval. Storage retrieval of text documents including search engines and keyword search.
2. Document clustering. Grouping and categorising terms, snippets, paragraphs or documents using clustering methods.
3. Document classification. Grouping and categorising snippets, paragraphs or documents using data mining classification methods, based on labelled examples.
4. Web mining. Data and text mining on the Internet with a specific focus on scale and interconnectedness of the web.
5. Information extraction. Identification extraction of relevant facts and relationships from unstructured text; the process of making structured data from unstructured and semistructured text.
6. Natural language processing. Low-level language processing and understanding tasks (e.g. tagging parts of speech); often used synonymously with computational linguistics.
7. Concept extraction. Grouping of words and phrases into semantically similar groups.

If these areas were mutually exclusive, this typology would represent a useful basis for the classification of resources and materials. However, these areas are interrelated to a variable extent. For example, document clustering and concept extraction may both make use of similar clustering approaches, whilst many areas may make use of resources or software libraries drawn from natural language processing. Here we have kept to a simpler approach, listing software and resources by similarity.

In this appendix and the those following, we provide a brief overview of types of tools and materials available covering a number of popular use cases, such as data collection, data preparation (or as David Mimno calls it, data carpentry), processing of textual data, analysis of results and visualisation or representation of data. As has been discussed in this book, it is important to remember that these steps are only part of the process of developing a text mining project, just as the creation of source code is only part of the process of developing a piece of software. Reaching the stage of data collection, preparation, processing or visualisation suggests that your project has already passed through the processes described by Nisbet et al. (2009): choosing the purpose of the study, designing or identifying appropriate data sets, and so forth. The full text mining process flow is defined by Nisbet et al. as follows:

- Phase 1. Determine the purpose of the study.
- Phase 2. Explore the availability and the nature of the data.
- Phase 3. Prepare the data.
- Phase 4. Develop and assess models.
- Phase 5. Evaluate the results.
- Phase 6. Deploy the results.

Any ethical issues that arise from the work should also have been identified and appropriate steps taken to ensure that the issues have been handled before the project proceeds.

The reader is warned that because many tools are designed and built by researchers at academic departments it is not unusual for projects to eventually disappear. We have attempted to identify a subset of projects that are still alive and active, or in some cases projects that are, although moribund, still useful as representative examples for testing, learning and teaching.

In the final section of this series of appendices (Appendix D), a number of relevant academic courses and learning resources are listed, along with some popular textual resources.

A.2 TEXT MINING SOFTWARE AND LIBRARIES

There are text mining packages for almost every configuration. You will often hear about text mining packages that are particularly popular in certain communities; this does not necessarily imply that they are the best text mining packages available overall. Some may offer functionality that is not available elsewhere. Others may be optimised for a given use case or may be designed to support the working practices of a given community.

As with any software development process, the choice of software depends on a number of factors. Damsgaard and Karlsbjerg (2010) remarks that in the infancy of the software industry, the software used tended to be developed in-house; that software then became commercially available through proprietary packages; and that finally standardisation of products has permitted customers to source software components from a large number of suppliers. In some cases, software packages become almost ubiquitous in a given sector, making a choice of software package (or at least category) almost inevitable.

In text mining, the software landscape is far from settled. Whilst commercially available software packages can be procured, text mining tends in general to be most relevant in cases in which reasonably large amounts of data are available. Consequentially, text mining projects tend to benefit from some level of centralisation. Commercial software packages for large-scale centralised work (such as business intelligence) are likely to be specialised, large, expensive and consequentially procured through a process that reflects the scale of the investment. Smaller projects are consequentially less likely to benefit from the use of monumental software packages of this type, benefiting instead either from the use of freely available software packages or from the use of pay-per-use services.

Customisation and development: Text mining projects often involve significant customisation or development. If the composition of the development team is set, then this will have an impact on the choice of software platform to be used.

Often the choice of platform or framework will relate to the disciplinary background. Some broad rules of thumb exist. The programming language R, for example, is popular among statisticians, and hence individuals from this background will have a greater familiarity with this language. Python is more popular in computer science, as well as in the digital humanities. Putting aside broad generalities, tailoring the choice of platform to the existing skillset of the development team confers significant benefits. This is particularly true in smaller projects with limited resources, such as pilot projects designed to evaluate the use of text mining in a given platform.

If a convenient platform is chosen, less training is required, so that the project proceeds faster and costs less. Developers with greater familiarity with a given platform are at an advantage when developing or debugging software, as they are better able to separate the familiar programming errors from issues resulting from unfamiliar libraries or functions.

Because the small–scale project is a common approach to evaluating text mining projects and processes, there is a risk that text mining projects do not deliver on inflated user expectations due to the use of basic packages.

Interface: Developers will find that different packages often take varying approaches to aggregation of functionality. It is often necessary to aggregate functionality taken from various packages to implement a given effect, but the interfaces available do not always facilitate this process.

Usability and "learning curve": Different software packages provide quite different levels of usability. Some require programming ability or expect the user to make use of the command line. Others provide graphical user interfaces or web-based wizards that help the user to work through the material.

Services, APIs and software packages are often multitalented. For convenience, packages for text analysis often provide easy access to data sources. So we will not attempt to classify exhaustively by functionality. Rather, we provide brief introductions to the functionality for which packages are best known and the primary audiences for each.

A.3 TEXT MINING FRAMEWORKS AND PACKAGES

A.3.1 UIMA

UIMA (unstructured information management architecture) is both a standard and an implementation. UIMA is formally an industry standard for content analytics, having been accepted as an OASIS standard in March 2009. As an implementation, UIMA offers an overarching software architecture enabling the user to make use of a variety of libraries/packages. It was initially developed by IBM in 2001 to improve the interoperability of the various text analysis components built across the enterprise (Kow, 2013), and is essentially an umbrella covering many other libraries and resource sets.

UIMA is *modular*, enabling the user to combine various software components to achieve their intended outcome. Developers may make use of existing components (annotators) in various configurations, as well as authoring their own *annotators*. As a popular implementation, UIMA is used for many purposes, including search and business intelligence applications.

In principle the UIMA architecture supports annotation of any type of data, including audiovisual material. Document artifacts may be passed through various annotators to extract and add further annotations, stored within the document metadata held by UIMA.

As UIMA is intentionally designed as a generic architecture, it is able to tie together a broad variety of components, including components from

OpenNLP, Stanford NLP Group, Alias-i's LingPipe, Weka (via the Mayo Weka/UIMA integration library) and others. GATE and UIMA are connected via an interoperability layer, making it possible to apply resources from one to another.

UIMA is an Apache project and may be downloaded from http://uima.apache.org.

Ferrucci, D.A., Adam, L., 2004. UIMA: an architectural approach to unstructured information processing in the corporate research environment. Nat. Lang. Eng. 10.3–4, 327–348.

A.3.2 GATE: Text Mining in Java or on the Desktop

GATE (the general architecture for text engineering) is both a desktop software and a set of APIs. As the software is written in Java, it is multiplatform as a desktop GUI.

GATE is free and open source. It may be downloaded from https://gate.ac.uk/download/.

See Cunningham, H., Tablan, V., Roberts, A., Bontcheva, K., 2013. Getting more out of biomedical documents with GATE's full lifecycle open source text analytics. PLoS Comput. Biol. 9(2), e1002854. http://dx.doi.org/10.1371/journal.pcbi.1002854 – http://tinyurl.com/gate-life-sci/.

Cunningham, H., et al. (2011). Text Processing with GATE (Version 6). University of Sheffield Department of Computer Science. 15 April 2011. ISBN 0956599311.

GATE provides access to a number of tools, many of which may also be used outside the GATE GUI. These include:

* an information extraction system referred to as ANNIE (a nearly new information extraction system);

  see Cunningham, H., Maynard, D., Bontcheva, K., Tablan, V., 2002. GATE: a framework and graphical development environment for robust NLP tools and applications. Proceedings of the 40th Anniversary Meeting of the Association for Computational Linguistics (ACL'02). Philadelphia, July 2002.

* tools for extraction and markup of information from social media, including TwitIE;

  see Bontcheva, K., Derczynski, L., Funk, A., Greenwood, M.A., Maynard, D., Aswani, N., 2013. TwitIE: an open-source information extraction pipeline for microblog text. Proceedings of the International Conference on Recent Advances in Natural Language Processing (RANLP 2013).

- machine learning tools, including classifiers and functionality intended to support evaluation of classifiers;

  see Li, Y., Bontcheva, K., Cunningham, H., 2009. Adapting SVM for data sparseness and imbalance: a case study on information extraction. Nat. Lang. Eng. 15(02), 241–271.

A.3.3 OpenNLP

OpenNLP is "a machine learning based toolkit for the processing of natural language text". It is written in Java. It allows developers to access common NLP functionality: tokenisation, sentence segmentation, parts of speech tagging, named entity extraction, chunking, parsing and coreference resolution.

According to Baldridge (2013), one of the authors of the package, OpenNLP was created in 2000 at the Division of Informatics, University of Edinburgh. Baldridge and another graduate student, Gann Bierner, hoped to create an organisational infrastructure packaging a broad spectrum of tools for natural language processing. OpenNLP provided a Java API allowing access to a number of components. In 2004, OpenNLP was developed into a toolkit supporting many natural language processing tasks.

OpenNLP has been an Apache project since 2012 (accepted for incubation in 2010) and may be downloaded from http://opennlp.apache.org.

See Hockenmaier, J., Bierner, G., Baldridge, J., 2004. Extending the coverage of a CCG System. Res. Lang. Comput. 2, 165–208. PDF.

Ingersoll, G.S., Morton, T.S., Farris, A.L., 2013. Taming Text How to Find, Organize and Manipulate It.

The OpenNLP Java tools have been ported to C# by Richard Northedge, and released as SharpNLP (see http://sharpnlp.codeplex.com/).

A.3.4 NLTK: Text Mining in Python

NLTK, the natural language toolkit, is a text processing library of use with Python.

NLTK is an extensive suite of libraries intended to support working with unstructured data written in human languages. It is ready for use as a training platform, as it provides easy access to existing corpora such as the Brown corpus and resources such as Wordnet. However, it is also useful for those looking to access libraries for classification, tokenisation, stemming, tagging, passing and semantic reasoning.

NLTK is free and open source, and may be downloaded from www.NLTK.org.

See Bird, S., 2006. NLTK: the natural language toolkit. In: Proceedings of the COLING/ACL on Interactive presentation sessions, pp. 69–72. Association for Computational Linguistics.

A.3.5 Stanford Parser and Part of Speech Tagger

The Stanford natural language processing group have created a great deal of software, a proportion of which is made available to the public under the GNU general public licence. Commercial licencing is also available. The majority of the software distributed is written in Java, although APIs are also often made available for other languages, including Python. This software is regularly updated to take advantage of the state-of-the-art in the research field.

The primary software package made available is **CoreNLP**, an integrated suite of natural language processing tools for English, Spanish and Chinese. Components available include:
- Stanford POS (parts of speech) tagger, supporting English, Arabic, Chinese, French, German and Spanish
- Stanford Named Entity Recogniser, supporting English, German, Chinese and Spanish.
- Stanford Parser, implementing probabilistic natural language parsing.

All Stanford software may be downloaded from http://nlp.stanford.edu/software/.

A.3.6 Weka

Weka (Waikato environment for knowledge analysis) is a set of machine learning tools provided alongside a graphical user interface. An accompanying book has been published by Morgan Kaufmann Publishers (Witten et al., 2011). Teaching material is available on the Weka homepage at http://www.cs.waikato.ac.nz/ml/weka/book.html.

Weka is written in Java.

Weka is free and open source and may be downloaded from Sourceforge: http://sourceforge.net/projects/weka/.

A.3.7 UIUC NLP Tools

The Cognitive Computation Group at the University of Illinois Urbana-Champaign provides access to a large number of tools, including tools designed for learning and classification, named entity taggers, chunkers, coreference extractors and so forth. A pipeline designed to integrate several of these tools into a coherent text processing service, the Illinois NLP Pipeline, is also provided.

These tools may be downloaded from: http://cogcomp.cs.illinois.edu/page/software.

A large set of associated publications is available at http://cogcomp.cs.illinois.edu/page/publications

An accessible overview of the CCG NLP tools is available at http://cogcomp.cs.illinois.edu/presentations/UIUC_NLP_2014.pdf

A.3.8 LingPipe

LingPipe is a toolkit able to support a variety of text mining operations, such as text classification and entity extraction. It is a commercial project available under a number of licences, including the AGPL (GNU Affero general public licence) and a number of commercial licences. Alias-i, the company behind the technology, was founded by Breck Baldwin in 1999 on the basis of outcomes from the 1995 U Penn Message Understanding Conference (MUC-5), and was originally known as Baldwin Language Technologies. The company has received funding from various agencies, including DARPA.

LingPipe, released in 2003, was initially "a fairly straightforward XML-based pipeline for doing sentence detection, entity extraction, within-document coreference and then cross-document coreference" (LingPipe, 2014).

LingPipe is written in Java and may be downloaded from http://alias-i.com/lingpipe/

Clear API tutorials are available at http://alias-i.com/lingpipe/demos/tutorial/read-me.html

A.3.9 The TM Package: Text Mining in R

The TM (text mining) package is a library available for R: this package contains a text mining framework that implements a number of useful functions for exploring or transforming the data, and analysing corpora. TM provides functionality enabling commonplace functions such as the elimination of white space, conversion of text, lowercase removal of stopwords, stemming and filtering. The TM package also provides a straightforward way of accessing various operations that can be of use on term document matrices such as those held within TM, such as clustering and classification approaches.

The TM package is free and open source.

See Feinerer, I., Hornik, K., Meyer, D., 2008. Text mining infrastructure in R. J. Stat. Softw. 25(5), 1–54. ISSN 1548-7 660. URL: www.jstatsoft.walk/V25/I05.

A.3.10 SpaCY

SpaCY is a library for text processing in Python, available either commercially or under the AGPL (GNU Affero general public licence). It is written by Matthew Honnibal, a researcher in NLP; whilst currently at an alpha-release stage, it is fast and efficient by comparison to many other text processing platforms. It is also written to take advantage of recent research in the domain.

SpaCY may be downloaded from http://honnibal.github.io/spaCy/index.html.

A.3.11 Mallet

MALLET, the Machine Learning for LanguagE Toolkit, is designed to support statistical natural language processing using various machine learning techniques. Several document classification algorithms are implemented in MALLET, as are tools designed for sequence tagging/named entity extraction and topic modelling. MALLET is written in Java.

MALLET is released under the GPL and is available at http://mallet.cs.umass.edu/.

See McCallum, A.K., 2002. MALLET: A Machine Learning for Language Toolkit. http://mallet.cs.umass.edu.

A.3.12 MontyLingua

MontyLingua was developed between 2002 and 2004 by Hugo Liu at MIT Media Lab. It was originally released under a dual licence, permitting non-commercial use under the GPL, whilst commercial use required separate agreements. It is billed as an "end-to-end natural language understander" capable of providing a semantic interpretation of raw English text.

MontyLingua is a self-contained natural language processor written in Python and may be downloaded at https://pypi.python.org/pypi/MontyLingua/2.1.

See Liu, H., 2004. MontyLingua: an end-to-end natural language processor with common sense. Available at: web.media.mit.edu/hugo/montylingua.

A.3.13 Textmining 1.0 (Python)

This package covers the functionality necessary to transform a collection of documents into a matrix (term-document matrix). This can then be read into a statistical package such as R for further analysis. Whilst much less capable than NLTK, the package is also very simple to use and may therefore be useful for training purposes.

This package is available free and open source and may be downloaded from http://pypi.python.org/pypi/textmining.

A.3.14 Sempre

Sempre (semantic parser with extraction) is a toolkit for training semantic parsers, which effectively supports the development of question answering systems. Beginning with natural language utterances (typically questions), the statement given is mapped to a logical form, which is then executed to extract a return value (i.e. the answer to the question). Sempre is primarily written in Java and is licenced under the GNU GPL v2 or later.

It is available from https://github.com/percyliang/sempre.

See Berant, J., Chou, A., Frostig, R., Liang, P., 2013, Semantic parsing on freebase from question-answer pairs. Empirical Methods in Natural Language Processing (EMNLP), 2013.

A.3.15 OpenEphyra

OpenEphyra is an open framework for question answering, developed by Nico Schlaefer at the University of Karlsruhe and later Carnegie Mellon. Following participation in the 2006 and 2007 TREC conferences, Open-Ephyra was placed into open source in 2008. It is designed to retrieve answers to questions using material taken from the web and other sources. The software depends on web APIs that no longer exist, but is otherwise functional.

It may be downloaded from http://sourceforge.net/projects/openephyra/.

See Schlaefer, N., Ko, J., Betteridge, J., Sautter, G., Pathak, M., Nyberg, E., 2007. Semantic extensions of the Ephyra QA system for TREC 2007. In: Proceedings of the Sixteenth Text REtrieval Conference (TREC).

Schlaefer, N., Gieselmann, P., Sautter, G., 2006. The Ephyra QA system at TREC 2006. In: Proceedings of the Fifteenth Text REtrieval Conference (TREC).

A.3.16 MEAD

MEAD, developed at the University of Michigan, is designed to support multilingual text summarisation and evaluation. It has been tested on a variety of languages, including English and Chinese.

MEAD is written in Perl and may be downloaded from http://www.summarization.com/mead/.

See Radev, D., et al., 2004. MEAD-a platform for multidocument multilingual text summarization. Proceedings of the 4th International Conference on Language Resources and Evaluation (LREC 2004).

A.3.17 Open Text Summarizer

Open Text Summarizer (OTS) was developed by Nadav Rotem. It is capable of summarizing texts in a variety of languages including English, German, Spanish, Russian, Hebrew and others.

OTS may be downloaded from http://sourceforge.net/projects/libots/files/.

A.3.18 MinorThird

MinorThird is a framework designed to support information extraction and data visualisation activities. Although a graphical user interface is provided that makes it possible to set up experiments using the algorithms provided in the SDK, the graphical user interface is not intended to be intuitive for a beginner. MinorThird can also be called directly via the command line, MinorThird can be downloaded from http://sourceforge.net/projects/minorthird/.

A.4 WEB MINING PACKAGES

A.4.1 Boilerpipe

HTML pages drawn from the web tend to include a large amount of extraneous material intended for design (templating) purposes or to carry background information about the site, such as copyright notices. Boilerpipe, written in Java by Christian Kohlschütter, provides a set of strategies designed to extract relevant text from the accompanying boilerplate material.

Boilerplate is released under the Apache License 2.0 and may be downloaded from https://code.google.com/p/boilerpipe/.

See Kohlschütter, C., Fankhauser. P., Nejdl, W., 2010. Boilerplate detection using shallow text features. Proceedings of the third ACM international conference on Web search and data mining. ACM.

A.4.2 Python-Goose

Like Boilerpipe, Python-Goose is designed to extract relevant material from an article (such as the main text and image), ignoring irrelevant material. Originally written in Java, Goose was rewritten in Python. Python-Goose is able to handle material in various languages, including Spanish, Chinese, Arabic and Korean.

It is licenced under the Apache 2.0 License and may be downloaded at http://github.com/grangier/python-goose/.

A.4.3 Bixo

Bixo is designed to run on top of a distributed computing framework, Hadoop. It is a web mining toolkit intended to "efficiently, yet politely" crawl a number of websites, which is designed to operate alongside the Cascading application development platform. It is used by a number of companies for data collection: for example, EMI Music (who cosponsored the project) uses the application to collect music and artist popularity information from social media platforms.

Bixo is released under the MIT licence and may be downloaded at http://bixo.101tec.com/.

A.5 DATA MINING PACKAGES

A.5.1 KNIME

KNIME (Konstanz information miner pronounced "naim") is an open-source data mining platform based around the Eclipse development platform. It is developed by KNIME AG, in collaboration with Michael Berthold at the University of Konstanz. The platform includes modules for data access, transformation, mining, visualisation and exploitation (i.e. reporting, writing to output format, etc.). KNIME is designed to be accessible to data mining novices, enabling "easy visual assembly and interactive execution of a data pipeline".

KNIME's text processing feature provides access to various natural language processing tools, including document access/parsing, parts of speech tagging, named entity recognition, processing filters such as word stemmers, keyword extraction and so forth. Once text is transformed into numerical data (i.e. word counts, document vectors, etc.), it is then possible to apply regular data mining KNIME nodes.

KNIME is licenced under the GPL and is available from https://www. knime.org/knime.

See Berthold, M.R., et al., 2008. KNIME: The Konstanz information miner. Springer, Berlin Heidelberg.

Berthold, M.R., et al., 2009. KNIME-the Konstanz information miner: version 2.0 and beyond. AcM SIGKDD Explor. Newsl. 11.1, 26–31.

A.5.2 RapidMiner

RapidMiner is a partially open-source data mining toolset. As a general purpose data mining platform, RapidMiner is not specifically focused on text mining. However, using text-specific extension functionality it is possible to perform many text mining functions with RapidMiner, such as commonplace preprocessing operations, automated classification, evaluation of similarity and so forth.

Note that RapidMiner now uses the *business source* model for licencing, making available the most recent version of RapidMiner under a business licence and releasing previous versions under an OSI-certified software licence. Hence, the most recent version may be used only as a trial version unless a commercial licence is procured. Open-source licenced versions may be found at http://sourceforge.net/projects/rapidminer/.

See Shafait, F., et al., 2010. Pattern recognition engineering. RapidMiner Community Meeting and Conference, vol. 9.

A.5.3 Orange

Orange is an opensource data mining, visualisation and analysis toolkit. Orange is designed to be accessible for those new to the field, providing both visual programming interfaces and Python scripting.

Orange may be downloaded at http://orange.biolab.si/.

A.6 A SELECTION OF COMPONENTS AND PACKAGES

A.6.1 SecondString

SecondString, is a library that implements a number of metrics for evaluating string similarity. SecondString was developed by researchers at Carnegie

Mellon University, including William W. Cohen, Pradeep Ravikumar, Stephen Fienberg and Kathryn Rivard.

SecondString can be downloaded from http://secondstring.sourceforge. net/.

See Cohen, W.W., Ravikumar, P., Fienberg, S.E., 2003. A Comparison of String Distance Metrics for Name-Matching Tasks. Retrieved 2013-07-01 from http://secondstring.sourceforge.net/doc/iiweb03.pdf.

A.6.2 SimMetrics

SimMetrics, like SecondString, provides metrics for evaluating string similarity. It is available under the GPL, and can be downloaded from http:// sourceforge.net/projects/simmetrics/.

A.6.3 The Bikel Parser

Multilingual statistical parser – Dan Bikel.

A.6.4 The Brill Tagger

Created by Eric Brill (1995), the Brill tagger depends on supervised learning. It is available under the MIT licence.

See Brill, E., 1992. A simple rule-based part of speech tagger. In: Proceedings of the third conference on Applied natural language processing (ANLC '92). Association for Computational Linguistics, Stroudsburg, PA, USA, 152–155. http://dx.doi.org/10.3115/974499.974526.

A.7 WEB INTERFACES FOR TEXT MINING
A.7.1 ScraperWiki

ScraperWiki describes itself as "a platform for doing data science on the Web", and is a UK-based web startup intended to support the collection, extraction and republication of data. The site also provides a repository (wiki based) for code sharing and publication.

The site's title refers to the process of "screen scraping". The site includes information extraction tools for Excel, PDF and webpages. For some time, ScraperWiki provided a Twitter scraping service, but this has now been discontinued: the organisation explained in a blog post that Twitter "have no route to market [that is, no viable plan] to sell low volume data for spreadsheet-style individual use".

ScraperWiki offers a variable pricing structure. http://www.scraperwiki.com/.

A.7.2 MonkeyLearn

MonkeyLearn offers services for various text mining tasks via web APIs, including classification and sentiment analysis. The MonkeyLearn platform is discussed in some detail in an interview (see Chapter 13). http://www.monkeylearn.com.

A.8 DISTRIBUTION AND SCALING

Text mining projects tend to rapidly grow in scale as the project proceeds from initial proof-of-concept sample or training data sets to full-scale implementations. Because many steps in text mining projects are processor-intensive to a greater or lesser extent, virtualisation and/or parallelisation approaches can be useful in rendering such projects practically achievable. In particular, elastic virtualisation technologies can be useful, as elastic virtualisation permits the growth or reduction in scale of platforms in a manner responsive to demand. This means that projects can pay for the resources they require at the time, rather than building the infrastructure to follow the expected demand in the future.

A.8.1 Amazon EC2

Amazon's EC2 (Elastic Compute Cloud) is widely known, so a detailed introduction is out of place here. Like other cloud-based solutions, it is a valid option for hosting larger-scale text mining projects, including parallelised architectures. Available virtual machines run a variety of operating systems, from Windows Server/SQL server environments to a broad spectrum of Linux distributions. A temporary expansion in infrastructure requirements can be handled using virtual machines without the need to invest in physical infrastructure; furthermore, temporary increases in demand can be handled even if they have not been forecast in advance.

EC2 is often used in combination with architectures such as Hadoop to permit the distribution of processing tasks across several machines.

A.8.2 Hadoop

This Apache project is a framework providing a scalable architecture permitting distributed processing of large data sets across clusters of computers.

Hadoop is designed to permit highly available services to be built on the basis of large clusters of computers. A Hadoop cluster can be likened to a high-performance computing (HPC) cluster (i.e. a supercomputing cluster) in some ways, although there are significant differences. For example, a HPC installation will typically, although not always, make use of shared storage to enable all nodes to work within a common data storage space. Hadoop clusters generally store data locally to each node.

An HPC installation cannot in general support the continuation of partially completed jobs – which is to say, if a large data processing software application fails on a HPC installation due to a transient error such as lack of CPU time or a system error, the HCP installation cannot in itself recover and resume the partially completed process. For that to occur, the software application that governs the data processing task must itself be able to recover state information (for example, using log files and data snapshots stored on the system) and continue the task. Therefore, in HPC it is typically up to the software developer to ensure that a lengthy task is fault-tolerant by providing checkpoint information and state restoration functionality.

Hadoop, on the other hand, is governed by a master job tracker process (a scheduler), which hands out individual tasks to partner task trackers operating on individual nodes. Therefore, if a node fails, Hadoop is able to recover from this error and hand the task to another node for completion.

Text mining processes are often well suited for processing using Hadoop, as one of the prerequisites for effective use of Hadoop is that the data to be processed must fit well into the MapReduce model and implementation. MapReduce requires that data be processable in small, bite-sized chunks and have no interdependencies. Textual documents respond well to this approach in general.

Hadoop is often used alongside cloud instances to support text mining processes on large data sets. It may be used alongside a wide variety of text mining frameworks and languages. For example, R provides the RHadoop packages, which facilitate the use of Hadoop alongside the R programming language. There are many Python frameworks for Hadoop, such as Hadoop Streaming, mrjob and pydoop.

Hadoop is available under the Apache Licence, Version 2.0, at http://hadoop.apache.org/.

See Dean, J., Ghemawat, S., 2008. MapReduce: simplified data processing on large clusters. Commun. ACM 51.1, 107–113.

A.8.3 Mahout

Once data is successfully retrieved and preprocessed, then it is desirable to have a similarly scalable method for processing the data. Apache's Mahout project is a Java library providing a number of scalable and distributed machine learning algorithms in linear algebra, classification, clustering and pattern mining. These can be used for common text mining problems, such as classification, clustering, collaborative recommendation, topic modelling and so forth.

Mahout can be used in stand-alone applications, or via Apache Hadoop; Mahout provides utilities that support the ingestion of data into Hadoop in a format accessible by the Mahout library.

Mahout is available under the Apache Licence, Version 2.0, at http://mahout.apache.org.

A collection of reference reading about the topics covered by Mahout has been published by the authors of the Mahout project, and is available at https://mahout.apache.org/general/reference-reading.html.

A.8.4 GATECloud

GATE facilities include a scalable cloud-based virtualisation platform allowing variable-scale text processing. Two primary service types are offered by GATECloud: the provision of specialist virtual machines with various GATE software preinstalled, and application/service-level provision of specialist text mining software pipelines. Such an approach reduces the setup cost and time investment in developing a relevant infrastructure.

See Tablan, V., Roberts, I., Cunningham, H., Bontcheva, K., 1983. GATECloud.net: a platform for large-scale, open-source text processing on the cloud. Phil. Trans. R. Soc. A 371. http://dx.doi.org/10.1098/rsta.2012.0071. A pre-print.

REFERENCES

Aziz, M., Rafi, M., 2012. PBM: a new dataset for blog mining. http://Arxiv.org/abs/1201.2072.

Baldridge, J., 2013. History – chalk. Retrieved Jan 20, 2014 from https://github.com/scalanlp/chalk/wiki/History.

Damsgaard, J., Karlsbjerg, J., 2010. Seven principles for selecting software packages. Commun. ACM 53 (8), 63–71.

Kow, E., 2013. UIMA annotation model. Retrieved 21-01-2014 from http://erickow.com/posts/anno-models-uima.html.

LingPipe, 2014. http://alias-i.com/lingpipe/web/about.html.

Miner, G., Elder, J., Fast, A., Hill, T., Nisbet, R., Delen, D., 2012. Practical Text Mining and Statistical Analysis for Non-Structured Text Data Applications. Academic Press/Elsevier, Waltham, Massachusetts. ISBN: 978 0-12-386979-1.

Nisbet, R., Elder, J., Miner, G., 2009. Handbook of Statistical Analysis & Data Mining Applications. Academic Press/Elsevier, Waltham, Massachusetts. ISBN: 978-0-12-374765-5.

Witten, I.H., Frank, E., Hall, M.A., 2011. Data Mining: Practical Machine Learning Tools and Techniques, The Morgan Kaufmann Series in Data Management Systems. Morgan Kaufmann; 3rd Edition (January 20, 2011). Burlington, Massachusetts.

APPENDIX B

Databases and Vocabularies

B.1 SAMPLE DATA SETS

Various data sets have been made available under text mining-friendly licences. Of these, a proportion have become a popular choice of data set for testing approaches to text and data mining. One benefit of using standard data sets is the ability to benchmark directly against other approaches to the same problem, which permits standardisation in evaluation.

In this section we list a number of standard data sets and competitions, referencing the areas in which they are primarily used. This list is not exhaustive, and is intended to serve as an introduction. We indicate the availability and licencing of each data set where relevant. Although data sets are often used for more than one purpose we have attempted to separate them by the purposes for which each data set is most commonly used.

It is worth noting that data sets are often created for specific purposes, such as challenges, conference workshops and competitions. Aziz and Rafi trace the collection of data for the performance of data or text mining experiments with the specific aim of blog mining back to TREC 2006, which distributed a data set entitled Blog06 at a cost of between £200 and £500. It was suggested that this cost was excessive and limited participation in the task. In most cases, competition data sets are freely available to participants.

B.1.1 Biology and Medicine

All journals published by Biomed Central have a policy of open access to the research articles they publish. These cover major subject areas within biology and medicine. These are freely licensed. Images from these journals can be reused in other places, and the text is openly available for text mining and analysis purposes. Biomed Central was founded in 2000 as part of the current science group.

Biomed Central was a founding member of the open-access scholarly publishers association (OASPA). The OASPA requires as one of the criteria for membership that publishers must use liberal licenses that encourage the reuse and distribution of content. The OASPA strongly encourages the use of the CC-by licence. This license allows unrestricted reuse of content

subject only to the requirement that the source work is appropriately attributed. As the CC–by licence permits derivatives, it becomes possible to create
and share data visualisations, text mining enhancements and other derivative
works on the basis of the material. Biomed Central is a popular data set for
academic research in the area of text mining.

Biomed Central data can be retrieved from www.biomedcentral.com/
about/datamining.

B.1.2 Parallel Corpora

The Opus Project collects translated texts from around the web, converts
them into appropriate formats, annotate's the texts with linguistic annotations, and provides them in a publicly available data set format. Data made
available in this way includes a number of books, financial documents from
the European Central bank, proceedings from the European Parliament, and
technical manuals. A large number of languages are represented.

http://opus.lingfil.uu.se

B.1.3 Blog Corpora

The **Blogs06** data set was distributed at TREC 2006, and consists of
3,215,171 permalink documents.

The **Blogs08** data set was distributed at TREC 2008, and consists of
28,488,766 permalink documents.

These are distributed for a fee (currently between £500 and £600) by the
University of Glasgow. http://ir.dcs.gla.ac.uk/test_collections/access_to_
data.html.

Data sets primarily used for text categorization.

B.2 DATASETS PRIMARILY USED FOR TEXT CATEGORIZATION

B.2.1 The Reuters Text Data Set

There are in fact a variety of versions of Reuters text data sets.

The **Reuters–21578** text data set is a popular test set for text categorisation tasks and contains over 21,000 Reuters News documents from the year
1987. These have been manually categorised with labels by Reuters. In total
672 categories are represented in the data set. This is often reported as the
most widely used test collection for text categorisation research in general.

It is available from http://kdd.ics.uci.edu/databases/reuters21578.

Copyright for this test collection resides with Reuters; it is distributed for
research purposes only.

The Reuters Corpus volume 1, or **RCV1**, is commonly used today. This consists of 806,791XML files in NewsML format, around 3.7Gb worth of data. A number of corrected versions are available.

The Reuters Corpus, Volume 2 or **RCV2**, is a multilingual corpus distributed on a single CD, containing almost 500,000 Reuters News stories in a variety of languages: Chinese, Danish, Dutch, French, German, Italian, Japanese, Latin American Spanish, Norwegian, Portuguese, Russian, Spanish and Swedish. These are not parallel translations, however: each language stands independently of the others.

The Thomson Reuters Text Research Collection, or **TRC2**, is 1,800,370 news stories dating from 2008 to 2009. This was originally distributed at the Text Retrieval Conference (TREC).

Information on the Reuters corpora can be found at: http://about.reuters.com/researchandstandards/corpus.

B.2.2 The Enron Corpus

Klimt and Yang (2004) proposed the Enron corpus be used as an appropriate data set for e-mail classification research.

As the name suggests, the Enron e-mail data set originates from senior management of Enron. It was originally made public and posted to the web by the Federal Energy Regulatory Commission during its investigation of the Enron Corporation following the company's collapse. This data set was purchased by Andrew McCallum at MIT at a cost of $10,000 (Markoff, 2011).

It is distributed by William Cohen at CMU. The most recent version of the database is August 21, 2009. This is around 423 MB and is distributed as a zip file. It contains e-mail data from around 150 users, which is described as mostly comprised of senior management of Enron. This contains around half a million messages.

This data set has been used for a variety of purposes, including spam filtering (Medlock, 2006), sentiment tracking (Muhammad and Yang, 2011) and social network analysis. Visualisations have also been developed on the basis of this data set. The Enron data has also been used for classification purposes (Hutton 2012; Bekkerman, 2004).

https://www.cs.cmu.edu/~./enron

SOURCES

Markoff, J., 2011. Armies of expensive lawyers, replaced by cheaper software. New York Times, March 5, 2011.

Klimt, B., Yang, Y. The Enron Corpus: a new data set for email classification research.

USES

Hutton, A., Liu, A., Martin, C.E., 2012. Crowdsourcing evaluations of classifier interpretability. In: Proceedings of the 2012 AAAI Spring Symposium on Wisdom of the Crowd.
Mohammed, S.M., Yang, T.W., 2011. Tracking sentiment in mail: how genders differ on emotional axes.
Bekkerman, R., 2004. Automatic categorisation of email into folders: benchmark experiments on Enron and SRI corpora.

B.3 USEFUL TERTIARY DATA SETS

B.3.1 DBPedia

DBPedia is a data set that contains structured information extracted from Wikipedia. It is the result of the aggregation of structured information embedded in articles taken from Wikipedia such as info-box tables and categorisation of pages, images and tables, alongside the text taken from the pages themselves. This information is encoded into RDF and shared as a data set. Because DBPedia is extremely extensive, it is often used as a convenient source of identifiers to connect other linked data sets. DBPedia, just like Wikipedia itself, is a useful resource for text mining.

Wikipedia is often used as a source of parallel corpora. See, for example, Ell and Harth (2014).

DBPedia has been used for a large number of purposes. For example, the DBPedia Spotlight tool annotates mentions of DBPedia resources in natural language text. This is useful for named entity recognition, name resolution and other information extraction tasks. A number of services have been built using DBPedia data, such as the Alchemy API cloud-based text mining platform. This makes use of semantic tagging via natural language processing to extract named entities, evaluate sentiment, tag relevant concepts, extract relevant authors, extract relations and so forth.

DBPedia data is licensed under the terms of the Creative Commons attribution share alike license and the GNU free documentation license. This information is provided as n-triples and n-quads; the latter contain provenance information.

This data set can, at the time of writing, be downloaded from wiki. dbpedia.org/downloads39.

SOURCES

Ell, B., Harth, A., 2014. A language independent method for the extraction of RDF verbalisation templates. Eighth International natural language generation conference. The Association for computer linguistics.

APPENDIX C

Visualisation Tools and Resources

The overview presented here is brief, but hopefully suffices to demonstrate the diversity of the visualisation ecosystem. In most cases there are several software packages in a variety of languages available to support the developer in achieving any given aim. One significant point to bear in mind when choosing between packages and languages is the need to choose a development environment within which the researcher, student or team is comfortable, or to factor in the time taken to become familiar with new languages and frameworks. It is recommended that visualisation be built into the process of text mining, as visualisations are a convenient method of exploring data sets and can often support the user or development in understanding the data set, including any weaknesses that may be present in the data collection or analysis phases.

C.1 D3 – DATA DRIVEN DOCUMENTS

This powerful JavaScript-based visualisation library is capable of supporting many types of visualisation, from traditional graphs such as boxplots and bar charts to rich interactive and animated graphs. With the use of WebGL extensions, D3 is even capable of rendering three-dimensional models. It is based around web standards including HTML, CSS and SVG.

Whilst D3 is extremely powerful, it is a reasonably complex framework and is likely to take time to learn. Several tutorials are available covering aspects of this library. D3 is available from http://d3js.org/.

A series of sample visualisations and tutorials may be found on the D3 gallery at https://github.com/mbostock/d3/wiki/Gallery. This page is also a good source of inspiration for others designing visualisations.

C.2 PROCESSING AND PROCESSING.JS

Processing itself is a visualisation language intended for interdisciplinary use. It provides a straightforward, usable graphical user interface and development environment alongside a programming language designed for ease of use. Processing is used primarily in the visual arts, in design and as a research and teaching tool. Overall, Processing is likely to be a great deal more accessible for interdisciplinary users than command-line software or full-featured scripting languages such as Python and R.

Processing is not a JavaScript-based language and hence cannot be used directly on the web. However, the sister project, **Processing.js**, allows code written in the Processing language to be run using web standards, meaning that it is possible to embed Processing code directly into HTML pages and run them in a web browser.

Processing is available at http://processing.org and Processing.js may be found at http://processingjs.org/.

C.3 MAP DISPLAY

Leaflet is an open source JavaScript-based framework designed to support the development and display of interactive maps on the web. Leaflet is optimised for use on mobile devices and is lightweight and accessible with good cross-platform compatibility. Plugins are also available designed to allow maps to be enhanced with additional visual elements such as heat maps, informational overlays and functionality to support improved interaction design. Leaflet is able to make use of information encoded in GeoJSON (geographic content encoded in JavaScript object notation).

Leaflet is available from http://leafletjs.com/, where accompanying tutorials are also provided.

OpenLayers provides comparable functionality to Leaflet and is a mature library made available by the developers of the OpenStreetMap resources (see below). It is significantly larger than Leaflet, but provides broader functionality for information display and manipulation. As well as GeoJSON, OpenLayers is natively able to make use of information delivered in formats such as GeoRSS, GML (geography markup language), KML (keyhole markup language) and others.

Tutorials for OpenLayers, as well as the library and relevant extensions, are available at http://openlayers.org/.

C.3.1 Map Tile Providers

To use map frameworks such as Leaflet or OpenLayers, it is necessary to make use of geographic data drawn from elsewhere. Notably, segments of the map under display ("map tiles") must be made available, or an existing mapping provider selected. There are a number of map providers, including **OpenStreetMap** (http://openstreetmap.org), a collaborative effort to create and distribute free geographic data worldwide. Alternative map providers include **OpenMapQuest** (http://open.mapquest.com/) and **Mapbox** (http://mapbox.com).

Many commercial providers, generalist and specialist, are available, who will typically charge according to projected usage. Those intending to make heavy use of map tiling services may either choose to select or negotiate a contract with a service provider or consider the installation and maintenance of a local server based around OpenStreetMap data. The choice of data provider, terms and contract will depend on usage, funding and sustainability concerns.

C.4 COMMAND LINE VISUALISATION TOOLS

C.4.1 R (http://www.r-project.org)

The programming language R is a popular choice for statistical computing and for data science, in part for its statistical features, but also for its visualisation capabilities. Although it is typically thought of as a relatively old and "staid" language, the breadth of R use in research and industry has led to widespread development of specialist modules and packages. Consequentially, many graphing and visualisation libraries are available with differing strengths and application areas.

R is often thought of as usable for traditional visualisations, such as bar charts, scatterplots, box plots and so forth. Using libraries such as **ggplot2**, it is possible to generate professional and aesthetically pleasing results. It is also capable of spatial analysis and presentation of geographic data using relevant libraries. For example, choropleths, maps displaying information as colours over geographic or geopolitical regions, may be generated using libraries such as **ggplot2**, **rworldmap** or **rchoropleth**. Processing, generation and presentation of social network data is also possible using libraries such as **igraph**. R also provides libraries suitable for time series analysis.

With a little ingenuity it is also possible to build time-based visualisations in R, usually by generating output images frame-by-frame and combining the result into a single video. Images may be combined using an appropriate software package such as **ffmpeg**.

R is powerful but, at least initially, reasonably difficult to use. Graphical user interfaces exist that may increase the accessibility of the language for new users.

Those with an interest in the use of R for time series data may wish to look at the *Little Book Of R For Time Series*, http://a-little-book-of-r-for-time-series.readthedocs.org/en/latest/.

C.4.2 Python (http://www.python.org)

As with R, Python is widely used for scientific computing and therefore has attracted significant development effort from a variety of fields. Python may also feel more familiar than R to developers with a background in scripting languages, or in languages such as C# or Java.

Beginners to Python, or those seeking to teach Python to beginners, may wish to explore the use of **ipython-notebook**, a user-friendly "lab book" for working with Python.

Traditional 2-D graphs of publication quality can be generated in Python using **matplotlib** (http://matplotlib.org/). Matplotlib is also capable of a good deal more, including 3-D graphs, animated graphics and interactive charts. Real-time data may be visualised using **vispy** (http://vispy.org/), which makes use of the capabilities of current graphics hardware to deliver fast interactive visualisations. Using an extension to matplotlib, **basemap** (http://matplotlib.org/basemap/), it is possible to plot data on map projections, including points, contours and heat maps.

Using **NetworkX** or **igraph** allows developers to manipulate graph structures such as social networks. Once calculated, graphs can be visualised using associated libraries such as **graphviz**. Python permits advanced interactive elements using graphical user interface libraries, including **networkx_viewer**, **graph-tool** and **Ubigraph** (http://ubietylab.net/ubigraph/).

C.5 GRAPHICAL TOOLS

An alternative to the above packages for the creation of geographic visualisations is the use of **QGIS** (http://www.qgis.org), a free and open-source geographic information system application. Straightforward visualisations such as choropleth charts are reasonably easy to create using the QGIS software package.

QGIS is also useful for many other tasks in geographic information system development and management, including the creation of new resources, the digitisation of paper resources and the conversion of data between formats, standards and coordinate systems. As such, QGIS is a useful tool for anybody working in the visualisation of geographic data.

C.6 GEOGRAPHIC DATA SETS

Those with an interest in geographic data and localisation will find that there are a number of data sources available to support their work. There is an extensive set of physical and human geography data sets available at freeGISdata.ArtieWilson.com. A few examples have been identified here.

C.6.1 The GeoNames Geographical Database

The GeoNames database is a freely available geographical database, published under a Creative Commons attribution license. It is also accessible through a number of web services, which provide relevant functionality such as name search (which provides the ability to search for place name or postal code and receive a list of postal codes and places in return, thus essentially providing the ability to geocode), place name look up from postal code, reverse geocoding or the ability to find nearby postal codes, finding populated places near a certain set of coordinates and so forth. It is also useful as a gazetteer, which is to say, essentially a list of place and feature names available for each country.

The GeoNames data set may be searched, browsed, queried and downloaded from www.geonames.org.

C.6.2 Gridded Population of the World

The Gridded Population of the World (GPW) data set is distributed by the Socioeconomic Data and Applications Center, hosted by the Center for International Earth Science InformationNetwork (CIESIN), Columbia University. This useful data set provides "gridded" estimates of global population for 1990, 1995 and 2000; that is, the surface of the Earth is represented by a grid, within which each square is assigned a population estimate.

This data set is available from http://sedac.ciesin.columbia.edu/data/collection/gpw-v3.

APPENDIX D

Learning Opportunities

There exist a variety of courses covering text mining at the time of writing, the majority of which explore the subject as part of a broader topic area such as data analytics. A few are listed below. Inclusion in this list does not constitute a recommendation and failure to include courses should not be taken as deliberate exclusion.

D.1 UNITED KINGDOM

MSc in Information Management, University of Manchester
Technical and organisational challenges of "Big Data"; text mining is covered as an optional element.MSc in Computer Science with Speech and Language Processing, University of Sheffield
Run by the Department of Computer Science in collaboration with the Speech and Hearing and Natural Language Processing groups, this course combines text processing, speech processing, machine learning, speech technology, natural language processing and research methods.
MSc in Data Mining, University of Westminster
"The entire data mining process", with a focus on SAS Enterprise Miner, SAS Text Miner and Oracle Data Mining Suite. Text mining is covered as an elective.

D.2 IRELAND

MSc in Computing, DCU (Dublin City University)
Data analytics, cloud computing, software engineering and human language technology; includes an introduction to linguistics.MSc in Data Mining and Business Intelligence, ITB (Institute of Technology Blanchardstown)
Business intelligence and data mining, data preprocessing; web content, text mining, geographic information system and multimedia mining are offered as electives.

D.3 SWEDEN

MSc in Statistics and Data Mining, Linköping
This course includes data analysis, machine learning, text mining and statistical methods in bioinformatics.

D.4 FRANCE

Master of Science in Informatics, University Paris 13
Second-year elective in Data Mining, Analytics and Knowledge Discovery; electives include neural networks, statistical and machine learning, social networks, time series analysis, bioinformatics and text mining.
Master in Business Analytics, EISTI (Ecole Internationale des Sciences du Traitement de l'Information)
A multidisciplinary MSc including statistics, data mining, operational research and architecture; methods include opinion mining, social networks and Big Data, optimisation. The course is taught in English.
DKM2 – Master in Data Mining and Knowledge Management
Offered by a consortium of universities – France (University of Pierre and Marie Curie Paris 6, University of Lyon Lumière Lyon 2, Polytec'Nantes), Romania (University Polithenica of Bucharest), Italy (University of East Piedmont) and Spain (Technical University of Catalonia). Beginning with the technical and mathematical prerequisites, the course includes data mining with social science applications, statistical modelling and data mining.

D.5 UNITED STATES

MSc in Computer Science, Stanford University
Text mining is a topic in the Information Management and Analytics track.
Data Mining M.S., Lewis University
Data Mining MSc, CCSU
M.S. in Analytics, Georgia Tech
Web Search and Text Mining module is an elective element of this M.S.
M.S. in Intelligent Information Systems, Carnegie Mellon University
Text mining is an elective in this Computer Science degree.

D.6 SHORT COURSES, TRAINING COURSES AND MOOCs

Short courses are an appealing alternative to postgraduate courses for those currently in education or research. A variety of short courses are held on a yearly or occasional basis as "summer (or autumn or winter) schools". These are sometimes a relatively inexpensive option.

Training courses are also available on various topics; these vary greatly in price depending on the subject matter and organiser, from free to extremely expensive. The developers and maintainers of popular text mining tools often run courses on their use. GATE training courses, for example, are currently held yearly in Sheffield; course material from previous years is freely available online.

MOOCS (massive open online courses) are available in several topics of relevance to text mining. A disadvantage of the MOOC format is the periodic unavailability of these courses. However, it is often the case that where courses are not currently running, material from courses remains openly available and can be used for self-directed study.

Data Mining with Weka, University of Waikato
    This course covers the Weka toolkit.

Corpus Linguistics, University of Lancaster (FutureLearn)
    Run by Tony McEnery, Professor of English Language and Linguistics (and author of a canonical textbook on corpus linguistics), this MOOC introduces the essentials of corpus linguistics.

Natural Language Processing, Stanford (Coursera)

Information Visualisation, Indiana University
    This course is part of Indiana's Online Certificate in Data Science, but can be followed for free.

Mining Massive Datasets, Stanford (Coursera)
    This class teaches algorithms for extracting models and other information from very large amounts of data. The emphasis is on techniques that are efficient and that scale well.

Process Mining: Data science in Action, Eindhoven University of Technology (Coursera)
    Process mining connects data-centric observation of behaviour with process analysis in order to develop an understanding of how event data and process models interact.

The University of Illinois at Urbana-Champaign currently runs a Data Mining specialisation on Coursera, including the following courses:

- Pattern Discovery in Data Mining
- Text Retrieval and Search Engines
- Cluster Analysis in Data Mining

- Text Mining and Analytics
- Data Visualization
- Data Mining Capstone (project)

INDEX

Note: Page numbers followed by *f* indicate figures, *b* indicate boxes and *t* indicate tables.

Printed in the United States
By Bookmasters